First World War
and Army of Occupation
War Diary
France, Belgium and Germany

29 DIVISION
88 Infantry Brigade
Worcestershire Regiment 4th Battalion,
Royal Scots (Lothian Regiment) 5th Battalion,
Hampshire Regiment 2/4th (T.F.) Battalion, 15th (Service)
Battalion and 51st (Y.S.) Battalion
1 March 1916 - 30 April 1919

WO95/2309/2-6

The Naval & Military Press Ltd
www.nmarchive.com
Published in association with The National Archives

Published by

The Naval & Military Press Ltd

Unit 10 Ridgewood Industrial Park,
Uckfield, East Sussex,
TN22 5QE England
Tel: +44 (0) 1825 749494

www.naval-military-press.com

www.nmarchive.com

This diary has been reprinted in facsimile from the original. Any imperfections are inevitably reproduced and the quality may fall short of modern type and cartographic standards.

© Crown Copyright
Images reproduced by permission of The National Archives, London, England, 2015.

Contents

Document type	Place/Title	Date From	Date To
Heading	WO95/2309/2		
Heading	29th Division 28th Infy Bde 4th Bn Worcs Regt Mar 1916-Apr 1919		
Heading	29th Division 88th Infantry Brigade. Arrived Marseilles From Egypt 20.3.16. 4th Battalion Worcestershire Regiment March 1916		
Heading	Worcester Regt Vol I BEF From MEF		
War Diary	Suez	01/03/1916	12/03/1916
War Diary	Suez	03/03/1916	20/03/1916
War Diary	Marseilles	20/03/1916	21/03/1916
War Diary	France	22/03/1916	22/03/1916
War Diary	Pont Remy & Haucourt	23/03/1916	23/03/1916
War Diary	Haucourt	24/03/1916	31/03/1916
Heading	29th Division 88th Infantry Brigade. 4th Battalion Worcestershire Regiment April 1916		
Heading	29 Worcester Regt Vol 2		
War Diary	Gorenflos	01/04/1916	30/04/1916
Heading	29th Division 88th Infantry Brigade. 4th Battalion Worcestershire Regiment May 1916		
War Diary		01/05/1916	31/05/1916
Heading	29th Division. 88th Infantry Brigade 4th Battalion Worcestershire Regiment June 1916		
War Diary		01/06/1916	01/06/1916
War Diary	Firing Line (White City)	02/06/1916	07/06/1916
War Diary	Louvencourt	08/06/1916	15/06/1916
War Diary	Englebelmer	16/06/1916	23/06/1916
War Diary	Louvencourt	24/06/1916	30/06/1916
Heading	29th Division 88th Infantry Brigade. 4th Battalion Worcestershire Regiment July 1916		
Heading	War Diary Of 4th Bn Worcestershire Regt. For July. 1916		
Heading	War Diary Of 4th Bn Worcestershire Regt. From 1st July 1916 to 31st July 1916 Volume 5		
War Diary	Auchonvillers Sector	01/07/1916	14/07/1916
War Diary	Mailly Wood.	15/07/1916	17/07/1916
War Diary	Acheux Wood	18/07/1916	23/07/1916
War Diary	Beauval	24/07/1916	27/07/1916
War Diary	Poperinghe	28/07/1916	29/07/1916
War Diary	Ypres	30/07/1916	30/07/1916
War Diary	Ypres Salient	31/07/1916	31/07/1916
Heading	29th Division 88th Infantry Brigade. 4th Battalion Worcestershire Regiment August 1916		
War Diary	In Ypres Salient	01/08/1916	09/08/1916
War Diary	Ypres	10/08/1916	19/08/1916
War Diary	In "A" Camp	20/08/1916	30/08/1916
War Diary	Ypres	31/08/1916	31/08/1916
Heading	29th Division. 88th Infantry Brigade. 4th Battalion Worcestershire Regiment September 1916		
Heading	War Diary of 4th Worcestershire Regt for Period. Sept 1st 1916 to Sept 30th 1916 (Volume 7)		

War Diary	Ypres	01/09/1916	08/09/1916
War Diary	Firing Line	09/09/1916	11/09/1916
War Diary	Firing Line Ypres	12/09/1916	18/09/1916
War Diary	Vlamertinghe "B" Camp.	19/09/1916	28/09/1916
War Diary	Firing Line Ypres	29/09/1916	30/09/1916
Heading	29th Division. 88th Infantry Brigade. 4th Battalion Worcestershire Regiment October 1916		
Heading	War Diary Of 4th. Bn. The Worcestershire Regt For Period October 1st 1916 to October 31st 1916. Volumn No 8		
War Diary	Ypres Salient	01/10/1916	05/10/1916
War Diary	In Camp. (Brandhoek)	06/10/1916	07/10/1916
War Diary	En Route	08/10/1916	08/10/1916
War Diary	Corbie	09/10/1916	10/10/1916
War Diary	Camp. Pommieres	11/10/1916	11/10/1916
War Diary	Geandecourt	12/10/1916	20/10/1916
War Diary	Bernafay Camp	21/10/1916	27/10/1916
War Diary	Guendecourt	28/10/1916	29/10/1916
War Diary	Bernafay Camp.	30/10/1916	30/10/1916
War Diary	Pommiers	31/10/1916	31/10/1916
Heading	29th Division. 88th Infantry Brigade. 4th Battalion Worcestershire Regiment November 1916		
Heading	War Diary of 4th Worcestershire Regt For Period Nov 1st 1916 to Nov 30th 1916 Volume 9		
War Diary	Ville-sous-Corbie	01/11/1916	15/11/1916
War Diary	Ville-Sous-Corbie Sandpits	16/11/1916	16/11/1916
War Diary	La Briqueterie	17/11/1916	17/11/1916
War Diary	Lesboeufs	18/11/1916	21/11/1916
War Diary	Carnoy Camp	22/11/1916	24/11/1916
War Diary	Bernafay Camp	25/11/1916	27/11/1916
War Diary	Lesboeufs	28/11/1916	30/11/1916
Heading	29th Division. 988th Infantry Brigade 4th Battalion The Worcestershire Regiment December 1916		
Heading	War Diary of 4th Battn The Worcestershire Regiment for Period December 1st to December 31st 1916. Volume 10.		
War Diary	Bernafay	01/12/1916	02/12/1916
War Diary	Carnoy Camp	03/12/1916	04/12/1916
War Diary	Bernafay Wood.	05/12/1916	06/12/1916
War Diary	Les Boeufs	07/12/1916	08/12/1916
War Diary	Bernafay	09/12/1916	11/12/1916
War Diary	Mericourt	12/12/1916	14/12/1916
War Diary	Moulliens	15/12/1916	15/12/1916
War Diary	Vidame.	16/12/1916	17/12/1916
War Diary	Moulliens Vidame	17/12/1916	30/12/1916
War Diary	M. Vidames	30/12/1916	31/12/1916
Heading	War Diary for period 1st January to 31st January 1917. of 4th Bn The Worcestershire Regiment. Volume II.		
War Diary	Molliens-Vidame	01/01/1917	11/01/1917
War Diary	Corbie	12/01/1917	12/01/1917
War Diary	Meaulte	13/01/1917	15/01/1917
War Diary	Carnoy No 5	16/01/1917	16/01/1917
War Diary	Guillemont	17/01/1917	17/01/1917
War Diary	Morval	18/01/1917	20/01/1917
War Diary	Carnoy	21/01/1917	22/01/1917
War Diary	Guillemont	23/01/1917	23/01/1917

War Diary	Morval	24/01/1917	26/01/1917
War Diary	Carnoy	27/01/1917	28/01/1917
War Diary	Guillemont	29/01/1917	29/01/1917
War Diary	Morval	30/01/1917	31/01/1917
Heading	War Diary of 4th Battn The Worcestershire Regiment for period 1st February 1917 to 28th February 1917. Volume 11		
War Diary	Morval	01/02/1917	01/02/1917
War Diary	Carnoy	02/02/1917	03/02/1917
War Diary	Guillemont	04/02/1917	04/02/1917
War Diary	Morval	05/02/1917	07/02/1917
War Diary	Carnoy Mansel	08/02/1917	08/02/1917
War Diary	La Houssoye	09/02/1917	21/02/1917
War Diary	Bronfay	22/02/1917	22/02/1917
War Diary	Combles	23/02/1917	23/02/1917
War Diary	Saillisel	24/02/1917	25/02/1917
War Diary	Fregicourt	26/02/1917	26/02/1917
War Diary	Bronfay	27/02/1917	28/02/1917
Heading	War Diary of 4th Battalion The Worcestershire Regiment. for period 1st March 1917 to 31st March 1917. Volumn 13		
War Diary	Bronfay Camp No. 2	01/03/1917	01/03/1917
War Diary	Combles	02/03/1917	02/03/1917
War Diary	In The Trenches (Sailly Saillisel)	03/03/1917	03/03/1917
War Diary	Bronfay Camp No. 1	04/03/1917	04/03/1917
War Diary	Meaulte	05/03/1917	18/03/1917
War Diary	Molliens-Vidame	19/03/1917	28/03/1917
War Diary	La Chausee	29/03/1917	29/03/1917
War Diary	Vignacourt	30/03/1917	31/03/1917
Heading	War Diary for 4th Battn The Worcestershire Regt for Period 1st April 1917 to 30th April 1917 Volumn 16		
War Diary	Beauval	01/04/1917	02/04/1917
War Diary	Mondicourt	03/04/1917	04/04/1917
War Diary	Le Souich	05/04/1917	06/04/1917
War Diary	Couturelle	07/04/1917	09/04/1917
War Diary	Gouy-en-Artois	10/04/1917	11/04/1917
War Diary	Ronville	12/04/1917	12/04/1917
War Diary	In Trenches S. of Monchy Le Preux	13/04/1917	14/04/1917
War Diary	Ronville	15/04/1917	19/04/1917
War Diary	Brown Line Trenches	20/04/1917	20/04/1917
War Diary	Trenches S of Monchy Le Preux	21/04/1917	24/04/1917
War Diary	Simencourt	25/04/1917	25/04/1917
War Diary	Gouy En Artois	26/04/1917	27/04/1917
War Diary	Coigneux	28/04/1917	30/04/1917
Operation(al) Order(s)	Appendix B Operation Order No 16 by Lt Col A.C. Halahan	12/04/1917	12/04/1917
Miscellaneous	Appendix C Special Order by Brig Genl. Cayley C.M.G. Comdg 88th Bde.	11/05/1917	11/05/1917
Miscellaneous	88th Brigade Instructions No. 1	20/04/1917	20/04/1917
Miscellaneous	29th Division Instructions No. 3	20/04/1917	20/04/1917
Operation(al) Order(s)	88th Brigade Operation Order No. 69 By Brigadier General D.E. Cayley, C.M.G. Commanding 88th Brigade.	21/04/1917	21/04/1917
Operation(al) Order(s)	Operation Order No. 1. By Lieut Col E.J.T. Kerans Commanding 4th Batt The Worcestershire Regt.	22/04/1917	22/04/1917
Miscellaneous	Appendix To Division Instructions No. 5		

Map	Map Barrage		
Heading	War Diary of 4th Battn The Worcestershire Regiment, for period 1st May to 31st May 1917 Volumn 15		
War Diary	St Amand	01/05/1917	02/05/1917
War Diary	Arras	03/05/1917	07/05/1917
War Diary	Berneville	08/05/1917	14/05/1917
War Diary	Hangest Work	15/05/1917	16/05/1917
War Diary	Lancer Lane	17/05/1917	20/05/1917
War Diary	Front	21/05/1917	24/05/1917
War Diary	Railway Triangle	25/05/1917	28/05/1917
War Diary	Front	29/05/1917	31/05/1917
Heading	War Diary 4th Worcestershire Regt. From 1st June 1917 To 30 June 1917 (Volume No. 18)		
War Diary	Front	01/06/1917	01/06/1917
War Diary	Arras	02/06/1917	04/06/1917
War Diary	Bonneville	05/06/1917	26/06/1917
War Diary	Doullens	27/06/1917	27/06/1917
War Diary	Proven	28/06/1917	28/06/1917
War Diary	De Wipp Cabt	29/06/1917	30/06/1917
Heading	War Diary of 4th Worcestershire Regt From 1st July 1917 To 31st July 1917 (Volume No 19) Vol 17		
War Diary	De Wipp Cabt	01/07/1917	01/07/1917
War Diary	International Corner	02/07/1917	06/07/1917
War Diary	Yser Canal	07/07/1917	11/07/1917
War Diary	L. Camp	12/07/1917	13/07/1917
War Diary	Crombeke Camp	14/07/1917	19/07/1917
War Diary	N. of Proven.	20/07/1917	24/07/1917
War Diary	Crombeke Camp	25/07/1917	27/07/1917
War Diary	Caribou Camp	28/07/1917	29/07/1917
War Diary	Crombeke Camp	30/07/1917	31/07/1917
Heading	4th. Battalion The Worcestershire Regt. War Diary. August 1917		
War Diary	Crombeke Camp (P.2.)	01/08/1917	05/08/1917
War Diary	Forest Area	06/08/1917	06/08/1917
War Diary	Bedford Farm	07/08/1917	15/08/1917
War Diary	Trenches (Cannes Farm)	16/08/1917	16/08/1917
War Diary	Black Line	17/08/1917	17/08/1917
War Diary	Boesinghe Chateau	18/08/1917	18/08/1917
War Diary	Trenches	19/08/1917	22/08/1917
War Diary	Elverdinghe	23/08/1917	23/08/1917
War Diary	De Wippe Capt	24/08/1917	26/08/1917
War Diary	Proven No 2 Area	27/08/1917	31/08/1917
Heading	War Diary of 4th. Battn. The Worcestershire Regiment. From 1st. September 1917 To 30th. September 1917. (Volume No. 21)		
War Diary	Proven No 2 Area	01/09/1917	01/09/1917
War Diary	Piccadilly Camp	01/09/1917	12/09/1917
War Diary	Herzeele	13/09/1917	16/09/1917
War Diary	Piccadilly Camp	17/09/1917	21/09/1917
War Diary	In The Line	22/09/1917	25/09/1917
War Diary	Rugby Camp	26/09/1917	28/09/1917
War Diary	De Wippe Camp	29/09/1917	30/09/1917
Heading	War Diary of 4th. Battn. The Worcestershire Regiment From 1st. October 1917 to 31st October 1917. (Volume No. 22)		
War Diary	De Wippe Camp	01/10/1917	05/10/1917

War Diary	Roussol Camp	06/10/1917	07/10/1917
War Diary	Trenches N. of Lange Marck	08/10/1917	08/10/1917
War Diary	Front Line Trenches N.	08/10/1917	08/10/1917
War Diary	Langemarck	09/10/1917	09/10/1917
War Diary	Harrow Camp	10/10/1917	10/10/1917
War Diary	Sarawak Camp	11/10/1917	16/10/1917
War Diary	Berles-Au-Bois	17/10/1917	31/10/1917
Heading	War Diary of 4th Worcestershire Regiment From 1st November 1917 To 30th November, 1917 (Volume No 23)		
War Diary	Berles-Au-Bois	01/11/1917	17/11/1917
War Diary	Moislains	18/11/1917	18/11/1917
War Diary	Sorel	19/11/1917	20/11/1917
War Diary	Sorel And In The Attack	20/11/1917	20/11/1917
War Diary	Near Masnieres	21/11/1917	21/11/1917
War Diary	In Trenches Near Masnieres	22/11/1917	23/11/1917
War Diary	Marcoing	24/11/1917	25/11/1917
War Diary	In Trenches	26/11/1917	28/11/1917
War Diary	Marcoing	29/11/1917	30/11/1917
Heading	War Diary 4th. Battn. The Worcestershire Regiment 1st. December 1917 to 31st. December 1917		
War Diary		01/12/1917	31/12/1917
Heading	War Diary of 4th Worcestershire Regiment From 1st January, 1918 To 31st January, 1918 (Volume No. 25)		
Heading	War Diary of 4th. Battalion The Worcestershire Regiment. From January 1st. 1918. To. January 31st. 1918		
War Diary		01/01/1918	31/01/1918
Heading	War Diary of 4th. Battalion The Worcestershire Regt. From 1st. February 1918 To 2nd. February 1918. (Volume No 26)		
War Diary		01/02/1918	28/02/1918
Heading	War Diary 4th. Battalion The Worcestershire Regiment. From 1st March 1918 To 31st. March 1918 (Volume No 1)		
War Diary		01/03/1918	31/03/1918
Heading	88th Brigade. 29th Division. 1/4th Battalion Worcestershire Regiment April 1918		
War Diary	Passchendale Sector	01/04/1918	10/04/1918
War Diary	La Creche.	11/04/1918	13/04/1918
War Diary	Mont de Lille	14/04/1918	15/04/1918
War Diary	Croix de Poperinghe.	15/04/1918	16/04/1918
War Diary	St. Jans Capelle.	16/04/1918	18/04/1918
War Diary	Abeele North East of Bailleul.	19/04/1918	21/04/1918
War Diary	Hondeghem	22/04/1918	23/04/1918
War Diary	North of Wallon Capelle.	24/04/1918	25/04/1918
War Diary	Nr. Sercus.	26/04/1918	28/04/1918
War Diary	East of Hazebrouck.	29/04/1918	30/04/1918
Heading	To Be Put Away With Diary 4th Batt. Worcestershire Regiment April 10th to 15th, 1918, by Captain J.E. Thorneloe, M.C. Late Adjutant.		
Miscellaneous			
Heading	War Diary of the 4th. Bn. The Worcestershire Regiment. From 1st. May 1918. To 31st. May 1918. (Volume No 3)		
War Diary	Reserve Trenches East of Hazebrouck.	01/05/1918	05/05/1918

War Diary	Strazeele Sector.	06/05/1918	09/05/1918
War Diary	Front Line	09/05/1918	10/05/1918
War Diary	Front Line. Strazeele Sector.	11/05/1918	15/05/1918
War Diary	Le Grand Hasard Camp.	16/05/1918	19/05/1918
War Diary	In Support South East of Hazebrouck.	20/05/1918	24/05/1918
War Diary	Front Line South East of Hazebrouck.	25/05/1918	28/05/1918
War Diary	Morbecque, South West of Hazebrouck.	29/05/1918	31/05/1918
Operation(al) Order(s)	4th. Battalion The Worcestershire Regiment. Operation Order No. 24 by Major R. Ratliffe.	19/05/1918	19/05/1918
Heading	OC 2nd Royal Fus		
Heading	War Diary 4th. Bn. The Worcestershire Regt. From 1st. June 1918. To 30th. June 1918. (Volume No 4)		
War Diary	In Support to 88th Infantry Brigade Near Bois D'aval and La Motte.	01/06/1918	04/06/1918
War Diary	In Camp Between Grand Hasard & Hazebrouck.	05/06/1918	07/06/1918
War Diary	In Camp Between Le Grand Hasard and Hazebrouck.	07/06/1918	12/06/1918
War Diary	Front Line, Vieux Berquin Sector.	13/06/1918	20/06/1918
War Diary	La Kreule	20/06/1918	21/06/1918
War Diary	In Camp At Val De Lumbres.	21/06/1918	30/06/1918
Heading	War Diary 4th. Battalion The Worcestershire Regiment. From. 1st July 1918. To. 31st. July 1918. (Volume No 5)		
War Diary	In Camp. Val de Lumbres.	01/07/1918	05/07/1918
War Diary	In Camp. Val de Lumbres.	06/07/1918	10/07/1918
War Diary	In Camp. Val de Lumbres.	11/07/1918	19/07/1918
War Diary	In Camp Pont D'Asquin.	20/07/1918	23/07/1918
War Diary	In Billets Near Zuypteene. (West of Cassel.)	22/07/1918	31/07/1918
Heading	War Diary of 4th Battalion The Worcestershire Regiment From 1st August, 1918 To 31 August, 1918. (Volume No. 6) Vol 30		
War Diary	La Kreule (N. of Hazebrouck)	01/08/1918	02/08/1918
War Diary	Front Line, Strazeele Sector.	03/08/1918	04/08/1918
War Diary	Front Line, Strazeele Sector. (Merris).	05/08/1918	15/08/1918
War Diary	In Camp Near La Kreule (N. of Hazebrouck)	16/08/1918	18/08/1918
War Diary	In Support Near Strazeele.	18/08/1918	18/08/1918
War Diary	In Strazeele Defences & "Z" Line.	18/08/1918	21/08/1918
War Diary	In Front Line Outtersteene.	21/08/1918	22/08/1918
War Diary	Front Line Outtersteene.	22/08/1918	24/08/1918
War Diary	In Front Line, Outtersteene.	25/08/1918	27/08/1918
War Diary	In Camp Near La Kreule, N. of Hazebrouck.	27/08/1918	31/08/1918
Heading	War Diary of 4th Battalion, the Worcestershire Regiment. From 1st September To 30th September, 1918. (Volume No 7). Vol 31		
War Diary	In Action South West of Bailleul.	01/09/1918	05/09/1918
War Diary	In Camp South West of Bailleul.	06/09/1918	11/09/1918
War Diary	In Billets, Hazebrouck.	12/09/1918	16/09/1918
War Diary	In Billets At Hazebrouck.	17/09/1918	21/09/1918
War Diary	In Camp At St. Janter Biezen.	22/09/1918	24/09/1918
War Diary	In Front Line, Zillebeke Sector.	25/09/1918	25/09/1918
War Diary	In Line Zillebeke Sector	26/09/1918	26/09/1918
War Diary	In Support, Bobstay Castle (Ypres).	26/09/1918	26/09/1918
War Diary	Bobstay Castle, East of Ypres.	27/09/1918	28/09/1918
War Diary	Advance On Gheluvelt From Ypres, Along Menin Road.	28/09/1918	28/09/1918
War Diary	Au Rossignol Cabt. (K.31.a.)	29/09/1918	30/09/1918
War Diary	Koelenberg Ridge. (K 32. c & d.)	30/09/1918	30/09/1918

Heading	War Diary 4th. Battalion The Worcestershire Regiment. From 1st. October 1918. To 31st. October 1918. (Volume No 8) Vol 32		
War Diary	In Support Keelenberg Ridge.	01/10/1918	01/10/1918
War Diary	Oude Kruisuicke	02/10/1918	02/10/1918
War Diary	Dirty Bucket Camp. (Near Brandhoek)	03/10/1918	05/10/1918
War Diary	In Billets Ypres.	06/10/1918	06/10/1918
War Diary	In Camp at Westhoek.	07/10/1918	09/10/1918
War Diary	In Front Line Ledeghem Sector.	10/10/1918	10/10/1918
War Diary	In Camp Becelaere	11/10/1918	14/10/1918
Miscellaneous	General Advance on Courtrai.	14/10/1918	14/10/1918
War Diary	General Advance On River Lys.	15/10/1918	17/10/1918
War Diary	Advance On & Crossing of The Lys.	17/10/1918	20/10/1918
War Diary	Crossing of River Lys, Advance on Stacegehem & St. Louis.	20/10/1918	20/10/1918
War Diary	In Billets at Staceghem	21/10/1918	22/10/1918
War Diary	In Billets at Staceghem.	23/10/1918	26/10/1918
War Diary	Neuville.	27/10/1918	29/10/1918
War Diary	In Billets At Croix (Near Roubaix).	30/10/1918	31/10/1918
Heading	War Diary Of 4th Battalion The Worcestershire Regiment From 1st November, 1918 To 30th November. 1918. (Volume No. 9). Vol 33		
War Diary	In Billets At Croix.	03/11/1918	05/11/1918
War Diary	Petit Tourcoing	06/11/1918	07/11/1918
War Diary	In Line Near River L'Escaut	07/11/1918	08/11/1918
War Diary	In Line Advance on St Sauveur.	09/11/1918	10/11/1918
War Diary	St Sauveur	10/11/1918	11/11/1918
War Diary	Lessines	10/11/1918	13/11/1918
War Diary	In Billets Lessines	14/11/1918	17/11/1918
Miscellaneous	March Lessines-Enghien	18/11/1918	18/11/1918
War Diary	In Billets Enghien	19/11/1918	21/11/1918
War Diary	In Billets Braine-Le-Chateau	22/11/1918	22/11/1918
War Diary	St Lambert	23/11/1918	24/11/1918
War Diary	Limelette	25/11/1918	26/11/1918
War Diary	Walhain St Paul	27/11/1918	27/11/1918
War Diary	Eghezee	28/11/1918	28/11/1918
War Diary	Antheit	29/11/1918	29/11/1918
War Diary	Warzee	30/11/1918	30/11/1918
Heading	War Diary 4th. Battalion The Worcestershire Regiment From 1st. December 1918 To 31st. December 1918. (Volume No 10) Vol 34		
War Diary	Malmedy La Reid Aywaille	01/12/1918	05/12/1918
War Diary	Elsenborn	06/12/1918	06/12/1918
War Diary	Simmerath	07/12/1918	07/12/1918
War Diary	Embken	08/12/1918	08/12/1918
War Diary	Lechenich	09/12/1918	11/12/1918
War Diary	Frechen	12/12/1918	12/12/1918
War Diary	Mulheim	13/12/1918	14/12/1918
War Diary	Berg Gladbach	15/12/1918	15/12/1918
War Diary	Altenberg	16/12/1918	18/12/1918
War Diary	Wermelskirchen	18/12/1918	31/12/1918
Heading	Southern (Late 29th) Divn 88th Infy Bde 4th Bn Worcester Regt Jan-Apr 1919		
Heading	War Diary Of 4th Battalion The Worcestershire Regiment From 1st January To 31st January, 1919. (Volume No. 11) Vol 35		

War Diary	Wermels-Kirchen.	01/01/1919	31/01/1919
Heading	War Diary 4th. Battalion The Worcestershire Regiment. From 1st. February 1919 To 28th. February 1919. (Volume No. 12) Vol 36		
War Diary	Wermelskirchen	01/02/1919	10/02/1919
War Diary	Dhunn	11/02/1918	28/02/1918
Heading	29 Division 88 Infantry Brigade 4 Battalion Worcestershire Regiment March 1919 Missing		
Heading	War Diary. 4th Battalion The Worcestershire Regiment. From 1st April. 1919. To. 30th April. 1919. Vol 39		
War Diary	Mulheim (Germany)	01/04/1919	10/04/1919
War Diary	Ath (Belguim)	11/04/1919	30/04/1919
Miscellaneous	WO95/2309/3		
Heading	29th Division 88th Infy Bde 1-5th Bn Royal Scots 1916 Mar-June 1916 To 32 Div 14 Bde Amalgamated 6, R Scots.		
Heading	29th Division 88th Infantry Brigade. Arrived Marseilles From Egypt 22.3.16 1/5th Battalion Royal Scots March 1916		
Heading	1/5 Royal Scots Vol I BEF From MEF 29 Div 88 Bde		
War Diary	Suez	09/03/1916	13/03/1916
War Diary	H.M.T. "Alawnia"	14/03/1916	21/03/1916
War Diary	Marseilles	22/03/1916	24/03/1916
War Diary	Ailly l'Clocher	25/03/1916	01/04/1916
War Diary		01/03/1916	08/03/1916
Heading	29th Division. 88th Infantry Brigade. Battalion Went to G.H.Q. 24th April 1916 1/5th Battalion Royal Scots April 1916		
War Diary		02/05/1916	08/05/1916
War Diary	Rouen	09/05/1916	13/06/1916
War Diary	Hesdin	13/06/1916	13/06/1916
War Diary	Le Quesnoy	13/06/1916	17/06/1916
War Diary	Amiens	17/06/1916	17/06/1916
War Diary	Rubempre	17/06/1916	17/06/1916
War Diary	Puchevillers	19/06/1916	30/06/1916
War Diary	Ailly L'Clocher France	01/04/1916	01/04/1916
War Diary	Bonneville	02/04/1916	04/04/1916
War Diary	Arqueves	05/04/1916	13/04/1916
War Diary	Beaussart	14/04/1916	24/04/1916
War Diary	Doullens	25/04/1916	30/04/1916
Heading	WO95/2309/4		
Heading	Southern (Late 29th) Divn 88th Infy Bde 2/4th Bn Hampshire Regt May-Oct 1919 From 62 Div 186 Bde		
Heading	War Diary of The 2/4th Battalion, The Hampshire Regiment. Period From. May 1st, 1919 To May 31st, 1919 Volume No. 23		
War Diary	Wermelskirchen	01/05/1919	31/05/1919
War Diary	Wermelskirchen	23/05/1919	27/05/1919
War Diary	Wermelskirchen	12/05/1919	30/05/1919
Heading	War Diary Of 2/4th Battalion, The Hampshire Regiment From:- 1st June 1919.To:- 30th June 1919 Volume. 25		
War Diary	Wermelskirchen	01/06/1919	13/06/1919
War Diary	Dhunn.	16/06/1919	16/06/1919
War Diary	Wermelskirchen	18/06/1919	18/06/1919
War Diary	Hunger	19/06/1919	30/06/1919

Heading	War Diary of The 2/4th Battalion The Hampshire Regiment. Period. From:- To:- 1st July 1919 31st July 1919 Volume No. 26		
War Diary	Hunger	01/07/1919	03/07/1919
War Diary	Suppelbach	03/07/1919	02/08/1919
Heading	2/4th Battalion, The Hampshire Regiment. War Diary August 1919 Volume No. 28		
Heading	War Diary of The 2/4th Battalion, To Hampshire Regiment. Period. From:- 1st August 1919 To:- 31st August 1919 Volume No. 27		
War Diary	Suppelbach	01/08/1919	02/08/1919
War Diary	Wermelskirchen	03/08/1919	02/09/1919
War Diary	Suppelbach	01/08/1919	02/08/1919
War Diary	Wermelskirchen	03/08/1919	31/08/1919
Heading	War Diary of The 2/4th Battalion, The Hampshire Regiment Period. From:- September 1st, 1919. To:- September 30th, 1919 Volume No. 28		
War Diary	Wermelskirchen	01/09/1919	31/10/1919
Heading	WO95/2309/5		
Heading	Southern (Late 29th) Divn 88th Infy Bde 15th Bn Hampshire Regt May-Sep 1919 From 41 Div 122 Bde.		
War Diary	Suppelbach	03/05/1919	15/05/1919
War Diary	Wermelskirchen	15/05/1919	19/06/1919
War Diary	Burg	20/06/1919	01/07/1919
War Diary	Wermelskirchen	02/07/1919	04/08/1919
War Diary	Suppelbach	05/08/1919	04/09/1919
War Diary	Wermelskirchen	05/09/1919	30/09/1919
Heading	WO95/2309/6		
Heading	Southern (Late 29th) Divn 88th Infy Bde 51st Bn Hampshire Regt 1919 May-Oct		
War Diary	Wermelskirchen	01/05/1919	31/05/1919
War Diary	Wermelskirchen	30/04/1919	30/04/1919
War Diary	Wermelskirchen	26/05/1919	26/05/1919
War Diary	Wermelskirchen	03/05/1919	03/05/1919
War Diary		01/06/1919	30/06/1919
War Diary	Kellshammer Burg on the Wupper	01/07/1919	02/07/1919
War Diary	Wermelskirchen	03/07/1919	31/07/1919
War Diary	Wermelskirchen	28/07/1919	28/08/1919
War Diary	Wermelskirchen	01/08/1919	05/08/1919
War Diary	Dellbruck	06/08/1919	16/08/1919
War Diary	Wermelskirchen	17/08/1919	30/09/1919
War Diary	Wermelskirchen	05/09/1919	30/09/1919
War Diary	Dhunn	01/10/1919	07/10/1919
War Diary	Wermelskirchen	29/10/1919	29/10/1919

W0051230912

29TH DIVISION
88TH INFY BDE

4TH BN WORCS REGT
MAR 1916 - ~~DEC~~ APR 1919

29th Division.
88th Infantry Brigade.

Arrived MARSEILLES from EGYPT 20.3.16.

4th BATTALION

WORCESTERSHIRE REGIMENT

MARCH 1916

29

4 Worcester Regt

Vol I BEF
from MEF

? Duplicate

INTELLIGENCE SUMMARY   March 1916

Sheet I

(Erase heading not required.)

Place	Date	Hour	Summary of Events and Information
Suez	1st		Brigade and Divisional Training
	2nd		
	3rd		2nd Lts R.C. Broughton, A Ramsden, B.M Storey, E.H Stroud, & J Scott (10th Leicesters) joined the Bn for duty
	5th		Divine Service parade in Bn lines was attended by the Corps Commander Lieut Genl Sir J Francis Davies K C.B etc, Major Genl De Lisle, 29th Division & Brig Genl. D.E Cayley 88th Brigade. 2nd Lts E.P Daw, D.L Todd, Y.M Field rejoined the Bn.
	6th		Brigade Ceremonial parade. Major Genl De Lisle inspected the Brigade. He remarked that the general bearing, the handling of arms, and march past of the Worcesters was excellent.
	11th		Divisional Field scheme took place 2 miles from the ruins, close to Wellmachinery lines. Genl De Lisle unmounted before each parade
	12th		Divine Service parade for the whole Brigade on the Football field. The Service was conducted by the Bishop in Jerusalem, The Corps Commander, Lieut De Lisle and other generals attended.

S Kerans Major O.C. 4th Worc Regt

WAR DIARY or INTELLIGENCE SUMMARY

Sheet 2   March 1916

(Erase heading not required.)

Instructions regarding War Diaries and Intelligence Summaries are contained in F.S. Regs., Part II. and the Staff Manual respectively. Title Pages will be prepared in manuscript.

Place	Date	Hour	Summary of Events and Information	Remarks and references to Appendices
S.S. Ivernia	13th		Orders were received to entrain on the 14th.	
"	14th		General fatigues. All outside tents much as. Sgts Mess, O Room, etc were struck at 2pm the remainder of camp was struck at 4.30pm. 1st Train arrived 11.10pm X.Y.Z. Coy and the following officers entrained: — Major Kenans (Commanding) Lt M. Pfizshue Lt Branch, 2nd Lt Knight, O'Neill, Harris, Broughton, Ramsden, Bannister, Turnbull, Moorhead, Johnson, Davis, Rothe, New, Field, Lt + Q.M. Butler, Capt Campbell, O.4 1st Train Lt Snag. 1.10 A.M. ENTRAINING was done very quickly. Arrived Alexandria 12.20pm. Party was paraded & went on board H.T. Transylvania. The men were told off to their messes. 2 Platoons of J Coy worked in loading the baggage. W Coy Lt Snag in 2nd Train at 4 AM Arrived Alexandria 3pm. The Coy was paraded & went on board & were told off to their messes. Two Platoons of Z Coy worked loading the baggage. When embarkation rounds, 1st Essex Rgt, 2nd Hants, 86 Brigade Machine Gun Coy + 56 Brigade Head Quarters left Alexandria 6pm.	
	15th			
	16th 17th 18th 19th		At Sea. Rounds at 10.30 A.M. daily. Very pleasant voyage. Physical Training for Capt & Subaltern Officers Lectures hall & officers by Lieut Cayley at 11.30 AM in Smoking Room. Trench Warfare on the 19th. Lieut Bell was never through the voyage.	
	20th		Arrived Marseilles at 7.45 AM Fatigue parties were detailed to unload ship.	

E. Kenans Major O.O. 4th Worc. Rg.

WAR DIARY or INTELLIGENCE SUMMARY

Sheet III March 1916

(Erase heading not required.)

Place	Date	Hour	Summary of Events and Information	Remarks and references to Appendices
Mavrovista	March 20th		The following officers went with the Battn. Major E.T.T. Kenna (Commanding) Lt-C. Felix M. Adjutant, Lt-C. M. Walker, Capts A.E. Stokes-Roberts, A.W. Brooke, R.C. Wynter, T.C. Hambling, Lt-C. T.Y.U. Beard, J.A. Smithson, 2/Lt-S. Bannister, 2/Lt-Y.W. Field, E.G. Daw, D.C. Dunglay, A.V. Johnson, E.M. Penhorn, R.H. Nunn & C.T. Woodward, S.S. Hanna, L.A. Brechen, L.A.W. Knight, Lt-R.C. Rooke 3rd K.O.S.B, 2/Lt-R.C. Brompton, A. Ramsden, B.M. Stoney, E.H. Sturrock, T-Sgt.14,10 Leahms 2/Lt R.G. Nield, 10 M.G. Staff 2/Lt E Tremlett & 9" Devons, & Capt N.H.W. Saw R.A.M.C. Fatigues were detailed to unload the ships.	
"	21st	10.15	Train left Anne Station (Pont One) at 4.36 pm consisting of M.G. Coy. + 72 N.C.O.s + men of "Y" Coy. Arrived Pont-Remy 11.30 p.m. 22/3/16. The Train was unloaded and the baggage brought to Hancourt in Motor Lorries. The party marched to Hancourt & were billeted by the interpreter	
"		2nd	2nd Train consisting of Z Coy & not remainder of "Y" & Head Quarters left Anne Station (Pont One) at 11.12 PM	
France	22nd		En Route (Train)	
Pont-Remy & Hancourt	23rd		1st Train are 20K. 2nd Train arrived Pont-Remy 3.15 AM. Train was unloaded Pont-Remy. Party marched to Hancourt & was billeted by interpreter in Motor Lorries. Party marched to Hancourt & was billeted by the interpreter. Ordnance Ordnance Lorries. At 2 p.m. the C Ormipshed the Bn. in front of billets. The W.O.C. 88 Brigade (Major D.E. Cayley) inspected the Bm. The Onwards on the Chapean at 4 p.m.	E. Kenna Major O.C. 4 M. Worc Regt

WAR DIARY or INTELLIGENCE SUMMARY

Sheet 4

March 1916

(Erase heading not required.)

Place	Date	Hour	Summary of Events and Information	Remarks and references to Appendices
Haucourt	24th		Bn. Route March at 9 A.M. Snowing fast & very cold. Lt A.C.R. Kearns (of Glasgow) rejoined the Bn. from 58th Brigade Staff.	
-"-	25th		Bn. Route March at 8.30 A.M. Route march of the times, cold march, returned 1 p.m.	
-"-	26th		Very wet day. The C.O. attended a congress of Brigade The Orchestra at 3pm in Bois de L'Abbaye	
-"-	27th		Bn. Route March at 9 A.M. Distance marched 16 miles. Some Rain.	
-"-	28th		Brigade Route March, concentrated at Bois de L'Abbaye at 9 A.M. Bn paraded 7.15 A.M. All Transport, Lewis Gun Team & R.A. [?] to Manoeuvres attended the parade. Major General de B—de inspected the route	
-"-	29th		at YAUCOURT. Bn Route march.	
-"-	30th		Party of five Officers + 18 other Ranks left on 8 days leave for England.	
-"-	31st		Proceed to new billets at SOREN FLOS. Weather much milder, sunny morning	

S. Kearns Major O/C
No 2/HLBMRC Regt

29th Division.

88th Infantry Brigade.

4th BATTALION

WORCESTERSHIRE REGIMENT

APRIL 1916

29

4 Worcester Regt
Vol 2

Army Form C. 2118.

WAR DIARY or INTELLIGENCE SUMMARY

(Erase heading not required.)

4. Worcesters

April 1916

Place	Date	Hour	Summary of Events and Information	Remarks and references to Appendices
Sorenflos	1st		Left Sorenflos and marched in Brigade to Bonneville, distance about 12 miles. Billets at Bonneville not as good as at Sorenflos or Vaucourt.	
	2nd		At Bonneville. Church parade. Conference of C.O's at 58" Brigade Hd. Qrs.	
	3rd		At Bonneville. Billets. Busy getting ready for a move to-morrow. At Bonneville remained in Billets. Inspection of Lewis gun teams of Sig. M. Transport by C.O.	
	4th		Left Bonneville & marched to Toutencourt distance of 16 miles. Dinner carried on the march, for which halt was given. The Brigade marched past the Corps Commander Lieut-Gen Sir. B. Thurston Woolcon, K.C.B., D.S.O. was accompanied by the O.C. 29th Division, Major-Gen H. de B. de Lisle C.B., D.S.O. Gen. Thurston Weston congratulated the C.O. Major Kerans on the way the Bmn. marched by & he also asked that it be made known to all Officers, N.C.O's + men of the 4th Worc. Rgt. who had served under him in the Gallipoli Peninsular, how pleased he was to have them march under his command. The men were given a ration of rum which was carried in their tea. Fine weather but very cold. Billets June something firing line only 6 miles to our front – Bmn in Reserve Area. 58' Bgd present, 87" Support, 86" firing line.	
	5th		At Toutencourt — in Reserve. Training of two extra Lewis Guns commenced, also entire bombers & snipers. A very good Field Force Canteen is attached or Toutencourt.	

S. Kerans
Major O.C. 4 "Worc"
Rgt.

104

Sheet II April 1916.

WAR DIARY
or
INTELLIGENCE SUMMARY
(Erase heading not required.)

Place	Date	Hour	Summary of Events and Information	Remarks and references to Appendices
April	4th		M. Townscourt. Bn & Coy training continued, also various classes of instruction. Poultry of 4 Officers & 5 other ranks left on leave to England, also various classes of instruction. A party of 4 Officers & 4 N.C.O's of M.G. Corp inspected the trenches on firing line held by 87th Brigade, noted the S.S. model rifle often in town. The Sgt Lt & M.O. of the Bn is very good. Strength 30 Offrs and 900 other ranks. Rations are excellent.	
	5th		M. Townscourt: Bn made march distance about 10 miles. Classes continued on bridging in trenches and continued. A party of 4 Officers & 6 N.C.O's went to firing line, a party to 2nd line of O.C. Corp & 8 N.C.O's	
	6th		M. Townscourt- Coy. on the disposal of their Commanders for Drill &c. One party marched the trenches and the 1st one to 2nd line	
	7th		M. Townscourt- Divine Service parade. Major Reeves left for Florescourt- (& "Army School").	
	8th		M. Febva, 2/Lt Kay to Bonmahen reported from leave	
	9th		M. Townscourt. One Officer & 5 other ranks left on leave to England. The Bn. marched to 2 knots of trenches at 5.45 p.m to move in position by 8 pm. Lt. Cayley marched the line of 87th going northward, about the Bn. to mount Park the Townscourt- The parade now done in order that everyone should know the position in case of having to reinforce. 3 Offrs & 44 N.C.O's marked firing line.	
	10th		M. Townscourt. Lecture on Jar & the use of the Ger. Helmet was given at 11.15 AM at Bgde Hd. Qrs. Offrs Lecture on chambers was fitted up with two cylinders, when the chamber got (Kearn) Major O.C. 4 M Worc. R.g.t

(NEXT SHEET)

WAR DIARY or INTELLIGENCE SUMMARY

Army Form C. 2118.

Sheet III April 1916

Place	Date	Hour	Summary of Events and Information	Remarks and references to Appendices
	11" (contd)		Full of gas. Officers + men fired on the gas helmet + went through, thus getting an idea of the kind of gas used by the Germans. Rain all day.	
	12"		M Tournecourt. Orders were received to move to Mailly Maillet. Everything now nearly dry. Moved out 5.45pm. arriving at Mailly Maillet 8pm. Rain the whole time, the men were very cheerful in spite of the fact that everyone was certain that Billets at Mailly Maillet 3000 were +92 2nd month not on leave to England.	
	13"		M. Mailly Maillet. Orders were received to the effect that the Bn was to form work in 4 + 5 Avenues leading up to the firing line. At 2.30pm the army C.O. + 4 Corp Commanders met up to inspect these avenues to ascertain what amt of work to be done W/Lt Corps marches to their trenches at 7.30pm + marched till 12.15 AM (14") X + 9 Corp moved on at 11.30pm I went not from 12.15 AM (14") till 5.15 AM. Notices of work, returning + watering 4 + 5 Avenues, also fixing them with .... + stones. The condition of these avenues was very bad, in same ?? + fat with mud. Great progress was made, especially with the Cav. Gen. deny to draw trenches. The Germans were very active on the left of our division, a great deal of heavy gun fire, being done by the enemy which was answered by our machine guns wh. replied. Very bad day, rain most of the time. 2" H.D. Troops + Workshops regained	

S. Kerona Major
O.C 4" Worc R.G.C

Sheet 4.

WAR DIARY
or
INTELLIGENCE SUMMARY

April 1916

(Erase heading not required.)

Instructions regarding War Diaries and Intelligence Summaries are contained in F.S. Regs., Part II. and the Staff Manual respectively. Title Pages will be prepared in manuscript.

Place	Date	Hour	Summary of Events and Information	Remarks and references to Appendices
Mailly Maillet	14th		The C.O. walked by the H.A. Div. at 11 A.M. & received instructions in connection with work to be done in Communication trenches. No 5 Minen was allotted to the Bn. At 12 Noon orders were received to send one Coy to relieve one Coy. Royal Fusiliers at Auchonvillers, the village is on road Beaumont-Hamel & Mailly Maillet distance 1000ft from firing line. Duty of this Coy to watch on improving the defences of the village & defend it in case of attack. This village has recently shelled by the Germans. 2/Lt Nairn reported from leave. 2/Lt O'Neil reported with party of N.C.O.s & men from course of instruction in trench mortars. X Coy proceeded to 5 Avenue at 7.30pm & great amount of work was done by these Companies. At 12 M. at 9.30pm. 2.d. At 11.30pm Railway was completely destroyed. Coy proceeded to Auchonvillers in relief of a Coy Royal Fus. at 7.30pm. Relief was completely ?—— Ram in torrents most of the day.	
Mailly Maillet	15th		Intelligence Officer & Company Officer 2.N.C.O.s per Coy. 1.N.C.C. Snipers marched the firing line at 10.30 A.M. 2/Lt Storey reported to 5 Avenue at 7.30pm ack with 2 Coy proceeded to 5 Avenue at 7.30pm to continue work in communication trenches. M Coy moved off at 7.30pm. X Coy at 12. Making up men in communication to 5 Avenue was marked and sent by ? Coy. The C.O? My marked the trenches, every night great progress was made in all trenches very changeable weather, rain & snow, occasional sunshine, very cold by R.E.	
Mailly Maillet	16		Divine Service in the village, R.O. & Englishmen 2/Lt O'Neil & 12 other ranks proceeded to Englebelmer to form trench mortar battery. M Coy & Auchonvillers were finding party in three reliefs working & taking orders from R.E. officer & from Q.M. T.E. Hambling and from ? when no men reported from leave.	

S. Kerans Major O.C.
"H" Bn. ? R.I.F.

Army Form C.2118.

Sheet 2. **WAR DIARY** April 1916

or

INTELLIGENCE SUMMARY

(Erase heading not required.)

Instructions regarding War Diaries and Intelligence
Summaries are contained in F. S. Regs., Part II.
and the Staff Manual respectively. Title Pages
will be prepared in manuscript.

Place	Date	Hour	Summary of Events and Information	Remarks and references to Appendices
	16th and 17th		Work was continued. W & X Coy moved off 7.30 pm; Z 10.30 pm; Rain all day. Major Kerans rejoined	
	18th	7.30 pm	Monday. Battal. Bn engaged in work in communication trenches from 6.15 pm to 3.30 am 17/18. Rain most of the day & night.	
	18th		Orders were received for the Bn to relieve the R.M. Fusiliers & part of R Dublin Fus in firing line.	
		11.30 pm	Many Reliefs, time & part of the line men on duty relieved. Relief commenced at 7.30 pm & was completed by 11.30 pm. Head Qrs, Sig Qr, Bombers, Snipers, Lewis guns were relieved in they 2 fd. a. Raining all day & night.	
	19th		In firing line. 2nd D.A.C. Roberts reported. Two Coys 1st Newfoundland Regt. arrived & took up position in Support trenches under the orders of O.C. 4th Worc Regt. Bn. worked during the day in repairing the trenches which were in a very bad state owing to the rain. At night work was carried out on the new firing line, front of forward lines, men were going through about. Very wet day & night.	
	20th		In firing line. Work continued in trenches & new firing line. Rain day & night. Very expensive. Work carried on by Lieut under German Machine guns & fire early part of the evening. O.C. 29th Bde Major Gen. De Lisle visited the firing line.	
	21st		In firing line. Work on repairing trenches carried on during day & night. Enemy fired 8 range shells from trench mortars which fell into left of redoubt. One dug out was demolished killing 4 men. Rain incessantly from 11 am & kept on all night.	

L. Kerans Major
O.C. 4th Worc Regt

WAR DIARY or INTELLIGENCE SUMMARY

Sheet 76

Place	Date	Hour	Summary of Events and Information	Remarks and references to Appendices
	22nd		In firing line. Still running. Artillery very active on both sides during day. During night the Norfolk and Reg't took part of the firing line held by J & K Coys who came back into Support trenches. From 10 to 11 am artillery very active on our right. Lt. York (Yorks Regt) reported Hd Bn.	
	23rd		In firing line. Fine day at last. Work carried on during wet weather from trenches & manoeuvring round. Lt. & Lt. Regt. C. Felix Liewer (or C. Ferrer Army School of Instruction at Flixecourt. Men from the Bn. were relieved by the Hampshire Regt & marched into billets at Englebelmer. Men were given 24 hrs rest & were eventually returned. Revd Sadler (the 3 meeting of Stokes on War) worker arrived.	
	24th		Day at Englebelmer. Spent in drying clothes & generally cleaning up. Bn. detailed for work on Communication trenches. C.O. & Coy Commanders inspected work to be done by Coy marched for 4 hours left at 9 pm. 2nd Lt. Strange joined the Bn. for duty.	
	25th		At Englebelmer. Following were received from Corps Commander. It-Yen Sir Aylmer Hunter Weston K.C.B. D.S.O.:— My kindest greetings to those the anniversary of your great achievement. He who met all officers & men at Bhq H.Q. One who had been present at the landing on the 25 April was informed on Tipperary Avenue. Coys marching in relief to honor this toast-day and my all. A new line was reconnoitred for a communication trench to be closed at to endeavour. Major Kerans went on leave to England.	
	26th		At Englebelmer. Work started & carried on continuously on Whittington Avenue a new communication trench. W Coy continued work on Tipperary Avenue & 1st Avenue 10th Yorkly Capt. Kerans reported from leave.	

S. Kerans Major O.C.
4th Bn. Norf. Regt.

WAR DIARY
or
INTELLIGENCE SUMMARY

(Erase heading not required.)

Sheet 7 April 1916.

Instructions regarding War Diaries and Intelligence Summaries are contained in F. S. Regs., Part II. and the Staff Manual respectively. Title Pages will be prepared in manuscript.

Place	Date	Hour	Summary of Events and Information	Remarks and references to Appendices
	27th	M.	Englebelmer. Work carried on as before. A beautiful day.	
	28th	"	Work as usual, enemy guns more active, partly on our my B? was shelled & reserved men kild.	
	29th	M.	Englebelmer. Work on as before. Snipers were given Mt. Range to test near my 81th Enemy heavy guns very active in the early morning, several shells dropping near village. Our guns bombard enemy lines from 2330 to 0030, his ranets were attempted but mostly with much success on the enemy show in great force. No work was allowed at night. 2/4 - Bn. now returned from leave.	
	30th	M.	Englebelmer. Work as on 26th. C.O. attended conference at Bgde. Head Qr. being num o2 1600. M. 1945 enemy shelling was heard on our own right & appeared to be chiefly from the enemy channel guns. Voluntary Church service was held in the library.	

E. Kerans
Major O.C.
4th Bn. Worcestershire Regt.

29th Division
88tbh Infantry Brigade.

4th BATTALION

WORCESTERSHIRE REGIMENT

M A Y 1 9 1 6

WAR DIARY or INTELLIGENCE SUMMARY

Army Form C. 2118.

4 Worcesto R[egiment]
May 1918

Sheet 3

Place	Date	Hour	Summary of Events and Information	Remarks and references to Appendices
May	1st	AM	Eng[lish]men C.O. & party of 6 officers marked the trenches to warn & for relief. Quiet on our front. Work on roads	
"	2"	AM	Eng[lish]men Party of 6 officers marked the trenches. Heavy showers & thunder	
"	3rd		Fine day. C.O., Adjt & Coy Commanders left H.Q. Englishmen for the trenches at 2.30pm. R.Map commenced to leave Englishmen at 4.30pm at 10 minutes intervals to have relieved by R.E.[?] men were concentrated from 0100 - 0230 and relief by 11.30 PM. Capt. Wynter & 2/Lt Johnson with 4 men out guide on patrol went with wounded. No enemy at the southern road.	
"	4th		In firing line. Quiet day. Much work done. Capt Wynter, 2/Lt Bond & 2/Lt Johnson out on patrol with 10 men. 2/Lt Craven Johnson in in [?] of 31 Rounds	
"	5th		In firing line. Quiet day. D.L.N. Moore & few stretcher bearers by Von Appleby & Sanders [?]M.130AM. Capt Wynter, 2/Lt Bond, 2/Lt Trench, 2/Lt Hounslow, McApp & Bommaker hits 30 men on patrol. Pte. Ferrard wounded. Capt Wynter & some [?] officers & Pte. Reilly. The following returned	
2/"			2"PM. Major Huntbury, Mr 2 P[ar]ty Capt Wynter & remaining guns + completed. Sundown. Un returning at 3AM it Sgt Reed was killed by trench mortar & gun & completed. Mr Boyne & Sgt Wynn R.E. we in Canada left VA R. Porks left A.A. Monbyne	
		4	was found. MNo. Y/R. Hounsberry wounded. Pte Wood were missing. 21st R. 11 C. Porks left	
	H.Q.	5.13		
"	6"		In firing line. X. Coy relieved 2 in firing level. M. returned & Coy. 2"Bomb & 2/7 R. Bommaken	9
			[?] of 4 m.g. men to be in attendance & Section R.E. had thing Conrad 24 Pan in the Red d.	114
			and schedule of items to be examined on No apr 1/2 75	
	7" N		P.Mode morning at 11AM. A patrol the [?] and to perform night & patrol Capt Wynter Major	
	H.Q.	S.13	completed with & one in the field & [?] with [?] 2/Lt Wood	

Army Forms/C.2118.

Army Form C. 2118.

WAR DIARY or INTELLIGENCE SUMMARY

Sheet II

(Erase heading not required.)

Instructions regarding War Diaries and Intelligence Summaries are contained in F. S. Regs., Part II. and the Staff Manual respectively. Title Pages will be prepared in manuscript.

May 1916

Place	Date	Hour	Summary of Events and Information	Remarks and references to Appendices
	May 7th		In firing line. Worked round Mouse & Perrin St. 1pm C.O. & Mess-Adm B got information 3pm Capt Stephen. Relief on front the day. Enemy's front unknown as men on sentry on all night. Relief came punctual. Quiet day on front.	
	" 8th		Inspecting lines. 3 am day the Bn was attacked by 2nd Line Turc. Rein. reinforced by 1/1 from Bn. 2nd units into battle. A Achava Wood. moved at 7.5 under Hd. Qrs. & were ordered to take no arms. Time estab. in firing line Q. & 1/9/16 & Q. & 1/2 Bn. Hol Q. on White Q.H.S.	
	" 9th		At Achava Wood. Quiet not cold. The Bn had a general clean up 2/Lts Togman & Newman joined for duty.	
	" 10th		At Achava Wood. Fine day. The Bn. moved with Bdes A Roadly Madlah X & 3 Coy moved off 10.4M reported pushed as reinforcements and Bde on northerly 2 Coy arrived bivouac Madlah W Coy moved the Roadly Madlah & have bottle supplies. Action before morning to Madlah Madlah W Coy moved the Roadly Madlah & have bottle supplies. Action Schenn camp. 2 M. Formed workings party of 3 & 20 left Camp at 7.15 pm. worked union P.E. by gas. twin the Elle. W that no compl. outlies were to supply two meals with the duty	
	" 11th		In Huth. Fine day. A/L. worked prt twice from 9 M X. & 1 prt twice from 1am X Coy men and hired M. Jun. hebrenthern at the short range. to balance grown for duty.	
	" 12th		In Huth. Working further as usual. Bombing my day. war as usual out M.C. S.G. last all worth of Sgt. Repeat Could any Straight 8 Bn. M.C. Rubbe 1020 S/Neum Major H. Mount R.B. OC 1st M. Mount R.B.	

2449 Wt. W14957/Mgo 750,000 1/16 J.B.C. & A. Forms/C.2118/12.

WAR DIARY or INTELLIGENCE SUMMARY

(Erase heading not required.)

Army Form C. 2118

Sheet III   May 1916

Place	Date	Hour	Summary of Events and Information	Remarks and references to Appendices
	May 13th		Cold. Monday day. No working parties found during day. 6.40 men proceeded to "Open Road" pump-shaft with Capt. [?] R.E. At 11.15 P.M. Return parties & the B.S. At 11.30 P.M. an enemy shell burst just outside hut Sgt containing 8 men around amongst whom a miller had exploded killing 1 man & wounding Pte. Sgt [?] & 19 men, 10 of these were reported seriously wounded, 5 of these to hold. The C.O. inspected & another hut found in Brigade	
	14th		Cold weather. Had no men held Open Road all day. M & X Coys played a football match and during afternoon & 32 men worked in Coys trenches for clearing up the debris. 2/Lt Monteith 20 men gone for duty off [?] Survey course v 12 Midnight [?] loading 3 Coys 2/Lt Morris [?] 20 men gone for duty.	
	15th		Very mild day. May inspection [?] during day at 10 a.m. Coys had full hut inspection. 3 men killed by shell fire yesterday. Pte & Cash were conveyed to their party as return. During night all 4 Coys 6.31 a.m. [?] & 7.15 p.m. [?] of 4th [?] by 24th Div. During [?] trench work on the left of the line held by 24th Div. W Coy & 2/Lt Sedgewick were CO of 9 men left over after 4.30 p.m. Ltr Capt & the O. pre. forces report	
	16th		Fine day. Coy marched Camp at 12 Noon. No mention very truly was found as usual.	
	17th		Mild & [?] as usual	
	18th		Fine day. Bn served with Bath & Eng Platoon as S.P.O. Day spent in training Coy ground. M & Z Coys joined Eng Platoon & term report on time attacked ground & removed Officers at 4.30 p.m. R.E. Officer returned 12. 2.30 M Pts 4 hrs. 100 mm & 2 Officers & 1 Coy of morning dragging water from French & food control	

E. Neams

Major O.C.
4th M.C. Reg

WAR DIARY or INTELLIGENCE SUMMARY

Sheet 4   May 1916

(Erase heading not required.)

Instructions regarding War Diaries and Intelligence Summaries are contained in F.S. Regs., Part II. and the Staff Manual respectively. Title Pages will be prepared in manuscript.

Place	Date	Hour	Summary of Events and Information	Remarks and references to Appendices
May 19th			Inglebelmer Fine day. C.O. & Adjt inspected Yellow line & forts during morning. At 2.30 pm C.O. inspected work to be done by the Bn. "X" Coy went out at 8 pm to commenced work at 9 pm. Commencing with 'X' the work continuously day and night connecting 7 JP and 8 JP and Fanny lane to up in Fanny Lane in Knightsbridge.	CO
" 20th			At Inglebelmer. Fine day. Work carried out as before C.O. & Adjt went to Flaxcourt to attend demonstration of Bayonet fighting, bombing etc. given by Statenhoef at the end of warnw.	
" 21st			At Inglebelmer. Fine day. C.O. inspected the trenches & various working parties. Lt & Adjt C Felton returned from the 4th Army School at Flaxcourt.	
" 22nd			At Inglebelmer. Work as usual. C.O. visited the detachment at Fork Prowse & Moulin à feu & shells fell in Fork Prowse. At 10.30 pm a heavy bombardment by the Germans was heard on our left followed by what appeared by the sound, repeated machine gun fire from British. Troubles it may be of day.	
" 23			At Inglebelmer. Work as usual, carried on day & night. CO inspd. round the trenches day & night. Another fine day.	
" 24th			At Inglebelmer. Work as before. 2nd in Command & Adjt inspected the forts CO visited the Parks. Rain began 12 to 5 pm & continued nearer in of day & all night.	
" 25th			At Inglebelmer. Still raining. Work as usual 2nd in command & Adjt visited as usual the working parties in morning. Adjt visited parties at night in Festubert St. Bayonet trench. Very little shelling from artillery. day & night.	

E. Kennis Major O.C.
4th Manc. R.E.

WAR DIARY or INTELLIGENCE SUMMARY

Sheet 5   May 1916

Place	Date	Hour	Summary of Events and Information	Remarks and references to Appendices
At Inglebelmer	May 26th		Very dull day. C.O. went out to reconnoitre way of taking Bn to White City, line of trenches to be taken up from 16th Middlesex on Saturday. Work was carried on as ordinary. Orders were received in connection with move.	
※	28th		The Border Regt relieved the Bn at Inglebelmer from Monturn & Reconnoitring the day. Adjt, R.S.M. left 2 for firing line at 11.30 a.m. C.O. & Hd. Qrs. personel left 12.45 P.M. W Coy left 1.30 p.m. By platoons at an interval of 10 minutes between them. This Coy took up left of firing line occupied by 16th Middx. "Z" Coy left at 2.30 p.m. & took over on W & took over right of firing line. Y Coy left at 3.15 p.m. Taking up support line in Tenderloin (they are support line at St. Helena). X Coy left at 4 p.m. Taking up support line on the other side. The Relief was completed by 5.30 p.m. Both the Coys adopted a new order of March with the exception of Fort Prowse, which was relieved at 5.30 p.m. arriving at White City. 1 PM (29th) 1 Platoon 'Z' Coy worked during night R2 in deepening & opening up Healey St. Tenderoin Tenderloin to firing line. 2 Platoons X Coy worked in Esaw May from 8.30 to 11.30 p.m. making traverses & repairs. 2 Platoons Y Coy at 11.30 p.m. worked till nearly daylight 2 Platoons X Coy at 11.30 p.m. deepening. 2 Platoons Y Coy relieved "X" Coy & worked in Turn & Down & area Sts, widening & deepening, were relieved by Platoons of Middlesex worked in Lum & Down & area Sts, widening & deepening, were relieved by Platoons Y Coy 2 11.30 p.m.	
※	27th		A fine day & night R2. Capt. Vann Storey joined for duty. Mr. Inglebelmer. Coy Commander, C.S.M's & guides marched trenches to be taken over from 16 "Middlesex" at the White City. Work was carried on hill 1 p.m.	
	29th		In firing line. White City received 4th round dose of Lemmon shells about 8 a.m. 90 men marched back a great number of shells failed to explode. A great amount of work was done in the Salient occupied by the Bn.	

SKean Major O.C. 4th Manc Regt

WAR DIARY or INTELLIGENCE SUMMARY

Sheet 6   May 1916

(Erase heading not required.)

Place	Date	Hour	Summary of Events and Information	Remarks and references to Appendices

May 29: continued:- Our artillery active early part of night. More German shells fell in White City about 6 p.m. 1 Officer + 9 men went on to move. Capt. Ripley, 2nd Lieut Bauch, M.G.O. joined for duty. A very wet night after a fine day. Lieut Cayley visited the trenches.

" 30th: In firing line. Still raining. Trenches very muddy. A new communication trench between Munden & firing line was started by "Z" Coy. Great progress was made with this work on hand, especially on 4th Avenue R. Great deal of Artillery fire was done by the Germans, has no damage was done in our Sector. Our artillery who did a great deal of firing, caused this 11 am to during night.

" 31st: In firing line. A very nice day. Lieut De Lisle 29 "Divn" & Lieut Cayley 66 "Bgde" visited the line & inspected work done for special work to be carried out. 5th Avenue was shelled by the Germans twice during the day, with no effect. About 200 shells were fired at one of our aeroplanes with no result, the plane kept hovering round over the German lines just like a bird, eventually returning to our own lines. Wonderful flash of the aviators. Great deal of work was done digging day & night.
2 2nd Lt & 14 men joined 13th; 2 Lieuts Field + Todd & 9 men reported off duties

L. Knowes Major
O.C. 4th Worc Regt

29th Division.
88th Infantry Brigde

4th BATTALION

WORCESTERSHIRE REGIMENT

JUNE 1916

WAR DIARY or INTELLIGENCE SUMMARY

Army Form C. 2118.

Sheet I June 1916

4 Worcester Regt

Place	Date	Hour	Summary of Events and Information	Remarks and references to Appendices
June 1st	1st		In firing line. Fine day. Great deal of work done especially in constructing bridges as overhead cover in all communication trenches and firing line. Gen. Cowley inspected the firing line. Two gas alarm horns were placed in position, one in the White City, one in firing line. Artillery on both sides active. Casualties 1 man.	
Firing line (White City)	2nd		Dull day. 4th Avenue shelled by Germans at 4 A.M. Several shells fell right in the trench. Our aeroplanes were out very nearly. Germans directed machine gun fire and shrapnel on them, with no effect. Several bridges for overhead cover were erected in 4th Avenue and King St. 5th Avenue was shelled at 6 P.M. no casualties. Lt. A.C.R. Kearns to Hospital.	
— " —	3rd		Erection of overhead cover carried on in all trenches. A mine was carried out by the 6.6th Brigade on that part of German trenches called "The Hawthorne Redoubt." Artillery bombarded enemy's trenches from 12 Midnight to 12.30 A.M, then left off to 2 A.M. line. Raiding party discharged "Bangalore" torpedoes thro' cutting the wire. At 12.45 A.M. the party entered the German trenches + found them empty. They did not penetrate into the 2nd line. A few rounds were brought back which gave the information that the 119th Reserve Regt were holding the trenches in front of us. At 12.15 A.M. the German artillery replied to our bombardment, + very heavily shelled the White City. Two huts were hit. Casualties 11 Killed, 2nd Lt. New + 27 other Ranks wounded. Raiding party returned ↑ 1.30 A.M. Artillery ceased firing 1.30 A.M. Divine service on evening 9th D.	

Lt. Col. D.C. 4th Worc. Regt.
E. Kerans

124

Sheet II

INTELLIGENCE SUMMARY
June 1916

(Erase heading not required.)

Place	Date	Hour	Summary of Events and Information	Remarks and references to Appendices
Iringlind – White City	4th	At 6 A.M.	The eleven bodies were got out from the debris, and taken down for burial to Auchonvillers cemetery. 18 officers and 9 men returned from leave.	
"	5th		Great deal of work was done in erecting overhead cover. Two communication trenches were commenced from Minden to Funny lines, and from Landwick to Funny line. Jerries shelled firing line with H.E. from 11.30 A.M. to 1 P.M. very little damage was done. June day. Very wet day. C.O. went to Bogie Trench & oo at 12 Noon. Heavy bombardment was kept on night between 10 P.M.–12 M.N. Front line badly damaged by German artillery between 11 P.M. & 1 P.M. No casualties. Work carried on as usual. Cold wind, rain all night.	
"	6th			
"	7th		Showery weather. The Bn. was relieved by the 1st Lancashire's two front party arrived White City. The Bn. relief was completed by 5.30 P.M. Up to this time German artillery very quiet. The Bn. marched to Louvencourt where the men were billeted. The last party (transport) arrived Louvencourt where the men were billeted. Rain very heavy early part of night.	
Louvencourt	8th	1 A.M.	Several working parties were found from the morning. Deep regret was felt by all ranks death of Lord Kitchener. Working parties of 8 officers and 400 men supplied, working in the neighbourhood of Auchonvillers Wood R.E.	
"	9th		The Bn. was practised in the attack on Bengate Training ground during the morning. Fatigue parties were found at Acheux Wood & Acheux Amonoy. Wet day.	

S. Kevans
Lt-Col. O.C. 4th M Gore Rg.

June 1916   Sheet II

INTELLIGENCE SUMMARY
(Erase heading not required.)

Place	Date	Hour	Summary of Events and Information	Remarks and references to Appendices
LOUVEN-Court	10th		Working parties were found for Achicourt Wood, Achicourt Quarry, Water Supply & Railway Crossing Court. Very wet day.	
—"—	11th		Divine Service parade at Bogs. The Gen. Showery weather.	
—"—	12th		The 58th Brigade was practised in the attack on the training ground, marked out by Staff, own line of trenches and German trenches being marked. 2/Br. Bevans. Bevans rejoined. Staff were not. Working parties were found as on the 10th.	
—"—	13th		Brigade Training. Gen. De-Lisle 29th Dun. was present. After the parade he remembered that he was pleased with the men. A few working parties were found. Time was advanced one hour. 11 am became 12 Midnight.	
—"—	14th		Brigade Training 6.30 AM. Gen. De Lisle and the Corps Commander Sir Hunter Weston were present. Three large working parties were found. Orders received for the Battalion to move to Englebelmer to-morrow to relieve S.W.B's 2/R.W. Johnson rejoined.	
—"—	15th		Three large working parties were found. The Bn. commenced moving at 1 P.M. The working parties moved direct to Englebelmer after their Coys had been comp. relief. Party of 250 worked during night filling in Cable Trenches. Last party arrived Englm. 4.30 P.M. Brevet Major M. C. Sandhouse – Clarne arrived.	
Engelbel-mer	16th		Working parties 10 Officers 750 men were found, to build tramway lines, filling in Cable Trenches & deepening dug outs. Showery weather.	

S/Keram   Lt-Col O.C. 4th Worc Rgt

Sheet 4   June 1916

INTELLIGENCE SUMMARY
or
(Erase heading not required.)

Instructions regarding War Diaries and Intelligence Summaries are contained in F.S. Regs., Part II and the Staff Manual respectively. Title Pages will be prepared in manuscript.

Place	Date	Hour	Summary of Events and Information	Remarks and references to Appendices
Englebelmer	14th		C.O. & Adj.t visited trenches to be occupied by the Bn. that night previous to the advance. Large working parties were found as on previous day. A few shells fell in Englebelmer.	
— " —	18th		Working parties as usual were found. 2/Lt. Scott, Stewart, returned from 29th Divl School. Capt Ripley rejoined from Flixecourt. Fine day.	
— " —	19th		During night working parties were found carrying bombs etc. Bn. worked on overhead cover in the trenches.	Bn. worked in Trenches
— 12 —	20th		Working parties for working & sleep dug-outs were found during day. Bn. worked in own trenches during the night. 4 Lemans artillery kept firing at one of own Batteries just behind Englebelmer. Fine day.	
— " —	21st		Good deal of overhead cover was erected in own trenches during night. Working parties were detailed to take (Rogers) Johnston to the trenches during the night. 2/Lt. Wyatt proceeded to 2/9th Divisional School. Another fine day. Moorhead, Croom-Johnson.	
— " —	22nd		Topping day. Working parties were found at night taking (Rogers) to the trenches & cutting gaps in wire.	
— " —	23rd		The Bn. moved to Louvencourt after dinners hour, & took over billets from S.W.B.s. Very heavy rain came down about 4.30 p.m.	

E. Kerans
Lt. Col. O.C. 4th Worc. Regt.

Sheet 1

INTELLIGENCE SUMMARY

(Erase heading not required.)

June 1916

Place	Date	Hour	Summary of Events and Information	Remarks and references to Appendices
Lucien Camp	24th		The G.O.C. 88th Brigade had all Bn. Commanders & Coy Commanders of all Bns. at	
		10 P.M.	his views on the forthcoming attack. First stage of the attack commenced. Own artillery opened fire on German wire. All Battle stores moved nearer to Coy. The stores consisting of trench bridges, bombs, picks, shovels, Bangalore torpedoes etc, etc.	
—"—	25th		The Brigade was practiced on the training ground with R.F.Corps. Our aeroplanes made a raid on German observation balloons, three were destroyed. Our artillery continued bombarding the German trenches. Germans did not reply so vigorously as was expected. Our casualties practically no A few shells fell in Mailly Maillet, one accounting for 30 casualties. Practically no damage was done the own trenches. Showery day.	
—"—	26th		Bn was formed up in training ground, & received Genl. De Lisle who delivered an address on his departure. Three cheers were given. The General responded by giving three cheers for the Worcesters. Artillery bombardment continued along and night.	
—"—	27th		Brigade parade at 0900 pm last time before the advance. Bombardment continued.	
—"—	28th		Very bad weather. All ranks very cheerful marching to forming up area in the trenches. At 3 pm orders were received that all moves were cancelled for 48 hrs. The C.O. gave an address to the Bn. which through three managing good cheer from all ranks.	
—"—	29th		The Bn. paraded in the training ground for steady practice during morning. Heavy bombardment by own Artillery continued day & night.	Lt-Col O.C 4th Worc Regt S. Kearns

Sheet 6

INTELLIGENCE SUMMARY
or
June 1916.

(Erase heading not required.)

Instructions regarding War Diaries and Intelligence Summaries are contained in F. S. Regs., Part II. and the Staff Manual respectively. Title Pages will be prepared in manuscript.

Place	Date	Hour	Summary of Events and Information	Remarks and references to Appendices
Louencourt	30th		Handing in packs etc. and getting ready to proceed to trenches in the evening. Men going about singing, and as cheerful as could be. The C.O. went to a conference to Bgde 7th Div. Bn left Louencourt at 4 pm en route to the trenches. A halt was made at Acheux Wood where tea + rum was served to the men. Left Acheux Wood at 11 pm 1st & 2nd Bombardment at this time very heavy. at 1am arrived in the trenches 3.30 AM	Men

E. Kerans Lt-Col O.C. 4th Worc Rgt

"(29th Division
88th Infantry Brigade.

4th BATTALION

WORCESTERSHIRE REGIMENT

JULY 1916

War Diary

of

4th Bn Worcestershire Regt.

for

July. 1916

War Diary

of

4th Worcestershire Regt

from

1st July 1916 to 31st July 1916

volumn 5

E. Kevans Lt. Col.
4/Worc. Regt

Army Form C. 2118.

WAR DIARY or INTELLIGENCE SUMMARY

(Erase heading not required.)

Sheet 1.   July 1916

Instructions regarding War Diaries and Intelligence Summaries are contained in F.S. Regs., Part II. and the Staff Manual respectively. Title Pages will be prepared in manuscript.

Place	Date	Hour	Summary of Events and Information	Remarks and references to Appendices
Auchon-villers Sector	1st		The Battn was formed up as follows working its turn to advance. "X" Coy in Redoubt Line. "Z" Coy in Pompadour, "Y" Coy in Connell, and "W" Coy manned Haymarket, Bm. Hd. Qrs. in "The Tenderloin."	
		At 6 A.M.	a terrible bombardment was begun on the German Trenches. The Germans shot most reliable very much at this period. 4th Division on our left, 36 Division on our Right.	
		At 7.30 A.M.	the advance was begun by 86th & 87th Brigades. At 9 A.M. 88th Brigade received orders to reinforce. Newfoundland Regt went first and suffered heavy casualties from Machine Gun fire, Essex Regt also pushed on suffering casualties.	
		At 11.30 A.M.	the Worcestershire Regt and the Hants Regt received orders to push forward and occupy front-line and prepare for a fresh attack. The Bn. suffered the following casualties in moving up 5 Officers 96 other Ranks. At this time the Germans were bombarding all our trenches very heavily with all kind of shells. Telephone wires were cut & communication with Brigade was kept up by runner. At about 1 pm the attack was postponed. At this period communication in the trenches was very difficult owing to the dead and wounded, the trenches, dug outs, were badly knocked about. At 2.30 p.m. orders were received to hold the line at all cost, as the Germans would in all probability deliver an attack. Every one worked hard in repairing the broken trenches under most trying conditions. At 4 pm orders were received to make	

WAR DIARY or INTELLIGENCE SUMMARY

Army Form C. 2118.

Sheet 2 July 1916

Place	Date	Hour	Summary of Events and Information	Remarks and references to Appendices
Authuille Section	1st Continued.		preparations for an attack we found at 3.15 A.M. tomorrow. Everything was ready, but we had orders at 11.45 p.m. cancelling the advance. This order I am sure was disappointing as we were looking forward to capturing the German front line. The 13th remain in the Trenches hoping the Germans would attack, but no luck came our way. The 10th Reserves rejoined the 13th. Germans continued to shell our trenches day and night. C/-	
	2nd		In firing line. Germans unfilling very active, our lines were continually shelled during day. Commenced to rain very heavily at 8 A.M. The Trenches got in a very bad state and the work of clearing the dead and wounded, repairing trenches, parapets etc became very difficult. Small parties went over into no mans land and brought in the wounded. One of our men got to a wounded man close to the German trenches, when a German Officer (who must have been on the Staff by his dress) shouted to him, you must not stop there with him, if you want to come in, come along on else go back to your own trenches, the lad replied "I'll go back to my own trenches Sir". Two stretcher bearers were caught out and brought in the wounded man. At this time the Germans were acting straight, and allowed our fellows to bring the wounded from no mans land. Parties worked in reasonably trumping and Railing the water out, repairing the trenches, and burying the dead + xxxxx xxxx during the day, + xxg 22 burying	

Army Form C. 2118.

WAR DIARY or INTELLIGENCE SUMMARY

Sheet III   July 1916.

(Erase heading not required.)

Instructions regarding War Diaries and Intelligence Summaries are contained in F.S. Regs., Part II. and the Staff Manual respectively. Title Pages will be prepared in manuscript.

Place	Date	Hour	Summary of Events and Information	Remarks and references to Appendices
Authuille Section.	2nd continued:-		The dead in no man's land. German artillery still bombarding our lines. CY	
	3rd		Raining in torrents. Bn. Head Qrs moved from Limerick Junction to deep dug outs in Thiepval St. These dug outs were used by 88th Brigade on 1st July. The work of repairing trenches carried on. Trenches in places were three feet deep in water. German artillery more active than yesterday. Heavy fighting going on in our right in the vicinity of Pozieres Ridge. Casualties yesterday and to day 21 killed & wounded. CY	
"	4th		Still raining. Trenches in a terrible state, and the work done did not seem to make any impression as regards getting the water away as the rain came down very heavy. More wounded were brought in from no man's land. Lt. Brevet was killed by a sniper. About 4.0 Northumberland Fus. (Pioneer Bn) came up at night & commenced digging a fresh trench in front of our lines. Heavy shelling during the day. Casualties 21 NCOs & Men. 1 Rabbit. A mule damage was to have been sent up at 8 P.M. unfavourable wind prevented this taking place. B.N. Hd. Qrs moved back to "The Three Acres" CY	
"	5th		Still raining, but not so heavy as yesterday. Pumps were used & plenty of water got away. More bodies were buried during the night. Great deal of salvage was done, four zinc huns were recovered. Pioneer Bn. came up during night & continued work on new trench. Signs of improvement.	

Army Form C. 2118.

WAR DIARY *or* **INTELLIGENCE SUMMARY**
(Erase heading not required.)

Sheet 4   July 1916.

Place	Date	Hour	Summary of Events and Information	Remarks and references to Appendices
Auchonvillers Section	6th		Showery weather. Great quantities of rifles, equipt. &c were collected, and the trenches began to look something like. Yemen artillery very active, a lot of damage was done to Essex St-sparks of the old firing line. Casualties 2 Killed 4 Wd. Off.	
"	7th		Fine weather at last. Trenches getting dry. Parties working in repairing trenches day & night. Lots of equipt & rifles &c collected. 12 night 12 parties burying dead in no mans land. Casualties 1 Killed, 1 Wd. Off.	
"	8th		Fine day. Great improvement could be seen in the state of the trenches. Artillery active on both sides. Casualty 1 Killed. Off.	
"	9th		Another fine day. Strong working parties were put on in Essex St, this being the worst affected part of the area. Pumps were worked & nearly all the water got away. Dead were thrown during night. More salvage done. Yemen artillery more active than yesterday, this was in answer to our own Artillery. Yemen artillery 10 minutes heavy firing. Casualties 2 Killed 5 Wd. Capt T.P.S. Moreland joined for duty. Off.	
"	10th		Usual work carried on, on all the trenches, especial attention given to Essex & Jephson St. Our artillery fires very heavily at intervals. Yemen continued their usual above during the day and night. Casualty 1 Wd. Off.	

WAR DIARY or INTELLIGENCE SUMMARY

Army Form C. 2118.

Sheet 5   July 1916

Place: Auchonvillers Sector

Date	Hour	Summary of Events and Information	Remarks and references to Appendices
11th		Quiet day. In Esau St. & Fethard St., several places, no sooner is wire repaired than knocked about by German artillery, who continues to be active. O.T.	
12th		Work carried out as usual. Orders were received to prepare a march on the German trenches. The C.O. ordered 2/Lt Penhorn in charge, 2/Lt Bunney Thorne & 2/Lt Horn all up to the point where the party was to start from i.e. Mary Redan, & from there bombed out the points of entrance to the German trenches. 2/Lt De Isle marked the trenches to German artillery extremely active during day and night. Orders were attached to the Coy Commanders to K. now that he was pleased with all K. work, & also to say more attention to trench discipline. O.T.	
13th		Germans active. Everything was prepared for the march to night. German artillery M.G. very active during the day. 2/Lt Bunney Thorne discharged another chough at 3.15 P.M. M.G. (14th) Raiding party left 9.25 p.m. consisting of 3 Officers & 30 other ranks. The C.O. & 2d in Comd & Adj & members at Brigade Hqrs went to deep dug outs on Fethard St. 2d in Comd & Adj & members the Germans were very quick in finding this out, a red flare was sent up in quick succession another 3 mins. after the gun was discharged. They also opened heavy machine gun firing but very little rifle fire. At this time our own artillery opened a heavy bombardment, the Germans retaliating & vigorously all along our line.	

Army Form C. 2118.

Sheet 6

WAR DIARY
or
INTELLIGENCE SUMMARY

(Erase heading not required.)

July 1916

Instructions regarding War Diaries and Intelligence Summaries are contained in F. S. Regs., Part II. and the Staff Manual respectively. Title Pages will be prepared in manuscript.

Place	Date	Hour	Summary of Events and Information	Remarks and references to Appendices
	13th	continued.	They did considerable lot of damage to own trenches. The working party during heavy damage the Germans put up in front of Many M[en] were units not go further than new trench. B.M. the gas and smoke shells went off very well. At 2 p.m. it was noticed that Shrapnel Wood was on fire. Casualties 3 Wd. during day. C4	No
Authuille Section	14th		Genl. Conyley inspected Bm. Head Quarters. Battn. was relieved from firing line by the Newfoundland Regt. during the afternoon. Relief was completed by 5 p.m. Bn. marched to Camp in Mailly Wood Shonaymaston. C4	
Mailly Wood	15th		Fine morning. At 9 AM six German aeroplanes were seen over the wood one dropping but doing no damage. Day spent in a general clean up of Equipt; Clothing ets. Heavy rain during front of the night. C4	
—"—	16th		The C.O. inspected the Bm. in Marching Order at 10 AM. A working party of 3 Officers + 240 Other Ranks was found to carry Rogers to firing line. Orders were received to prepare a move for to-morrow night. C4	
—"—	17th		The Bm. was relieved from Mailly Wood by the Borders Regt. after dinner. Route marched to Achemoi Wood in Thelm. Relief completed by 6 p.m. The Officers encamped in the Wood reached the trenches + reconnoitre the ground as far as it	

WAR DIARY or INTELLIGENCE SUMMARY

Army Form C. 2118.

Sheet - 7

July 1916.

Place	Date	Hour	Summary of Events and Information	Remarks and references to Appendices
	14th		Continued:- Party left in Meroun Bivs at 5.25 p.m. The C.O. meeting them at Englebelmer was possible. Party left in Meroun Bivs at 5.25 p.m. The C.O. meeting them at Englebelmer. Heavy rain during the night. C/F	
Acheux Wood	18th		Dull morning. Raiding party returned at 5.30 A.M. Result:- Entered the German trenches, killing 5 or 6 Germans, no prisoners being taken which was their aim. The C.O. attended conference at Bgde Hd Qrs at 11 A.M. & was told the Bn. moved do an attack probably in a few days time. Draft of 68 Other Ranks joined from the Base, some of them being men who had been in Gallipoli. C/F	
"—"	19th		Fine day. Bn. marched to training ground at Lowrencourt & practiced the March. Returned to Camp at 1.30 p.m. In the afternoon the Bn. was formed up in the football ground & received an address from the Corps Commander Lieut Gen. Sir A. Hunter-Weston C/F	
"—"	20th		The Bn. was formed in the same place as yesterday & received an address from the Bungadier Gen. Cayley, who spoke words that will be remembered by all who are running this campaign. After inspection Bn. marched to Lowrencourt for training. 2/Lt O'Neill rejoined the Bath. from T.M. B. Coys paraded for ½ hour bayonet practice, ½ hour rapid loading during the afternoon. C/F	

Army Form C. 2118.

WAR DIARY or INTELLIGENCE SUMMARY

Sheet 8   July 1916

(Erase heading not required.)

Instructions regarding War Diaries and Intelligence Summaries are contained in F. S. Regs., Part II. and the Staff Manual respectively. Title Pages will be prepared in manuscript.

Place	Date	Hour	Summary of Events and Information	Remarks and references to Appendices
Acheux Wood	21st	12 Noon	Bn. (except D Coy) marched to Tournencourt to training ground & 3.0 A.M. Five German aeroplanes passed over the Wood, & were dispersed by our own artillery. The C.O. inspected the Transport at 10 A.M. 2/Lt Denham to hospital.	A
— " —	22nd		Coys were placed at disposal of Coy Commanders for drill etc. during the morning. Bayonet practice & Rapid loading was done in the afternoon. Orders were received that the Brigade would march to Beauval to-morrow. Very heavy artillery fire during day & night.	O.K.
— " —	23rd	7 A.M. 8.40 A.M. 1.45 p.m.	Breakfast. Bn. moved out. First-line transport marched in rear of Bn. 4 S. Waggons were brigaded & followed in rear of the Brigade. Arrived Beauval at 1.45 p.m. Four halts were made during the march. No one fell out. Billets at Beauval were good.	O.K.
Beauval	24th	10 A.M.	Morning up to dinner hour was spent in washing clothes etc. 2nd in Command inspected the Lewis Guns & teams, also Transport Limbers 10 A.M. Bombers were taken for instructions in the afternoon.	O.K.
— " —	25th	9 P.M.	Bde Route march at 9 P.M. Distance about 11 Miles. Fine day.	O.K.

2449 Wt. W14957/Mgo 750,000 1/16 J.B.C. & A. Forms/C.2118/12.

Army Form C. 2118.

WAR DIARY
or
INTELLIGENCE SUMMARY

Sheet 9   July 1916

(Erase heading not required.)

Place	Date	Hour	Summary of Events and Information	Remarks and references to Appendices
Beauval	26th		C.O's inspection in marching out order at 10 A.M. "Z" Coy best turn out of the Bn. Football match Officers of the Bn v Officers 2/Hants. Result 1–1. Another fine day.	O/-
"	27th	8.0A.M.	Bn. left Beauval at 9.40 A.M. and marched to Condas, where it entrained en route to Poperinghe. Arrived Poperinghe at 6pm, left Condas 12.57pm. Bn. was billeted as follows 3 Coys in a large Convent, 1 Coy in small Convent (opposite each other) Bn. H.Q. (in a small house opposite Convent) General Bullen (late C.O.) came to see the Bn. Off. at Condas.	O/-
Poperinghe	28th		The C.O. with the Brigadier (88th Bde) visited the front of the line to be taken up in Ypres salient.	O/-
"	29th		Party of Officers, N.C.O's, Sniping Officer, Bombing Officer visited the trenches in the morning. Bn. entrained at 9pm + proceeded as follows:- "X" + "Z" Ecole, "Y" & "W" Malmaison. Bn. arrived at 9.36pm. Coys were accommodated as follows:- "X" or "Z" Ramparts, Bn. Hd. Qn. in Allers opposite Convent.	O/-
Ypres	30th		Adjutant visited the trenches + took over all documents etc from Majr "Y" + L. Regt. 9.30pm Coys began to move off at intervals of 3 minutes between platoons. Relief was completed by 12 Midnight. Beautiful day.	O/-

Army Form C. 2118.

WAR DIARY or INTELLIGENCE SUMMARY

Sheet 75   July 1916.

(Erase heading not required.)

Place	Date	Hour	Summary of Events and Information	Remarks and references to Appendices
Ypres Salient	31st		Lieut. Cayley went round the line with the C.O. at 5 A.M. At 11 A.M. the C.O. had Coy Commanders, Sappers Officer, Bombing Officer & issued out-orders in accordance with instructions received from the Brigadier. Western Line: Artillery on both sides quiet. Parties worked mining in front, repairing communication trenches, & building machine-places. OF	

L. Knox. Lieut-Col.
O.C. 4th Bn Worc R⁹ᵗ

29th Division.
88th Infantry Brigade.
9------

4th BATTALION

WORCESTERSHIRE REGIMENT

AUGUST 1 9 1 6

Army Form C. 2118.?

Sheet I

WAR DIARY
or
INTELLIGENCE SUMMARY

August 1916 4 Worcester Regt Vol 6

Place	Date	Hour	Summary of Events and Information	Remarks and references to Appendices
In Ypres Salient	1st		Fine day. Great deal of work was done during the day in West LANE, Moseley LANE, Duck Walk, where boards were covered with wire netting. Artillery activity on both sides nothing to speak about. 2nd Lt. Wilson arrived from Base for duty. OH	
— " —	2nd		Hot day. Several shells dropped in No I A Crater. No Casualties. OH	
— " —	3rd		Another fine day. No I A Crater again was shelled, 1 Officer + 1 O.R. wounded by shrapnel. 2nd Lt. Holman joined for duty, also 2/Lt. Youngman. Parties worked in New Trenches from H20 to Railway, and trenches leading to No I Crater. Parties worked during the day running chalk towards new trench line. Our aeroplanes very active between 5 & 8 p.m. 1 M. killed on night working party. OH	
— " —	4th		Dull day. 3 German aeroplanes bossed over our lines at 5.30 AM. Followed by 3 more about 6 PM going in the direction of Ypres. During day parties worked on clunk towards M might. Parties worked as follows :- Mining in front of new Trench on night 2 of our line. Mining two to two trenches leading to No I A Crater, improving barriers in Moseley LANE, Making five steps in No I Crater, Collecting salvage. M + Z Corp relieved X + Y in firing line. Some shells in No I X No 7 13. OH	
— " —	5th		Yesterday bombs bossed the line at 5 AM. & remarked that not enough mining had been done, and bombed what part of the line he guessed improving at once. German aeroplanes very active between 5 & 9 AM. German artillery active with H.E. shells bursting as from our own lines, 7 NE & NW of the Salient. Usual morning barrier on chalk mounds	124

INTELLIGENCE SUMMARY

Sheet 1

August 1916

(Erase heading not required.)

Place	Date	Hour	Summary of Events and Information	Remarks and references to Appendices
In Ypres Salient	6:		were found during the day. Bungalow Gen Cayley visited the line early in the morning. Working parties at night as follows:- Entrance No Crater No.I commenced, new trench continued from #14 towards entrance of Gulfpoint Farm, also running party in front of above trench, party in new trench from H 20 to Railway line, party worked in Sap from 1½ 1A crater, & from 1A crater to firing line. Mine in front No 2 Crater ampresses (?) the front of the H 28 shewy trench with marie. CH	
			Quiet day. German aeroplanes again active between 5 & 9 A.M. Our guns opened fire but no hits seen. Their many. Working parties were found as before during day & night. Between 6 & 7 p.m. 5 German planes were seen over our lines, & about 8 p.m. a number (about 12) of our planes were seen coming back from over the German lines, evidently from a raid, German empty covered the whole sky with shells, but all the planes got well away without accidents. German artillery active between 4 & 8.30 p.m., our own artillery retaliating. 3 patrols went out during the night, 1 reconnd no man's land between posts 54 & 69. They found the ground full of shell holes, much loose wire hidden by long grass, which would impede greatly, progress in a raid or attack; another patrol examined ground in front between H 20 & Railway & found old firing line obliterated, this mine in front in good condition. The ground in front with few shell holes. 3? Patrol recommd old firing line North of Tombsters LANE, this could not enter it owing to the enemy having bombing posts there CH.	
—	7:		Dull morning. 12.10 A.M. Germans put a few shells into West-LANE. Working parties improving defences of craters during the day. Great deal of work was done in new trenches, entrance No.I Crater, & running front-line during the night. 2 Patrols went out during the night, 1 reconnd North of Tombsters LANE & one No patrol in O.8	

WAR DIARY or INTELLIGENCE SUMMARY

Army Form C.2118

Sheet III   August 1916

Place	Date	Hour	Summary of Events and Information	Remarks and references to Appendices
In Ypres Salient	8th		with a view of effective raid on German lines. OC Artillery not very active on both sides. Usual working parties found during day and night. At 10.30 pm the gas alarm horns were sounded on our left, by the 4th Divison it appeared to the 4th Division front. It was soon found out that the Germans had discharged gas. No gas approached our front line, but Bn. H.Qrs. & X Coy in Reserve & 7, 13 grd St, Helmets were found worn immediately the alarm was given and all were well. The gas alarm sounded 11.45 pm. & Helmets were then taken off. Our artillery kept up a heavy bombardment on the German lines during the whole time. Our working parties resumed work at 12.30 am.	
"	9th		Fine day. Officers 1st Newfoundland Regt. came & inspected the line during the morning OC as they were relieving the Bn. at night. 1st Coy arrived at 10 pm & relief was completed by 12.30 am. The Bn. went back to Ypres in Brigade Reserve. OC	
At Ypres	10th		Weather all fine. German aeroplanes active over Ypres. Heavy bombardment by our artillery took place by the Canadians line. 12 mgts. a party of 260 worked in the new X line crossing west. LANE. Party of 52 worked under O.C 88th M.G. Coy. & 56 under O.C 86th M.G. Coy. OC R.E. Party of 20 under R.E. during the day. 15 men were attached to	
"	11th		Very dull morning. Partly thundery. New X line was increased to 320. 17 few shells fell in the Ecole, no casualties. Same parties were found for work as on the 10th. 5 men were sent to Trench Mortar Battery. OC	
"	12th		Little Rain. German planes active over Ypres. Usual working parties were supplied. OC	

WAR DIARY or INTELLIGENCE SUMMARY

August 1916

Sheet 4

(Erase heading not required.)

Instructions regarding War Diaries and Intelligence Summaries are contained in F. S. Regs., Part II. and the Staff Manual respectively. Title Pages will be prepared in manuscript.

Place	Date	Hour	Summary of Events and Information	Remarks and references to Appendices
M. Ypres	13th		Fine day. Work carried on as on previous days. Lt-Morgan + 3 other Ranks left for Divisional School of Instruction.	29"
"	14th		Usual working parties were found, also the following sorties over:- 6 permanent No Wheel new O.P. 20 under R.E. turning m.g.t.s in Menin Rd. Potije Rd. German aeroplane dropped two bombs just behind Infantry B.H.Q. close to Bn. Head Qrs + also fired Machine Guns into the trench about 5 P.M.; no damage done, only a few old mattresses hit. O.K.	
"	15th		The C.O. + Coy Commanders visited the firing line with O.C. 8th Bgde at this time (11 AM) Germans shelled Sunken Rd, all being manoeuvre-shrapnel. Orders were given for a new trench to be commenced in front of S.18. W.X. + Y Coys worked on this new trench digging the night. Y Coy finishing then working parties in "X" line by West-LANE. The Regt. number "3" Camp, as orders had been received H.Q. the Bn. would be occupying this Camp when the new Camp come. As Divisional Reserve. O.K.	
"	16th		C.O. went to firing line trenches to see the works done in new Trench front of S.18. Usual working parties found. D.2. 3.15 P.M. the gas alarm horns were heard, but it was observed mostly afterwards that it was a false alarm. A German aeroplane was heard over the regiment, about O.R. the engine stopped two bombs, and fail to explode. O.K.	
"	17th		Showery morning. 2nd in Command went to "A" Camp also found working parties as	

WAR DIARY
or INTELLIGENCE SUMMARY

Sheet 5

August 1916.

(Erase heading not required.)

Instructions regarding War Diaries and Intelligence Summaries are contained in F.S. Regs., Part II and the Staff Manual respectively. Title Pages will be prepared in manuscript.

Place	Date	Hour	Summary of Events and Information	Remarks and references to Appendices
Pop Ypres	18"		No details of officers & Sgt's messes during the 10 days the Bn would be in Div. Reserve. The Camp was changed from "B" to "A". Working parties as usual were found.	C.4.
— " —	19"		Still showery weather. Working parties were found for X line only, besides the usual R.E. parties. Wiermight.	C.4.
			Fine day. Party of 7th Royal Fus. (2nd Bn.) & 1 Officer arrived to relieve this Bn. relieving us during the night. The Bn. arrived at Poperinghe at 11 p.m., & eventually got away by train at 1.10 am. Arrived "A" Camp, Flamertinghe 1.40 AM.	C.4.
"A" Camp	20"		Raining. A most extensive programme was drawn up for the Bn. to follow during the 10 days. Divine Service paraded at 11 A.M. in field close to 29" Div. Canteen. 2/Lt Strang returned from Hospital.	C.4.
— " —	21st		Fine day. Camp commenced training. In the evening 30% were allowed to go to Poperinghe on pass; there was very little.	C.4.
— " —	22nd		Dull day. Gen. De Lisle inspected the Camp, when he gave the guard, he remarked it was the smartest guard he had seen in the Division the morning. Training in bombing, Lewis guns, Rapid Wiring, Company, & C.O.'s R.C. continued.	C.4.
— " —	23"		Training as usual. Party of 1 Officer & 50 men went to handle transport lines at 2-0 am.(?) on the drainage of Camp. 2/Lt Scott joined.	C.4.

Sheet 6

INTELLIGENCE SUMMARY

August 1916

(Erase heading not required.)

Place	Date	Hour	Summary of Events and Information	Remarks and references to Appendices
In A Camp	24th		Training carried on as before. Bayonet fighting course was improved by "D" Coy, by erecting frame for hanging nosebags & a trench dug.	
-"-	25th		Great improvement seen in the Bn. through the training. Party of 100 found for dig.g gun cable trench in front of Ypres during the night.	
-"-	26th		Dull & rainy day. Training carried on till 1 pm. Brigade Marshall or Arms commenced exam. The Bn. Meck. Ist party for transport, Snipers, & Officers Servants. Party of 200 found for digging cable trench.	
-"-	27th		Showery day. Divine Service parade at 11 A.M. Armd. Day. Holiday.	
-"-	28th		Training as usual. Party of 400 found to finish Cable trench during the night.	
-"-	29th		Still showery weather. Camp marked in takeing up all shell proofs, & laying a double line across the Camp. Orders for the move to-morrow to Ypres were received to all concerned.	
-"-	30th		Raining. A violent storm broke out about 10 A.M., & it commenced to rain very heavily. 1 Coy of the Camp got flooded. The Bn. moved by trains from H.B.A. 8.15 pm & arrived at Ypres by 10 P.M. Parties of 40, 20, & 18 were formed by 8 pm & 4.10 pm. All Coys were in position by 2 midnight.	
In Ypres	31st		Nice morning after yesterday's storm. German artillery very active during the morning. The 18 arms to last night till now found for work also one of 40 & 20 to R.E. & one of 75. Artillery which in RGA were observing evening.	

S. Kearns Lt-Col. O.C. 4th Monm Regt

29th Division.

88th Infantry Brigade

4th BATTALION

WORCESTERSHIRE REGIMENT

SEPTEMBER 1 9 1 6

Confidential

War Diary

of

4th Worcestershire Regt.

for period

Sept 1st 1916 to Sept 30th 1916

(volume 7)

WAR DIARY
or
INTELLIGENCE SUMMARY September 1916

Sheet I

(Erase heading not required.)

Instructions regarding War Diaries and Intelligence Summaries are contained in F.S. Regs., Part II. and the Staff Manual respectively. Title Pages will be prepared in manuscript.

Place	Date	Hour	Summary of Events and Information	Remarks and references to Appendices
Ypres	1st		During the day 130 men worked under the R.E. on different parts of the line, and 200 men worked in front of the line during the night. German artillery manned Cavalry B's about 6 pm. Our aeroplanes active the whole day. Gas alarm was given at 10.30 pm, but after an hour it was found to be a False Alarm. OC	
"	2ND		Working parties were found in various parts of the line and Ypres under the R.E. by day and by night. 1 man dead was done in Trenching parties from Servants and Orderlies at Bn Head Qrs in Ypres. Showing weather OC	
"	3rd		Usual working parties under the R.E. by day and by night. 12 men found. Lt-T. Grgann and 5 O.Rs returned from Divisional School on completion of course. Mild night. OC	
"	4th		Fine day. One extra working party was found to work in Murdoch LANE. German aeroplanes active between 5 & 6 pm. Very quiet day. Capt. Matthews and 5 O.Rs proceeded from Etaples, Lewis gun Course. OC	
"	5th		Servants and Orderlies room nearly completed. Working parties found as on previous days. Capt. & Col. Mr H. Parker to Hospital. OC	207L
"	6th		O.C. Coys and 2/In Command worked the Right Sector of the Firing line. About 6 pm German Artillery shelled behind Infantry Bln with H.E's, evidently directed at some of our batteries. OC	
"	7th		8.30 AM. bombers of our aeroplanes were seen going over the German lines, they were shelled very heavily, but they all went their way unharmed. Platoon officers worked the firing line. Orders were received for the Bn to move up to the Right Sector to morrow night. OC	

WAR DIARY or INTELLIGENCE SUMMARY

Sheet II Sept. 1916

(Erase heading not required.)

Instructions regarding War Diaries and Intelligence Summaries are contained in F.S. Regs., Part II. and the Staff Manual respectively. Title Pages will be prepared in manuscript.

Place	Date	Hour	Summary of Events and Information	Remarks and references to Appendices
Ypres	8th		C.O. visited the firing line at 5 A.M. At 9 A.M. orders were received for Coy. Commander as to line to move up. Coy began to move off at 4.45 p.m. The following was the order of move up:- Z Coy, right of LINE, W Coy left of LINE, X Coy in Support, Y Coy in Reserve. Relay was completed by 10.30 p.m. Very damp + muddy night. O4.	
Firing LINE	9th		Very foggy morning, but cleared up at 11 A.M. Brigade Major, Major Bailey R.E. & C.O. men 2 round the line, & made programme of work which required immediate attention. Patrol of 10 O.Rks. taken out last night by 2nd & 3rd Wgrtts in connection with enemy work reported. They plainly heard the Germans working and by the sound heard they must have been using concrete. Very quiet day on the whole. Night flying by our aeroplanes took place at 10 p.m. O4.	
-"-	10th		Very dull day. At 5 p.m. our heavy guns registered on German lines in front of H 19, 20, 21. The Germans retaliated with small trench mortars and Minnenwerfen, no casualties, but the parapets in Sunken Rd, S21 & H20 were blown in. Most important work in progress. Building New Bm. Head Qrs in 711, & Coy. Hd. Qrs in S18, and Platoon Commanders dug outs in both Right & LEFT Coys in firing line. Very little activity shown by aeroplanes. Patrol of 1 Officer + 10 men examined enemy's wire in small salient I 11 B 95.60. Wire appears to be rib of scrap wire closely piled together. Small Elephant iron accessories brought up during the night. O4.	
-"-	11th		At 9. C. 88th Brigade visited the firing line at 7 A.M. The C.O. accompanied the General round. Our aeroplanes active during the hours of 8 & 12 Noon. German artillery fired a few shells between 10 & 11 A.M. Great deal of work was done in connection with	

WAR DIARY or INTELLIGENCE SUMMARY

Sheet III   Sept. 1916

Place	Date	Hour	Summary of Events and Information	Remarks and references to Appendices
Firing Line. Ypres	12th	2 A.M.	Coy Head Qrs in Right Coy & Platoon Commanders quarters in firing line. Parapet in S.2.1. was heightened & thickened for a distance of 30 yards. Rain during the night. Parapet from 10.P.17 No 2 Md St. Broadway & I.O.R. repaired from bombing school, Teagleham. O⊥	
			Dull morning. Yeomans artillery fired about 30 shells most shrapnell on left and west of firing line over Artillery retaliated very quickly with four times as many shells. Heard amount of timber was carried from Hell Fire Corner to 7.11 Jan Bn. Head Qr. Our heavy guns registered on German lines opposite H.19, 20 & 21, at least 80% of the shells were observed. German artillery very active especially their trench mortars during the afternoon, shells falling on Sunken Rd, 7.11. The whole of S.18 was more a ruin. By Coy during the night. A strength of 4 men. Yeomen. O⊥	
—"—	13th		Dull morning. Yeoman artillery active between 11 A.M. & 1 P.M. Very heavy shift came over falling in 7.11, Duck Walk. Two men wounded, retaliation was ordered from Yeoman about 1.30 p.m., round in our favour. General De L'Isle 29th Division visited the line & Bn Head Qr. On this remark in the Coy Mess Room "My next his the Right Bn was generally satisfactory. He ordered more firestep to be made in the front line & the parapet to be thickened. Patrol of 1 Officer & 10 B. Ranks went in front of No 2 A Cross & examined the ground & reported no enemy being. That the Germans were at work. Hell Fire Corner was shelled between 4 & 5 p.m. 2 n.c.os & 10 Ranks left for England Zn in course in Machine Yun & Trench Mortar. Firing up of Coy Head Qrs & Platoon Commanders quarters in firing line nearly finished. Very cold night. More wiring done in front of S.18, & another march and thickened in S.21. O⊥	

WAR DIARY or INTELLIGENCE SUMMARY

Sheet 4   Sep 2 1916

Place	Date	Hour	Summary of Events and Information	Remarks and references to Appendices
Firing LINE Somme	14th		Extremely cold morning. Wind high, but in our favour. Between 4 & 6 pm German artillery very active, no casualties, but the parapet in several places were badly knocked about. Our trench mortars and artillery retaliated. A great deal of work was done all round.	
—	15th		C.O. went to Brigade Head Qrs to see marching party products from the last line. Everything was fixed for the raid to take place to-night. During the whole day our artillery very active. The Germans with the exception of a few shells from Trench Mortars, showed no retaliation in connection with the raid. The following was very much the order:- At 2.15 pm orders were received in connection with the raid. The following was the order:- At 11 pm our artillery and Trench Mortars commenced bombarding front of enemy line ending I/12 A.0.8. and on five places where mines have been previously exploded. At 11.30 pm the marching party moved forward to enter the German trenches, at the time Artillery lifted. Party consisted of 3 Officers & 30 O.R's. 2/Lt. Wyatt + 5 men (his party) entered German trenches, he was shot by a German Officer in the stomach, who then ran into a dug out; 2 men of the party threw mills bombs down into the dug out, and then got 2/Lt Wyatt out of the trench. On the way back a party of Germans were encountered, some taken prisoners, two 2 of them were wounded. Killed + one lousing to death with the British lines, which was ultimately was required for identification purposes. The whole of the marching party returned at 1.30 AM. We had 1 Officer + 3 men wounded. During the raid the Germans were kept up a heavy bombardment on our trenches with artillery + minenwerfers and other trench mortars. Our trenches were badly knocked about. Tommies T.M. Battery were failed.	Lt R.C. Wyatt injured the Battn. C.f.

INTELLIGENCE SUMMARY Sep-7-1916

Sheet 5

(Erase heading not required.)

Place	Date	Hour	Summary of Events and Information	Remarks and references to Appendices
Firing LINE Mones	16th		Cold morning. Our aeroplanes very active. Germans continually firing at them with no result. One German aeroplane flew over our lines at 9 A.M. but the observer could not possibly see much owing to the heavy mist which was flying. 2nd Lt. J.C. Durrant, D.N. Moulds, joined the Bn. for duty. Captain Ripley rejoined. At 10.30 A.M. Germans shelled Rly Wood, Muddy LANE & 713. Whereabouts of A Frames were found in positions in firing line & Manoby LANE C.R.	
	17th		Showery up to 5 p.m. when it began. The rain very heavy. Trenches soon got in a bad state. Germans extremely active both in the morning and afternoon. Work carried on as usual. 2/Lt. J. Hall joined for duty. C.R.	
	18th		Lendrie Cayley visited the firing line at 6 A.M. C.O. went round with him at 4.50 P.M. The Germans commenced bombarding our trenches, which increased very heavily at 8.10 A.M. & one Minenwerfer up to about three hours. 2nd Lt. De Loste (who had only just come down) was hit through the arm. About the Bn. H.Q. Orderlies and told the C.O. who had only just come down R.E. he thought the Germans would attack. Orders were given at once from the platoon on N° 711 & two platoons in 711 (left) went to S.21. One platoon went to Muddy LANE Trench, 2 in 76 St. M. Coy and 711 (right 22) and S.15. X Coy were holding the left + of Aug the night of the firing line. The C.O. met the Adjutant went round the whole of the line and ascertained the damage done, which was severe. In Muddy LANE the band was about 60 yards was completely flattened down and impassable. In 711 two bays were destroyed + the ground behind 711 became full of shell craters. In Railway Trench at the junction of Sunken Rd up to Duck Walk a very large shell fell and by the amount of wreckage and the size of the window, it must have been an 8" or 11" shell. In the firing line from bays in H.14 + 16 were flattened, two bays in 7.19 + 20. Our artillery retaliated as far as the field guns were concerned, but the heavier port a long time before retaliating. Our casualties were 10 killed 11 Wd. 1 Missing. Other casualties occurred in accounts of fire of other trenches. During the whole time many came down in torrents, the gas trenches	3 M 1

Forms/C.2118/12.
2449 Wt. W14957/M90 750,000 1/16 J.B.C. & A

WAR DIARY or INTELLIGENCE SUMMARY

Sept 1916 Sheet 6

(Erase heading not required.)

Instructions regarding War Diaries and Intelligence Summaries are contained in F. S. Regs., Part II. and the Staff Manual respectively. Title Pages will be prepared in manuscript.

Place	Date	Hour	Summary of Events and Information	Remarks and references to Appendices
Flourbaix "B" Camp	19th		got very muddy and slippery. After the bombardment working parties were detailed to clean up. This was done throughout, and with the exception of two traps in H.19 & H.21, the whole line was cleaned up & made passable. The Bn was relieved during the night by the 2nd Royal Fusiliers. The men were very much disappointed because the Germans did not attack, a glorious chance for killing Germans if they had. Relief was completed by 10.30pm. Bn moved back into "B" Camp close to Ploegensteghe arriving there at 12 midnight.	CF
" "	20th		Showery weather. The men were given a day off for cleaning up rifles, equipt etc. A training programme was drawn up to commence tomorrow. Party of 1 Officer and 4 & 6 O.R. were sent to work early in the Transport lines. Owing to Companies being under opens only 2 Bn Officers and the established Cmdrs & Sub Offrs also established. Very wet and cold night. 2nd Lt Gray & Thomas joined for duty. Y.O. & 29" Bn moved to Brigade Rev in the morning.	CF
" "	21st		Still morning. Training commenced. Classes in bombing, Lewis Gun, Bayonet fighting &c also started, and working parties were found on an enemy double line of switch trench. Drafts of 6 joined.	CF
" "	22nd	4.30 PM	Dull morning. 4 Officers and 4 N.C.O.'s attended a lecture on Gas at Divisional School. Training continued till 4pm. The Bn. paraded to work on cable trenches in front of Ypres at 4.30 pm. Returned to Camp	CF
" "	23rd		Showery day. Training carried on as usual. German aeroplanes flew over the Camp at a very high altitude, our artillery fired but no luck resulted. 2nd day. Training carried on till 3pm. Football matches :- 2 Lewis, 1 - Lt Col F.W. Capt Coys 870 Rec Roberts won the Officers Revolver Compn. Major a score of 32 out of a possible 48.	CF
" "	24th	10.45 PM	Glorious day. Divine Service 2nd Lt Stewart to R.F. Corps. 2nd Lt Burnt to England. Cont: remained at Fochan, Sun. at Grantham.	CF

Sheet 7

INTELLIGENCE SUMMARY
Sept 1916
(Erase heading not required.)

Place	Date	Hour	Summary of Events and Information	Remarks and references to Appendices
Flauville "B" Camp	25th		Another fine day. Training went on till 12 Noon. In the afternoon all Coys practised with Small Bore Respirators. Football Match 2nd v 21st. Bath. proceeded to work on cable trenches in front of Ypres at 4 pm. Returned to Camp 11 P.M. O4	
"	26th		Beautiful day. Bn. attended lecture on the Small Bore Respirator at the Divisional Top School and then entered the Chamber. Coy Bombing & Bn. Bombing Officers & N.C.O's attended lecture on Lewis bombing and gymnasium. Boxing Tournament (Brigade) in the afternoon in C. Camp. One final was decided. Pte Murch beat Pte Morris winning Gold night. O4	
"	27th		Training as usual. Great day, news received of Counter Attack. Boxing in the afternoon Pte. Darby 4" Morse Rgt winner. L/8tc Wright. Bn. lost 2 & won 2 events. Orders were received from the move to firing line to morrow night. O4	
"	28th		Dull morning. Room heavily about 12 Noon. B.N. entrained at 2 Brandhoek 4 pm. arrived Asylum Ypres 4.20 pm. Relieved 13th Lanc Fus in Right Section. Relief completed by 10.20 pm. Rain during night. The King of Belgium with General Sixt. A Number-Westom marked the line in the morning when the Somme culture two were occupying the line. Draft of 2 Officers & 11 men joined. O4	
Firing Line Ypres	29th		Very dull morning & showery. Six of our aeroplanes passed our line at 2 p.m. 4 enemy formed up heavily but the planes all got away. Mind moving. German artillery shown several times during the day. O4	
"	30th		Nothing unusual occurred during the morning. At 5 pm our trench mortars & artillery opened on German line from O.4. A raid was made by the 13th Lanc Fus at 5.30 pm. The morning & early evening the trenches & found the Germans had left the front line, leaving rifles, equipt, coats &c, which the raiding party brought back, evidently a relief was being carried out. Lt-Myrddin + 2nd Lt-Morpher + O4	

L.S. Evans
Lt-Col G.C. M O.C.
F&G

29th Division.

88th Infantry Brigade.

4th BATTALION

WORCESTERSHIRE REGIMENT

OCTOBER 1916

Confidential

War Diary

of

4th Bn. The Worcestershire Regt

for period

October 1st 1916 to October 31st 1916.

volumn No 8.

E. Kevans Lt. Col.
4/Worc. Regt.

Army Form C. 2118.

Sheet I

WAR DIARY or INTELLIGENCE SUMMARY

(Erase heading not required.)

October 1916

Place	Date	Hour	Summary of Events and Information	Remarks and references to Appendices
Ypres Salient	1st		Nice morning. One of our aeroplanes was seen to bring down two German observation balloons in flames, a grand bit of work. In the afternoon another balloon was seen coming down in flames, but unfortunately it was reported to be Belgian. Aeroplanes very active during the whole day. Artillery very quiet on both sides during the day. Your men put in position on F.11, Sunken Rd, + Sap leading to Craters. O4.	
"	2nd		Very quiet day, especially after the march of the 30th. Began to rain at 11 AM. C.O. grounds of leave. Great amount of work was carried out during the day and night, materiel had to be carried on distance of 2000 yds through trenches. Very wet night, parapets in many places fell in, trenches in a bad state. Draft of 4.5.6. Rs joined from 1/9 Bn 5th officers + 8 N.C.O.s 64 Kings Liverpool R5 moved. Marched to the Bn. O4	
"	3rd		A few Minnenwerfer shells fell in F.11, but shot no damage. Our aeroplanes very active during the hours of 5 + 6 pm. Germans fired very heavily at them with no result. Rain most of the day + night. Work was greatly hindered owing to bad weather.	
"	4th		Artillery very active on both sides during the day especially between farm + shrub. Rain the whole day, and very strong, caused aeroplane scouting almost impossible. Draft of 65 O.Rs joined from Worcestershire Yeomanry. O4.	
"	5th		Germans artillery very active with H.E. during morning. West LANE, Ry LINE by 7.13, received special attention, no damage was done. The firing came from both sides of Salient. The Bn was relieved by the 5th Bn. Kings Liverpool "R5" relief completed by 9.30 pm.) The Bn. moved back into Camp near Vlamertinghe. Heavy rain during the night. O4	21st

WAR DIARY or INTELLIGENCE SUMMARY

Army Form C. 2118.

Sheet 2

October 1916

Place	Date	Hour	Summary of Events and Information	Remarks and references to Appendices
In Camp (Brandhoek)	6th		The men were given the day to clean up equipment & dry their clothes. Orders were received in time from the Bn. to move to Poperinghe to entrain from 10 a.m. to 2 a.m. On the whole a fine day. C/.	
" "	7th		The transport and & Lewis gun teams with hand carts left at 11.30 a.m. for Hopoutre siding. The Bn (less X Coy which proceeded with the transport or brought to entry) left Camp at 12.45 P.M. and arrived Rly Siding (Hopoutre) at 2.30 p.m. The men had tea before departing. Train left 4.30 p.m. arriving (Longeau) at 10 p.m. arriving at 6 a.m. 8". C/.	
En Route	8th		L/R Longeau at 7 A.M. after the men had breakfast & marched to Coulre. Rain very heavily during the march, arrived at 11.20 A.M. Billets excellent. Two Regts of French Infantry marched through Coulre in the afternoon, every one noticed what a smart & well built lot they looked, also clean. Our men very soon made friends with the French soldiers. Draft of 30 O.R. joined from the Royal Warwickshire Regt. C/.	
Coulre	9th		Cloudy day. Orders were received for a portable move to-morrow. M. 10.10pm orders received for the Bn.Mn. to move by motor to Pommien Redoubt. Everything was got ready & the Bn.Mn. was ready to move at 7 th notice. C/.	
" "	10th		The Bn.Mn. moved out at 5 A.M. Coys marched at intervals of 200x & the transport 500x behind the Coys. St Helen & 10 minutes later horse was made. Dinners en route. Arrived in Camp at 4.15 p.m. Bivouaced for the night. C.O. returned from leave at 11.30 pm. Orders were received for a further move to-morrow. Our artillery continual shelling enemy trenches all day & night. C/.	3/6/1

Army Form C. 2118.

WAR DIARY or **INTELLIGENCE SUMMARY**

Sheet III   October 1916

(Erase heading not required.)

Place	Date	Hour	Summary of Events and Information	Remarks and references to Appendices
Camp in Pommiers	11th		The Battn received orders to move up to Switch Trenches, these trenches are situated on the high ground North of Delville Wood. Two Coys were not to occupy Switch Trench, & two Coys in Pioneer Trench. Battn left Camp at 8 p.m. & arrived at new positions about 10.30 p.m. All arrangements were made for an attack on the German lines in front of Gueudecourt. Shows and bombardment by own artillery. OK	
Gueudecourt	12th		Heavy artillery firing day & night. The German lines. The Essex Regt & Newfoundland Regt formed various bombardments on the German lines. The Essex Regt & Newfoundland Regt formed the attacking line, 2nd Hampshire Regt in Support & the Battn in Reserve. Objective was gained but the whole was not kept; men, hundred prisoners were taken. OK Our men were killed when in Lewis & infantry parking up ammunition at night.	
" "	13th	Bn 10.10	The Battn moved to forming line in the evening & relieved the Essex Regt. One Coy in firing line, 6 Lewis guns, one Coy in Sunken Portion of Gueudecourt, Two Coys in York Lane trench. B'n in Pilgrims Way. Our artillery activity day and night. The German several times during the day & night placed a heavy barrage on the Sunken Rd, & North Side of Gueudecourt. Cocoa Alley from Pilgrims Way to firing line was completely flattened. Several German prisoners came in during the early hours of the morning (14th) OK	
" "	14th		On the firing line. Bombardment still continues on both sides. Working parties were sent on reforming & deepening Cocoa Alley to firing line from Pilgrims Way, & making fire steps in front line. 2 more German Prisoners came in to a Post of 1 Officer & 6 men recovered from & covered in front of our line but no definite information was obtained as the prisoners got badly injured at OK	

WAR DIARY or INTELLIGENCE SUMMARY

Army Form C. 2118.

Sheet 4

Ovillers 1916

Place	Date	Hour	Summary of Events and Information	Remarks and references to Appendices
Yeomanbank	15th		In firing line. Heavy artillery bombardment lying on several times during the day. The Germans retaliated heavily on two occasions the Sunken Rd & Leavilecommunication Rd receiving special attention. Lieut. Cayley reported B.M. H.Q. On & had a conference with the C.O. & the C.O. 9.2nd Hampshire Regt. on the attack to take place on the 18th. 2 officers, 3 O.R.'s & 1 Lewis Gun went into no mans land to occupy the Sunken Rd. Only three Germans were seen & were shot on approaching our men. Posts were placed in each half the Sunken Rd. No 3 Plat commanding the Southern Rd, & a communication trench from No 3 Plat to our firing line was dug. In No 3 Plat, in a deep dug out 3 M.G. N.C.O's, 1 Sub Lieutenant, Soldiers & 1 Yeoman were found. The Essex Regt relieved the Wilts Corps in the firing line. These Corps came back to Lord Trench & Gower Trench to move forward as the attack on the 18th Oy.	
"	16th		In the trenches. Artillery firing continued incessantly. Everything was got ready for the attack. Four German aeroplanes flew very low over our lines early in the morning. Germans kept up a heavy bombardment practically the whole day all over our sector. (Wd on the 2nd 8/16) Commenced to man Support trenches. 21st Bavarn regiment from the trench Oy about 8.30am & it got very cold Oy	
"	17th		Very cold morning. Everything was ready for to-morrow. The C.O. (Lt-Col Kirwan) had a Conference & explained once more everything in connection with the attack. Every one was eagerly awaiting for the hour to come. It began to rain very heavily about 5 p.m. Corps moved into the firing line relieved the Essex Regt & took up position. The 2nd Hampshire Regt on our own immediate right, Essex in Support, Newfoundland Regt in Reserve. Every one in position by the Mg HO Cy	

Sheet 5 . October 1916 .

Army Form C. 2118.

WAR DIARY
or
INTELLIGENCE SUMMARY
(Erase heading not required.)

Place	Date	Hour	Summary of Events and Information	Remarks and references to Appendices
Gueudecourt	18th	5.A.M	Side morning. The whole night of the 17th our artillery kept up a somewhat heavy fire throughout the night of the 17th on Yvan Trench. M.3. 4 & M.4. a barrage was placed on the German trenches & our troops advanced under the cover of our barrage. At 3.45 PM the Germans go lifted & own troops assaulted the German trenches. This assault was most successful & though the enemy much outnumbered our troops + over 208 prisoners taken, including 2 officers, one of them found that he had only come to the trenches with his Coy the night before. The formation of the Bn was X obtained from the Lem. P.M. M.G. & Z Coy. funded. Everas trench was captured, consolidated & manned & possible & many bomb blocks. The Battn managed to get formed "to the good" old Worcesters + once more upheld the name of the "Incomparable 29th Division". Operations were hampered very much by the tradition of the ground being very wet and made going heavy, but this state of things did not make our men & the ground of difference to our lads, they were all eager, & sorry they could not go further than their objective. Communication with Bn. HQ quarters was successfully kept by means of runners, they were joined by a gave of heavy artillery fire our own trenches & no wire during two communications was kept. Twice in the day the Germans were seen forming up for a counter attack, the C.O. got information, promptly telephoned to our artillery who let the bricks & most effective barrage which confounded & made the counter attacks impracticable, communication trenches in places 2 ft deep in mud, some of the men had to be pulled out. Our Casualties so far as could be ascertained this day were 2 Officers killed 2 Missing & Wd. Other Ranks. 16 Killed 80 Wd. & 30 Missing. O.K.	

WAR DIARY
INTELLIGENCE SUMMARY

Army Form C. 2118.

Month: October 1916

Place	Date	Hour	Summary of Events and Information	Remarks and references to Appendices
Guedecourt	19th		Watched enemy: communication trenches worse than ever. The enemy's artillery was busy all day on Corn Valley, Pilgrim's Way and Sunken Road, the company of the 1st Essex Regt in the latter supping heavily. The 2nd in Command & the S.M. Watts Bodkin and Company Commanders noted the line in the morning with a view to taking over. There first company arrived at 1.30 AM. It had rained since the enemy began to shell Count Alley front with light and then with heavy H.E. Their fire was very heavy indeed, unfortunate units must wait until the South there. Bodkin learnt very thoroughly how the relief was being made arranged.	W.S.
"	20th		By daylight more of the Companies & the relieving unit were in positions. As very awkward pass as a relief by daylight in the face of the time is very unwelcome. Our Companies had orders to send their men there in relief in small parties. This was done. There was started from Bn. H.D. to Brigade H.A. and orders to Camp near Bernafay from a distance of 4 miles. Relief was completed at 7.45 AM. Having taken 18 hours intently, enemy fire during the day was not heavy. The Battalion found small bivouacs at Bernafay Camp and had tea and rum on arrival. The last party arrived at 1.30 AM, 21st. No small relief to be there.	W.S. Copies Inspection German prisoners for early
Bernafay Camp	21st		Very calm day; men in considerable discomfort owing to lack of protection, but cheery generally. Thirty two spent up cleaning up. The Battalion is under orders to move at an hours notice about 11 AM & German airplane passed the camp but were brought down by our machines. The Battalion is ordered to hold itself in readiness to parties for road repairing in the morning.	W.S.
"	22nd		The Battn paraded at 5.30 AM and worked for 4 hours on the LONGUEVAL - FLERS Road, repairing & levelling the surface. Parties of 1 officer and 50 O.R. reported to 87/T.A. for work preparing trucks for light Railway between LONGUEVAL and FLERS. Hostile aeroplanes dropped 6 bombs on the camp all night, doing no damage	W.S.
"	23rd		Very little done but two each. Heavy rain at 10 pm. "Z" Coy worked on LONGUEVAL - FLERS light railway from 8 to 11 PM to 8 PM.	
"	24th		Very heavy artillery on LONGUEVAL very active all day.	
"	25th		Rain all day. 4 "Coy sent 1 officer and 50 O.R. at 5 pm to work for 87/T Ambulance.	W.S.
"	26th		Still raining. A few German shells on camp, but no damage. Two days work during the day, 45 from the By/a and 100 from the 5 Staff Regt. The Battalion found 150 men at night for carrying material to the front line.	W.S.
"	26th		G.O.C. 88th Brigade inspected the huts at 10.30 AM. Two parties of 1 Major and 100 O.R. were found during the day for constructing new road W. BERNAFAY 10 pm. Several more German Shells dropped in the vicinity of camp, but did no damage. The Battalion received orders to move to the trenches next day, in relief of 1 units of the 87/Bde.	
"	27th		The Battalion is ready to move. "M, Z and X" Coys moved at 5 pm. The 2nd in command remained in camp under Brigade Orders.	

Army Form C. 2118.

Sheet 7

WAR DIARY
or
INTELLIGENCE SUMMARY

October 1916

(Erase heading not required.)

Instructions regarding War Diaries and Intelligence Summaries are contained in F. S. Regs, Part II. and the Staff Manual respectively. Title Pages will be prepared in manuscript.

Place	Date	Hour	Summary of Events and Information	Remarks and references to Appendices
Bernafay Camp	27th cont.		The relief of the South Wales Borderers was complete by 12 midnight, very good time considering how heavy going it was. Disposition of Coys as follows: "W" Coy in the captured German Trench north of Lesboeufs. "X" Coy in SUNKEN ROAD and "Z" in Great Trench.	W.S.
Trenches	28th		Very heavy rain. The artillery of both sides were very active. The Germans, as usual, shelling Guedecourt very heavily. The trenches are in a very bad state, especially between Bn.H.Q. and Sunken Road. The new trenches up to the firing line were frankly impossible.	W.S.
~	29th		Still raining. Artillery on both sides quieter than usual. During the evening the battalion was relieved by the 5th and 6th Prussians. Relief complete by 5.20 A.M, which time very suitable, considering that the Prussians had marched up all the way from Bernafay Camp. The foot company arrived at 4.45 and the last at 8.30 am. That enough, tea and rum for the men on return.	W.S.
Bernafay Camp	30th		The battalion moved off at 10.30 am for 'C' Camp, Pommiers Redoubt. The going was very bad indeed on the route now by the ever congested, ever muddy and broken Mametz - Montauban - Longueval Road. The last company did not arrive till 3.30 pm. Distance only 2 miles. Very little accommodation was found in the Camp. Orders were received very late for a move to VILLE-SOUS-CORBIE on the morning.	W.S.
Pommiers	31st	10.30 am	The battalion moved at 10.30 am, companies at 200 yards distance. The Transport moved by a different route. The battalion moved over MAMETZ - FRICOURT - MEAULTE. Going was very bad indeed owing to congestion of traffic and state of roads, especially from the end of FRICOURT. Z Company arrived late at 3.30 pm. The last of the transport arrived at 6 pm. The billets were good, there being plenty of room and in many cases wire beds for the men. Everything was relieved at getting away from the sound of the guns.	W.S.

S. Kearns Lt.Col.
4 Monc. Regt. 1/11/16

29th Division.

88th Infantry Brigade.

----- ---

4th BATTALION

WORCESTERSHIRE REGIMENT

NOVEMBER 1 9 1 6

Vol 9

YP 174
22nd
8B

Confidential

War Diary

of

4th Worcestershire Regt

for period

Nov 1st 1916 to Nov 30th 1916

Volume 9.

E Kerans Lt. Col
4/Worc. Regt.

WAR DIARY or INTELLIGENCE SUMMARY

Army Form C. 2118.

Sheet No 7

Place	Date	Hour	Summary of Events and Information	Remarks and references to Appendices
VILLE-SOUS-CORBIE	Nov. 1918			
"	Nov 2nd		The day was spent cleaning up, in the men arrived very muddy from the trenches. Lewis Gun carts and transport were also cleaned. A draft of 121 O.R. arrived under a conducting officer. W.S.	
"	3rd		Very wet. The Battalion continued cleaning up. Arrangements were made for training Lewis Gunners and Bombers and Snipers in accordance with the Brigade Programme issued. The G.O.C. 88th Brigade went round billets. The Bn. Parade all clases. One Company did a route march and another went on the range. The cleaning and un-muddying of kits was continued. Tindall was down for the testing of Snipers for the Bn. W.S.	
"	4th		The G.O.C. 29 Div. visited VILLE and inspected Offr. Gr. new Brigade Transport Lines. The Battalion marched by Coys to VILLE Baths. W.S.	22M
"	5th		Route March from town to VILLE Baths. W.S.	
"	6th		The Battalion Transport Animals were inspected by the A.D.V.S. Church parade at the Y.M.C.A. at 10 a.m. W.S. Dry and fine day. Training and Transport training. The Battalion was inspected in men by G.O.C. 88th Brigade. All Lewis Gun carts and Transport on parade. Afterwards the Battalion marched past to billets. W.S.	
"	7th		Early on the morning Smoke was thrown over the vicinity of hostile aircraft. They displayed an unusual anxiety at the A.A. fire and the Battalion Coys were kept in during the morning and the afternoon was spent in interior economy and lectures. Training interfered with by weather. Many were casualties. W.S.	
"	8th		Wet & cold. Training in the afternoon. Training interfered with in the morning by the falling of snow repeatedly. A draft of 6 O.R. arrived. D.T.F. Hasberty, H.E. Gance, H.B. Willmann, M.K. P.J. Bud, T.F. Brownshill. W.S.	
"	9th		Still wet, cleaning and refitting material to troops. Many more casualties. W.S.	
"	10th		Weather much improved. Training in full progress. A German aeroplane was brought down at E.B. VILLE at 11.30 a.m. W.S.	
"	11th		Two Companies were employed in work at Brigade Stables at VILLE and Hampton stables at NEULCOURT. W.S. LIMARS. Two Companies went for a Route march into VILLE - BOIRE - TRAIN - VILLE. W.S. It is a mystery the Battalion we were in the ground above the range. Attempts are to advance under Barrage Barrage by every class. W.S.	

Army Form C. 2118.

WAR DIARY or INTELLIGENCE SUMMARY

(Erase heading not required.)

Sheet II

Place	Date	Hour	Summary of Events and Information	Remarks and references to Appendices
VILLE-SOUS-CORBIE	13th		Sunday. Church Parade at Y.M.C.A. hut at 10am. Three companies marched to baths at VILLE. Orders received for inspection of the Battalion on 14th by G.O.C. 29th Division. W.S.	
	13th		The G.O.C. 29th Division inspected the Battalion at 10am in the football ground. Afterwards he watched an inspection salute by the Newfoundland Regt. carried out whilst further inspections were carried out. In the afternoon the Battalion carried on a Brigade Field day by Companies at their own discretion. W.S.	
	14th		Orders received for a move to SANDPITS. The move to SANDPITS on the 15th. The morning was spent by Companies at their economy, inspection and lectures by the M.O. The G.O.C. Brigade sent round orders in the morning and Times with please with the improvements made by this Battalion — particularly referring between one Coy and improvements. Mon was very cold that am and Two Lectures, no intention to report breeze and incineration. Lieut. N.K. R.J. Carpenter reported for duty. W.S.	
	15th to		The Battalion left VILLE at 9.10am, Yorkshire Brigade HQ, and marched via MEAULTE to SANDPITS Camp.	
SANDPITS	16th		A very cold day. The Cols being Bivoluac and isolated at LESBOEUFS with orders to take over. The Battalion was inspected by the Adjutant to LA BRIQUETERIE camp by BERNAPAY WOOD. Bn/c - FRICOURT - MAMETZ - MONT - AUBAN. Arriving at 3.15 pm. Gen'l B commences to apt S.M. C-HIGHAM & C.S.M. F. Hinchgan M.C.	224L
LA BRIQUETERIE	17th		Very cold morning. One day's rations were brought up from CARNOY for a party of 40 men per Coy. Holding cape were moved to trenches at 3.45pm. The Battalion moved to LESBOEUFS. W.S.	
			via GUILLEMONT - GINCHY - DUCKBOARDS - LESBOEUFS Trenches in front of LESBOEUFS. Protocols or multiplying Shootouts carrier. Relay of 2nd E lanes complete by 10.45am. H	
LESBOEUFS	18th		Both the CO and the G.O.C. 87th Bde visited the front line in the morning. The G.O.C. noticed that trenches in the front line - FALL YAUTUMN Trenches and that the whole front the correct. W	

2449 Wt. W14957/Mg0 750,000 1/16 J.B.C. & A. Forms/C.2118/12.

Army Form C. 2118.

WAR DIARY
or
INTELLIGENCE SUMMARY

Sheet III

(Erase heading not required.)

Instructions regarding War Diaries and Intelligence Summaries are contained in F. S. Regs., Part II. and the Staff Manual respectively. Title Pages will be prepared in manuscript.

Place	Date	Hour	Summary of Events and Information	Remarks and references to Appendices
LESBOEUFS	19th		"Y" Coy supplied a party Tr carrying material for arriving from a dump found near Bn. H.Q. They carried up enough for arriving the front line. Rations & water came up by truck to COW TR.	W.I
"	20th		The O.C. 14 Essex H.C. Coys visited the line with a view to relieving. O.C. Coys went onto the firing line. The O.C. 4th Wilts Regt was on the line at the time and did not see the O.C. 14 Essex. Enemy artillery was a good deal more active than usual, shelling LESBOEUFS, WINTER and DEWE Trenches. Battalion reliefs for and continued. Work done; hands dumps in WINTER Tr. and trenches in MAIL and HUTTON. Y Coy carried up rations to front line. X + Z meet the front line.	W.I
"	21st	5:30 AM	Very poor morning. The G.O.C. 29 Divn. visited the line. The battalion was relieved by the 14 Essex Regt. Our guides made 2/Lt Thomas met the 14 Essex Regt at GINCHY. Coy guides Tr. over from them at COW Tr. Relief was complete at 11pm. The battalion marched by Companies to CARNOY Camp, some men having tea on the way at the Dump. Aun on the duck-boards. The Battalion was in bivouac in shell ... Good elephant huts for the men, one for platoon with a bivouac in shell about 30 cries Trench feet in all. Each man had one blanket & outside kit for day on the line, and one for them beside M - every day.	W.I
CARNOY CAMP	22nd		CARNOY CAMP. The day was spent in cleaning up. 2/Lt. C.W. Horton reported for duty. The following working parties went to TRONES WOOD for work at the station - Y Coy and No 5. Platoon at 6:15 am ; Nr6 Platoon at 6:15am ; 2 Coy + No 7 Platoon at 1pm ; N0 8 Platoon at 8pm. Another party of 50 men sent to Rear Dump, H.Q. - The C.O. inspected "W" Coy on fatigue.	
"	23rd	12 noon	Working parties were forwarded as follows: 20 men for Town Camp Commandant; 1 Officer and 50 O.R. for Rear Dump, H.Q. Carrying across-boards and a carrying party of 50 men To C.R.E. Coys, crown storage and the Quartermaster inspected "X" "Z" Coys on fatigue duties. The battalion marched to ABERNETHY Camp. Reported by the A.R. Dublin Fusiliers, arriving MR at 3 p.m. and MATAJAMM took over their accommodation.	23rd W.I

2449 Wt. W14957/M99 750,000 1/16 J.B.C. & A. Forms/C.2118/12.

Army Form C. 2118.

Sheet IV

WAR DIARY
or
INTELLIGENCE SUMMARY
(Erase heading not required.)

Instructions regarding War Diaries and Intelligence Summaries are contained in F.S. Regs., Part II. and the Staff Manual respectively. Title Pages will be prepared in manuscript.

Place	Date	Hour	Summary of Events and Information	Remarks and references to Appendices
BERNAFAY CAMP	25th		Rain without ceasing. The following working parties were found from "X" & "Z" Coys. One platoon to B.M.[?] and 50 at TRONES WOOD Station. 1 Officer and 50 for carrying RE materials from SINCENY [?] and a party of 30 for work under 8th H.G.C. "W" & "Y" Coys made good use of the drying rooms for drying wet clothes, mud, and got rubbed in comfort. W[?]	
"	26th		Weather rather finer. "X" & "Z" Coys used the drying rooms, taking up working parties as above. W[?] Found fatigues as above. W[?]	
"	27th		Bright with mist clearing. Preparations made for relieving 1st Dublin Fusiliers in the naval sector. Each Coy to go up 100 strong, plus S.B. plus signallers. Each platoon looked up 1 bottle of Port oil and 1 Primus stove for cooking. Each man took up 1 pair of dry gum boots to be put on immediately on arrival. The first Coy left Bernafay at 2.30pm. Return journey made at the dump. The last Coy was clear in the trenches at 5.30 pm. Relief was delayed by casualties to the leading Coy, including 2/Lt. T. Flynn wounded — Relief not complete till 2.10 a.m. W[?]	
LESBOEUFS	28th		9th [?] received Div. A.O.S. Baynes for a maintenance party in PRUE Tr. between Coy and the trenches. Orders received. THISTLE trenches. Trenches in a very bad state owing to their falling in in many places. Drains were necessary for the clearing of communication to avoid a night and left. Two were provided as far as possible, especially on the [?]. Rations were served up to WINTER Tr. Z coy in COW Tr. first as trouble. The junk made took them back from there to the drying rooms, as well as empty water tins. Owing to no Pioneer came in ready until the morning and was sent to Brigade. A German relief was reported for the night of 29/30th and our H.Q.s and special fire in warning the 7th Connaughts[?] relieved by 5 Borders. W[?]	
"	29th			
"	30th		Battalion was relieved by the 11th Essex Regt. Guide water 7/1st Batt. met to relieve on the duck boards and handed over to Coy guides at Coy Tr. Relief completed at 12.45 a.m. Guides not to relief at 8 p.m. A quiet relief. The men had tea in the huts there and toward the remainder of the night at G.H.Q. camp. W[?]	

S. Kearns Bt. Col.
4/[?] Irish Regt.

Forms/C.2118/12.

29th Division.

988th Infantry Brigade

4th BATTALION

THE WORCESTERSHIRE REGIMENT

DECEMBER 1 9 1 6

CONFIDENTIAL.

WAR DIARY
of
4th BATTN THE WORCESTERSHIRE REGIMENT
for period

DECEMBER 1st to DECEMBER 31st 1916.

Volumn 10.

Army Form C. 2118.

WAR DIARY
INTELLIGENCE SUMMARY.
(Erase heading not required.)

Place	Date	Hour	Summary of Events and Information	Remarks and references to Appendices
BERNAFAY	Dec 1.		The Battalion marched by Companies to Carnoy Camp, replacing the 1st R. Dublin Fusiliers. W.D.g. St Clair Roberts returned from Hospital + took over Command of X Coy. L.N.R. 2nd Lt. B. Perkins joined for duty + was posted to X Coy. L.N.R.	
	Dec 2.		Working parties were found from Z & X Coys for work at TRONES WOOD. Rly station. Another party were found to work at Advanced Div. HQ at BERNAFAY and another party to work at Rear Div. HQ³. L.N.R. 20 men were sent to TRONES WOOD for attachment to the 256 Tunnelling Coy. During the day the Batt: were cleaning up, subming feet + oiling boots. All Lewis Gun Ammunition + Transport limbers were cleaned. L.N.R. Lt. & Ady C Felix rejoined from leave. Capt J.B.W. Perryman 1st Bn R.O.S.B. joined the Batt. as second in Command. L.N.R.	
CARNOY CAMP.	Dec 3			
	Dec 4.		The Batt. moved to BERNAFAY WOOD being relieved by the 1st ESSEX Rgt. Working parties were found to the extent of 400 men to work in various parts of the line L.N.R.	
BERNAFAY WOOD.	Dec 5		Working parties of 350 men were supplied to R.E. Officers. Camp was heavily shelled in the afternoon between 4 & 5 P.M. L.N.R.	22A

WAR DIARY
INTELLIGENCE SUMMARY

(Erase heading not required.)

Army Form C. 2118.

Place	Date	Hour	Summary of Events and Information	Remarks and references to Appendices
	6/12/16		The Batt ordered to relieve the R. Dubln Fusiliers in the front line at LES BOEUFS during the evening. W Coy proceeded to work in OZONE TRENCH from the relieved W Coy of the R Dublin Fusiliers at 4 P.M. Remainder of the Batt left at 3 P.M. Relief was completed by 7 P.M. Disposition X & V Coy, left of firing line Z & Coy right of firing line BENNETT TRENCH. Y Coy Support 2 Platoons WINTER TR^H + 2 Platoons in FROSTY. W Coy Reserve in COW TR^H Lewis Guns were distributed as follows X Coy Guns in FALL TR. Y Coy Gun in AUTUMN. Z + W Coy Guns in BENNETT. Vat Guns BENNETT TR. supports making a continuous firing up communication between WINTER & FROSTY, and FROSTY & BENNETT TR. Notice Boards giving map ref: of action of front line trench were put up. Orders for work were issued as follows Z Coy to make BENNETT Continues + Y to dig a communication between FROSTY + BENNETT & FROSTY & WINTER. X Coy to improve trench from FALL to AUTUMN and AUTUMN & WINTER W Coy form a permanent party for OZONE AVE. digging dump pits + clearing a 2' Berm. W Coy also found a party (about?)	
LES BOEUFS	7/12/16			

WAR DIARY
INTELLIGENCE SUMMARY

Army Form C. 2118.

Place	Date	Hour	Summary of Events and Information	Remarks and references to Appendices
	8/12/16	6.45 AM	Bodies lying behind WINTER T^s. In the afternoon G.O.C. 67 Bde. General BRAY visited Bn H.Q^s. J.M.R. G.O.C. 67 Bde visited the front line in the morning meeting the C.O. & officers of BENNETT T^R at 6.45 AM. All Trenches worked on uncovering parapets & by from Bn.D. Orders received for a relief by 1st ESSEX Reg^t. Relief was completed in record time by 6.10 PM. Bn^t marched by Coys to BERNAFAY. 74 men sent to 29th Divl Labour Batt at GUILLEMONT. J.M.R.	
BERNAFAY	9/12/16		2 Coys paraded to relieve INFLD^s. Z & X Coys left at 2.30 PM & rested at the at 4 PM. W & Y Coys paraded with Pack in OZINET^s Drying Rooms & Trench Mor Dug outs. J.M.R.	
	10/12/16		Bn^t marched to camp at THE CITADEL arriving about 4 PM. Z,Y X Coys arriving at 6 PM. being relieved in the line by 6th O.L.I. J.M.R.	
	11/12/16		Bn^t marched to the PLATEAU & there entrained for MERICOURT arriving at 6 PM. Corps at Disposal of O.C. Corps for general clean up. Col. KEARNS proceeded on leave at 4 PM. Major Pennyman 2^d I/C. taking over command Capt Winford & 2nd Lt Lewis (joined) for duty. J.M.R.	
MERICOURT	12/12/16			

WAR DIARY
INTELLIGENCE SUMMARY.
(Erase heading not required.)

Army Form C. 2118.

Place	Date	Hour	Summary of Events and Information	Remarks and references to Appendices
MERICOURT	13/2/16		C.O. & Adjutant visited Billets & found them in a satisfactory state. Coys kept busy cleaning up, inspect rifles etc. PAUL	2316
	14/2/16		Batt paraded at NOON & marched to EDGEHILL to entrain for HENGIST. 1st line Transport proceeded by Road direct to MOULLIENS VIDAMES under 2 Lt Bamville. Batt entrained at 1 P.M. Train left up to time at 2 P.M. HENGIST 5.15 P.M. Marched to MOULLIENS VIDAME (12 ½) & stayed in HENGIST for the night no provision arrang. Officers & Lewis Guns & Cntts & a party left behind at the School until the morning. Batt moved off at 7 P.M. arrived at MOULLIENS VIDAME at 9.45 P.M. PAUL	
MOULLIENS VIDAME.	15/2/16		Divisional Conference. C.O attended. PAUL	
	16/2/16	2.30 PM	Batt inspected by C.O. in marching order. Conference of C.O's at 5 P.M. at Bn H Q's at 2.30 P.M. PAUL. Capt. Saul R.A.M.C. proceeded on leave. also 2 Lts Skaug & I.W. Johnson & 8 men. PAUL.	
	17/2/16		Batt at use of Baths & every man obtained clean underclothing	

Army Form C. 2118.

WAR DIARY
or
INTELLIGENCE SUMMARY.

(Erase heading not required.)

Instructions regarding War Diaries and Intelligence Summaries are contained in F.S. Regs., Part II and the Staff Manual respectively. Title pages will be prepared in manuscript.

Place	Date	Hour	Summary of Events and Information	Remarks and references to Appendices
MOULLIENS VIDAME	17/12/16	9.30am	Batt paraded for Divine Service. L.N.R.	
	18/12/16		Batt fitted with new clothing. Coys went for Route March between 6 + 6 miles during the morning. Batt Run + Physical Ex before Breakfast to take place daily whilst the Batt was in the area of H.V. Dame. Class of instruction in Bombing, Signalling, Lewis Guns, Snipping, Scouts, Commenced L.N.R.	
	19/12/16		B.A.C. Bombing class started in the Bogie arrangements. Drill Parade at 9 AM when Coy Commanders & Arabic Lecture gave 2nd class Lecture for duty L.N.R.	
	20/12/16		The Range was allotted to W + X Coys. Firing aimed 3rd class figure Target + 3rd Class chequered Target. The Coys also carried out Bayonet fighting. Extended order drill + also judging distances L.N.R. 2nd Lt Weatherhead joined for duty. L.N.R.	
	21/12/16		Training carried on as usual. Lecture by M.O. on cleanliness at 2 P.M. 2nd Lt Marriott proceeded on leave. L.N.R. 2nd Lt Bannister proceeded on leave.	237
	22/12/16		Training Continued + organizing. W + X Coys. Route march 5 - 6 miles. Y + Z in the Range L.N.R.	

Army Form C. 2118.

WAR DIARY
or
INTELLIGENCE SUMMARY.
(Erase heading not required.)

Instructions regarding War Diaries and Intelligence Summaries are contained in F. S. Regs., Part II and the Staff Manual respectively. Title pages will be prepared in manuscript.

Place	Date	Hour	Summary of Events and Information	Remarks and references to Appendices
MOULLIENS VIDAME	23/12/16		One Officer & 95 other ranks proceeded by motor lorries to Musketry Camp 14th Corps at 10.A.M. C.O's Parade 9-10 A.M. training interfered with by Rain. S.A.H.R.	
	24/12/16	11.A.M.	Divine Service at 11.A.M. Bath allotted to Batt.	
	25/12/16	9.30A.M.	Divine Service. C.O + A.M. Westmans Birds at dinner hour. S.A.H.R. Lawton (attached to the Batt) proceeded on leave. S.A.H.R.	
	26/12/16		Route march + practised "Advance Guards" distance 7 miles. Classes in Sen instruction continued as usual. S.A.H.R.	
	27/12/16		C.O's Parade 9 a.m. Training in attack from Trenches + consolidation of Captured Trenches. Classes carried on as usual after C.O's Parade S.A.H.R.	
	28/12/16		Adjutants Parade 9-9.45. (following) the am as yesterday S.A.H.R. except that all class joined in the attack from Trenches S.A.H.R. 9th Perkins + Lewis proceeded on 2 days leave to Paris. Riding Class for Officers in Sen C.O. in the afternoon. S.A.H.R.	
	29/12/16		Lecture by C.O. 6.30 pm on outposts. Route march 10 A.M. + on Outpost scheme Lt. & Alacfystt proceeded to Divisional School on instruction. S.A.H.R.	2/3/2
	30/12/16	11.15	Route march + Tactical Scheme. Hand Grenade Lt L Burlinghate	

Army Form C. 2118.

WAR DIARY
INTELLIGENCE SUMMARY.
(Erase heading not required.)

Instructions regarding War Diaries and Intelligence Summaries are contained in F. S. Regs., Part II and the Staff Manual respectively. Title pages will be prepared in manuscript.

Place	Date	Hour	Summary of Events and Information	Remarks and references to Appendices
H. VIDAME S.	30/1/16		over Aladj. Van 31 Febix. B.M.72.	
	31/1/16		Divine Service at 11 A.M. C.O's riding class for Officers in the Afternoon. SAKN.	

Mhenryson
Major 11KOSB
O.C. 4 Worcestershire Regt.

2742
VB

CONFIDENTIAL.

WAR DIARY
for period
1st January to 31st January 1917.
of 4th Bn The Worcestershire Regiment.

Volume II.

WAR DIARY or INTELLIGENCE SUMMARY

January 1917 — Sheet I

Army Form C. 2118.

Place	Date	Hour	Summary of Events and Information	Remarks and references to Appendices
Mollieus Vidame	January 1st		Weather dull and rainy. The usual training carried on. Adjutant's parade. Tactical scheme - an exercise on "Wood fighting" CO's riding class for officers in the afternoon. WJ	
"	2nd		Training and Schemes as usual. In the afternoon CO and OC Coys went to look at the ground over which the attack before GOC Division would be carried out next day. 2/Lt R.R. Fullarghs and 2/Lt Aitken joined for duty and were posted to "Y" Coy. WJ	
"	3rd		Inspection by GOC Division at 9 AM at place of assembly on the RIENCOURT – LE QUESNOY Road. The General expressed satisfaction at the turn out. Afterwards an attack practice was carried out, barrage being represented by flags on the usual way. WJ	
"	4th		Night operations at 4 pm an outpost scheme under Major Pennyman. WJ	
"	5th		Route march to training ground Nr. 7 RIENCOURT an attack through a wood and an advanced guard Scheme on the way home. WJ	
"	6th		Attack by 1st Essex and Newfoundland Rgts before GOC Division. Similar to that of the 3rd. We supplied 1 officer and 138 men to act as "snapping-up" party. WJ	
"	7th		Sunday. Divine Service in the Hôtel de Ville at 11 AM. A football match, Officers v. Sergeants in the afternoon at which Major Forrest Hickman, GOC 34th Div. was present. WJ	
"	8th		A lecture by Major Pennyman to the battalion on "Wood-fighting" at 9 AM in the Hôtel de Ville. Training	

Army Form C. 2118.

Sheet II

January 1917 WAR DIARY or INTELLIGENCE SUMMARY.
(Erase heading not required.)

Instructions regarding War Diaries and Intelligence Summaries are contained in F. S. Regs., Part II. and the Staff Manual respectively. Title pages will be prepared in manuscript.

Place	Date	Hour	Summary of Events and Information	Remarks and references to Appendices
Méaulte Risoure	8th		As usual. Special attention being paid to the sifting of strong points. Brigade Cross Country Run in which the Battalion took place. WJ	
"	9th		A French aeroplane forced to land just outside the village by the high winds. WJ	
"	10th		Training as usual. Capt. A.E. Stokes-Roberts reported from Corps for Senior Officers at ALDERSHOT and took over 2nd in Command. WJ	
"	11th		The Battalion moved to HANGEST to entrain for CORBIE arriving at 4 P.M. Running had No train arrived till 12 midnight and not leave till 4 P.M. arriving at CORBIE at 6 P.M. Very cold. Very good billets in good Café. WJ	
CORBIE	12th		Orders received to move to MÉAULTE. Halts on the 13th, the rest of the Brigade remaining at CORBIE. 7th T.D.F. MacCarthy takes over Town Major of LA NEUVILLE and BONNAY. WJ	
MÉAULTE	13th		The Battalion moved off at 10AM and marched to MÉAULTE HUTS arriving at 2PM WJ	6 7/1
"	14th		Very cold. Snowing. Y and Z Coy under Capt. Stokes-Roberts left for MANSEL CAMP to take over Corps Fatigues (4 Officers and 311 O.R.) arriving at 9 P.M. WJ	
"	15th		Freezing hard. Y and Z Coy on completion of Fatigues moved to ETINEHEM CAMP No 5. W and X Coys improved transport lines at MÉAULTE digging new standings. WJ	
CARNOY No 5.	16th		9.30 Freezing. W & X Coys moved to CARNOY leaving at 9.30am. Lt. Col. E.T.F. Murrow reported from leave. WJ	104

2353 Wt. W2541/1454 700,000 5/15 D.D.&L. A.D.S.S. Forms/C. 2118.

Army Form C. 2118.

January 1917 WAR DIARY Sheet III
             INTELLIGENCE SUMMARY
             (Erase heading not required.)

Place	Date	Hour	Summary of Events and Information	Remarks and references to Appendices
GUILLEMONT	17/16		Very cold and snowing hard. The Battalion moved to [illegible] back later at GUILLEMONT. Clearing huts very wet without floors. Accommodation small. MM	
MORVAL	18th		The Battalion relieved the 11th Manchesters on the left sub-sector of the right or MORVAL sector. The advanced front movement up on duckboards carrying 2 days' rations food and bedding etc. was slow. Brigade ordered the army from GINCHY to BeQuil Coy HQ. The C.O. and O.C. Coys went on an advance from COMBLES. Duckboards very slippery owing to frost. A very rapid relief complete by 6.20 PM. One front in Bn H.Q. Cavalry. JQ a strong support platoon on rear support. 9 platoons and 2 K.G.m front line; 3 platoons in supports and 2 + 5; 3 + 5 in H.Q. Dug-outs 3 Coys in Winter Line supplying X in Centre Z on left. Each Coy 100 strong. Transport very wet owing to temporary [illegible] and [illegible] very quiet part of the line. Impossible to send stretch.	
—	19th		Front very quiet.	
—	20th		G.O.C. divng visited Bn. H.Q. at 6 P.M. whilst chief was on purpose and gave orders for the comg [illegible] of new support posts. Battn relieved by 11th R Dublin Fus relief complete by 6.20 PM. Bn all moved on CARNOY Nos. by 11.30 PM MM	
CARNOY	21st		Battn held normal front in climbing up. 100 movement to MONTAUBAN Battn in the afternoon MM	
—	22nd		Battn out in Fatigues just enlarging the camp of the Bn. Went to Battn at MONTAUBAN MM	
GUILLEMONT	23rd		Battn then moved to GUILLEMONT in the afternoon. Can't work compound - heavy knocks near Lumbe. from the men put in on some huts. The 88th Bde tons over the left of MORVAL sector from the 88th Bd.	
MORVAL	24th		These Coys moved to the trenches to relieve the 11th Manchesters 50 men of Bn [illegible] Coy remained at GUILLEMONT to carry rations and stores over the new support posts. Relief complete by 3.15 P.M. in both. MM	6762

WAR DIARY or INTELLIGENCE SUMMARY

Army Form C. 2118.

January 1917   Sheet IV

Place	Date	Hour	Summary of Events and Information	Remarks and references to Appendices
MORVAL	25th		Wind, frost still continues. The men had plenty of fuel & rugs in our dug outs at M.H. Two days. The girls now dry our available blankets. Have caused inroads. Very disheartening of fires and shortening time.	
—	26th		Clear continues. A Kings 8 67 D.R. Tunnel began in CARNOY. A Victoria Cross party in CAIRO AVENUE to work in the afternoon termed attacks by the Left of LESBOEUFS. Progress made. BN. in line was relieved by the 1st R. Dublin Fusiliers & just enough light before the arrival of the Coy of the relieving unit the neighbourhood of Bn. H.Q was heavily shelled for 20 minutes. Luckily there were no casualties during time but back on CARNOY by M 8.30pm. Wt	
CARNOY	27th		Still over protection of Coys by the C.O. New recruits to the 11th B.n in Res. Rgt and 1st R Inniskilling Fus during normal time another today & officers and 276 O.R. previous. In to relief for the N.West Fus. 1 Con Res. Wt	
—	28th Sunday		Divine Service at 11 AM in Church Army Hut. Wt	
GUILLEMONT	29th		Very Warm. Bn. moved to GUILLEMONT BARRACKS. 1st Bn. leaving at 3.30pm. "Z" Coy supplied 50 men for carrying and The remainder except at CARNOY. Capt H. Crow-Johnson being O.C. Details. Wt	
MORVAL	30th		Still cold weather moved to the Life Saleman to relieve the 2nd Manchesters by this 2nd in Coy Coy relay a Patrols War night if no greater & in sight to enable C. 6.30 men under Wt Sn, were accompanied as usual by rate Patrols passed and careful of pictures will slightly short of terms. The weather the time & top & types another shelling this respect and established a trust in the New frontwar. Wt	
—	31st		Heavy shelling of trenches between Co. 119 and Right trenches Ra. 110 between Co. 114 in men has being time. Prisoners Sorin O. Baker Pte P. McClusky got wounded grenade attack got killed by a German grenade. Wt	

E. Kenard Lt. Col.

CONFIDENTIAL.

WAR DIARY

of

4th BATTN THE WORCESTERSHIRE REGIMENT

for period

1st FEBRUARY 1917 to 28th FEBRUARY 1917.

volumn 11.

E. Kerans Lt. Col.
4th Worcestershire Regt.

Army Form C. 2118.

February 1917   Sheet 1

WAR DIARY
or
INTELLIGENCE SUMMARY.
(Erase heading not required.)

Instructions regarding War Diaries and Intelligence Summaries are contained in F. S. Regs., Part II. and the Staff Manual respectively. Title pages will be prepared in manuscript.

Place	Date	Hour	Summary of Events and Information	Remarks and references to Appendices
	1917			
MORVAL	1st		The Bn. was relieved by the 1st Kr. Dublin Fusiliers, relief being completed by 8.00pm. The enemy bombarded our back during the relief but fortunately no casualties were shown. Weather still very cold. No traces of trench foot during the tour. After relief the Bn. marched to CARNOY and rested.	
CARNOY	2nd		Major Bonnyman rejoined from leave. Still cold, though fine. Two live Cpls. The men cleaned up and during the afternoon & officers N.C.Os. & men to attend a Cinematograph performance at the Church Army Hut.	
"	3rd		Still cold. Fatigues to a total of 5 officers and 220 O.R. were found for work on the Carnoy Battle Line. At 12.00pm. paraded in full order under Major Bonnyman for route march over the snow en route to Junction of MORCOURT.	
TUILLEMONT	4th		The Bn. marched to TUILLEMONT Camp, "X" Coy finding the usual carrying party of 50 men for	
MORVAL			Orders were received for the Relieve Party to leave Bernus The Bn. at 9.00 next morning to proceed to the new billeting area by	
"	5th		The Bn. relieved the 8th Middlesex Regt. in the usual manner. Arguments were kept but to H.Q. Party were delayed by heavy shelling of Bn.H.Q. 2nd Lt Wilkinson took command of the McCann carrying party, and 1 N.C.O. 10 men were left at LONE TREE to act as water party. Lieut R.G. Wynter rejoined from England. Lieut Honeycutt & Lieut Benzystic and 2/Lt Bateman reported.	
"	6th		Enemy more active. Heavy shelling of front line specially on the right. Very little damage done as to	

Army Form C. 2118.

WAR DIARY or INTELLIGENCE SUMMARY

Part II

(Erase heading not required.)

February

6801

Place	Date	Hour	Summary of Events and Information	Remarks and references to Appendices
MORVAL	6th		Enemy number had the range of our front line at night. Enemy parties later on by Verey-flare. C.O. and O.C. Coys of the 6th Bedfords. Bricks L.I. visited the line each relief to taking over.	
MORVAL	7th		Frost continues. British again heavily shelled from 11am to 12.30pm and from 2.30 - 3.30. The Bn was relieved by the 6th Bedfords and Bricks L.I.: relief complete at 8.15 pm. The Bn marched to EPINOY having tea at GUILLEMONT en route as usual. 9/Lt Nicholson rejoined from Hospital.	
CARNOY MANSEL	8th		The Bn moved to MANSEL Camp at 12 noon. 9/Lts Dann, Croston, Aitken and Bradman rejoined at LA HOUSSOYE from course. Lt. Col. E.T.I. Reeves proceeded on short leave to PARIS.	
LA HOUSSOYE	9th		The Bn paraded at 12 noon to proceed by bus to new billets at LA HOUSSOYE. Owing to mismanagement some vehicles did not arrive till late so that the men were not complete till 8.30pm. As no rations for the day could be obtained, owing to some mistake, the men were authorised to eat their iron rations. Two days rations were drawn at LA HOUSSOYE.	
—	10th		Weather fine but cold. Coys were placed at the disposal of O.C. Coys for the day. Training programme was prepared, to commence 12th inst. Capt. D.G. St Clair Roberts commanded in the absence of the Col.	
			R.T.I. Reeves. Lieut Wynter joined the Staff of the 89 Div.	
—	11th		Sunday; no Divine Service. No Tumble away by the Bn. Long wanted from other units. The Division, though at present rather quiet, is at intervals. Billets in LA HOUSSOYE fair though unproductive for training and Scanty; there being no range or bombing ground. No bombing arrangements to make the Bn at HEILLY.	
—	12th		Training for the day cancelled owing to either arrangements to hand out route march under Capt. Roberts. Inspection of transport	
—	13th		Training & [...] in earnest. Adjutant & the A.D.V.S. The Bn played football against 19th R.F.C.S. at HEILLY and lost 6-1 by G.O.C. 8th Bde and The 1.0.	

2449 Wt. W14937/Mgo 750,000 1/16 J.B.C. & A. Forms/C.2118/12.

Army Form C. 2118.

WAR DIARY
or
INTELLIGENCE SUMMARY.

February. Sheet III

Place	Date	Hour	Summary of Events and Information	Remarks and references to Appendices
2A HOUSSOYE	14th		The Adjutant and O.C. Coys attended a lecture on Contre-Attacks at HEILLY in the morning.	
"	15th		The Commanding Officer returned from leave. WY	
"	16th		Training as usual. All Officers under 2/Lt Perkins for P.T. at 9am. WY New class in Training commenced: an attack under cover of barrage for this in the afternoon.	
"	17th		Agmnt. 2nd Divnl. school at DOURS. WY Three continuous marching tests over training ground in a very bad state. Company route march via PONT NOYELLE and FRÉCHENCOURT. The Bombing and Stokes Gun class gave a demonstration on the A.N.Z.A. Corps School at BOIS D'ESCARBONNEUSE, the only ground available for the purpose. WY	
"	18th		Sunday. Divine Service in the school at 11AM for one Coy. The Bn had baths at HEILLY and exchanged soiled clothing. 2/Lt Storry proceeded on 48hrs leave to PARIS. Inspection of the Bn. in fighting order by R.C.O. on the Aerodrome. WY	
"	19th		Special classes as usual. Orders received for the Bn. to move next day. The Transport moved to an avenue at 3pm. and parked in MÉAULTE for the night, travelling via HEILLY, RIBEMONT, BUIRE, VILLE. WY	
"	20th		2/Lt. Storry returned from leave. WY	
"	21st		The Transport moved to at 8.30 am for BRONFAY Fm, unloaded at Camp 158, on reaching	

Army Form C. 2118.

WAR DIARY
or
INTELLIGENCE SUMMARY.

(Erase heading not required.)

February   Sheet IV

Place	Date	Hour	Summary of Events and Information	Remarks and references to Appendices
LAHOUSSOYE	7th		Detail camp. The Bn. paraded at 7 AM and marched to CORBIE to entrain for PLATEAU, arriving at 1.30 pm. At the camp are large huts, each holding a Coy, but permanent R.H. stoves and a detail hut. The camp is stared with 16 H.L.I. less 1 Coy and 11th R. Inniskilling Ins. Mr Ramden took over duties of Lewis Gun Officer from W.L. Williamson.	
PRONAY	2nd		The Bn. settled down and cleaned up. The C.O. and Intelligence Officer went to reconnoitre the new sector, noting COMBLES. Route to line and PRESTICOURT taking our dispositions from O.C. 1st E. York / W	
COMBLES	23rd		The Bn. moved to COMBLES via MARICOURT and MAUREPAS. "W" "X" Coys accommodated in HAIE WOOD Rd in good dugouts. "Y" + "Z" were allotted an open trench but later dugouts and shelters were found, sufficient to house both companies. Capt D.G. St.C. Roberts and O.C. Coys went into the line. "Y" + "Z" Coys	
SAILLISEL	24th		The Brigade Major went round the line but a view to sorting them. New companies drew gum-boots from the line and all returned for anti-trench foot treatment. The Bn. relieved the Ennis Fus in the right Sub-sector; a speedy relay. During line, "Y" in the right, "Z" in the left, in relation posts; "X" in support on BETTYE Tr. and "W" in support on the BAPAUME Road. Small accommodation for R.H.Q. Work carried on near Stray Point in the right of BETTYE Tr.	

WAR DIARY or INTELLIGENCE SUMMARY

Army Form C. 2118.

February. Sheet V

Place	Date	Hour	Summary of Events and Information	Remarks and references to Appendices
SAILLISEL	25th		In the trenches. A difficult line to sort as it is impossible to approach by day. The Bn. took over right group, including the strong point at BETHE. This took long owing to the Flamenceult Regt, and the Bn. refused to dig a communication trench from D.14.a.4.4 to the right of GREEN HOWARD Tr. The line kept out and works badly kept up by "W" and "X" Coys before orders were received for "X" to stand by and "W" to send out a patrol of 3 officers and 50 O.R. to ascertain if at all, and if so, how strongly the Huns were holding the s-- Emergence of a suspected opened and gradual retirement of the enemy. They found the line held by small parties of 3 or 4 men. W. Perhin and Rickett were in charge of the patrol. Much damage was done - duckboards and wire.	
FRETCOURT	26th		A heavy barrage was put into the front, support and reserve lines during the relay being observed. The Huntingdon Fusiliers arrived too early. H. Fosse at 5.45 and by 5.30 things were quiet. The Bn. marched to FRETCOURT Wd.	
BRONFAY	27th		The Bn. moved to TRONES WOOD to entrain for PLATEAU, leaving S-- at the station.	
BRONFAY	28th		In the afternoon all camp went for Anti Trench foot treatment. A party of 3 Officers and 200 O.R. paraded for work at PLATEAU under Capt Roberts at 5.00am. The Bn. went to baths in the afternoon.	68/3/2

E. Kenzie B--O.C

CONFIDENTIAL.

WAR DIARY

of

4th BATTALION THE WORCESTERSHIRE REGIMENT.

for period

1st MARCH 1917 to 31st MARCH 1917.

volumn 13.

E. Kerans Lt. Col.
4/Worc. Regt.

Army Form C. 2118.

WAR DIARY
or
INTELLIGENCE SUMMARY
(Erase heading not required.)

March   Sheet I

Place	Date	Hour	Summary of Events and Information	Remarks and references to Appendices
Bronfay Camp No 2	March 1st		Companies paraded for anti-trench feet treatment in the morning. In the afternoon moved to Combles to the same billets as on the former occasion arriving at 5 pm	
COMBLES	2nd		Enemy shelled TEUZE WOOD. Advance party of 4th Grenadier Guards arrived to take over at 3 pm. at 5.30 pm the Battalion moved off to occupy the right subsector, relieving the Essex. Relief was over by 8.15 pm. Work was commenced at once, the support & reserve company being sent up to connect up CANARY TRENCH with No 7 Post & Right Coy H.Q.	
IN THE TRENCHES (SAILLY SAILLISEL)	3rd		A quiet day - sniping by the enemy round Right Coy H.Q. The Battalion was relieved by 1 Coy of the 1st Coldstream Guards and 2 Coys of 4th Grenadier Guards. relief complete by 9.15 pm. Batt was last of the 29th Division to be relieved and proceeded to TREGICOURT Rejumed.	
BRONFAY CAMP (No 1)	4th		Battalion marched to TRONES WOOD and came by train to LE PLATEAU. arriving from there into camp. On arrival plenty of hot water was obtained for feet washing and cleaning up. No both Rgi.	
MEAULTE	5th		Battalion moved on foot to MEAULTE via BRAY arriving 12.15 pm Billets poor and insufficient the whole BRIGADE being in the same village. Rgi.	
"	6th		Day spent in cleaning up; Training programme drawn up, with special attention to platoon organization. Special classes commenced. Rgi.	
"	7th		Training proceeds on ground WEST of ALBERT ROAD. LECTURE by major S.Graz-Roberts on MAP READING. Rgi.	

21.4.

WAR DIARY or INTELLIGENCE SUMMARY

Army Form C. 2118.

March. Sheet II

Place	Date	Hour	Summary of Events and Information	Remarks and references to Appendices
MÉAULTE	8th		Half the Battalion had baths during the day. Lecture by the C.O. to officers & Senjts on the training programme. Lecture on the Lewis Gun. R.9.	
"	9th		Range allotted to the Battalion for the day. Divisional training as usual. R.9.	
"	10th		12 pm Lecture to all officers by Col Beckwith D.S.O. on "6th Division". R.9. Battalion route march in the morning MÉAULTE – ALBERT – LE CARILLOT – FILIER – MÉAULTE. R.9.	
"	11th		Sunday. Church parades for all denominations in Y.M.C.A. Church army hut or village church. R.9.	
"	12th		Training as usual – W and X Coys a route march. Y & Z practice for the attack. Cinema in the afternoon. "Conference of officers at 5 pm. R.9.	
"	13th		Training – Battalion fired on the range and every officer fired the Lewis Gun. R.9.	
"	14th		The Battalion all had baths at the Divisional baths – having also inspected with. Night operations 5.30 pm to practice OUTPOSTS. R.9.	
"	15th 16th		Training training as usual R.9. Training as per programme. R.9.	

Army Form C. 2118.

WAR DIARY
or
INTELLIGENCE SUMMARY

Month: March   Sheet III

(Erase heading not required.)

Instructions regarding War Diaries and Intelligence Summaries are contained in F.S. Regs., Part II. and the Staff Manual respectively. Title Pages will be prepared in manuscript.

Place	Date	Hour	Summary of Events and Information	Remarks and references to Appendices
MÉAULTE	17th		Usual training - classes in the afternoon.	
"	18th		Owing to orders for move on the 19th, Baths and Services cancelled. Inspection of Companies by the C.O. Transport stages for MOLLIENS-VIDAME with orders to spend night at DADOURS and ARGOEUVES Ry.	
MOLLIENS-VIDAME	19th		Battalion left MÉAULTE at 5.45 AM entraining at EDGE-HILL at 7.0 AM. They detrained at AIRAINES marching from there to MOLLIENS-VIDAME. They arrived at 2.30 pm - same billets as on previous occasion. Ry.	
"	20th		Training commenced on training ground. Ry.	
"	21st		Training on the Y ground near LE QUESNOY. Companies in the attack advance made practice on the way out. Baths in the afternoon. Ry.	
"	22nd		Training on the Y training ground. Lewis Gunners on the range. Ry.	
"	23rd		Practice of attack formation on Battalion training ground. All Rifle Grenadiers fired No 20 and No 23 Grenades. Lewis Gunners on the range. Wire cutting demonstrations in the afternoon. C.O inspected transport 3/pm Ry.	
"	24th		Y training ground, attack as a Battalion on 400 × front. Gas from Gas Ry. MONTAIGNE towards LE QUESNOY. Transport accompanied the Battalion Ry.	

WAR DIARY
or
INTELLIGENCE SUMMARY

Army Form C. 2118.

Month: March Sheet IV

Place	Date	Hour	Summary of Events and Information	Remarks and references to Appendices
MOLLIENS VIDAME.	25th		Sunday. Service in the Town Hall 9.30 am. Bombers Lewis Gunners and Signallers practiced during the day. Regt.	
"	26th		88th Brigade attacked by 86 & 87 on Y training ground during day. Batt arrived on the ground at 8.30 AM and dug in from J till 10.45 AM on the scheme left. They were slightly attacked by 86th Brigade and forced to relieve. Operations ceased 3 pm. Regt.	
"	27th 28th		Battalion training. companies on the range. Regt. No training. Day given over to interior economy preparing to departure. Regt. On the 29th Lewis officer and men fired a rifle grenade. Regt.	
LA CHAUSÉE	29th		Battalion paraded 9.30 AM and marched via OISSY and PICQUINY to LA CHAUSÉE where they stayed the night. Billets cramped during an Australian Bn School in town. Regt.	
VIGNACOURT	30th		The Battalion marched from LA CHAUSÉE to VIGNACOURT arriving at 12.30 pm. Billets better, alarm posts fixed, latrines dug at once etc. Regt.	
"	31st		Companies at disposal of O.C. Coy during morning. Draft of 133 other Ranks arrived in the early morning at 12.15 AM.	

S. Kearns Lt-Col.
4/Worc. Regt.

CONFIDETIAL.
───────────

WAR   DIARY

for

4th BATTN   THE   WORCESTERSHIRE   REGT

for

period

1st APRIL 1917 to 30th APRIL 1917

VOLUMN 16.

Army Form C. 2118.

WAR DIARY
or
INTELLIGENCE SUMMARY.

(Erase heading not required.)

Instructions regarding War Diaries and Intelligence Summaries are contained in F. S. Regs., Part II. and the Staff Manual respectively. Title pages will be prepared in manuscript.

Place	Date	Hour	Summary of Events and Information	Remarks and references to Appendices
BEAUVAL	1.4.17	2.30 p.m	After a march of 12 miles the Battalion reached the Town and was billeted in the North End. Rain ceased.	
	2.4.17	8.30 a.m.	Battalion left BEAUVAL at this hour and marched to MONDICOURT via LE BON AIR, HULEUX, FRESCHVILLERS, ORVILLE, HALLOY, GRENAS, and was killed in a hut camp originally intended for German prisoners. The camp had water laid on and a so well fitted up Bath Hut.	
MONDICOURT	3.4.17		Three inches of snow in morning. Further training of companies in the attack with and without a barrage. Demonstrations of wire cutting and infantry diggings.	
"	4.4.17		Rain all day. Every man given a bath and clean change of underclothing.	
Le SOUICH	5.4.17		The Battalion left MONDICOURT at 4.15 p.m. and marched to Le SOUICH via LUCHEUX and BRÉVILLERS. Very good billets and transport lines. Met several of the 2nd Bn The Worcestershire Rgt. who had taken over some of our billets at MONDICOURT.	
"	6.4.17		Church parade 10 a.m. Rain all afternoon.	
COUTURELLE	7.4.17		Marched to this village via IVERGNY - SUS ST LEGER - WARLUZEL - COULLEMONT arriving at 2:30 p.m. Good billets - 2 Coys in Huts, H.Q. and 2 Coys in a chateau.	
"	8.4.17		Church Parade 10 a.m. Brigadier General Cayley present. Two cavalry divisions marched through village. Fine day.	
"	9.4.17		Bn warned to be ready to move at 6 hours notice. Demonstration of contour patrol work by aeroplane. Rain all day.	

Army Form C. 2118.

WAR DIARY
or
INTELLIGENCE SUMMARY.
(Erase heading not required.)

Place	Date	Hour	Summary of Events and Information	Remarks and references to Appendices
SOUY-en-ARTOIS	10.4.17		The Bn marched to this village via LABRET and BAVINCOURT. On entering the village the head of the column was held up by a party of 2000 prisoners marching to the Corps Cage. Extract from XVIIIth Corps Orders d/7/4/17:— The Field Marshal Commander-in-Chief today called upon Lieut Genl Ivor Maxse and requested him to convey to the Divisional and Brigade Commanders of the XVIIIth Army Corps his best wishes for the success of their units during the forthcoming operations. He expressed his conviction that the confident fighting spirit which obviously pervades all ranks in the army is mainly due to the moral influence exerted by the Commanders and to the high tone which obtains amongst the Officers. There qualities lead to success and the C-in-C would have liked to express his appreciation personally to Divisional Commanders though time however, would not permit of this and therefore this remarks are forwarded by the Corps Commander. Signed P.M. Davies B.G. D.A+Q.M.G. XVIIIth Corps. Battalion was warned to be ready to move at 2 hours notice. Battle stores and reserve rations issued.	
"	11.4.17			
RONVILLE	12.4.17	3 a.m.	The Bn marched to F+q RONVILLE via DAINVILLE taken dinners was served and then Km of ARRAS. At 6.30 p.m. Bn moved down CAMBRAI ROAD to FEUCHY CHAPEL enroute when it was met by guides who led companies to their respective trenches South of MONCHY le PREUX just E of the village of LA BERGÈRE.	

Army Form C. 2118.

WAR DIARY
or
INTELLIGENCE SUMMARY.
(Erase heading not required.)

Instructions regarding War Diaries and Intelligence Summaries are contained in F. S. Regs., Part II. and the Staff Manual respectively. Title pages will be prepared in manuscript.

Place	Date	Hour	Summary of Events and Information	Remarks and references to Appendices
In trenches S. of MONCHY le PREUX	13.4.17		The 11th Middlesex Regt was relieved. Companies were distributed as follows. Z Coy in right, W on left of firing line. Y Coy in support. X Coy in reserve. The CAMBRAI ROAD was much congested with traffic and the relief was not completed until 2 a.m. During the morning orders were received to be prepared to attack at 2 p.m. The B'de in reserve. This was cancelled later as the 2nd Hampshire Regt had not been able to dig the jumping off trench the night before. At 5.30 p.m. the 3rd Div on our right attacked on a line running from the CAMBRAI ROAD to a point S of GUEMAPPE. We could see which attack receipt of the extreme right. GUEMAPPE was carried but the Germans eventually reoccupied the village. A Bn of the West Yorks Regt on the extreme right of the attack passed over the trench occupied by Z Coy and suffered heavy casualties from machine gun fire and the enemy's barrage. Z Coy also lost 7 O.R. It was noticed that the German barrage was late in starting and that when they did open fire the majority of their shells fell behind the advancing troops. Machine gun fire was the main factor which disorganised the advance.	
"	14.4.17		At 2 a.m. W Coy and 1 platoon Y Coy took over the line occupied by the N.F.L.D. Regt. The remainder of Y Coy took over W Coy line and Z Coy took over the line vacated by Y Coy. The line recently occupied by a company of the 2 S.W.B.	

2353 Wt. W2514/1454 700,000 5/15 D. D. & L.   A.D.S.S. Forms/C. 2118.

WAR DIARY or INTELLIGENCE SUMMARY

Army Form C. 2118.

Place	Date	Hour	Summary of Events and Information	Remarks and references to Appendices
In Trenches S of MONCHY le PREUX	14.4.17		Meanwhile the 1st Essex and N.F.L.D Regt found up in a trench just E of MONCHY dug by the 2nd Hants on the previous night. At 5.30 a.m. the battalion advanced under cover of a barrage and gained their objective. At 10 a.m. about 2000 Germans were seen advancing towards us with small parties of our troops retiring before them. The artillery was informed and barrage fire was immediately opened. When the retreating troops had cleared our front W Coy opened fire with rifles and Lewis Guns, and the attack was completely shattered by 12.30 p.m. although the enemy reached a point within 100 x from our trenches. After the Z Coy was moved up in support of W in case of another attack. The Essex & NFLD lost about 70% of their total strength. We lost Capt S. BANNISTER & 2/Lts HACKETT and BRUNSKILL wounded, but remaining with unit. 50 O.R. killed and wounded. 2/Lt AITKEN wounded, died of wounds. In connection with these operations the following Special orders were issued:— From VIth Corps:— Corps Commander congratulates you and your division on your defence of MONCHY on 14 and on the gallant manner in which strong counter attack was repulsed. SPECIAL ORDER OF THE DAY. The commanding officer has much pleasure in publishing the following to all ranks of the Bn his high appreciation of the work performed by them on the 14th Inst which he considers was most creditable to the regiment, adding to the reputation gained by all	

Army Form C. 2118.

WAR DIARY
or
INTELLIGENCE SUMMARY.
(Erase heading not required.)

Instructions regarding War Diaries and Intelligence Summaries are contained in F. S. Regs. Part II. and the Staff Manual respectively. Title pages will be prepared in manuscript.

Place	Date	Hour	Summary of Events and Information	Remarks and references to Appendices
RONVILLE	15.4.17		Extract from Special order of the day by Brigadier General Cayley commdg 88th Infy Bde d/14/4/17 "During the operations on the 14th inst the conduct of the 4th Worc Regt and 2nd Hants Regt and M.G.C. was most admirable. The 4th Worc Regt: dispersed with heavy loss two strong counter attacks made on their position in the course of the day. The Bn was relieved by 2 Coys 2nd S.W.B. and 1 Coy 1st Inniskillen Fusiliers. Relief complete by 2 a.m. when Bn marched back to billets in RONVILLE. Day spent cleaning up clothing etc.	
"	16.4.17		A quiet day, nothing — Rain in the evening.	
"	17.4.17		Battalion warned to be ready to move at 2 hours notice. Dull weather with showers.	
"	18.4.17		A few shells on ARRAS and environs from H.V. Guns. No casualties.	
"	19.4.17		Orders were received to take over part of the Reserve trenches in the BROWN LINE S. of the CAMBRAI ROAD. Bn marched off at 3.35 p.m. at 3.45 it was found that a half of a point 300x W of FEUCHY CHAPEL was roads owing heavy enemy shelling. The trenches which were in fair condition were taken over at 4.45 p.m. Bn H.Q. in old A.A. gun pit. No casualties.	
BROWN LINE TRENCHES	20.4.17		These trenches were spent in front of the heavy artillery positions and as there in a good deal of intermittent shelling.	

Army Form C. 2118.

WAR DIARY
or
INTELLIGENCE SUMMARY.
(Erase heading not required.)

Instructions regarding War Diaries and Intelligence Summaries are contained in F. S. Regs., Part II. and the Staff Manual respectively. Title pages will be prepared in manuscript.

Place	Date	Hour	Summary of Events and Information	Remarks and references to Appendices
TRENCHES of MONCHY LE PREUX	21.4.17		Casualties:— Lt J.M. ALDANA killed. 2/Lts LEWIS and MORGAN wounded. 2/Lt THOMAS wounded still stuck. 20 O.R. killed and wounded. Q.M. Stores and transport lines at RONVILLE were shelled during the night, one horse killed. During the day some shelling in near trenches. 2/Lt ROUND killed 9 O.R. wounded.	
"	22.4.17		At night the Bn relieved the 2nd Hants Regt in front line. 13 O.R. killed wounded on way up. Bn H.Q. also that of 2nd Hants Regt was in a large chalk cave near LES FOSSES Fm Coys distributed as follows. Y on left X on right of firing line W Coy in support Z Coy in cave with Bn H.Q.	See Appendix X Copies of Operation Orders Map etc.
"	23.4.17		A quiet but busy day as preparations had to be made for attack on the following day. 2/Lt MORTON wounded. By 4 a.m. the Bn was formed up in the "jumping off" trench as follows:— Y Coy on left and X Coy on right in the trench W Coy on left and Z Coy on right behind the parados of the same trench. Bn H.Q. was established in the shaft of a dug out in a sunken road about 10x in front of the entrance left of the Bn. At 4.45 a.m. the barrage started, although it was supposed to fall 200x in front of our trench a great many shells dropped in close proximity both in front and in rear of our trench. 2/Lt ACTON was killed just before our barrage opened and was wounded shortly on our front line 15 very few minutes after our mum attack.	

Place	Date	Hour	Summary of Events and Information	Remarks and references to Appendices
	23.4.17	4.45 A.M.	The Bn advanced under cover of the barrage to the BLUE LINE taking Pick and Shrapnel Trenches in its stride as no Machine gun and about 80 prisoners were captured. On arrival at the first objective (BLUE LINE) companies were very much disorganised owing to the very high percentage of losses among Officers and N.C.O.'s. Z Coy on the right in front of the Copse at O.8. central had their right flank in the air owing to the attack by the 15th Div on our right, having failed. Consolidation of the position was immediately commenced but was considerably hampered by examine sniping from the direction of the BOIS DU VERT. During this period the Germans an Artillery searched all the ground between our original front line and the new position at the same time keeping a large number of guns to counter battery work and to hindering communication on the CAMBRAI ROAD and approaches to MONCHY. At 9 a.m. Bn H.Q. moved up to the Cross Roads at point 8.6. At about 10 a.m. the Germans made a counter attack which was beaten off mainly by rifle their Guns fire but came of the advanced posts occupied by Z Coy were made up. In their shelling and emptying continued through out the day. At 3.45 p.m. 1 Coy 16th Middlesex Regt was detailed to form a defensive flank between Z Coy and the 4th Hants Regt who were in Pick and Shovel Trenches. At 4 p.m. another Infantry counter attack was launched by the Germans who made to force their way round the	

WAR DIARY
or
INTELLIGENCE SUMMARY.
(Erase heading not required.)

Place	Date	Hour	Summary of Events and Information	Remarks and references to Appendices
	23.4.17	4 p.m.	Copse at O 8 central. Part of A & B Coys were forced back from in front of the copse but the remainder of the line held good and heavy casualties were inflicted on the enemy by fire from Shrapnel Trench. Col KERANS rear gained the men who had fallen back from the Blue Line and led them together will all available men at Bn HQ to Shrapnel Trench. At 5 p.m. a third attack was attempted by the enemy but our S.O.S. signal was answered by the artillery within 30 seconds and the attacking enemy wave was completely broken up. At about 6 p.m. the C.O. of the 2nd Hants Regt was badly wounded and Lt Col KERANS took command of the Brigade front. At dusk 1 Coy 16th Middlesex Regt and 40 2nd Hants Regt attempted to reoccupy the part of the Blue line which had been lost, but finding the position too strongly held had to withdraw. Shortage of flares and ammunition was now felt and under extreme difficulties the line was reorganised as follows. 1 Coy 1/5th Middlesex on the right, 40 tanks in the centre, 4 Wore Regt on left. 1 Coy 2nd Hants in Shrapnel Trench. The work of consolidation was continued and 2 sections Field Coy R.E. and 1 Coy Monmouth Regt were sent up to this purpose this remain being to make strong points but owing to later arrival and having to clear again by 2 a.m. only put up wire in front of Shrapnel Trench,	

WAR DIARY or INTELLIGENCE SUMMARY

Army Form C. 2118.

Place	Date	Hour	Summary of Events and Information	Remarks and references to Appendices
	23.4.17		Rations were brought up to FOSSES Fm 2 limbers and 10 horses were lost by shell fire at this hour.	
	24.4.17	2 A.M.	Orders were received that the battalion would be relieved by the Royal Fusiliers. The relief was completed before dawn with the exception of 42 men under 2Lt WILLIAMSON who were not relieved until the following night. Casualties in the above operations were:— Killed 2Lt Weatherhead, 2Lt BIRD, 2Lt BRUNSKILL, Lt WILLS; Missing 2Lt PITT, 2Lt BATEMAN, Wounded & missing 2Lt NICHOLSON, 2Lt HOLLAND. Wounded Capt PERKINS, 2Lt GAMLEN, Lt CROOME-JOHNSON, Other Ranks Killed 34 Missing 53, Wounded 325. On relief the Bn marched down the CAMBRAI ROAD to RONVILLE, when the men were given tea and rum, and hence to SCHRAMM BARRACKS in ARRAS. At 4 p.m. the Bn was conveyed in Motor Buses to SIMENCOURT a distance of about 10 miles, but owing to congestion of traffic did not arrive until 10 p.m. Billeted in Huts. The following wire received from C.-in-C. referring to the fighting on 23rd :— Attended Third Army. The fine fighting yesterday has carried us another step forward. I congratulate you and all under you on the result of it and on the severe punishment you have inflicted upon on the enemy.	
SIMENCOURT	25th			

WAR DIARY
or
INTELLIGENCE SUMMARY.

Army Form C. 2118.

Place	Date	Hour	Summary of Events and Information	Remarks and references to Appendices
SIMENCOURT	25th		Following wire received from Lt Gen Sir Aylmer Hunter-Weston K.C.B. D.S.O. Cmdg 8th Corps:— "My thoughts are with you and all my old comrades of the 29th Div both living and dead on this the anniversary of the Great Landing." 2nd Lt WILLIAMSON having been relieved on the previous night rejoined with 42 O.R.	
GOUY EN ARTOIS	26th		The Bn marched to this village at 11 a.m. the same billets being occupied as on 10th inst. leaving at 10.30 a.m. the battalion marched via BAILLEUVAL STA, BAILLEUMONT, LA CAUCHIE, HUMBERCAMP, ST AMAND, SOUASTRE to COIGNEUX — good billets in barns etc.	
	27th			
COIGNEUX	28th		A beautiful spring day was spent in reorganization and cleaning up. Draft of 109 arrived. Church parade 11 a.m. Another fine day.	
"	29th		Morning spent training — inspection of rifles by armourer. Advance party went on to ST AMAND to take over billets for tomorrow. Extract from Orders:— The Corps Commander has awarded the Military Medal to the undermentioned N.C.O. for an act of gallantry in the field. i.e. on 14th inst.	
"	30th			

Appendix B

Operation Order No 16
by
Lt Col A. C. Halahan

12-4-17

Map Reference- Special Map 1:10000
Monchy-Le-PREUX
3rd Field Survey Co. R.E. (1523.

1. The 88th Bde will attack at a time Zero to be notified later.
2. The 2nd Hants will dig an assembly trench during the night and Companies will move & be in position by 4.30 am as follows:-
   "W" Coy with their right resting on a point 50ˣ north of track at O.a.5.5.
   "Z" Prolong this line to the left.
   "Y" Prolong this line to the left.
   "X" Will move up through Monchy wood & take up their position on the left of "Y" Coy
3. On Zero & the Barrage falling all Coys will get up to the barrage and form up in two lines.
   Z & Y first line
   W & X second line
   The barrage will move forward at the rate of 100 yds in 4 mins.

The right of Z Coy will be directed in the centre of the small wood at O.2.d.8.5. and the left of "Y" Coy on a point O.2.b.4.2.

"X" Coy will be responsible for the defence of the left flank and will detail strong points of 1 (one) platoon as follows.

(a) at Zero one strong point O.1.b.7.9.
(b) During the advance one at O.2.a.8.6.
2 platoons will follow "Y" but will be used for defence of flank if necessary

"Y" Coy will detail two strong points.
(a) O.2.b.5.4.
(b) O.3.c.2.9.

4. The Newfoundland Regt will be on the right of "Z" and "W" Coys and will be responsible for the strong point at O.3.c.2.5.

5. On arrival at objective O.C. Coys will report progress.

6. Bn Hdqrs & Aid Post will remain in present positions in Monchy.

Appendix C

Special Order
by
Brig: Genl. Cayley. C.M.G.
Comdg 88th Bde.

The Brigadier wishes to place on record his appreciation of the gallant work done by the 88th Bde in the hard fighting of 14th April.

The Attack carried out by the 1st Essex & by the 1st N.F.L.D was entirely successful, the Objectives being brilliantly gained.

It seems certain that the enemy had planned an attack in force on Monchy on the morning of the 14th. This attack fell on the two battalions which had advanced, and though they were nearly destroyed in doing so they appear to have completely broken up & disorganised the German attack.

The hostile troops consisted of a fresh Bavarian Division which had not been in the previous fighting.

The Brigadier deplores deeply the heavy losses suffered by these two battalions which were brought about

by no fault of their own.
He wishes all ranks to understand that their sacrifices were not in vain and that by their gallantry they undoubtedly defeated an important attack on MONCHY.

Ernt Stirling
Con? of Essex Regt
11.5.17

SECRET.   COPY NO. 8

88th BRIGADE INSTRUCTIONS NO. 1

Reference Special Map MONCHY-LE-PREUX.

20th April 1917.

1. Orders have been received from 29th Division that the general advance will be continued at ZERO on a date to be notified later.

2. The objectives of 29th Division will be :-

   1st Objective (BLUE LINE) O.8.Central - COPSE O.8.B.1.2. (inclusive) A line running up the spur through O.8.B.3.4. and O.8.B.4½/9½.

   2nd Objective (RED LINE) O.9.B.5.0. - O.9.B.5.5. - O.3.D.5.0. - O.3.D.2.0. - Eastern edge of BOIS DU SART - I.33.B.8-1.

3. The 15th Division will attack on the right, the 29th Division in the centre and the 17th Division on the left.
   The 88th Brigade will attack on the right of the 29th Divisional Line and the 87th on the left.
   Boundaries The boundaries between the 88th Brigade and 15th Division on their right will be An East and West line from N.12.Central to O.9.Central and thence to O.10.A.2.4.
   Between 87th and 88th Brigades - The East and West Grid Line between O.1 and O.7.
   Between 87th Brigade and 17th Division I.32.C.2.3. - I.33.D.6.8. - I.34.A.0.6.
   The 86th Brigade will be in reserve.

4. The 12th and 29th Divisional Artilleries will cover the Divisional front of attack.
   After the capture of the BLUE LINE the Divisional Artillery will move into previously prepared forward positions to cover the advance against the RED LINE.
   There will probably be a 6 hours pause after the capture of the BLUE LINE.

5. Dispositions at ZERO hour.
   88th Brigade Headquarters ... ... N.12.A.8.1.
   Worcestershire Regt. in SUNKEN ROAD in O.7.A.
   Hampshire Regt.   in front line trench in N.12.B.
   Essex and Newfoundland Regts. ... ARRAS

   87th Brigade Headquarters ... ... N.6.B.9.5.
   A. and B. battalions in front line in O.1.D. and B.
   C. and D. battalions in support in O.1.D. and B. and in)
) MONCHY.

   86th Brigade Headquarters. at H.54.C.5.5.
   A. and B. battalions in and forward of BROWN LINE.
   C. and D. battalions in ARRAS.

6. AT ZERO HOUR the Worcestershire Regt. and A. and B. battalions of 87th Brigade advance to the BLUE LINE. Their places in the front line trenches being occupied by C. and D. battalions 87th Brigade. The Hampshire Regt. will follow behind the Worcestershire Regt. and on the BLUE LINE being captured will dig in in rear of the BLUE LINE ready to go forward through the Worcestershire Regt. to the attack on the Red Line at O plus 7 hours.

7. The advance to the 1st objective will take place under a creeping barrage which will advance in front of 88th Brigade at the rate of 100 yards in 3 minutes. This creeping barrage on the Divisional front will be composed of the whole of the 18 pdrs available (90) and will be placed in the first instance in a line 200 yards east of our front line. A standing barrage of 4.5" howitzers will be placed on the German line and the Heavy Group will engage the trenches and woods in O.8.C.A and B. - O.2.D.B. and A.
   At 0.6 the barrage will commence to creep and it will reach the 1st Objective (BLUE LINE) and about 0.32.

-2-

At 0.32 the barrage will lift 100 yards in one bound and remain there while the troops are consolidating. This lift will be the signal for the troops to commence consolidating.

8. The advance will take place under a machine gun barrage of 28 machine guns, 16 of which will cover the front of the attack, while 8 cover the right flank and 4 cover the left flank. Mobile machine guns will accompany each Brigade in the attack.

9. The Field Artillery will move forward in bounds to positions in N.6., register and prepare for the barrage to cover the second advance, keeping three brigades always available to break up any counter attack by the enemy.

10. The reserve of machine guns (6 in number) will move forward to positions in O.2. and open fire on the second objective in conjunction with 14 other guns - A total of 20 machine Guns.

11. A. and B. battalions of 86th Brigade will take over the defences of MONCHY. C. and D. battalions from ARRAS will also move up to the BROWN LINE in the course of the morning to occupy trenches vacated by A. and B. battalions.

12. At ZERO plus 7 hours the advance will take place against the RED LINE, provided the Divisions on the flanks have attained their first objectives.
The signal for the advance will be the barrage falling at 0 plus 7 hours. This advance will be carried out in a similar manner to the first. The Artillery barrage will creep at the rate of 100 yards in 4 minutes. The bulk of the Artillery will be concentrated on the BOIS DU VERT and the BOIS DU SART, the GULLY in between receiving the attention chiefly from machine guns.
The Hampshire Regt. will advance on the right and C. and D. battalions 87th Brigade on the left.
On reaching their objective, the RED LINE, they will consolidate immediately pushing forward weak patrols to reconnoitre towards the GREEN LINE. Should the GREEN LINE be vacated the patrols will be supported by platoons and the GREEN LINE will be occupied.

13. ACKNOWLEDGE.

Issued at 1000

Captain,
Brigade Major, 88th Infantry Brigade.

Copy 1-5 Staff
6 Diary
7 File
8 Worcesters.
9 Hants.
10 Essex
11 Newfld.
12 M. Gun Coy.
13 T. M. Battery.

SECRET.   Copy No. 16

29TH DIVISION INSTRUCTIONS NO. 3.

19th April, 1917.

1. In order to fully utilise the fire power of the Brigade Machine Gun Companies the following scheme will be carried out during the operations on the 23rd instant.

2. There will be 2 main barrages, which will be referred to through this scheme as A and B.

A. A moving barrage to cover the advance of the Infantry, developing into a standing barrage to cover the consolidation of the 1st objective.
To open on a N. and S. line from O.8.central to O.2.b.0.7. at Zero, remaining on this line until Zero plus 8 mins. At O plus 8 minutes, O plus 16 minutes, O plus 24 minutes, O plus 32 minutes, and O plus 40 minutes, there will be a lift of 200 yards until the final barrage line is a N. and S. line from O.9.a.6.0. to I.33.c.0.4.6.

B. A protective barrage in front of the 2nd objective on a N. and S. line from O.10.Central to I.34.Central.

3. The grouping of guns and action will be as follows :-

86th Machine Gun Coy.

(1) A Group of 12 guns at N.12.b.8.8. To open fire at Zero and carry out the barrage A, remaining on the final barrage line of the 1st objective until O plus 7 hours.
At O plus 6 hours, however, 6 guns of this group move forward to the Sunken Road about O.8.c. to O.7.b. and carry out barrage B. from O.10.central to O.4.d.0.5.
The other 6 guns remain on the final barrage of the 1st objective until O plus 7 hours. They then cease fire and move up to positions in the 1st objective and will be prepared to open on to Barrage B. should they be required, owing to casualties placing other guns, detailed for this purpose, out of action.

(2) A Group of 4 Mobile Guns. To be in the Southern end of jumping off trench at Zero. To follow the 2nd wave of Infantry and take up a position about O.8.central and to control by direct fire the road and houses in O.14.a. when not masked by our infantry at O plus 7 hours to advance to 2nd objective in rear of infantry and engage such targets as may appear.

87th Machine Gun Coy.

(1) A Group of 4 guns about O.1.b.3.3. Target, valley in I.33.c.central. Range not less than 1500 yards. To fire from Zero to O plus 32 minutes. At O plus 32 minutes to lift 200 yards and at O plus 40 minutes to lift 200 yards, remaining on final barrage line of 1st objective until O plus 7 hours, when group ceases fire and moves up into 1st objective and carries out Barrage B. from I.34.d.0.0. to I.34.B.0.0.

(2) A Group of 4 guns about O.1.c.9.2. Target, valley in O.7.d. - Sunken Road and ruined Mill in O.8.a. and c. - Copse in O.8.b. To fire direct when not masked by our Infantry, from Zero. At O plus 40 minutes to lift on to final barrage line of 1st objective. To cease fire at O plus 7 hours and then move

/ up

- 2 -

up to 1st objective and carry out barrage B. from O.10.central to O.4.d.O.5.

(3) A Group of 4 Mobile Guns. To be in the Northern end of "jumping off" trench at Zero. To follow 2nd wave of Infantry and take up a position about the copse O.2.a.2.5. 2 guns to control by direct fire the valley in I.32. and 2 guns the valley in I.33.c. when not masked by our infantry.

As soon after the capture of the 1st objective to work forward as close to our Artillery standing barrage as possible and to control by direct fire the valley in I.33.c.central and the BOIS du SART.

These guns advance to 2nd objective in rear of Infantry and engage such targets as may appear.

86th M.G. Coy. and 87th M.G. Coy.

A Group of 8 guns, 4 of 86th M.G. Coy. and 4 of 87th M.G. Coy. under O.C. 86th Machine Gun Coy. at about N.6.d. Target, valley O.9.c. - BOIS du VERT - BOIS du SART. To cease fire at O plus 7 hours. The 4 guns of 87th Machine Gun Coy. then move up to 1st objective and reinforce barrage B. line as required.

86th Machine Gun Coy.

(1) A Group of 4 guns referred to in previous para.

Remainder of guns in Reserve - 8 of these guns to move up after capture of 1st objective to MONCHY and take over defences in positions vacated by 87th Machine Gun Coy.

4. For the above scheme it is roughly estimated that each gun will require 10 boxes S.A.A. Each Brigade will be responsible for dumping this together with tins of water as far forward as possible before operations commence. A carrying party of 50 Infantry should be attached to the 87th Machine Gun Coy. and to the 88th Machine Gun Coy. for carrying forward S.A.A. etc. after the operations commence.

5. Attached is a table for Machine Gun Fire orders, copies of which, if required, can be obtained on application to these Headquarters.

6. Mobile Machine Guns detailed to accompany the Infantry to the 2nd objective must keep their belt boxes full for the advance from the BLUE to the RED line.

7. The guns detailed to advance at O plus 7 hours to the first objective will only move forward when the Officer in charge has satisfied himself that the advance from the BLUE to the RED line has commenced.

8. Officers Commanding Machine Gun Groups must keep in touch with the situation and be prepared to cover the BLUE line, should for any reason the advance to the RED line not take place.

9. ACKNOWLEDGE by wire.

C. Fuller
Lieut-Colonel, G.S.,
29th Division.

Issued at 12 noon.

Copies 1 - 5   General Staff.   21   17th Divn.
       6 - 10   86th Brigade.   22   15th Divn.
       11 - 15 87th Brigade.   23   VI Corps M.G.O.
       16 - 20 88th Brigade.   24   VI Corps "G".

JRM

S E C R E T

COPY No. 8

88th Brigade Operation Order No. 69

by

Brigadier General D.E. CAYLEY, C.M.G. Commanding 88th Brigade.
****

21st April, 1917.

Ref. Special Map MONCHY LE PREUX, 1/10000.

1. The attack referred to in 88th Brigade Instructions No. 1, dated 20th April, 1917 will take place on a date and at an hour to be notified later.

2. The objectives will be as follows :-
   (a) <u>BLUE LINE</u> - The Worcestershire Regt. will capture and consolidate the line O.8.B.1/2 - O.2.D.3/0.

   (b) <u>RED LINE</u>. - At ZERO plus 7 hours, provided that the Divisions on the Flanks have captured the BLUE LINE, the Hampshire Regt. will advance through the Worcestershire Regt. and will capture the BOIS DU VERT, and will consolidate the line - O.9.B.5.0. - O.3.D.5.0.

3. During the attack on the 1st objective, the Hampshire Regt. will be in Brigade Reserve.
   During the attack of the Hampshire Regt. on the Red Line, the Worcestershire Regt. will be in Brigade Reserve.

4. The artillery barrage map of instruction has been today issued to all concerned.

5. The posts behind the Sunken Road in O.7.A. will be evacuated one hour before ZERO.
   The Worcestershire Regt. will form up for the attack in our present front line trench from N.12.b.6/0 to O.7.A.1/8, and the Hampshire Regiment will form up behind them in the trench in N.12.B.
   After the Worcestershire Regt. have left their forming up trench on the fall of the barrage, the 3 leading Companies of Hampshire Regt. will follow directly behind the Worcestershire Regt. until they reach the German trench in O.8.A. and O.7.B. which they will occupy and consolidate.
   The remaining 1 Company Hampshire Regt. will hold our present front line trench from N.12.B.6/0 - O.7.A.1/8.
   This Company will remain in that trench until ordered forward to take part in the attack on the RED LINE.
   Should the attack on the RED LINE be ordered, the Hampshire Regt. will be formed up behind the BLUE LINE by ZERO plus 7 hours ready to advance to attack the RED LINE on the fall of the barrage.

6. Formation to be adopted will be as follows :-
   The Worcestershire Regt. will attack on a frontage of 2 Companies in 2 waves.
   The Hampshire Regt. in its attack on the 2nd objective will, after passing BLUE LINE be covered by a line of skirmishers followed by sections in small column followed by remainder of battalion in waves.

7. The Worcestershire Regt. will construct strong points about :-
   O.8.B.1/2 - O.8.B.4/1½ - O.8.B.2.5. and O.8.B.5/6.

   The Hampshire Regt. will construct two strong points about 50 yds to the West of the Eastern Edge of the BOIS DU VERT, one towards the Northern End and one towards to Southern End, also a strong point about O.9.B. Central.

(2)

8. Each man will carry:-

    2 Sandbags
    1 Mills Bomb
    Unexpended portion of days ration and
    1 days ration in addition to the iron ration.
    75% of men going forward will carry a pick or shovel.

    Each man will carry 170 rounds S.A.A. except Lewis Gun and Rifle Grenade Section.
    Each platoon will be provided with 2 yellow and black flags as guides to artillery which will only be put up when troops finally reach their objective.

9. 4 mobile machine guns will go forward behind the 1st wave of the attack.

10. The S.O.S. signal is 2 red flares fired in rapid succession and repeated until acted upon by the artillery.
    This can be equally well used by day as by night.

11. The advanced dressing station will be at N.3 Central with relay posts at FOSSE FARM (N.11.b.9.4.) and at N.6 d.6.0.

12. A forward brigade Dump is established in the Cave, opposite Fosse Farm which contains all battle stores and water.

13. Brigade Headquarters will close at N.34 central at 1700, 22nd April, and will open at the same hour in the deep dugout at N.12.A.8/1.

14. Major CRUNE will act as Liaison Officer between 88th Brigade and 45th Brigade and will report at Headquarters, 45th brigade at N.10.D.3/8 by 4 a.m. on the day of attack.
    Lieut. HOLIDAY, Essex Regt. will perform a similar duty with 87th Brigade at N.6.B.8/3.
    Both these Officers will call at Brigade Headquarters beforehand to be told details of dispositions, etc.

15. The Newfoundland Regt. will find 1 N.C.O. and 3 men to form a stragglers post at the dressing station at FEUCHY CHAPEL.
    This post will be under the supervision of the A.P.M.

16. Infantry will light flares when called upon by Contact Aeroplanes either by sounding Klaxon Horns or by firing white lights.
    Flares will be called for about 7 a.m. and 2 p.m.

17. The Officer Commanding the composite battalion of Essex and Newfoundland Regts. will detail 1 officer and 50 men whom he will leave behind in the BROWN LINE. This party will act as carriers to 88th Machine Gun Company. The rationing of these men will be done under Battalion arrangements.

18. The 510th (London) Field Company R.E. will be at the disposal of 88th Brigade for consolidating the captured position after dark

19. The 10% reinforcements of Worcestershire and Hampshire Regts. will be accommodated during the day of attack in the trenches of the BROWN LINE S. of ARRAS CAMBRAI Road where the Reserve Battalion now is. The senior officer of the reinforcements of each of these 2 battalions will report at Brigade Headquarters at 5 p.m. on the day of attack.

20. Prisoners will be sent to the Prisoners Cage established at H.33.B.6.8 where they will be handed over to the A.P.M.

21. The composite battalion of Essex and Newfoundland Regts. will move back to ARRAS on the night 22/23rd.

22. Please acknowledge.

ISSUED AT........ 2045

CAPTAIN,
BRIGADE MAJOR, 88TH INFY. BRIGADE

Copies 1-5 Staff
       6 Diary
       7 File
       8 Worcesters
       9 Hampshire
      10 Essex
      11 Newfoundland
      12 Machine Gun Coy.
      13 Trench Mortar Bty.
      14 London Fd.Coy. R.E.
      15 29th Divl.Group R.A.
      16 29th Division "G"
      17 No. 4 Coy. A.S.C.
      18 45th Infy. Brigade
      19 87th Infy. Brigade.

SECRET

COPY   OPERATION ORDERS NO I.   COPY NO I.
BY
LIEUT COL E.J.T. KERANS
COMMANDING 4th BATT THE WORCESTERSHIRE REGT.

22.4.17.

1.   Orders have been received that the 88th Brigade will attack the enemy's BLUE LINE O.8.B.I.2. to O.2.D.3.0. objective, this line being the first objective; which will be taken & consiladated by the 4th WORCESTERSHIRE REGIMENT.

2.   The 2nd HAMPSHIRE REGT will advance through the Worcestershir Regt at ZERO plus 7 hours & will attack & consolidate enemy's RED LINE east of the BOIS DE VERT this line running from O.9.B.5.0. to O.3.D.5.0.

3.   The 15th Division will be in touch & attacking on the RIGHT of the 88th BRIGADE
    The 87th BRIGADE will be in touch & attacking on the LEFT of the 88th Brigade.
    The 17th DIVISION will be attacking on the LEFT of the 87th BRigade.

4.   The Worcestershire Regt will be formed up at 3.40 A.M. to capture the BLUE LINE as follows:-
X COY on the RIGHT. in the present front line.
Y COY on the LEFT in the present front line.
Z COY on the RIGHT immediately behind the parados of the present front line, & W COY on the LEFT.
    While proceeding to the forming up posts & during the period before ZERO strict silence must be maintained.

5.   The Hampshire Regt will be formed up in Trenches in N.I2. B.5.5. At ZERO the Worcestershire Regt will advance to the BLUE LINE & capture & consolidate same

6.   The advance will take place under a creeping barrage at the rate of 100 yards in 4 minutes, which in the first instance will come down 200 yards immediately in front of the forming up place; and at 04 will commence to creep forward at the rate of 100 yards in 4 minutes. This barrage will reach the BLUE LINE at varying times and will finally lift 200 yards in front of The BLUE LINE; which will be the signal to the troops to show that they have reached the BLUE LINE & to commence consolidating.
    Immediately on lifting there will be one minute's intense bombardment: it will remain there for 30 minutes.

7.   The RIGHT of the Battalion will marvh on the SMALL COPSE

at O.8.CENTRAL.

8. The Battalion will attack on a frontage of 500 yards with 2 COYS in 2 WAVES
Y COY on the LEFT (will constitute the first WAVE.
X COY on the RIGHT)
W COY on the LEFT (will constitute the second WAVE.
Z COY on the RIGHT)
The distance between lines will be about 10 yards, & between waves 100 yards.
   The 2nd wave will leave the forming up place at the same time as the first wave & will correct distance during the advance.

9. O.C.Y COY will ensure that touch is maintained thrughout with the 87th Brigade.

10. O.C.X Coy will tell off small party to block enemy's trench at O7 B2.2. and will hand over to "Z" Coy on arrival who will it turn hand over to the Hampshire Regt.
   The parties of "X" & "Z" Coys after handing over will rejoin their companies.
   O.C."Y" Coy will establish a block at O8A 2.8 and hand over to "W" Coy who will in turn hand over to the Hants Regt.   These two parties to rejoin their companies after handing over.
   2/Lieut Gamlin will advance close up to 2nd wave and establish Lewis G$_n$ positions as follows :-
       2 guns at O7 B2.2.
       1 gun at   O8 A 2.3.
       1 gun at   O8 A 1.9½

11. On capturing the BLUE LINE companies will at once send 1 Lewis Gun section per company at least 70 yards forward. Companies will be reorganised and the BLUE LINE consolidated
   "W" Company on the left, "
   "Y" Coy left centre,
   "X" Coy right centre.
   "Z" Coy on the right
   O.C.Coys will construct the following strong points.
       "W" Coy strong point at O.8.B.3.6.
       "Y" Coy stron point at O.8.B.2.5.
       "X" Coy strong point at O.8.B.I.2.
       "Z" Coy strong point at O.8.B.4.1½.
   These strong points must be capable of holding 1 platoon.

12. Any prisoners taken will be brought back by small parties and handed over to the Hampshire Regt.

13

13. Throughout the whole operations Coys will be responsible for the protection of their own flank.

14. Telephone wire will be carried forward by sibnallers with the 2nd wave. The signallers of "Y" & "X" Coy will advance with "W" & "Z" Coy respectively.

15. Battalion Headquarters will be established in the Sunken Road at O.7 A.2.7.
Reports to be sent frequently to Battalion Headquarters, not only giving the dispositions of the companies but also of troops on right and left if possible.
It is of the utmost importance to sent back information of this nature.

16. 75% of companies will carry picks and shovels; proportion to be 1 pick to every three shovels. Every man will carry 1 Mills bomb over and above the authorised amount carried by bombers.
Rifle grenadiers will each carry 8 grenades.
Companies will carry the authorized number of ground flares; full waterbottles, uncomsumed portion of the day's ration; 1 days iron ration.
Every man will carry 170 rounds S.A.A. with the exception of No 1 of Lewis Gun sections and rifle grenadiers who will each carry 120 rounds.
Each platoon will be provided with 2 black and yellow flags to put up on reaching the objective as guides to the artillery

17. Any German dug out encountered during the advance will be passed, with 2 men left at the entrance until the Hampshire Regt come up, when they will be handed over & the men left will rejoin their companies.

18. All posts in front of our present line now held by Y & X Coys will be vacated before Zero.

19   L/C Baggs & Cpl Fell will remain with the Medical Officer at the dressing station for the purpose of checking casualties.
Battn Head Qrs less the Commanding Officer, Adjutant, Signalling Officer 3 signallers and orderlies will remain in forming up trenches under the Regimental Sergt Major.
All stretcher bearers will be with this party.
O.C.Coys will each leave 1 lewis gun section in forming up trench which will come under the command of 2/Lt Gamlen.

20. The S.O.S. signal will be two Very lights as at present.

21. Dressing stations will be established at N.3 central.

22. Infaantry will light ground flares when called upon by the contact aeroplane either by sounding the Klaxon horns or by firing white lights.
Flares will be called for about 7.0 a.m. and 2.0 p.m.
The Regimental dump of S.A.A. Bombs water etc will be formed in the forming up place.

23. Previous to moving up in the forming up area great coats will be dumped as follows :-
"W" Coy in the trench at present occupied by them
"Z" Coy clear of the entrance to the caves.
"X" & "Y" in forming up trench.
O.C."X" & "Y" Coy will immediately make steps in the parapet of present front line trench to ensure quick exit
These orders must be committed to memory and destroyed before going into the attack.

(sd) L.A.W.Knight Lieut
A/Adjt 4/Worcestershire Regt.

Copies sent to
1. HEADQUATERS
2. O.C.HAMPSHIRES
3. O.C."W" COY
4. O.C."X" COY
5. O.C."Y" COY
6. O.C."Z" COY

APPENDIX TO DIVISIONAL INSTRUCTIONS NO. 5.

The arrangements for the Artillery Creeping Barrage are as follows :-

FIRST PHASE.

At Zero, a creeping barrage will be placed on the line A.B.C.D.E.F., as well as a standing barrage on the enemy's trenches.

At Zero, the troops advance from our front line, and get as close to the barrage as possible. If troops reach the barrage before it commences to creep back, they should kneel down; they must not however lie down.

The barrage on our front C.D.E.F. will creep at the rate of 100 yards in 4 minutes; that on the front A.B. of the troops on our right at the rate of 100 yards in 3 minutes, in order that they may catch up our right.

At 0.8 the barrage will lift off the enemy trenches on the front E.F., thus enabling our troops to enter the trench.

The barrage reaches the first objective BLUE Line at varying times, vide attached plan, and the signal to the troops that they have reached the BLUE Line, will be the a lift of 200 yards by the Artillery, followed by 1 minutes intense fire on the line G.H.J. The barrage will continue on the line G.H.J. for 30 minutes to enable them to consolidate.

After this period the artillery will fire bursts on the barrage line G.H.J., and also sweep enemy lines of approach, and places of concentration.

Should the S.O.S. call be made, while our troops are consolidating the BLUE Line, a barrage will be placed on the line G.H.J.F.

The enemy trenches South of point E. will be specially dealt with by howitzers, and machine guns, until the creeping barrage reaches them.

SECOND PHASE.

At Zero plus 6 hrs. and 48 minutes, the barrage will return to the line G.H.J., to enable the troops for the assault of the second objective RED Line to get into position on the BLUE Line. At Zero plus 7 Hours the troops advance from the BLUE Line.

The barrage commences to creep at Zero plus 7 hours and 4 minutes, and advances at the rate of 100 yards in 4 minutes to the line K.L.M.N.

When the barrage reaches the edges of the woods BOIS du VERT, and BOIS du SART, it will be intensified, and it will be preceded through these woods by a Heavy Howitzer barrage 200 yards in front of the shrapnel barrage, and a Field Howitzer barrage 100 yards in front of the shrapnel barrage.

The barrage reaches the second objective RED Line at varying times vide attached plan. The signal to the troops that they have reached the RED Line will be a lift of 200 yards by the Artillery, followed by 1 minute's intense fire on the line K.L.M.N.

The barrage will continue on the line K.L.M.N. for 30 minutes to enable the troops to consolidate.

It will then die away, and patrols can be sent forward to reconnoitre.

The S.O.S. barrage for the troops consolidating the RED Line, will be placed on the line K.L.M.N.

-o-o-o-o-o-o-

CONFIDENTIAL.

WAR DIARY,

of

4th Battn The Worcestershire Regiment,

for period

1st May to 31st May 1917

Volumn 15.

A. Hobart Roberts Major
O.C. 4th Worc R

WAR DIARY
or
INTELLIGENCE SUMMARY.
(Erase heading not required.)

Army Form C. 2118.

Place	Date	Hour	Summary of Events and Information	Remarks and references to Appendices
ST AMAND	May 1st		Bn left COIGNEUX at 7.30 a.m. and marched to ST AMAND via SOUASTRE. A fine day. Lewis Gun classes and training of scouts continued.	AWR
"	2nd		LAHERLIÈRE to SAULTY-LABRET station and thence by tactical train to ARRAS. Billeted in cellars in the GRANDE PLACE. Battle stores issued and all preparations made to move at 3/4 hrs notice. At 3 p.m. the Bn marched via HUMBERCAMP	AWR
ARRAS	3rd		Reveillé 4.30 a.m. Standing by from that hour. Owing to the operations by 1st, 3rd and 5th Armies not being so successful as anticipated the Bn was not required and notice was increased from 3/4 to 3 hrs. A number of shells from H.V. gun near our billets. R.Q.M.S. wounded. Ammunition dumps set on fire through careless — about 1/4 mile from billets but debris and fragments of shells fell near us. 1 D.R. wounded.	AWR AWR
"	4th		More shells than usual on the Town. Wire received that 2/Lt E. HACKETT had been awarded the Military Cross for gallantry during the operations of 11th April.	AWR
"	5th		About 100 shells fell near our billets between 2 and 4 a.m. Training programme carried out near the Race Course. A thunderstorm with heavy rain at 6.15 p.m. made the air much cooler. Systematic clearing out of billets commenced. 9 G.S. limbers of rubbish removed.	AWR
"	6th		ARRAS Church parade 11 a.m. Work on cleaning billets continued. [illegible]	

Army Form C. 2118.

Army Form C. 2118.

WAR DIARY
or
INTELLIGENCE SUMMARY
(Erase heading not required.)

Instructions regarding War Diaries and Intelligence Summaries are contained in F.S. Regs., Part II. and the Staff Manual respectively. Title Pages will be prepared in manuscript.

Place	Date	Hour	Summary of Events and Information	Remarks and references to Appendices
ARRAS	7th		A good deal of shelling during the early hours also bombs dropped near our billets. No casualties. At 2 p.m. Battn marched via WARLUS to BERNEVILLE, arriving at 5 p.m. Billeted in huts. Extract from Battn Orders:- The Corps Commander has awarded Military Medals to the undermentioned N.C.O. & men. Bar to Military Medal L/C. Elkins. " " " Pte Munden. " " " " Neale " " " " Haywood.	For distinguished conduct at Monchy Ap 23rd 1917
BERNEVILLE	8th		Rain all morning. Coys confined to huts for classes lectures etc.	
"	9th		Training carried out near old Trenches South of ARRAS - DOULLENS road. Conference at Div. H.Q. for Brigadiers & C.O.'s	
"	10th		Practise trench to trench attack as a Brigade. Bombing inspiration drill for draft & troops in afternoon.	
"	11th		From 9 a.m. 6/11a.m. Coys were on the range. At 2 p.m. Batt marched to ARRAS via BAC DU NORD. Arrived at GRAND PLACE 5 p.m. Five officers joined Batt.	
"	12th		3-45 a.m. 2nd i/c & O.C. Coys started out to reconnoitre strong posts N of CAMBRAI ROAD near LA BERGERE Fm which were to be wired at night. 9.30 a.m. Coys practised wiring on ground near the RACE COURSE. Wiring postponed to 13th. Dump of wire & stakes formed at LA BERGERE Fm.	
"	13th		Church Parade 2 Coys 9-30a.m, 2 Coys 11-30 a.m. 7.30 pm. 2 Coys marched up & wired strong points near LA BERGERE Fm & fork road N of HUSSAR LANE. B great many of salvage collected including 3 Lewis Guns. Many corpses buried. A good deal of shelling in the vicinity of working Party. Batt. received orders to go into reserve trenches at HANGEST WORK N of TILLOY.	
"	14th		These orders were cancelled but re-issued at 4-30 p.m. Four platoons left our strong points D.E.F.G. respectively. 200 men were found for carrying special proportions to front line. at 4.30 p.m.	

Army Form C. 2118.

WAR DIARY
or
INTELLIGENCE SUMMARY

(Erase heading not required.)

Instructions regarding War Diaries and Intelligence Summaries are contained in F.S. Regs., Part II. and the Staff Manual respectively. Title Pages will be prepared in manuscript.

Place	Date	Hour	Summary of Events and Information	Remarks and references to Appendices
HANGEST WARN	15th		Four platoons remained in occupation of the sitting points. Four more platoons going up in night to assist in construction of same. E Strong point settled N/of S.W. of MONCHY.	
"	16th		At about 7 p.m. they were visited by Gen. Sir H. de Beauvoir de Lisle. GOC. At 9 p.m. the Batt Hd Qrs all ranks moved up to occupy trenches S.E. of FEUCHY. From HANGEST WARN to LANCER LANE. We relieve the 6 Batt Queens who were 200 strong. Right guard his men fell heavily in a clump (Col) of Batt HQ to dump after. HR.	
LANCER LANE	17th		During the day S. part of our line was shelled. Casualties 2 men wounded. H.E. & Gas shells fell in the vicinity of Batt HQ to dump after. HR.	
"	18th		Day quiet. Spent in improving our trenches & supplying fatigue parties to Brigade & to the line. One officer wounded. WW	
"	19th		Day quiet. Our aircraft very active. 30 being up at one time.	
"	20th		On the night 20/21 it we were relieved by NEW FOUNDLAND REGT. - 200 strong. They only had Strong points. We in turn relieved the Composite Battn of NORTHAMPTONSHIRE IMPERIAL YEOMANRY & II CORPS CYCLISTS. in the front line system of trenches immediately S. of RIVER SCARPE. ELBOW TRENCH being our front line. HR	
FRONT	21st		Batt HQ. a captured enemy dugout was chosen from 10-30 p.m for about an hour no casualties. The Battn was visited by Gen. Sir H. de Beauvoir de Lisle.	
"	22nd		It was decided to establish four advanced posts in front of our front line ELBOW TRENCH. Four parties each consisting of 12 men & a N.C.O. (One officer to each party) (two parties) started at 12 p.m. The posts were lettered from left to right A.B.C.D. An enemy post near the river & only a short distance from A opened fire on A party. Every time they commenced work. After having lost one officer & two men wounded the post was found to be untenable & they returned. B.C. & D posts were established & held. RR	
"	23rd		During the night we established another post. C2 midway between & 35 yards in advance of C&D. Communication trenches were also dug from front line to C & D posts. A patrol I officer & 8 O.R. went to reconnoiter the German post near the river. They found a working party of 40 approximately with a covering party of about 20 men. They returned to cover & for some hours engaged them with Rifle grenades rifle & M.G. fire.	
"	24th		Batt HQ was heavily shelled from 5 to 9 p.m. At 5 p.m one man went over to a German Inf. Lieut (30th? R. 8.) on left of our line he found to our council but is continued a M.G. emplacement. He brought back a letter, cartridge, pocket book etc. During the night we were relieved by the Composite Batt (N I Y & II Corps Cyclists & went back to RAILWAY TRIANGLE & rest 1.30	

2449 Wt. W14957/M90 750,000 1/16 J.B.C. & A. Forms/C.2118/12

Army Form C. 2118.

WAR DIARY
or
INTELLIGENCE SUMMARY.
(Erase heading not required.)

Instructions regarding War Diaries and Intelligence Summaries are contained in F.S. Regs., Part II. and the Staff Manual respectively. Title pages will be prepared in manuscript.

Place	Date	Hour	Summary of Events and Information	Remarks and references to Appendices
RAILWAY TRIANGLES			Fine weather - Men cleaning up rifles, Equipment &c. 10% O.R. 50% officers allowed on 48 hours pass to ARRAS. The following Officers & N.C.O's have been mentioned in Dispatches - from extract from LONDON GAZETTE published in the TIMES of May 23rd. Lt.Col. E.T.J Kerans. 2/Lt. C.C. Helm. 2/Lt. Tyrer. 9377 R.S.M Morgan D.C.M. 10270 Rgt 2.M.S. Samson G. PMS	
"	26		Fine weather - during morning Rifles + Kit inspections - Baths - Afternoon musketry on the range. PMS	
"	27		Fine weather. Kit + Billet inspection by E.O. Church Parade 11 A.M. PMS	
"	28		On night 28/29th we again relieved the Composite Battn of N.I.Y + VII CORPS CYCLISTS on the same Sector as before. Strength of 40 men 2 officers arrived. 2.30.PM 3 men wounded by S.B.'s patrol in RAILWAY TRIANGLE. PMS Early in morning a Patrol reconnoitred Enemy post S. of PELVES LANE - I.25.d.4.8. - found to be strongly held + wire intact. By M.G's The wire was thin in places. Our trenches heavily shelled practically all day. Casualties:- 10 killed 6 wounded. PMS	
FRONT	29			
"	30		Order was received to attack + capture Enemy Post I.25.d.4.8. Heavy Thunderstorm at 4.PM flooded our trenches had + water been above our knees in many places. 11.20 pm. Attacked as follows 2 platoons in front line 1 platoon in second. 1 platoon in FINGER TRENCH to carry consolidating material unless + unable to capture position Attack was immediately observed by enemy at the outset + immediate heavy rifle + M.G fire. Enemy S.O.S Signal went up + an intensely heavy barrage was opened on our trenches. Eventually it was found impossible to advance + the attacking party were brought back to FINGER TRENCH. Our total losses under internal enemy fire + under pressure by enemy bombing raid	

Army Form C. 2118.

WAR DIARY
or
INTELLIGENCE SUMMARY
(Erase heading not required.)

Instructions regarding War Diaries and Intelligence Summaries are contained in F. S. Regs., Part II. and the Staff Manual respectively. Title Pages will be prepared in manuscript.

Place	Date	Hour	Summary of Events and Information	Remarks and references to Appendices
FRONT	30th		This was repulsed with loss to the enemy, & eventually things became quiet. From deserters taken from enemy dead it was discovered that the enemy had planned an attack on our trenches for the same time as we last attempted. Fortunately Wagner stalled them. Casualties 12 killed 27 wounded 2 missing. YPRS	
	31st		A quiet day – two artillery actings on both sides. 3pm a German came over & surrendered. He belonged to 141st I.R. YPRS.	

[signature] Major.
Comdg. A "B" Worcestershire Regt.

Confidential

War Diary

4th Worcestershire Regt.

From 1st June 1917   To 30th June 1917

(Volume No. 18)

WAR DIARY or INTELLIGENCE SUMMARY

Army Form C. 2118.

Place	Date	Hour	Summary of Events and Information	Remarks and references to Appendices
FRONT	June 1st/17		Considerable Artillery activity during the day. Our Heavy Artillery dropped several shells about into our front line 2-30 p.m. Casualties 2 men buried (killed). On the right of 1/Fus we were relieved by Composite Batt. W.I.Y. & W Corps Cyclists & we marched back to ARRAS in rest.	
ARRAS	2nd		Arrived in ARRAS by daybreak. Day spent in rest & cleaning and from clothing, equipment, rifles etc.	
"	3rd		Early this morning enemy aeroplane dropped bombs on ARRAS. Apparently little damage was done during the night 3/4. Hostile aeroplane again dropped bombs in the vicinity. Battn. entrained for BONNEVILLE at ARRAS. Stat. at 10 a.m. While entraining hostile aeroplanes again dropped bombs.	
"	4th		Aeroplanes stopped bombs on ARRAS, BILLETING party sent in advance to BONNEVILLE.	
BONNEVILLE	5th		Battn. entrained for BONNEVILLE & detrained at CANDAS at 3 p.m. & was met by guiding & marched to BONNEVILLE. Weather hot. Billets good.	
"	6th		Weather very hot. Parades 7 & 8 a.m. 9, 12. 2 p.m. under Coy. arrangements.	
"	7th		Owing to extensive parade will further move to be :- Reveille - 5.30. P.T. 6 a.m. & 8 a.m., 9 a.m. Lecture in afternoon or evening. P.T. The following building honour. Have been turned to Officers of 4th Batt. Worcestershire Regt. B.S.O. Lt. Col. Honour. Military Cross. Serjeant T.H. Toogs 95th Infantry Bde. Lieut R.C. Wynyate.	
"	8th		6 West 3rd officers & 27 O.R. joined the Batt. Whether very dim. Training in practice as usual. Published the Batt. Orders explaining award for gallantry in the field. Military Cross Lieut H. Crow Johnson	
"	9th		Battle drill 6 a.m. Onwards. Parade under C.O. Other parades as usual.	
"	10th		Weather very hot. Church Parade 9.30 a.m. Cricket played between Officers & Sergeants. A. won by 5 runs. Scores - 93 runs v 88. Officers v 28 O.R. joined Batt. from a.6. I.B.D.	
"	11th		Parades as usual. 1 Officer v 28 O.R. Joined Batt. from a.6. I.B.D.	
"	12th		Training as usual. Coys paraded to MONTRELET (d. Ratio)	
"	13th		Batt. paraded at 10 a.m. & marched to 95th Br. Training ground in CANDAS Copse and spent the morning in 2 hours and 2 hrs of Inner.	
"	14th		2 Officers & 75 O.R. joined the Batt. from a.6. I.B.D.	
"	15th		Day hot day. Parades at 7-11. 13th. 2 Officers & 75 O.R. joined the Batt. from 6. 2-45 a.m. Parade 9 a.m. Night operations at CANAPLES 9.30 p.m.	
"	16th		2 Officers. Horse show was held at BERNEUIL. The Batt. obtained 3rd Prize for First Aiders & 2nd for	
"	17th		Officers "Kitchen" event.	
"	19		Billeting army parade - 9.45 a.m.	
"	20th		Training as usual.	

R.W. Wynyate Capt & Adj
1st Worc. Regt.

Army Form C. 2118.

WAR DIARY
or
INTELLIGENCE SUMMARY.
(Erase heading not required.)

4 to 10 November Reg.

Place	Date	Hour	Summary of Events and Information	Remarks and references to Appendices
ONNEVILLE	21/6/17		Training as in previous days. ths	
"	22nd		Special instruction to NCOs. Lecture on "Bangalore Torpedoes" ths	
"	23rd		Wire Obstacles had to be carefully neg'd in every details. In Lecture party left for HOPPER NONE to arrange billets. ths	
"	24th		Good Parade. Man. followed by demonstration of wire cutting by Bangalore Torpedoes & of Fire from Lewis Gun. Memo. 20 pickets before 9 pm.	
"	25th		Training as usual. C.O. visited HQ D.O.E.N.q. YPRES. ths	
"	26th		Coys paraded 9 am & marched to DOULLENS & were billeted there for the night. ths	
ILLENS	27	10.20am	Batt. entrained at DOULLENS North for POPERINGHE. Detrained at HOPOUTRE SIDING at 7PM & marched to Camp in PROVEN. ths	
OVEN.	28		Batt. moved to bivouac in wood near YPRES C48 - two 10 PR. P party finding fatigue/ridding. ths	
WIPPERS C48	29		The Batt. supplied working parties to assist R.E. to dig gun pits & dugouts. also parties to R.E. ths	
"	30		Working parties carried on the usual work also engaged on the preceeding day. ths	

1577 Wt. W10791/1773 500,000 1/15 D. D. & L. A.D.S.S./Forms/C. 2118.

Rollophis Cafe
Algeut 4 Wore Regt

Confidential

War Diary
of
4th Worcestershire Regt.

From 1st July 1917 " To 31st July 1917

(Volume No 19)

Army Form C. 2118.

WAR DIARY
or
INTELLIGENCE SUMMARY.
(Erase heading not required.)

Instructions regarding War Diaries and Intelligence Summaries are contained in F. S. Regs., Part II. and the Staff Manual respectively. Title pages will be prepared in manuscript.

4 Batt'n Worcester Regt July 1917.

Place	Date	Hour	Summary of Events and Information	Remarks and references to Appendices
DE WIPPE 1/7/17				
INTERNATIONAL CORNER	2nd		Orders to look into N.W. portion of International Corner Z.	
			Relieving position of 2/Hunts Regt. Between 9 p.m. and 10 p.m. See International Corner Map	
"	3rd		Major C. Scobey 2/Hunts Regt Company Cmdr of the Relief Batt.	
"	4th		The relief was completed by 11 p.m. 3/7/17	
"	5th			
"	6th			
"	7th			
"	8th			
"	9th			
"	10th			
"	11th			
YSER CANAL	12th		Batt. relieved by 1 R.M.S. Wales on the Yser Canal (Bridge Lassen) N + Z Coys	
"	13th			
"	14th			
"	15th			
L. CAMP	16th			
"	17th			
"	18th		L Camp	
CROMBEKE CAMP	19th		The Batt. moved to Crombeke Camp	
N. of PROVEN	20th		M + Z Coys returned to this Camp. 2 a.m. Coy Training + C.O.'s Parade had to be abandoned on account of heavy rain	
"	21st		Church Parade. Coys to provide working parties.	
"	22nd		Coys practiced the Attack	
"	23rd		Coy Training + usual Classes held	
"	24th		Training continued as for 19th	
CROMBEKE CAMP	25th		Batt moved + pitched and area rest Camp at 19/A.25.c.d.5. (N. of Proven)	
"	26th		Coy Training + Classes as usual	
"	27th		Batt marched to Herzeele + practiced attack	

Army Form C. 2118.

WAR DIARY
or
INTELLIGENCE SUMMARY.
(Erase heading not required.)

Instructions regarding War Diaries and Intelligence Summaries are contained in F. S. Regs., Part II. and the Staff Manual respectively. Title pages will be prepared in manuscript.

Place	Date	Hour	Summary of Events and Information	Remarks and references to Appendices

CONFIDENTIAL.

4th. BATTN. THE WORCESTERSHIRE REGT.

WAR DIARY.

AUGUST 1917.

Army Form C. 2118.

4TH WORCESTERSHIRE REGT WAR DIARY or INTELLIGENCE SUMMARY.

(Erase heading not required.)

Instructions regarding War Diaries and Intelligence Summaries are contained in F. S. Regs., Part II. and the Staff Manual respectively. Title pages will be prepared in manuscript.

August

Place	Date	Hour	Summary of Events and Information	Remarks and references to Appendices
CROMBEKE CAMP (B.2.)	1st		Very wet day. No parades. R.9.	
"	2nd		Wet day. Company route marches in afternoon. R.9.	
"	3rd		Another wet day. Training rendezvous. R.9.	
"	4th		Still wet. Company route marches in the morning. R.9.	
"	5th		Church Parade 10 AM. Weather clearing. R.9.	
FOREST AREA	6th		Batt paraded 1.30pm and marched to No 5 camp near De Wippe Cabaret. Canvas camp. Very muddy. R9	
BEDFORD FARM.	7th		Battalion less 10% moved to another canvas camp. 10% could do lot. 10% moved to the Transport Lines R.9.	
	8th		Company Training. R9.	
	9th		Company Training. Map made of front. Went to stock when under R.9. attack was made.	lect
	10th		Company Training - Marching on a certain bearing in artillery formation and extended order. R9.	
	11th		Brig Gen Colley discussed the coming attack with all officers commanding Coys. Watched by means of model attacking B2 Coy.	

4TH WORCESTERSHIRE REGT WAR DIARY or INTELLIGENCE SUMMARY

Army Form C. 2118.

II August

Place	Date	Hour	Summary of Events and Information	Remarks and references to Appendices
BEDFORD FARM	12TH	10 AM	Church Parade R.9.	
"	13TH		Cross country marching on compass bearing R.9.	
"	14TH		Batt. practised crossing bridges and deploying on East side of the stream R.9.	
"	15TH		Final preparations for the attack. Move a very short dist.	
TRENCHES (CANNE'S FARM)	16TH		Batt. formed up for attack on West side of STEENBEEK (W of LANGEMARCK) Barrage started 4.45 AM. Battn. was in 2nd line at commencement. BLUE LINE (1st objective) soon taken. Final objective RED LINE taken by battalion without difficulty. Line consolidated & held. Advance to GREEN LINE continued in artillery formation. Casualties:- Capt. ADDISON, 2/Lt BOWDEN, 2/Lt WORDINGHAM killed, 2/Lt BONFIELD Capt. STACKE, 2/Lt GOODMAN, Lt VANCE (American Medical Corps) wounded. 95 other ranks casualties. Ground attacked over was in a very bad state, but very little resistance was met and the whole operation was a great success owing partly to the help keeping well up to the barrage R.9. Shelter	

4 WORCESTERSHIRE REGT WAR DIARY
or
INTELLIGENCE SUMMARY.

(Erase heading not required.)

Army Form C. 2118.

III

August

Instructions regarding War Diaries and Intelligence Summaries are contained in F. S. Regs., Part II. and the Staff Manual respectively. Title pages will be prepared in manuscript.

Place	Date	Hour	Summary of Events and Information	Remarks and references to Appendices
~~SHRAPNEL~~ BLACK LINE	Aug 17		Batt relieved Coal ingRt by 1.R.Dub Fus. They came back and spent the day in old German trenches. Heavy shelling. 2/Lt CC O M NEWCOMBE killed. 18 O R casualties.	
BOESINGHE CHATEAU	18th		The Batt came back here for 1 day and night to reorganize. No casualties here and men had a good nights sleep	
TRENCHES	19th		This Regt moved up into the Left sector walk. trench at 8pm and relieved the 16th Middlesex Regt. H.Q at WITTENDRIFT and header this side of BROENBEEK stream. Good relief.	
"	20th		2nd FRENCH DIV on our left. R.Dub Fus on our right. 2 Coy front by Fire day at end, went beginning to dry up a bit. We established a post over the BROENBEEK during the night. The N.T.L.D.N. are now on our right Coy.	
"	21st		Heavily shelled during the day. On our or right our dark & Ford Lewis Cop were relieved by outposting Coys. another post put over BROENBEEK. 2/Lt CALE wounded. 29 OR	
"	22nd		3rd post established over BROENBEEK. Quiet day. very fine PQ. Clinton Lt. Col	

4th WORCESTERSHIRE REGT
WAR DIARY or INTELLIGENCE SUMMARY
August

Army Form C. 2118.

Place	Date	Hour	Summary of Events and Information	Remarks and references to Appendices
ELVER-DINGHE	23		Batt was relieved by 2nd S.W.B's. Perfect relief, no casualties. Batt now in camp E of ELVERDINGHE in tents.	
	24		Batt paraded 2pm and marched to the camp. Ample accommodation in long trench huts.	
DE WIPPE	25		Baths and general clean up. 10% wksmen.	
	26		Church Parade 10AM & 2 Coys. Remaining Coys worked on track. 11 pg. After the day at Batt. ancled the camp by 12 Nthn. Tents.	
PROVEN M'ZAREN	27		Called PICCADILLY CAMP, 2 mile N.E. of PROVEN. By Rained hard all day. Special classes commenced. Platoon	
	28		sheet memory. N.C.O.'s under R.S.M. Profy of 7 officers and 57 sergeants in from BOLLEZEELE (?).	
	29		Men & Officers Coys. C.O's parade when men permitted. Complaints. Crawford accidentally wounded by revolve on later to hospital. 24	
	30		Weather still bad. Very little work possible. Py	
	31		Camp getting very muddy. owing to constantram. Company parades and classes during the morning. Py	

Hunton Lt Col

CONFIDENTIAL.

WAR DIARY

of

4th. BATTN. THE WORCESTERSHIRE REGIMENT.

From 1st. September 1917   To 30th. September 1917.

(VOLUME No. 21.)

Army Form C.-2118.

WAR DIARY
or
INTELLIGENCE SUMMARY.
(Erase heading not required.)

Instructions regarding War Diaries and Intelligence Summaries are contained in F. S. Regs., Part II. and the Staff Manual respectively. Title pages will be prepared in manuscript.

Place	Date	Hour	Summary of Events and Information	Remarks and references to Appendices
PROVEN N°2 WEP	1/9/17		Lt Bratton reported to the Reserve Brigade personnel duty	
Richmond Camp	19/9/17		Strength return B Ech. 1 Officer. R & F	7A
"	19/9/17		The Bde proceed to ceremonial parade & the composite Bty of 146/FA	7A
"	19/9/17		Division F.A. on good showing the review the dress & cleanliness	7A
	20/9/17		The Bde. 1/2 played the D.S. at the tactical exercise at 7/51 FA	7A
			for a Field Division of infantry in defence	
	2/9/17		Presentation of decorations by GOC. Division: Capt B. was awarded M.C.	7A
	9/9/17		The B. observed the internal discipline of training	7A
	9/9/17		B. route march followed by cleaning of harness & billets	7B
			& inspection of billets by OC Bde & orders	
	10/9/17		Brigade sports	7A
	12/9/17		Church parade & polo Bde won Cup Match defeating 7th at the	7A
			Corps Horse + hound parade & bivouac	
	11/9/17		Bde moving T 9 ar. Gre Q destination the hostile shop at lunch	7A
			York 1 OC Bde paraded for France + Maj Ory + Maj M V 5 Capt Wanbury + Capt Ogram.	7A
			Remounts &	

Army Form C. 2118.

WAR DIARY
or
INTELLIGENCE SUMMARY.
(Erase heading not required.)

Instructions regarding War Diaries and Intelligence Summaries are contained in F. S. Regs., Part II. and the Staff Manual respectively. Title pages will be prepared in manuscript.

Place	Date	Hour	Summary of Events and Information	Remarks and references to Appendices
PICCADILLY CAMP	1/9/17		Bn proceeded to the gallery in HERZEELE for 3 days musketry training. 7 Coy ban	17A
			Route test in the Knox renaming Coys. have been instructed by Brights	
			at the Moorslag. Capt Beirdy Cb attached to Brights	
HERZEELE	2/9/17		MUSKetry commenced. Coy exercises ranged "A" + "B" + "C" + "D"	17A
			morning fires	
			Continued training. Notice to the Bn arrangements	17A
	3/9/17			17A
	4/9/17		Various Offrs detailed to 88th Bgde for having to supervise	
			attached held in the O/Brigade orders. Offrs proceeded to a certain	
			of the attack to be held by all ranks on arrival	
	5/9/17		Bn left HERZEELE at 10.30 am entrained at H.W. HOUTKERQUE	17A
PICCADILLY CAMP				
PICCADILLY	6/9/17		Various arcs of company movements	17A
	7/9/17		Major of the Corps arrangements for issuing rations from T.O.	17A
	8/9/17		Primary reconnaissance by the 2/i/c to be kept by Bright	
	9/9/17		Orders issued Bn to parade at 10.15am to move forward to C.M.	17A

Aylandm Lt. G.R.
4 Worcestershire Regt.

WAR DIARY or INTELLIGENCE SUMMARY

Army Form C. 2118.

(Erase heading not required.)

Place	Date	Hour	Summary of Events and Information	Remarks and references to Appendices
NIEUPORT LINE	24/9/17		Hostile Coys Supp. Coy + BHQ shelled from 7.15 AM - 8.30 by 5.9s + 4.2s	A/8
			No damage. All well save one slight wound. Coy shelled again at	A/8
			4 am after the two front Coys & Z were relieved by battalion	A/9
			Capt W. H. Drummond left HQ + for HQ's with the K.R.R.	
	25/9/17		Relief completed about 9 am. Battalion took over support line	A/7
			& continued to be a force. Large shelling by enemy on our Coys	
			and on return during the evening of the 25th on our Coys	
			The 3rd Batt K. Regt during the evening relieved by K.R.R. Batt in	
			Nieuport. A light shrapnel hit at HQ was relieved by the K.R.R	
			Next morning Batt 26th 9.15 no casualties Breakfast & issue	
			Coys sent back to Rest Camp 27th.	
RUGBY CAMP	27/9/17		B. Battalion at D.35.b. Coy taken by Co Commander. Officers	A/8
	28/9/17		" B " paraded for bathe. Coy issue bully & tea. Baths & tomorrow.	A/8
	29/9/17		" B " paraded at 2 am marched to E. DE WIPPE CORNER CAMP	A/8
DE WIPPE CAMP	29/9/17		" B " paraded according to the routine of work	
	30/9/17		" B " paraded to Church Parade & the Padre who [?] commanding	

CONFIDENTIAL

WAR DIARY

of

4th. BATTN. THE WORCESTERSHIRE REGIMENT

from 1st. October 1917   to 31st. October 1917.

(VOLUME No. ZZ.)

Army Form C. 2118.

WAR DIARY
or
INTELLIGENCE SUMMARY.
(Erase heading not required.)

Place	Date	Hour	Summary of Events and Information	Remarks and references to Appendices
De WIPPE CAMP	1st Oct		Instructional Classes continued. Huts surrounded with sandbags/walls to protect the effects of hostile Bombs. During night E.A. came over when moon was very bright and dropped bombs in camp vicinity.	
"	2nd "		Classes continued. Each company worked for 2 hours on the improvement of Inspection Track II following their keeping parties digging during it. E.A. again active during hours dropped in our area.	
"	3rd "		Working Party of 150 Sent to BOESINGHE to bury cables. Two companies to baths. Rain during day.	
"	4th "		Companies practised attacking in waves under barrage represented by flags. Instructions for the Tournament.	
"	5th "		Heavy rain during morning. Training carried on later part of the afternoon. 250 reinfts. see Div. Tourn.	
ROUSSOL CAMP	6th "		Battalion paraded at 9 a.m. and marched to ROUSSOL CAMP. C.O. + 2nd in Command + other job remaining. Further part.	
"	7th "		Church parade 9.30 a.m. The "B" paraded at 5:30 p.m. marched to BOESINGHE and hence via RAILWAY STREET duck boards to front line when it relieved 2nd Bn S.W.B.	
TRENCHES N. of LANGEMARCK	8th "		Relief complete by 3.30 a.m. W.Coy left front line, X.Coy right - on either side of YPRES - STADEN railway in the LA German trenches known as BEAR and LEOPARD. Y.Coy left support, Z.Coy right.	
			H.Q. at SPRING FARM U.22.c.5.1.1. Patrols were out all to reconnoitre the BROEMBEEK and much useful information was gained concerning possible crossings of it. At 5:30 p.m.	BROEMBEEK Map 1:40,000
			B" H.Q. moved from SPRING FARM to a block house in BEAR TRENCH at U.17.c.8.1. behind LEOPARD TRENCH occupied by X.Coy.	Sheet No 2
			Z.Coy moved from MARTIN'S MILL to shell holes	Obg. Capt. H. H. GP.

Army Form C. 2118.

WAR DIARY
or
INTELLIGENCE SUMMARY.
(Erase heading not required.)

Place	Date	Hour	Summary of Events and Information	Remarks and references to Appendices
FRONT LINE TRENCHES N. of LANGEMARCK	8th		During the night tapes were laid out in front of the line the companies to form up on the tapes.	
	9th	2.30 a.m.	By this hour companies were found up on the tapes as follows:- W Coy LEFT Right leading wave, Y Coy Left, Z Coy Right, Z Coy Right. About 1 hour after this the 1st Newfoundland Rgt arrived and found up about 160ᵗ in rear of our lines. It had been raining hard during the preceding 24 hours. Zero hour was at 5.20 a.m. when it was just light enough to see across Battalion frontage about 600ˣ. The Barrage started at 5.20 a.m. moving at the rate of 100ˣ in 6 min. In BROEMBEEK there was sufficient obstacle to cause a good deal of disorganization among units. The Leading Coys (W & X) gained their objective to within about 6 a.m. - although mustering with a great deal of opposition. The advance was not hung up. During the first advance touch was kept with the Coldstream Guards on Left and 2ᵃᵈ Lancashire Fusiliers on Right. News that first objective had been captured reached Bᵗⁿ H.Q. at 6.15 a.m. At 7 a.m. Bᵗⁿ H.Q. moved forward to NAMUR CROSSING V.18.b.2.9. The barrage held for about an hour in front of 1ˢᵗ objective and then moved forward at the rate of 100ˣ in 8 min to the second objective. The second line	Ry. Capt. of Bn. Col.

Army Form C. 2118.

WAR DIARY
or
INTELLIGENCE SUMMARY.
(Erase heading not required.)

Place	Date	Hour	Summary of Events and Information	Remarks and references to Appendices
	9th		Companies pushed on close to the barrage and captured the 2nd Objective with rather less opposition. This line was also consolidated and touch gained with the Irish Guards on left and Royal Fusiliers on right. The 1st N.F.L.D. Regt. had formed up behind & this line and when afts on lines the barrage moved forward again this followed it and captured the 3rd Objective. The Bn took 6 officers and 200 O.R. prisoners and captured 5 machine guns. We lost killed 2 officers 20 O.R. Wounded 6 officers 107 O.R. Missing 40 O.R. The enemy barrage was dropped about 10 min. after zero and was very heavy, chiefly along the BROEMBEEK. At night the Bn were relieved as follows. The two coys. Y & Z on the 2nd objective were relieved by the 1st N.F.L.D. The two coys (W + X) on 1st Objective were relieved by 7th Bn. Lt. Shropshire R.gt. Relief complete by 3.50 a.m. Companies then marched down to HARROW CAMP near ELVERDINGHE. W 9.30 a.m. returned disposed of Intimated at Corner and then marched to SARAWAK CAMP. Rolls called	
HARROW CAMP	10th			

Army Form C. 2118.

WAR DIARY
or
INTELLIGENCE SUMMARY.
(Erase heading not required.)

Instructions regarding War Diaries and Intelligence Summaries are contained in F. S. Regs., Part II. and the Staff Manual respectively. Title pages will be prepared in manuscript.

Place	Date	Hour	Summary of Events and Information	Remarks and references to Appendices
SARAWAK CAMP	11th		Weather very unsettled. Day spent checking casualties, cleaning up etc. AHR	
"	12th		More rain. Companies proceed to Baths. 7 Officers and 164 O.R. join Bn from Corps Depot. AHR	
"	13th		Weather still bad. Companies reorganised as three platoons. AHR	
"	14th		Church parade 9.15 a.m. Fine day but SSR very muddy. AHR	
"	15th		Some rain. Camp cleared up preparatory to an early move. AHR	
"	16th	3 a.m.	Bn assembled to PESELHOEK STATION about 4 miles. Breakfasts in station and awaited entraining. Train only took 30 minutes including loading M Transport and animals. Train started two hours late and took 12 instead of 7 hours on the journey. Detrained at SAULTY-LABRET at 8 p.m. The Bn less W Coy left behind as entraining party to remainder of Brigade Group marched to BERLES-AU-BOIS. Very wet. AHR	
BERLES-AU-BOIS	17th		Instructional classes for NCO's, Lewis Gunners, Signallers & Scouts recommenced AHR	
"	18th		W Coy rejoin the Bn. Classes continued. C.O.'s conference at Div H.Q. re training. AHR	
"	19th		X Coy build a new 100' range. Classes continued. 2 Coy inter section football tournament. AHR	
"	20th		Musketry & classes continued. Second lecture re men lost to Lewis gunners to specialists. AHR	
"	21st		Fine day. Church Parade. Party detailed to up-keep of roads in vicinity. AHR	

Army Form C. 2118.

WAR DIARY
or
INTELLIGENCE SUMMARY.
(Erase heading not required.)

Instructions regarding War Diaries and Intelligence Summaries are contained in F. S. Regs., Part II. and the Staff Manual respectively. Title pages will be prepared in manuscript.

Place	Date	Hour	Summary of Events and Information	Remarks and references to Appendices
BERLES -AU- BOIS	22nd		Rain intermittently during day. Ceremonial parade. Classes in musketry.	BWR
"	23rd		Rain all morning. Classes in MLG. Musketry in afternoon.	BWR
"	24th		Ceremonial Parade 9-10.30 a.m. Afternoon classes. New lot of young persons.	BWR
"	25th		W/day employed improving roads & drainage. Remainder musketry, bayonet fighting etc.	BWR
"	26th		All afters in Bn inspected by Bde Commdr. Musketry. Rain all afternoon.	BWR
"	27th		Ceremonial parade. Coys start firing a classification musketry course.	BWR
"	28th		Church parade 9:15 a.m. Sharp frost. The following decorations were awarded the Bn to operations on 9th Oct. 4 Military Crosses 4 D.C.M. 30 Military Medals of the latter, two of these men were attached to other units on the day in question.	BWR
"	29th		Brigade ceremonial parade 10:30 a.m. Musketry in afternoon.	BWR
"	30th		Ceremonial parade. Bayonet fighting competition. Rifles found to pull sharp and sticking up.	BWR
"	31st		Brigade ceremonial parade 10.30 a.m. - 12.45 p.m. This day. Wire attached in B Coy to Bde foot ball tournament. Men all rested. Semi final X, Y & Z Coys	BWR

C.S. Linton Lt-Col
31st Oct 1917
9 Lincolnshire

CONFIDENTIAL

WAR DIARY

OF

4TH WORCESTERSHIRE REGIMENT

FROM 1st November 1917   TO   30th November, 1917

(Volume No 23)

4th Worcestershire Regt.   November 1917.   1st Sheet

Army Form C. 2118.

WAR DIARY
or
INTELLIGENCE SUMMARY.
(Erase heading not required.)

Instructions regarding War Diaries and Intelligence Summaries are contained in F.S. Regs., Part II. and the Staff Manual respectively. Title pages will be prepared in manuscript.

Place	Date	Hour	Summary of Events and Information	Remarks and references to Appendices
BERLES AU BOIS	1917 Nov 1.		88th Bde. inspected by Maj. Genl. S. Bisscoe on foot, K.C.B., C.S.O., who afterwards forwarded most wishes to Officers and many the men who had been awarded decorations in recent operations. A cold, cloudy day. Parade and march past went off very well, and the G.O.C. expressed satisfaction on the turnout, bearing of men, etc. Some rain in the evening.	
BERLES AU BOIS	Nov 2.		Day: misty morning, with some rain. W & X Coys. on rifle range. Z. Coy. bayonet fighting and ten mins drill. Y Coy. advance local Coy. found parties for collecting mines. Hopps again open to farmers.	
"	Nov 3		Foggy morning. Musketry.19. Lectures to Officers & NCO's on Gas. Shooting match between Officers and Sergts. Score of S. Patro in Snafed. Officers 218 – Sergts. 184.	
"	Nov 4.		Church parade 10 A.M. During afternoon C.O. & 2/Lt. rode over to see a demonstration of Lembs machine gun infantry. Capt. R.J.H. Macearthy reported from Army School.	
"	Nov 5		W, Y & Z Coys. on Musketry. Bayonet fighting and wiring. X Coy. on outpost scheme. Lt. Col. Linton, D.S.O., inspected & lecd to his D.S.O., for services during recent operations, probably Aug. 16.7, and Oct. 9.7.	
"	Nov 6		Drawing continued as above. W. Coy. on outpost scheme. C.O. attended a demonstration of the use of Stokes mortar. Rain all afternoon. Musketry competition between Coys. Rapid fit team of 5. Z. Coy came in 1st.	
"	Nov 7.		2 Cl. Henry and a draft of 6 O.R. joined the Batte. Draft included men from Cavalry. Batts. attached on account march, but returned to billets owing to heavy rain. Coys. inspected in their organization of Platoon & Sections. Officers and Platoon aergts. above scheme for movement and method of carrying and explained work across open.	
"	Nov 8		Slight frost in morning. At 10 A.M. the Battn. carried out a scheme advancing under barrage, two Coys for first objective, in two waves, and two Coys for 2nd objective, following in artillery formation at 150 x. 1200 y to final objective, 1700 y to 2nd objective. Attack was carried out and on system of bounds in direction of MONCHY AU BOIS, and was very creditably performed in spite of rough ground, mud, etc. Brigadier expressed his satisfaction.	
"	Nov 9		In the afternoon. Bayonet fighting & L.G. competitions. Z. Coy won the former, & Y Coy the latter. Coys on bombing, bayonet fighting, and musketry. Demonstration in use of smoke shells from 3" Stokes Guns not witnessed by D. & L., London, E.C., of reconstruction of G.O.C. Division. Lecture by Maj. Somerville, from G.H.Q., on Musketry.	

1st Worcestershire Regt. November 1917. Army Form C. 2118.

WAR DIARY
or
INTELLIGENCE SUMMARY.
(Erase heading not required.)

2nd Sheet

Place	Date	Hour	Summary of Events and Information	Remarks and references to Appendices
BERLES-AU-BOIS	Nov 10		Coys. carried out usual training programme. G.O.C. Division approved C.O.s and 2nd i/c's at Battle. In the afternoon the G.O.C. gave a lecture to all Officers and full N.C.Os of 88th Bde. on the forthcoming training and offensive - semi-open warfare, etc.	
"	Nov 11		Church Parade 9.30 A.M. in General Hazel Bath, a demonstration for all officers on the Bde. of the various formations to be adopted by infantry when working with tanks.	
"	Nov 12		All Coys. practiced advance Guard. Bombing practice continued. The C.O., 2 i/c, OC Coy. (Capt Bartlett) and 2/Lt Snow proceeded to recgd. new trench area and reconnoitre. Bt Gen Nelson held a conference of all Coy. Commanders at Bde. H.Q.	
"	Nov 13		Coys. practised advance Guard formation over broken and difficult ground. Party of officers saw a few microphones. Maj. A.E. Stokes-Roberts left to take Command of 7/8 Royal Scots. (65th Div.)	
"	Nov 14		Battn. assembled for Brigade practice in advance Guard formation in preparing for forthcoming operations. The Battn worked as R. Flank of Bde., and advanced in advanced formation to line of canal (marked by flags), crossed the canal under covering fire, and took up position on the crest beyond, rifleing in a similar attack and consolidating the position. At a conference after the operation, the Brigadier expressed himself as pleased with the work as a whole, but pointed out matters which could be improved.	
"	Nov 15		The operations of yesterday were repeated. The Brigade on this occasion worked as the R.Bn. of the Division in attack. The Battn. occupied the same position on the R. of the Bde. The main minor differences in the conduct of the advance, disposition of Coys. etc., but the general idea of the operation was the same. The G.O.C. in C. watched the advance, and in course of lecture delivered in the centre and L. of the Bde., The G.O.C. Division left notes with the Brigadier which were read to C.O.s + Staffs after the operation.	
"	Nov 16		Preparations for move. Spare kit dumped at Rail-Head DOMWERK. The transport left to new area by	

D.D.& L., London, E.C.
(A6601) Wt. W1771/M2931 750,000 5/17 Sch. 53 Forms/C2118/14

Army Form C. 2118.

4 Worcestershire Regt.

WAR DIARY
or
INTELLIGENCE SUMMARY.

(Erase heading not required.)

November 1917 .... 3rd Week

Instructions regarding War Diaries and Intelligence Summaries are contained in F.S. Regs., Part II. and the Staff Manual respectively. Title pages will be prepared in manuscript.

Place	Date	Hour	Summary of Events and Information	Remarks and references to Appendices
BERLES-AU-BOIS	1917 NOV 17		Battn. proceeded by march route to BOISLEAU-AU-MONT, and MONCHY-AU-BOIS and ADINFER. Entrained there after a hot meal, and proceeded to PERONNE – Thence by march route again to MOISLAINS, arriving about 3 AM 18/11/17.	
MOISLAINS	NOV 18		Billeted in Hutment Camp (YORK CAMP) and spent the day preparing to move further up towards the Line. Battn. paraded at 5 PM. and proceeded by route march from NURLU & FINS to SOREL, billeting there in bivouac shelters.	
SOREL	NOV 19		Day spent in drawing battle stores and warning them throughout the Battn., and making as much as possible preparatory to moving into the Assembly Position for the attack. Rifles under Lieut. Wyatt and 2/Lt Burton reconnoitred route up to and on to Assembly Area. Everything quiet along the front.	
SOREL and in the ATTACK	NOV 20		Reveille 12.45AM. Troops had breakfast, and Battn. paraded on road outside Camp at 3 AM, moving off with rest of Brigade through HEUDICOURT and GOUZEAUCOURT to Assembly Area No9 Batter village. Battn. reached Assembly Area and formed up without trouble by 4.45AM. Detail party remained at SOREL, also Q.M. Stores and new Battn. Hqrs. At Zero, the 88th Bde. moved forward to the forming up area (the British front line prior to Zero) and the Battalion moved into position between POPE AVENUE and FUSILIER AVENUE by 10.20AM. The enemy barrage was very weak. At 10.30AM (approx) the Brigade bugle sounded to advance. The Essex Battn. moved forward over the 1st Objective (HINDENBURG LINE) and 2nd Objective (HINDENBURG SUPPORT) which had been captured by the 20th DIVN, without trouble, and direction was kept well except for one platoon of Y. Coy. most of the L. The ESSEX REGT. at this point were not so far forward, though the Germ was that they should be on to the L. The 20th DIVN, after capturing their two objectives, had moved forward towards the Canal, still covering the advance of the 29th DIVN. – though this was not strictly according to plan – the Battn. moved straight on, over the 2nd Objective (the platoon of Y Coy regaining its place and direction on the move) and meeting mother to the R. crossed the CANAL crossing at the LOCK in front of the SUGAR FACTORY. Opposition to this point practically nil, except for occasional sniping. The Battn. had passed through the 20th DIVN. before reaching the CANAL. X Coy crossed the CANAL, followed by X Coy, W. Coy being on the R, covering the crossing. Z. Coy and Battn. Hd. Qrs. up now facing on W. L. facing the village of MASNIERES. One platoon of Z Coy followed the tanks up to the MAIN BRIDGE, and forming Rear Guard, one of the objectives of the ESSEX REGT. who were also taking the bridge. Having been partially blown up by the enemy collapsed beneath the weight of the tank.	

Army Form C. 2118.

1st Worcestershire Regt.

WAR DIARY
or
INTELLIGENCE SUMMARY.
(Erase heading not required.)

November 1917

Instructions regarding War Diaries and Intelligence Summaries are contained in F. S. Regs., Part II. and the Staff Manual respectively. Title pages will be prepared in manuscript.

Place	Date	Hour	Summary of Events and Information	Remarks and references to Appendices
IN the ATTACK (cont'd)	Nov 20		At this spot 2/Lt DIXON was shot in the head and died of wounds shortly afterwards. The 1/ESSEX REGT. and 2/HAMPS REGT. arrived. The 1/W.F.A.D. REGT. crossed the CANAL on the L. Owing to the MAIN BRIDGE being down, difficulties were experienced in supplying up the centre of the village of MASNIERES, and some lively opposition was met from there. About 2 A.M. the C.O. (Lt Col LINTON, D.S.O.M.C.) crossed the canal to see the position, and on his return was shot by a sniper and killed outright. The position at this time was: Y. and X. Coys across the CANAL on the R. of MASNIERES, (near the SUGAR FACTORY) and W + Z Coys covering their flanks from the near side of the CANAL. W. on the R., Y. on the L., with Batt. H.Q. At dusk, W. Coy relieved Z, and Z crossed the CANAL about 10.30 P.M. taking up a position near SUGAR FACTORY, in support of Y+ X Coys. .... Later on Z Coy was ordered in the mopping up of the village of MASNIERES, and completed that job by 12 A.M. Z Coy then moved forward and consolidated on this line which had been taken up by the 2/HAMPS R. and the two Coys. of 4/W.R.C.R. while crossed the CANAL first, covering MASNIERES from the CANAL, in advance of the SUGAR FACTORY towards the village of RUMILLY. Disposition at dawn :- X on R., Y in centre, Z on L. connected up with 2/HAMPS.R. Who reached	
MASNIERES	Nov 21		at 11 A.M., following orange and to 18th. Coys massed forming new advancing near ridge behind CRÈVECOEUR. In the direction of MON PLAISIR FARM. Batt. has not been able to advance." No action followed on both fronts. Day occupied in consolidation and dealing with snipers. 16 Civilians sent down to VILLERS PLOUICH. Relief arranged for Batt., but cancelled about 9 P.M. Start made in communication trenches between front line and support.	
In TRENCHES near MASNIERES	Nov 22		Day spent in consolidation and sniping. No further advance - No enemy action, beyond sniping, and occasional shelling near LOCK CROSSING. During night continued digging C.T. connecting front line with support.	
- do -	Nov 23		Day quiet. Consolidation continued. Soon after dark, the Battn. was relieved by the 1/ Surrey Rifle Infantry and proceeded to billets in MARCOING. Relief carried out without trouble.	
MARCOING	Nov 24		In billets in cellars at MARCOING. Day spent in cleaning up and overhauling equipment and dubbin shoes. Village shelled heavily by enemy all day.	
- do -	Nov 25		Enemy artillery quiet. After dark the Battn. relieved the 2nd S.W.B. in reserve trenches on the R. of MARCOING. STATION. Relief carried out without difficulty. Lt Col. B. C. S. Clarke took over command of the Battn.	
IN TRENCHES	Nov 26		The Battn. Continued consolidation of the reserve trenches. No enemy activity on Battn. sector. C.T. dug, connecting reserve trenches with front line, a distance of about 500 yds.	
- do -	Nov 27		C.T. dug, connecting reserve trenches with front line. After dark the working party to C.T. started on previous night. Z. Coy reported to O.E. 2/HAMPS.R. and formed working party to carry wire and dig C.T. connecting front reserve line in front of RUMILLY	

Army Form C. 2118.

4th Worcestershire Regt.

WAR DIARY
or
INTELLIGENCE SUMMARY.

(Erase heading not required.)

November 1917   3rd Sheet

Place	Date	Hour	Summary of Events and Information	Remarks and references to Appendices
IN TRENCHES	Nov 28		The Battn. completed consolidation of position and was relieved after dark by the 2/5 War. Marched back to MARCOING by Coys, and billeted in cellars. Blankets issued.	
MARCOING	Nov 29		Enemy shelling heavy all day, but casualties light. Men remained under cover Much needed rest.	
MARCOING	Nov 30		Orders received about 9AM. to move out of MARCOING to a sunken road behind the copse on the MARCOING - MASNIERES ROAD. As the Battn. was about to move information was received that the enemy had attacked and were shew on the outskirts of MARCOING. The Battn, with the remainder of the Bde., moved out to the high ground overlooking the CANAL valley, and drove the enemy back by a vigorous Counter attack. Consolidation of a line then commenced, and by 8 P.M. the Battn. was dug in, all four Coys being in front line, with 1/KOSB. on R. and in support and remainder of 88th Bde. on L. No further enemy attack during night.	

In the Field.
4 - 12 - 17.

W. Edmund Blake Lieut Colonel
Comdg 4/Worcestershire Regiment

CONFIDENTIAL

WAR DIARY

4th. BATTN. THE WORCESTERSHIRE REGIMENT

1st. December 1917 to 31st. December 1917.

(Volume No 24)

1/4th Worcestershire Regt.

Army Form C. 2118.

WAR DIARY or INTELLIGENCE SUMMARY.
(Erase heading not required.)

Place	Date	Hour	Summary of Events and Information	Remarks and references to Appendices
	1.12.17		Continued with Consolidation of the line taken on 30th inst. All four Companies still in front line with 1/K.O.S.B on our right and 1/Essex on our left. "X" Coy retained 3 Machine Guns and took up position with 1 platoon in an advanced post. 2/Hampshires in support. H.Q. 2/Hampshires & 4/Worcestershires in same deep dugout in sunken road about 800 yards S.W. MARCOING. No other infantry action on our immediate front, but attacks still in progress on both flanks. MARCOING & MASNIERES heavily shelled. Enemy aircraft very active. Communication trench from Hampshires to front line.	
	2.12.17		A lot of hard work done in improving our line. Two platoons of "X" Coy brought back into the support line. 1 platoon still being an advanced post. Continued work on Communication trench. Hampshires moved to reinforce left of 88th Inf. Brigade who were suffering heavy casualties. 2 platoons of the 16/Middlesex sent to support this Batn. 93 Infantry Action, but great Artillery & Aerial activity. MARCOING & MASNIERES again heavily shelled. Very cold.	
	3.12.17		6th Division attached by the Enemy & lost ground on the left of 88th Bde. Situation very serious. Left of 88th Bde. 13th. withdrawn & line readjusted. "X" Coy took over the front of the right Coy of the 1/Hants. "W" Coy took over the advanced post. Capt R.A. Manyatt, Lieut H. Groom Johnson M.C., 2/Lt. J. Watts & 2/Lt. R.S. Thomas arrived with 40 other Ranks, who were immediately formed into a 5th Coy with the two Middlesex platoons under Lieut H. Groom Johnson M.C. placed in the support line. Hd. Qn. moved to 1/K.O.S.B Hd.Qn. in deep dugout in HINDENBURG LINE & shared with 1/K.O.S.B. Frequent gas shelling & Trench Mortaring, also the usual heavy shelling. Bitterly cold. All ranks exhausted.	

1.h. Worcestershire Regt.

WAR DIARY
or
INTELLIGENCE SUMMARY.
(Erase heading not required.)

Army Form C. 2118.

Instructions regarding War Diaries and Intelligence Summaries are contained in F. S. Regs., Part II. and the Staff Manual respectively. Title pages will be prepared in manuscript.

Place	Date	Hour	Summary of Events and Information	Remarks and references to Appendices
	4.12.17		A very critical day. On account of successful attacks by the enemy on troops on our left flank arrangements were made for the left of the Brigade to be withdrawn during the night, the general line of defence being the HINDENBURG LINE with a line of posts two or three hundred yards in front. Withdrew and took up our new position "W" & "X" Companies holding out post line "Y" & "Z" Companies in support in the HINDENBURG LINE. Orders to hand over our posts to the 118th Division, which was delayed & could not arrive before midnight. A great deal	
	5.12.17		of sniping, mortaring & gas shelling. The Batt. was relieved by a Battn. of the Royal Irish Rifles (118th Division) at about 1 a.m. and withdrew from the advanced posts. Worked their way in parties down the HINDENBURG LINE to Transport Lines near Ribecourt, where a hot meal was served & each party immediately sent on independently to bivouac at ETRICOURT, where the Batt. rested during the afternoon. The Batt. entrained at about 7.30 p.m. with the remainder of the 88th Bde. & commenced their journey to MONDICOURT, being derailed by shell fire en route at BEUGNY (near BAPAUME), took engines & first four trucks being overturned. The Batn. was then transferred to a relief train which was again shelled. No casualties were incurred. Arrived at MONDICOURT about 9 a.m. where breakfasts were served. Marched to WARLUZEL, where we arrived at about noon & went into	
	6.12.17		billets. Rested the remainder of the day. In billets at WARLUZEL. General cleaning up & and settling down into billets. Lieut H. Groom Johnson M.C. posted to "Z" Coy. and took on command (Antidated to 30.11.17). 2nd Lieut H. F. Bodding ton posted to "W" Coy. (Antidated 30.11.17) 2nd Lieut V. C. Cornish posted to "X" Coy. (Antidated 30.11.17)	

Army Form C. 2118.

WAR DIARY
or
INTELLIGENCE SUMMARY.
(Erase heading not required.)

4th Worcestershire Regt.

Instructions regarding War Diaries and Intelligence
Summaries are contained in F. S. Regs., Part II.
and the Staff Manual respectively. Title pages
will be prepared in manuscript.

Place	Date	Hour	Summary of Events and Information	Remarks and references to Appendices
	7.12.17		In billets at WARLUZEL. Kit inspection & overhauling of all equipment. Billet inspection. Drums beat Retreat.	
	8.12.17		Capt. M. St. John Carpendale having rejoined the Battn. assumed command of "W" Coy [6.12.17] 2nd Lieut. R.S. Thomas appointed Battn. Intelligence Officer. The Battn. was paid out during the afternoon. A draft of 39 other ranks arrived for the Battn. In billets at WARLUZEL. Companies at the disposal of Company Commanders. C.O. & 2nd in Command attend Conference at Head Quarters, 29th Division. A draft of 13 other ranks joined the Battn.	
	9.12.17		In billets at WARLUZEL. Inspection of draft by the Commanding Officer. Divine Service cancelled owing to bad weather.	
	10.12.17		In billets at WARLUZEL. Commenced first phase of training. All Companies doing Platoon Drill, Handling of Arms from 9 - 9.45 a.m. "P.T. & B.F. 10 - 10.30 a.m." Company Drill & Musketry 10.45 a.m - 11.30 a.m. Special classes for Signalling, Lewis Gunners & B.O.R. Drums beat Retreat.	
	11.12.17		2nd Lieut. S.J. Pye joined Battn. & posted to "X" Coy. 2nd Lieut. B.A. Monks joined Battn. & posted to "Y" Coy. 2nd Lieut. J.H. Walt joined Battn. & posted to "Z" Coy. In billets at WARLUZEL. All Companies at Ceremonial Drill. P.T. & B.F. etc. Special classes as usual. Drums beat Retreat.	

4th Worcestershire Regt.

Army Form C. 2118.

WAR DIARY
or
INTELLIGENCE SUMMARY.
(Erase heading not required.)

Place	Date	Hour	Summary of Events and Information	Remarks and references to Appendices
	12.12.17		In billets at WARLUZEL. Parades for training as usual. Special classes as usual. A draft of 5 Officers & 36 other ranks joined the Battn. 2nd Lieut. G. W. Amesbury posted to "W" Coy. 2nd Lieut. A. E. Chatwin posted to "X" Coy. 2nd Lieut. S. Gray posted to "Z" Coy. 2nd Lieut. C.A.E. Elliott posted to "Z" Coy. Lieut. L. H. Pouch posted to "Y" Coy and assumed command.	
	13.12.17		In billets at WARLUZEL. Parades & classes as usual. A draft of 2 Officers and 14 other ranks arrived. 2nd Lieut. C. Mason posted to "W" Coy. 2nd Lieut. H. a. Ward posted to "Y" Coy. 2nd Lieut. J. S. Graves and 2nd Lieut. E. L. Booth having rejoined the Battn were posted to "X" & "Z" Companies respectively. The Battn had baths & change of clothing at Sus-St Leger on parties of 100 men per hour. Remainder of Battn did a route march via SUS ST LEGER.	
	14.12.17		In billets at WARLUZEL. (abt 6 miles) on drill order with the Drums. "W" & "X" Companies carried out training as usual. "Y" & "Z" Companies were allotted to ranges near SUS ST LEGER & carried out two practices (one application - one rapid) Final Brigade inter Coy. Football Match at 2 p.m. Result "Y" Coy. 2 goals "X" Coy 1 goal.	

4th Worcestershire Regt.

Army Form C. 2118.

WAR DIARY
or
INTELLIGENCE SUMMARY.
(Erase heading not required.)

Instructions regarding War Diaries and Intelligence Summaries are contained in F. S. Regs., Part II. and the Staff Manual respectively. Title pages will be prepared in manuscript.

Place	Date	Hour	Summary of Events and Information	Remarks and references to Appendices
	16.12.17		In billets at WARLUZEL. Sunday Divine Service was not held for C of E. Nonconformists service 10 a.m. R.C. Service 10.30 a.m.	
	17.12.17		A bright morning, but a snow storm in the afternoon which continued all night. In billets at WARLUZEL. A blizzard. 8 inches of snow. Batln. cleared the snow from the roads, working one platoon per Coy. at a time. Platoons were also instructed in billets at Box Respirator drill & musketry, and lectured on French Orders. 29th Division. Advance party of 1 Officer & 9 other ranks marched to new billeting area near BOUBERS SUR CANCHE.	
	18.12.17		Batln. marched from WARLUZEL at 9 a.m. over two miles of frozen plough, the road to SUS ST LEGER being impassible, owing to snow drifts at places 6 feet deep. Order of March. H.Qrs. "Y" "Z" "Bruno", "W", "X". Transport. Route. SUS ST LEGER - WANIN - REBREUVIETTE - FREVENT - BOUBERS- SUR- CANCHE - CONCHY - SUR - CONCHE - MONCHEL - BLANGERVAL - BLANGERMONT. (Over 17 miles) where we went into billets at 5.30 p.m. A bitterly cold day - roads extremely slippery & difficult. Halted for mid-day meal 1 mile West of FREVENT. Blanket lorries arrived up. No great coats or blankets this night. There were no stragglers.	

Army Form C. 2118.

4th Worcestershire Regt.

WAR DIARY
or
INTELLIGENCE SUMMARY.
(Erase heading not required.)

Instructions regarding War Diaries and Intelligence Summaries are contained in F. S. Regs., Part II. and the Staff Manual respectively. Title pages will be prepared in manuscript.

Place	Date	Hour	Summary of Events and Information	Remarks and references to Appendices
	19.12.17		The Batln marched independently of the remainder of Brigade, leaving BLANGERMONT at 10 a.m. Order of March. Hdqrs, "H", "X", "W", "Drums", "Z", "Y" via LINZEUX - WILLEMAN - VIEIL - HESDIN - LE PARCQ - GRIGNY where we went into billets at about 2.30 p.m. The 1st Line Transport marched at 10 a.m. via MONCHEL - AUBROMETZ - WAIL - VIEIL - HESDIN - LE PARCQ, arriving at GRIGNY about 9 p.m. A bitterly cold day, snow very deep, not possible to stick to the road all the way. Roads very dangerous difficult for marching & transport.	
	20.12.17		The Batln marched from GRIGNY at 10.30 a.m. independently of the remainder of Brigade, through the FORET D'HESDIN via LA LOGE into billets at WAMBERCOURT - ST MARTIN - CAVRON- ST MARTIN. The Transport arriving at 12.30 p.m. The Transport arriving shortly afterwards.	
	21.12.17		In billets at WAMBERCOURT - ST MARTIN and CAVRON ST MARTIN. Very scattered indeed, but on the whole good billets for the troops. Inspection of all Companies in billets from 11 a.m. - 1 p.m. by Commanding Officer.	

4th Woolwich Regt.

Army Form C. 2118.

WAR DIARY
or
INTELLIGENCE SUMMARY.
(Erase heading not required.)

Instructions regarding War Diaries and Intelligence Summaries are contained in F.S. Regs., Part II. and the Staff Manual respectively. Title pages will be prepared in manuscript.

Place	Date	Hour	Summary of Events and Information	Remarks and references to Appendices
	22.12.17		In billets at WAMBERCOURT - ST. MARTIN and CAVRON ST MARTIN. Four days Company Training. All Companies practised in shaking out into Artillery formation from Column of Route. Physical Games & Bayonet fighting. Special Classes under the Signalling Officer & Lewis Gun Officer.	
	23.12.17		In billets at WAMBERCOURT - ST. MARTIN and CAVRON ST MARTIN. Divine service at 11 a.m. in barn near "W" Coy billet.	
	24.12.17		In billets at WAMBERCOURT - ST MARTIN and CAVRON ST MARTIN. Battn. entered a second phase of training. Coy. training as follows. 9 - 11 a.m. "Y" Coy on range. 11 a.m - 1 p.m. "Z" Coy on range. "W" & "X" Coys Physical Games & Bayonet fighting. 9 - 9.30 a.m. "W" & "X" Coys Artillery formation & extension. 9.30 - 11 a.m. "W" & "X" Coys return of Return of Route. 11 - 11.30 a.m. "W" & "X" Coys Physical Games & Extended Charges.	
	25.12.17		Special classes as usual. Weather very cold, snow interfering with training. X'mas Day. In billets at WAMBERCOURT - ST MARTIN and CAVRON ST MARTIN. Divine Service 10.30 a.m. X'mas dinner was supplemented from Battn. funds with Turkey, Pork, Beef & Fruit. Day passed off very successfully.	

4th Worcestershire Regt.

Army Form C. 2118.

WAR DIARY
or
INTELLIGENCE SUMMARY.
(Erase heading not required.)

Instructions regarding War Diaries and Intelligence Summaries are contained in F.S. Regs., Part II. and the Staff Manual respectively. Title pages will be prepared in manuscript.

Place	Date	Hour	Summary of Events and Information	Remarks and references to Appendices
	26.12.17		In billets at WAMBERCOURT ST MARTIN - CAVRON ST MARTIN. "W" & "X" Coys. Musketry on the range. "Y" & "Z" Coys. Physical Games, Bayonet fighting & Artillery formations & Extension from Column of Route. Snow during the afternoon. Transport work very difficult. Rations very late.	
	27.12.17		In billets at WAMBERCOURT ST MARTIN - CAVRON ST MARTIN. A fall of snow during the night & a high wind caused the ST MARTIN - ROYON Road to become blocked. "W" & "X" Coys were employed clearing it doing good work. Weather very cold, made good shooting difficult. "Y" & "Z" Coys. Musketry on the range.	
	28.12.17		In billets at WAMBERCOURT ST MARTIN - CAVRON ST MARTIN. "Y" & "Z" Coys finished the clearing of ST MARTIN ROYON Road. "W" & "X" Coys on range. A light thaw during the day, made transport work a little easier.	
	29.12.17		In billets at WAMBERCOURT ST MARTIN - CAVRON ST MARTIN. Battalion march ST MARTIN - LA LOGE - ST AUBIN - CAVRON ST MARTIN. Distance 6 miles. Time 2 hours, good going, fine weather. The weather was on the whole, successful, despite bad conditions. At night a convoy was given by the Fragments Troupe. (88th Field Ambulance.)	
	30.12.17		In billets at WAMBERCOURT ST MARTIN - CAVRON ST MARTIN. Divine Service 9.30 a.m. Coys were paid out for the first time since Dec 8th. Rations did not arrive until 9.30 p.m. owing to the condition of the roads.	

Army Form C. 2118.

WAR DIARY
or
INTELLIGENCE SUMMARY.
(Erase heading not required.)

4th Worcestershire Regt.

Place	Date	Hour	Summary of Events and Information	Remarks and references to Appendices
In billets at WAMBERCOURT ST MARTIN – CAVRON ST MARTIN.	31/12/17		Batn. entered on another phase of training.	
		9.10 a.m.	"W" Coy. inspected by Commanding Officer.	
			"Y" Coy. practised Anti-Gas measures, all available men being present.	
		10.11 a.m.	"Y" Coy. inspected by Commanding Officer.	
			"W" Coy. practised Anti-Gas measures, all available men being present.	
		9.11 a.m.	"X" & "Z" Coys. Musketry on Range.	
		11.30 a.m.	Bombing by all Platoons.	
			A draft of 6 Officers arrived & were posted to Companies as follows:—	
			Major R. Radcliffe .... "Z" Coy. (2nd in Command).	
			Lieut. J. E. Thornelae ... "W" Coy.	
			2/Lieut. S. S. Kuper ...... "W" Coy.	
			2/Lieut. W. Cammont ..... "Y" Coy.	
			2/Lieut. E. R. Smith .... "Z" Coy.	
			2/Lieut. W. Hamer .... "Z" Coy.	
			8 N.C.O's & men also rejoined from Hospital and rejoined their respective Companies.	

CONFIDENTIAL

WAR DIARY

OF

4TH WORCESTERSHIRE REGIMENT

FROM 1st January, 1918   TO 31st January, 1918

(VOLUME NO. 25)

C O N F I D E N T I A L

W A R   D I A R Y

of

4TH. BATTALION THE WORCESTERSHIRE REGIMENT.

From January 1st. 1918.   To. January 31st. 1918.

Army Form C. 2118.

4th. Bn. The Worcestershire Regt.

WAR DIARY
or
INTELLIGENCE SUMMARY.
(Erase heading not required.)

Instructions regarding War Diaries and Intelligence Summaries are contained in F.S. Regs., Part II. and the Staff Manual respectively. Title pages will be prepared in manuscript.

Place	Date	Hour	Summary of Events and Information	Remarks and references to Appendices
	1918 Jan 1st		In billets at WAMBERCOURT, CAVRON ST MARTIN and ST MARTIN. Inspection of "Z" Coy. by Commanding Officer at 9 a.m. and of "X" Coy. at 10 a.m. In Drill - Handling of Arms and Anti Gas. "W" and "Y" Coys - Musketry on the range. Revolver practice for Officers on the range at 2 p.m. Ground still covered with snow. Lieut. E. R. Smith took over duties of Acting Adjutant.	
	Jan 2nd.		In billets as above. Companies on the Minature Range. "Z" and "Y" on "Z" Range "W" and "X" on "W" Range. Practice was carried out firing with the Box Respirator in Anti Gas was also practiced. Bitterly cold. Division prepartin to move to the TILQUES AREA. Battalion advance party - 1 Officer and 9 O.Rs. sent on to the new area at VAUDRINGHEM.	
	Jan 3rd		The Battalion marched from ST MARTIN at 8 a.m. to VAUDRINGHEM, a distance of 21 miles. Route - FRUGES, FAVQUEMBERQUES, LE LOQUIN, EQUIRE, VAUDRINGHEM. (Ref. Map 1/100,000 HAZEBROUCK and LENS), where we went into billets about 9.45 p.m. Transport arrived about 1.30 a.m. The journey was very slippery and tiring. Traffic on the main road greatly interfering with the marching.	
	Jan.4th.		The Battalion again paraded at 10 a.m. to march to MORINGHEM:- Route NIELLES, LUMBRES, SETQUES, QUELMES, MORINGHEM - distance 12 miles. At LUMBRES the Battn. halted for dinners. MORINGHEM reached at 5 P.m. H.Q. and "W" Coy. in Billets in the village. "X" and "Z" Coys. in PETIT DIFQUES and "Y" Coy. in GRAND DIFQUES.	
	Jan.5th.		General cleaning up. Commanding Officer inspected Coy. billets.	
	Jan.6th.		Divine service in the Y.M.C.A. Hut - PETIT DIFQUES.	
	Jan.7th.		The Battn. marched to ACQUIN to the Baths. 100 men per hour. Change of clothing issued.	

Army Form C. 2118.

WAR DIARY
or
INTELLIGENCE SUMMARY.
(Erase heading not required.)

Instructions regarding War Diaries and Intelligence Summaries are contained in F.S. Regs., Part II. and the Staff Manual respectively. Title pages will be prepared in manuscript.

Place	Date	Hour	Summary of Events and Information	Remarks and references to Appendices
	1918 Jan. 8th.		Heavy Snow Storm. Range practice cancelled on account of the weather. Coys. instructed in Musketry in billets. Brigade Armourer Sergt. visited Battalion. Draft of 99 O.Rs. joined the Battalion from the 14th. (Pioneer) Bn. Worcs. Regt.	
	Jan. 9th.		Two Companies "X" and "Y" practiced "Attack under a Barrage". "W" and "Z" Coy practiced wiring. Still snowing heavily.	
	Jan. 10th.		A rapid thaw set in. The Battalion paraded for Brigade Ceremonial practice. 2/Lieuts. T.P.Guy and B.G.M. Klee joined the Battn. and were posted to "X" and "W" Companies respectively.	
	Jan. 11th.		The Brigade paraded for Ceremonial practice. "W" and "X" Coys. practiced Bombing. "Y" and "Z" Map reading and Compass marching.	
	Jan. 12th.		Commanding officer went off early in the morning for a Course with the R.F.C. Companies lectured in billets on organization of shell holes and trench warfare. Brigade paraded for Ceremonial parade. Major Gen. Beauvoir de Lisle inspected the Brigade and distributed award ribbons.	
	Jan. 13th.		Divine service in Y.M.C.A. Hut PETIT DIFQUES.	
	Jan. 14th.		Whole Battalion on "A" Range PETIT DIFQUES. 32 Targets. Practices 13. 14. 17, 18, and 19 of part III fired. Gas precautions also practiced.	
	Jan. 15th.		The Battalion took part in a Brigade Field Day - attacking in the open from ZUDAUSQUES towards MORINGHEM. Major Gen. de Lisle was present and held a conference with C.Os., Adjutants, and Coy. Commanders afterwards. Was not impressed with the exercise. Raining hard and very heavy going across country. The men were soaked through.	

Army Form C. 2118.

WAR DIARY
or
INTELLIGENCE SUMMARY.
(Erase heading not required.)

Instructions regarding War Diaries and Intelligence Summaries are contained in F. S. Regs., Part II. and the Staff Manual respectively. Title pages will be prepared in manuscript.

Place	Date	Hour	Summary of Events and Information	Remarks and references to Appendices
	1918- Jan.16th.		All Coys. took steps to get their Coys. cleaned up and fully equipped in readiness for the move to the BRANDHOEK AREA. Mens' clothes were dried as much as possible. The advance party - 1 Officer (2/Lieut. A. Parry) 4 C.Q.M.S and 1 H.Q.Runner moved off to the new area. The transport left and proceeded by road.	
	Jan.17th.		The Battallion less Transport marched from MORINGHEM at 7.30 a.m. to WIZERNES where they entrained and proceeded by rail at 11.30 a.m. to BRANDHOEK, and detrained there at 2.30 p.m. and were situated in "B" Camp for the night of 17/18th. Heavy snow storm.	
	Jan.18th.		The Battalion moved at 3.15 p.m. to JUNCTION CAMP - ST JEAN - arriving at the Camp at 5 p.m. The Commanding Officer rejoined the Battalion for a Course in connection with the R.F.C. from	
	Jan.19th.		"X", "Y" and "Z" Coys. supplied 100 men each for working party for work under C.R.E. 33rd. Division. Locality of work (Sheet. 28 NW) C.23.d. Work done draining and salvage from 8.30 a.m. to 12.30 p.m. "W" Coy. draining, cleaning up and repairing huts in Camp.	
	Jan.20th.		Divine Service. "Y" and "Z" Coys. supplied 100 men each for working party. Work done as on the 19th. inst. "W" and "X" Coys, draining, cleaning up and repairing huts in camp. The Commanding Officer, O.C. "W" and "X" Coys., and one Officer each from "Y" and "Z" Coys. reconoitred the support Brigade defence line.	
	Jan.21st.		"W" and "X" Coys. supplied 100 men each for working party for work as on 19th. inst. "Y" and "Z" Coys. draining, cleaning up and repairing huts in camp.	

Army Form C. 2118.

WAR DIARY
or
INTELLIGENCE SUMMARY.
(Erase heading not required.)

Instructions regarding War Diaries and Intelligence Summaries are contained in F. S. Regs., Part II. and the Staff Manual respectively. Title pages will be prepared in manuscript.

Place	Date	Hour	Summary of Events and Information	Remarks and references to Appendices
	1918			
	Jan.22nd.		"W" and "Y" Coys. supplied 100 men each for working party for work as on the 19th inst. "X" and "Z" Coys. draining, cleaning up and repairing huts in camp. 80 O.Rs. of "X" Coy. Baths at DEAD END (Sheet 28 NW) I.2.c.2.3), 50 O.Rs. of "Z" Coy. inspection of Small Box Respirators by Bde. Gas. N.C.O. at WIELTJE.	
	Jan.23rd.		"X" and "Z" Coys. supplied 100 men each for Working Parties as on the 19th inst. "Y" Coy. and 50 O.Rs. of "W" Baths at DEAD END.	
	Jan.24th.		"W" and "Y" Coys. supplied 100 men each for work as on the 19th. inst. "Z" Coy. and the remainder of "X" Coy. Baths. ~~XXXxxxxXXXxxxxxxxpxxxxxxxxxxxx~~	
	Jan.25th.		"X" and "Z" Coys. supplied 100 O.Rs. each for work as on the 19th. inst. 80 O.Rs. H.Q. and Employed men and 80 O.Rs. "W" and "Y" Coys. Baths.	
	Jan.26th.		"W" and "Y" Coys. supplied 100 O.Rs. each for work as on the 19th. inst. One officer and 34 O.Rs. attached to 497th. (Kent) Field Company R.E. for 10 days. The Battalion moved from JUNCTION CAMP - ST JEAN - to CALIFORNIA CAMP, WIELTJE.	
	Jan.27th.		Cleaning up Camp. Treatment for prevention of "Trench Feet". 100 men per Coy. carrying R.E. Material to Front Line.	
	Jan.28th.		100 men per Company carrying screw pickets and duck boards to the Front Line. Treatment for prevention of "Trench Feet". Cleaning up Camp.	
	Jan.29th.		The 29th. Division extended its front westward as far as TOURNANT FARM (Sheet Trench Map C.1. 1/10,000) V.28 b.31. inclusive. "X" and "Z" Coys. and 2 platoons "Y" relieved the 4th. North Staffs. in the left sub sector of the Brigade front (GOUDBERG Sector). "X" Coy. less 2 sections, 2 platoons "Y" Coy. in front line and "Z" in support. Battn. H.Q. at KRON PRINZ FARM. "W" Coy. and 1 platoon "Y" remained at CALIFORNIA CAMP.	

Army Form C. 2118.

WAR DIARY
or
INTELLIGENCE SUMMARY.
(Erase heading not required.)

Instructions regarding War Diaries and Intelligence Summaries are contained in F. S. Regs., Part II. and the Staff Manual respectively. Title pages will be prepared in manuscript.

Place	Date	Hour	Summary of Events and Information	Remarks and references to Appendices
	1918 Jan.30th.		"W" Coy. and 1 platoon "Y" relieved the left company of the 2/Hants. Regt. coming up on the right of the Battalion front, and joining up with the 1/Essex Regt. on their right. Dispositions: "W" Coy. and 1 platoon "Y" on the right; "X" Coy. less 2 sections in the centre; "Y" Coy.minus 1 platoon on the left; "Z" Coy. in support; 2 sections of "X" Coy. in reserve. Battn. H.Q. moved to Pill Box No.83 (Sheet 28 NE.) D.4.b.0.6. D.L.I of 35th. Division on our left, 300 yds. between our left post and their right. Posts were joined up. Commenced wiring. "X" Coy. from right to left. Posts were joined up and revetting and cleaning up of trenches.	
	Jan.31st.		Weather foggy. Much work done joining up Posts. A large quantity of R.E. Material carried up to front line, and good progress was made with the wiring and duck boarding of Trenches. Strength. Total Strength. 45 Officers. 831 O.Rs. Ration Strength. 37 Officers. 610 O.Rs. Actual strength in trenches.... 21 Officers 481 O.Rs.	
	7. 2. 18.			

Lieut. Colonel.
Comdg. 4th. Bn. The Worcestershire Regiment.

C O N F I D E N T I A L

WAR DIARY

of

4th. BATTALION THE WORCESTERSHIRE REGT.

From 1st. February 1918   To 2nd. February 1918.

(VOLUME No. 26)

Army Form C. 2118.

WAR DIARY
or
INTELLIGENCE SUMMARY.
(Erase heading not required.)

Instructions regarding War Diaries and Intelligence Summaries are contained in F.S. Regs., Part II. and the Staff Manual respectively. Title pages will be prepared in manuscript.

Place	Date	Hour	Summary of Events and Information	Remarks and references to Appendices
	1/2/18.		Left Battn. of Brigade. GOUDBERG SECTOR./ Foggy weather which lifted about noon 3rd. day in the line. Enemy fairly quiet. Wiring of "X" Coy. was completed, and improvement to posts and approaches was carried out by "Y" and "W" Coys. The Battn. on our right, (1/Essex) were raided about 11.0 p.m. - the raiders were driven off leaving a wounded prisoner in their hands. A party of 200 other ranks NEWFOUNDLAND and HAMPSHIRE Regts. carried R.E. material from KRONPRINZ DUMP to our front line.	
	2/2/18.		4th. Day in the Line. Weather bright and clear. Enemy more active in all arms. "W" Coy. sent out a patrol of 1 N.C.O. & 2 men to reconnoitre the enemy's wire. The wire was found to be strong and made up of concertina wire in front of posts, and in between posts only trip wire was found, with tins attached to it. "Y" Coy. continued wiring its front, "X" and "W" Coy's. duckboarding their trenches. "Z" Coy. in support built a strong point on the WALLEMOLEN RIDGE. A working party of 200 other ranks, Hampshire Regt. carried R.E. material to our front line from the KRONPRINZ DUMP.	
	3/2/18.		5th. and last day in the Line. Weather clear and summerlike. Enemy did not show themselves as freely as on previous days. Were relieved by the 1st. Bn. K.O.S.B. at 9.30 p.m. and marched back to WIELTJE, where the Bn. entrained about midnight for BRANDHOEK. Casualties during the tour of duty in the Line.- 3 o.ranks Killed and 2 o.ranks Wounded.	
	4/2/18.		RED ROSE CAMP. - The Battalion detrained at BRANDHOEK, and marched to RED ROSE CAMP near VLAMERTINGHE, arrived in camp about 4 a.m. During the day, companies had a clean up and rest.	
	5/2/18.		RED ROSE CAMP. - A general clean up, scrubbing of equipment and making up of deficiencies. 3 Officers and 150 o. ranks found for working parties. Major General Sir Beauvoir de Lisle, K.C.B., D.S.O. lectured C.O's., 2nd.in comd's, Coy. Commanders and Adjts. on ceremonial.	
	6/2/18.		RED ROSE CAMP. - The Divisional Baths at VLAMERTINGHE allotted to the Battn. Change of clothing issued. 120 men per hour bathed. The Commanding Officer inspected the Battalion Lines.	

Army Form C. 2118.

WAR DIARY
or
INTELLIGENCE SUMMARY.
(Erase heading not required.)

Instructions regarding War Diaries and Intelligence Summaries are contained in F.S. Regs., Part II. and the Staff Manual respectively. Title pages will be prepared in manuscript.

Place	Date	Hour	Summary of Events and Information	Remarks and references to Appendices
RED ROSE CAMP.	7/2/18.		Raining in the morning. The Battalion formed up in mass for inspection by Brig. Gen. B.C. Freyburg, V.C., D.S.O., but owing to the weather it was postponed. Regimental classes for Lewis Gunners, Signallers, Scouts, Snipers and N.C.Os were commenced.	
RED ROSE CAMP.	8/2/18.		Again owing to the weather the G.O.C's parade was cancelled. 1 Officer and 50 o. ranks found for working party at VLAMERTINGHE.	
RED ROSE CAMP.	9/2/18.		Brigadier General B.C. Freyburg, V.C., D.S.O. inspected the Battalion and expressed his satisfaction in everything that he saw. "X" and "Y" Coys. march to the range near SIEGE CAMP, but owing to the wind xxxxxxxxx no firing of any consequence was carried out. 88th. Field Ambulance came and gave a concert to the Battn. in the evening.	
RED ROSE CAMP	10/2/18.		Divine Service for 50 o. ranks per company. Preparations made for the move to the STEENVORDE AREA. Advance party of 1 Officer and 9 o. ranks left for the new area. Draft of 2 Officers (Lieuts. A.H. Bowman & H.S. Smith) and 46 o. ranks joined the Battn. from the 2/7th. Bn. The Worcestershire Regiment.	
	11/2/18.		The Battalion marched from RED ROSE CAMP at 11.45 a.m. to BRANDHOEK STATION where it entrained. After half an hour's run, the Battalion detrained at GODEWAERSVELDE and marched through STEENVORDE to the new billets. Companies were very scattered and difficult to get at.	
WINNEZEELE AREA.	12/2/18.		The Battalion paradede as strong as possible for a Battn. Ceremonial Parade. Gas drill and musketry. Regimental xxxxxxxxxxxxxxxxxxxxxxxxxxxxxxxx ROSExGAMPxwerexconttinued. Falling in with the drum was practised and several Battn. manoeuvres were accomplished. Quite a good parade.	
WINNEZEELE AREA	13/2/18.		Owing to wet weather Companies remained in billets and practiced Gas Drill and Musketry. Regimental Classes started at RED ROSE CAMP were continued.	
WINNEZEELE AREA	14/2/18.		Companies practice Gas Drill, Bayonet Fighting and organised games under Company arrangements.	

Army Form C. 2118.

WAR DIARY
or
INTELLIGENCE SUMMARY.
(Erase heading not required.)

Instructions regarding War Diaries and Intelligence Summaries are contained in F.S. Regs., Part II. and the Staff Manual respectively. Title pages will be prepared in manuscript.

RR/

Place	Date	Hour	Summary of Events and Information	Remarks and references to Appendices
WINNEZEELE AREA.	15/2/18.		The Battalion paraded for a Brigade Ceremonial Parade at WINNEZEELE. Manoeuvres were limited on account of the state of the ground, which was very wet.	
WINNEZEELE AREA.	16/2/18.		The Battalion paraded for a Brigade Ceremonial Parade in a field near "Y" Coy's billet near ST. LAURENT. Major General Sir Beauvoir de Lisle K.C.B.; D.S.O. presented ribbons to recipients of awards won during the CAMBRAI operations. He inspected the Brigade and expressed his satisfaction. All P.H. Helmets returned to store.	
WINNEZEELE AREA.	17/2/18.		Divine Service on "X" Coy's parade ground. The Baths at STEENVOORDE were allotted the Battalion, clean clothing was handed out.	
WINNEZEELE AREA.	18/2/18.		"W" and "X" Coys. at Battn. H.Q. and "Y" and "Z" Coys. in "Z" Coy's. parade ground for musketry on the minature range. Gas Drill, wiring, saluting drill and physical games. All Officers and 8 N.C.Os. per coy. attended a lecture given by the Divisional Commander to Officers and N.C.Os. of the Divn. The advance party, 1 Officer and 5 o. ranks left for POPERINGHE to make arrangements for billets for the Battn.	
POPERINGHE. - WATOU - ST. JAN-ter-BIEZEN.	19/2/18.		The Battn. moved by route march to POPERINGHE via DROGLANDT - WATOU - ST. JAN-ter-BIEZEN. Transport moved with the Battn. A party of 5 Officers proceeded by motor lorry to reconnoitre the work on the Army Line near WIELTJE, and rejoined the Battn. at POPERINGHE. Details of 2 Officers and 36 O. ranks left behind at Headquarters Farm to complete work done on the ranges and specialist training (Lewis Gun).	
POPERINGHE.	20/2/18.		A working party of 270 o. ranks of "W", "X" and "Y" Coys. was sent to work on PLUM and UHLAN KEEPS on the Army Line. They were conveyed to and from WIELTJE by rail. "Z" Coy. was taken to the THEATRE to see the performance of "RUFFLES" given by the 2nd. Bn. Royal Fusiliers.	
POPERINGHE.	21/2/18.		270 o. ranks of "X", "Y" and "Z" Coys. sent on the working party. "W" Coy. taken to the theatre to see "RUFFLES".	

Army Form C. 2118.

WAR DIARY
or
INTELLIGENCE SUMMARY.
(Erase heading not required.)

Instructions regarding War Diaries and Intelligence Summaries are contained in F.S. Regs., Part II. and the Staff Manual respectively. Title pages will be prepared in manuscript.

R.P.

Place	Date	Hour	Summary of Events and Information	Remarks and references to Appendices
	22/2/18		POPERINGHE. - 270 O.Rs. of "W", "Y" and "Z" Coys. were sent on the Working Party. "X" Coy. tested their Box Respirators in Lachrymatory Gas, and also, with details, bathed at the Baths 200 men. "X" Coy. taken to the Theatre.	
	23/2/18		POPERINGHE. - "W", "X" and "Z" Coys. found the Working Party of 270 O.Rs. "Y" Coy. was passed through Gas in the morning, and baths in the afternoon. "Y" Coy. taken to the Theatre. A draft of 45 O.Rs. (transfers from A.S.C.) joined the Battalion.	
	24/2/18		POPERINGHE. - The Battalion less Working Party paraded for Divine Service at the Empire Hall, POPERINGHE. The Working Party was increased to 350 O.Rs., and was supplied by all Companies for work on PLUM and UHLAN KEEPS. "Z" Coy, and as many employed men as possible, bathed.	
	25/2/18		POPERINGHE. - All Companies found the Working Party of 350 O.Rs. Advance party of 2/S.W.B's., who were taking over our billets in POPERINGHE, arrived to look round. The Draft (A.S.C. Transfers) were practiced in Handling of Arms and Musketry - over 50% of them had had no previous experience.	
	26/2/18		300 O.Rs. from "W", "X", "Y" and "Z" Coys. were sent on the Working Party. Commanding Officer (Major R. Ratliffe) going with this party. The remainder of the Battalion, under Capt. H.L. GROGAN, M.C. marched back to their former billets in the WINNEZEELE AREA, via WATOU, and DROUGLANDT. The Transport moving independently. The Working party arrived back in POPERINGHE about 4 p.m. and received tea at the CORPS RAILHEAD REST CAMP, and entrained again at 5.30 p.m. on the metre gauge for STEENVOORDE.	
	27/2/18.		Companies were at disposal of O.C. Coys. for reorganization into four platoons per Coy., and for general cleaning up. O.C. Coys. went with the Commanding Officer to reconnoitre the ground to be used for the Brigade Field Day.	

Army Form C. 2118.

WAR DIARY
or
INTELLIGENCE SUMMARY.
(Erase heading not required.)

Place	Date	Hour	Summary of Events and Information	Remarks and references to Appendices
	28/2/18.		All Companies practiced Attack under a Barrage. Also specialists training - Wiring, Musketry, Bombing, rifle bombing and Lewis Gunnery was carried out under Coy. arrangements. Night operations for Anti Gass Training was practiced. The Draft (transfers from the A.S.C.) 45 O.Rs. leftthe Battalion for the Divisional Wing, BAILLEUL, for a course of training.	

R. Ratliffe Major.

Commanding 4th. Bn. The Worcestershire Regiment.

CONFIDENTIAL

WAR DIARY

4th. Battalion The Worcestershire Regiment.

From
1st. March 1918
To
31st. March 1918

(VOLUME No 1)

Army Form C. 2118.

WAR DIARY
or
INTELLIGENCE SUMMARY.
(Erase heading not required.)

Instructions regarding War Diaries and Intelligence Summaries are contained in F. S. Regs., Part II. and the Staff Manual respectively. Title pages will be prepared in manuscript.

Place	Date	Hour	Summary of Events and Information	Remarks and references to Appendices
WINNEZEELE AREA	1918 March 1st.		The Battalion practiced for the Brigade tactical scheme, attacking across open country, dotted with strong points, under a barrage, "Y" and "Z" Coys. taking the 1st. Objective and "W" and "X" the 2nd. The whole operation was done twice.	
IN BILLETS	March 2nd.		Baths allotted the Battalion at WINNEZEELE. Companies practiced the attack without a barrage (fire and movement), also Musketry, Close Order Drill etc.	
IN BILLETS	March 3rd.		Divine Service at STEENVORDE.	
IN BILLETS	March 4th.		The Battalion took part in the Brigade Tactical Scheme. The same Companies taking the same Objectives as on the 1st. After the final Objective was taken, a small party of the R. Newfoundland Regt. specially told off, attacked the Battalion on our left, the 2nd. Hants., and our left front, which had to withdraw. They were driven out again by the counter-attack made by the remainder of the R. Newfoundlands.	
IN BILLETS	March 5th.		Interior economy, cleaning up and ~~everything~~ preparing for the move back to the WIELTJE AREA.	
HASLAR CAMP	March 6th.		The Battalion moved to the WIELTJE AREA. By Route March to GODEWAERSVELDE, entrained there and proceeded by train to WIELTJE, and from there marched into HASLAR CAMP, ST. JEAN.	
HASLAR & CALIFORNIA CAMPS.	March 7th.		3 Officers each from "W" and "Z" Coys. reconnoitred Posts Nos. 7, 9, 10, 11, 13, 14, 15 & 16 on GRAVENSTAFEL RIDGE (Divisional Reserve Line). A working party of 6 Other Ranks from "W" and "Z" Coys. (38 each) supplied for carrying R.E. Material from WATERLOO DUMP to 13, 14, 15 and 16 posts. "W" and "Z" Coys. moved to CALIFORNIA CAMP. The Brigade moved into the Line.	
HASLAR & CALIFORNIA CAMPS	March 8th.		"W" and "Z" Coys. worked on the Divisional Reserve Line. "X" and "Y" Coys. on PICKLEHAUBE KEEP, ARMY BATTLE ZONE.	

Army Form C. 2118.

WAR DIARY
or
INTELLIGENCE SUMMARY.
(Erase heading not required.)

Instructions regarding War Diaries and Intelligence Summaries are contained in F. S. Regs., Part II. and the Staff Manual respectively. Title pages will be prepared in manuscript.

Place	Date	Hour	Summary of Events and Information	Remarks and references to Appendices
	March 9th.		HASLAR & CALIFORNIA CAMPS - All Companies worked on the Divisional Reserve Line, (KRONPRINZ - WATERLOO LINE), "X" and "Y" Coys. in the early morning, "W" and "Z" Coys. continued the work after midday.	
	March 10th.		HASLAR & CALIFOENIA CAMP - "W" and "Z" Coys. found the first working party, commencing work at 6.30 a.m. "X" and "Y" Coys.found the second party commencing at 1 p.m. Voluntary Services held in HASLAR CAMP. S.O.S. sent up on our left front, nothing happened.	
	March 11th.		HASLAR & CALIFORNIA CAMPS - "W" and "Z" Coys. found the first working party commencing at 6.30. a.m. "X" Coy. found the 2nd. party commencing at 1 p.m. "Y" Coy. found the 3rd. party commencing at 4.15 p.m. The first two parties worked on the KRONPRINZ - WATERLOO LINE and the 3rd. party worked on the C.T. over ABRAHAM HEIGHTS The Bosche attacked the whole Divisional Front about 5.45 a.m. In answer to the S.O.S. the Battalion stood to. Two Coys. ordered up to the Divl. Reserve Line. "W" and "Z" Coys. moved forward and remained for the work. The attack was everywhere repulsed.	
	March 12th.		HASLAR, CALIFORNIA & JUNCTION CAMPS. - Work on the Divisional Reserve Line as for 11th. inst. "W" and "Z" Coys. going with the first party, "X" with the second, "Y" the third. "X" and "Y" Coys. moved from HASLAR to JUNCTION CAMP. Headquarters moved to CALIFORNIA CAMP.	
	March 13th.		CALIFORNIA & JUNCTION CAMPS - Work as for the 11th. inst. "X" and "Z" Coys. finding 1st. party, "W" the 2nd, and "Y" the 3rd. The Bosche was busy shelling back areas with a H.V. Gun. About 5 p.m. one shell fell in CALIFORNIA CAMP, Killing 6 and wounding 6 of "Z" Coy. and wounding 1 of "X" Coy. Attack made on the Division on our Right. S.O.S. Sent up, Battalion stood to. The whole Battalion was ordered forward, which afterwards was cancelled.	
	March 14th.		CALIFORNIA & JUNCTION CAMPS - "W" and "Z" Coys. went on 1st. working party, "X" the 2nd. & "Y" the third. on the C.T. third. The whole Battalion moved into IRISH CAMP as the Brigade came out of the line into Brigade in Reserve. "X" Coy. moved first about 9.30 a.m., "Y" Coy. about 3.30 p.m. H.Q, and the remaining 2 Coys. about 5.0 p.m. relieving the 1st. R. Guernsey L. Infantry. Considerable amount	

Army Form C. 2118.

WAR DIARY
or
INTELLIGENCE SUMMARY.
(Erase heading not required.)

Instructions regarding War Diaries and Intelligence Summaries are contained in F. S. Regs., Part II. and the Staff Manual respectively. Title pages will be prepared in manuscript.

Place	Date	Hour	Summary of Events and Information	Remarks and references to Appendices
	March 14th. (Cont).		IRISH CAMP - of shelling by the Bosche H.V. Gun, in and all round the Camp. Two men wounded.	
	March 15th.		IRISH CAMP - The whole Battalion was employed in revetting round the huts in the Camp. A quiet day.	
	March 16th.		IRISH CAMP - The whole Battalion worked on the Army Line. "W" and "X" Coys. worked on SQUARE KEEP, "Y" & "Z" Coys. on LOW KEEP. 25 O.rks. of "Y" Coy. attached to 171st. Tunnelling Coy. A few shells fell in Camp.	
	March 17th.		IRISH CAMP & POPERINGHE - The Battalion worked on the Army Line and returned to billets in POPERINGHE. H.Q. and details moved to POPERINGHE by train leaving ST. JEAN at 9.45 a.m. No Church Services were held on account of the move.	
	March 18th.		POPERINGHE - The whole Battalion proceeded to the Baths at HOPOUTRE for a complete de-lousing treatment and sterilisation of greatcoats and blankets. No other work was done. 8 Officers and 8 N.C.Os. proceeded to Field Works School, BRANDHOEK, for a four days course. Massed Drums (Worcesters and Hants) only) played the "Retreat" in the Square. A draft of 61 o.rs. joined the Battalion.	
	March 19th.		POPERINGHE - "X" and "Z" Coys. proceeded by the Workmen's train leaving POPERINGHE at 8.0 a.m. for work on the Army Line. (PLUM and RAT KEEPS). "W" and "Y" Coys. Interior Economy. The Bde. Armourer Sergt. inspected the rifles of these two Coys. Massed Drums of the Brigade played the "Retreat" in the Square. "W" and "Y" Coys. Battalion Sing-Song at Concert Hall, TALBOT HOUSE, at 7.0 p.m. "W" and "Y" Coys. attended a S.O.S. Demonstration.	
	March 20th.		POPERINGHE - "W" and "Y" Coys. worked on the Army Line (PLUM and RAT KEEPS) "X" and "Z" Coys. had their arms inspected by the Bde. Armourer Sergt. and had various inspections. "X" and "Z" Coys. Officers and N.C.Os. attended a S.O.S. demonstration. The Corps Commander inspected the Mass Drums at 6 p.m. in the Square and expressed his satisfaction.	
	March 21st.		POPERINGHE - "X" and "Z" Coys. worked on PLUM and RAT KEEPS. The Corps Commander inspected the billets of the Brigade. Enemy offensive commenced.	

Army Form C. 2118.

WAR DIARY
or
INTELLIGENCE SUMMARY.
(Erase heading not required.)

Instructions regarding War Diaries and Intelligence Summaries are contained in F. S. Regs., Part II and the Staff Manual respectively. Title pages will be prepared in manuscript.

Place	Date	Hour	Summary of Events and Information	Remarks and references to Appendices
	March 22nd.		LINE - The Battalion relieved the 2nd. S.W. Borderers in the Left Sub-Sector of the Divisional Sector (PASSCHENDALE), three Coys. being conveyed from POPERINGHE by train to SPREE FARM and 1 Coy. to WIELTJE. Dispositions- Battn. H.Q. Pill-Box 83 (D.4.a.9.4.) "Z" Coy. Front Line holding Posts. 10 - 19 inclusive "W" Coy. in Support at WALLEMOLEN (V.28.c.6.4.) and INCH HOUSES (V.27.d.0.0.) "X" Coy. at KRONPRINZ, "Y" Coy. at ENGLISH CAMP. Relief complete by 11.50 p.m.	
	March 23rd.		LINE - Enemy artillery and M.Gs. very active between 12.30 a.m. and down on tracks. Artillery fairly active during day. 2nd. Lt. G.G. Royal wounded at INCH HOUSES. 1 O.R. "X" Coy. wounded. Front Line Coy. on strengthening wire in front of all posts and building up parados and parapets. Support Coy. 1 Off. 50 o.rs. carrying R.E. material from BELLEVUE to GOUDBERG, doing two trips. 1 Coy. carrying rations and R.E. material to Front and Support Coy. 1 Coy. work on Divl. Line.	
	March 24th.		LINE - 2nd. Lt. R.S. Thomas, 31130 Cpl. G.F. Coton, 2 men Killed and 1 man Wd. at Bn. H.Q. Artillery and M.G. not so active. Work as on 23rd. inst. All leave stopped.	
	March 25th.		LINE - Artillery fairly active. Work as on 23rd. inst. Casualties 1 o.r. Killed, 1 wounded. All Officers and N.C.Os. returned from Courses.	
	March 26th.		LINE - Enemy artillery very active during the morning on BELLEVUE and BN. H.Q. "W" Coy.relieved "Z" Coy. in front line in the middle of a S.O.S. barrage. 2nd. Lieut. L. Mason and 2 o.r. wounded. "Z" Coy. withdrawn to ENGLISH FARM. "X" Coy. moved to Support Line.at WALLEMOLEN, and "Y" Coy. to support at KRONPRINZ.	
	March 27th.		LINE - Enemy artillery very active. 1 o.r. wounded. Work as on 23rd. inst., with exception of 1 Coy. on Divl. Line. 44 o.r. rejoined from Divl. Wing. (Transfers from ASC). 10 o.r. joined Battalion.	
	March 28th.		LINE - Enemy artillery very active from 3 p.m. to 9 p.m., shelling Bn. H.Q., BELLE-VUE and tracks. 1 casualty. Rainy. Work as on 23rd. inst.	

Army Form C. 2118.

WAR DIARY
or
INTELLIGENCE SUMMARY.

(Erase heading not required.)

Instructions regarding War Diaries and Intelligence Summaries are contained in F.S. Regs., Part II. and the Staff Manual respectively. Title pages will be prepared in manuscript.

Place	Date	Hour	Summary of Events and Information	Remarks and references to Appendices
LINE	March 29th.		Enemy artillery very active during day, quiet at night. Enemy M.G. very active at night. Nos. 8 and 9 posts taken over from Battalion on our Right, (R. Newfoundland Regt). Good Friday. Services at Church Army Hut, BRAKE CAMP, at 5.30 p.m.	
LINE	March 30th.		Artillery very active from 7 a.m. to 8 a.m. Inter Company relief, Company Dispositions. Front Line "X", WALLEMOLEN "Y", KRONPRINZ "Z", ENGLISH CAMP "W".	
LINE	March 31st.		Slight enemy artillery activity.	

1st. April 1918.

Lieut. Colonel,
Commanding 4th. Bn. The Worcestershire Regiment.

88th Brigade.
29th Division.

1/4th BATTALION

WORCESTERSHIRE REGIMENT

APRIL 1918.

Army Form C. 2118.

WAR DIARY
or
INTELLIGENCE SUMMARY.
(Erase heading not required.)

APRIL 1918

Place	Date	Hour	Summary of Events and Information	Remarks and references to Appendices
PASSCHENDAELE SECTOR	1st.		IN LINE - Dispositions - Bn. H.Q. PILL BOX 83, "X" Coy. Front Line, "Y" Coy. WALLE-MOLEN & INCH HOUSES, "Z" Coy. in Support at KRONPRINZ, "W" Coy. in Reserve at ENGLISH CAMP. Apron wire fence put up from posts 10 to 14. Work on posts and trenches continued. "Y" Coy. found 1 Officer and 50 o.r. to carry R.E. material from BELLEVUE to GOUDBERG. "W" Coy. carried rations and R.E. material to "X" & "Y" Coys. "W" Coy. 4 hours work on Divisional Line. A carrying party found from details at ENGLISH CAMP to carry S.A.A. from MOSSELMARKT forward - a quiet day.	
	2nd.		Wet day, enemy artillery more active than previous day. New entrance built to Front Line Coy's. H.Q. Duckboard tracks repaired. "X" Coy. wiring and repairing line, remainder of work as on 1st.	
	3rd.		Inter company relief carried out during night, "X" Coy. moving back to ENGLISH CAMP "Y" Coy. to Front Line, "Z" Coy. to WALLEMOLEN and INCH HOUSES, "W" Coy. to KRON-PRINZ. Work as on previous day, but done by according to their new dispositions. Enemy artillery very active from about 5.30 p.m. to 6.15 p.m. on front line, Bn. H.Q. WALLEMOLEN and duckboard tracks.	
	4th.		Fairly quiet day. Our artillery fairly active. The 2nd. Hampshire Regt. made a raid on TEALL COTTS. which they found unoccupied. Very dark night. Work as on previous day.	
	5th.		Wet and quiet day. "Z" Coy. H.Q. at WALLEMOLEN had a direct hit from enemy shell. No casualties. "Y" Coy. captured a prisoner who had lost his way and wandered into our line. Work as on previous day.	
	6th.		A nice bright morning which changed to rain at midday. Quiet day. Work as on pre-vious day.	
	7th.		2 prisoners captured opposite No. 15 post by "Y" Coy. They are thought to have been carrying wire to the front line and lost their way. Enemy M.G. active firing at our low flying 'planes. A few shells round P.B. 83. Inter-Company relief carried out "Z" Coy. moving to Front Line, "W" to WALLEMOLEN, "X" to KRONPRINZ and "Y" to ENGLISH CAMP.	

Army Form C. 2118.

WAR DIARY
or
INTELLIGENCE SUMMARY.
(Erase heading not required.)

Place	Date	Hour	Summary of Events and Information	Remarks and references to Appendices
PASSCHENDAELE SECTOR.	8th.		Quiet and misty day. Officers of 23rd. Middlesex Regt. came to take over. One Officer stayed the night with each of our Coys.	
	9th.		During the early hours of the mroning the enemy bombarded our front line and tracks for an hour. Retaliation was called for. All details and Transport moved from SOULSBY CAMP, BRANDHOEK to SCHOOL CAMP, ST. JAN ter BIEZEN. Orders were received for the Bn. to entrain at about 4 p.m. 10th. inst. for ARRAS. These orders were cancelled and the following substituted. Owing to the enemy having broken through at ARMENTIERES the Bn. will be prepared to embuss at 12 noon 10th. inst. for an unknown destination.	
	10th.		The Bn. was relieved in the PASSCHENDALE SECTOR by the 23rd. Bn. Middlesex Regt. The Bn. arriving back in SCHOOL CAMP at 6 a.m. after having been in the line 18 days. The Bn. embussed at 2 p.m. for an unknown destination, leaving the 10 % at ROAD CAMP, ST. JAN ter BIEZEN. The Bn. then proceeded via ABEELE - BAILLEUL towards ARMENTIERES and debussed on the main road immediately NORTH of LA CRECHE at about 4 p.m. amidst a continuous stream of refugees, wounded, stragglers, guns, transport etc. moving back towards BAILLEUL. The Bn. with the remainder of the 88th. Brigade deployed immediately and advanced towards the village of LA CRECHE, establishing a position SOUTH of the village covering the approaches from STEENWERKE and the SOUTH EAST. Enemy M.Gs. and artillery active. The Battalion caught the enemy coming down the railway line in column of fours and dispersed him with Lewis Gun and rifle fire. The 3rd. Bn. The Worcestershire Regiment under the command of Major R.F. TRAILL in action on our RIGHT, and in close touch with us. The night was spent in consolidating our position and patrolling.	
LA CRECHE.	11th.		Maintained our position SOUTH of LA CRECHE with the 3rd. Bn. still on our RIGHT and the 2nd. Hampshire Regt. on our LEFT. Situation very obscure. At about 2.30 a.m. "W" Coy. moved forward and occupied STEENWERKE RAILWAY STATION, thus rendering our line more tenable.	
	12th.		Still maintained our position SOUTH of LA CRECHE. Heavily bombarded, many casualties. 2nd. Lieut. J.H. WATT Killed and 2nd. Lieut. C.H. GORRIE Wounded. Situation again very obscure.	

Army Form C. 2118.

WAR DIARY
or
INTELLIGENCE SUMMARY.
(Erase heading not required.)

Instructions regarding War Diaries and Intelligence Summaries are contained in F. S. Regs., Part II. and the Staff Manual respectively. Title pages will be prepared in manuscript.

Place	Date	Hour	Summary of Events and Information	Remarks and references to Appendices
LA CRECHE.	13th.		Maintained our position SOUTH of LA CRECHE. Heavily bombarded all day. Severe fighting all round, no successful advance against the front held by the Battalion. A very anxious time for all, and position extremely dangerous owing to pressure on both flanks. Orders received for a withdrawal to another line by night. From the 10th. to 13th.inclusive the 88th. Brigade was attached to the 25th. Division.	
MONT de LILLE	14th.		The Battalion carried out a successful withdrawal to MONT de LILLE, commencing at 12.15 a.m., in conjunction with the troops on our flanks. Took up a position at dawn, holding MONT de LILLE, "X" and "Y" Coys. being on the forward slope, and "W" and "Z" Coys. on the reverse slope, on a frontage of 1200 yards. 3rd. Bn. on our RIGHT, 2nd. Hampshire Regt. on our LEFT. All our positions very heavily shelled during the whole day. Enemy made several attempts to get forward, but failed. 2 M.Gs. and 11 prisoners captured.	
CROIX de POPERINGHE.	15th.		The Brigade Front taken over by a Battalion 2/5th. Lincolns of 59th. Divn., at about 2 a.m. Relief complete by 5.30 a.m. Immediately after our Companies had been relieved the enemy managed to push forward into part of our late position with a M.G. which caused great consternation. The Battalion marched back to CROIX de POPERINGHE, where it went into camp for a few hours rest and a hot meal, during which time we were constantly shelled. Orders were then suddenly received to move forward into a position of assembly ready (300 yards SOUTH of CROIX de POPERINGHE) to make a counter-attack with the remainder of the 88th. Brigade at dawn. Spent a very cold, wet and miserable night in a hop field, digging in. Both flanks were again threatened. Signs of a heavy enemy attack. Enemy artillery and M.Gs. very active.	
ST. JANS CAPELLE.	16th.		Remained in position of assembly until dusk, when the Battalion again changed position, moving 1000 yards WEST, "W" and "Z" Coys. taking up a position in Army Support Line in direction of ST. JANS CAPPEL, "X" and "Y" Coys. digging in support to "W" and "Z" Coys. on the reverse slope. Battalion held as counter-attack Battalion for 101st. and 147th. Brigades. French cavalry and armoured cars arrived. The cavalry digging in to our rear, supported by three batteries of 75's.	

Army Form C. 2118.

WAR DIARY
or
INTELLIGENCE SUMMARY.
(Erase heading not required.)

Instructions regarding War Diaries and Intelligence Summaries are contained in F. S. Regs., Part II. and the Staff Manual respectively. Title pages will be prepared in manuscript.

Place	Date	Hour	Summary of Events and Information	Remarks and references to Appendices
ST. JANS CAPELLE.	17th.		Battalion remained in Support to 101st. and 147th. Brigades as counter-attack Bn. Very heavily bombarded morning and afternoon. Suffered a good many casualties. French Troops assisted our stretcher bearers in carrying back our wounded. Five enemy attacks beaten off by front line troops, a very critical day.	
BAILLEUL. NORTH EAST OF	18th.		The 88th. Brigade relieved the 103rd. Brigade in the LEFT sector of the 34rd. Divl. Front. The Bn. in close support to the 2nd. Hampshire Regt. and 1st. R. Newfoundland Regt. who were in position N.E. of BAILLEUL. A quiet day. Another attack succesfully driven off by this Brigade.	
	19th.		Enemy and our own artillery active, but not on our portion of the front. Hostile aircraft flying low over our line was fired on by Lewis Guns.	
	20th.		The 88th. Brigade was relieved by the 401st. French Regt. at night. This Battalion was not relieved, but received orders to withdraw at 2 a.m. on 21st. inst. From 14th. to 21st. April the 88th. Bde. was attached to 2 34th. Divn. 2/Lt. H.A. Ward Killed.	
HONDEGHEM ABEELE	21st.		The Bn. withdrew from Support line at 2 a.m. and moved back by march route to ABEELE where the men were provided with a hot meal and had a few hours' rest. Arrived back at ABEELE at about 7 a.m. The Bn. embussed at 4 p.m. and proceeded by motor lorries via STEENVORDE to HONDEGHEM, where they debussed and marched yo an old aerodrome, arriving there about 6 p.m. The men xxxxxx were accomodated in 2 hangars	
	22nd.		General cleaning up and re-organisation. 10% rejoined Battalion.	
NORTH of WALLON CAPELLE.	23rd.		The Bn. moved at 10.15 a.m. to new area, 1 mile NORTH of WALLON CAPELLE, where the Bn. was under canvas. Lewis Gun Class commenced. In the evening sports were held, which were a great success. Bn. payed out.	
	24th.		Lewis Gun Class continued. Coys. at the disposal of O.C. Coys. for Musketry, Drill and ceremonial.	
	25th.		The Bn. moved at 10.15 a.m. to 1 mile EAST of SERCUS where tents were pitched for the Bn. Lewis Gun class continued in afternoon. the 1st. Royal Newfoundland Regt. left the Brigade and was replaced by the 2nd. Bn. Leinster Regt.	

Army Form C. 2118.

WAR DIARY
or
INTELLIGENCE SUMMARY.
(Erase heading not required.)

Instructions regarding War Diaries and Intelligence Summaries are contained in F.S. Regs., Part II. and the Staff Manual respectively. Title pages will be prepared in manuscript.

Place	Date	Hour	Summary of Events and Information	Remarks and references to Appendices
Nr. SERCUS.	26th.		The Battalion found the following working parties for work on the Divisional Line. "W" Coy. 70 o.r., "X" Coy. 80 o.r., "Y" Coy. 100 o.r., "Z" Coy. 50 o.r. The following Officers joined the Battalion: Lieuts. C.W. Morton, M.C., J.V.P. O'Connor, W. Strang, C.G. Sneade, M.R. Foster, G.T. Uren, 2nd. Lieuts. T.L. Gillespie and H.T. Crawley.	
	27th.		The Bn. relieved the 15th. Bn. West Yorks Regt., 31st. Divn. 88th. Brigade was in support to the Division in the front of HAZEBROUCK, "W" on left, "Z" on right, in reserve line of 1st.Zone. "X" on left and "Y" on right of "B" line. The left of "Y" Coy. and Battalion H.Q. heavily shelled in the evening. 2 o.r. Killed and 15 o.r. wounded of "Y" Coy. All H.Q. staff cleared out of building to trench to right of "X" Coy.	
EAST of HAZEBROUCK.	28th.		In reserve trenches EAST of HAZEBROUCK. A quieter day on our own front. Very heavy fighting immediately to our NORTH. Three Coys (W, X, & Z) worked on the reserve defences.	
	29th.		Battle still raging to the NORTH. Comparatively quiet day on our own front. A thorough reconnaissance of this area carried out by Company Commanders. "W" & "Z" Coys. withdrawn to a switch line 1000 yards in rear of the front system. "Y" & "Z" Coys. worked on the defence.	
	30th.		Heavy bombardment by our guns at 3.30 a.m. on Assembly Areas. Commanding Officer and Company Commanders made a reconnaissance of GRAND SEC BOIS and PETIT SEC BOIS and approaches. "W", "X" and "Y" Coys. worked on reserve defence.	

1st. May 1918.

R. Rudcliffe Major for Lieut. Colonel,
Commanding 4th. Bn. The Worcestershire Regiment.

To be put away with diary

- o -

4TH BATT. WORCESTERSHIRE REGIMENT.

April 10th to 15th, 1918,

by

CAPTAIN J.E. THORNELOE, M.C.
late Adjutant.

- o -

A few miles from BAILLEUL the Staff Captain met the convoy and stopped it proceeding any further in the direction of ARMENTIERES. We were informed that everybody was in full retreat and that there was nothing between us and the advancing enemy other than a few stragglers and refugees. The only map of the area was that in possession of the Staff Captain. Colonel Clarke who was in command of the convoy at the time immediately gave orders for the three Battalions (4/Worc, 2/Hants and Monmouths) to disembark at once and sent the busses away. Being entirely dependent on that one map and the information received from the Staff Captain, he decided to seize the village of LA CRECHE and the station and railway embankment to the South of it.

The objective was pointed out on the ground as far as possible. The 4/Worc R advanced to the attack of the above mentioned objectives. The 2/Hants were deployed on their left and advanced with them to make good the high ground between LA CRECHE and the BAILLEUL-ARMENTIERES road. The Monmouths being kept in reserve for the time being.

The enemy were advancing in considerable strength towards the village and along the railway embankment, and the 4/Worc were soon heavily engaged, but managed to inflict severe loss on the enemy and reached all objectives. The fighting was severe at the station, which changed hands three times during the day but eventually remained in possession of the 4/Worc.

Both battalions were able to consolidate their positions and all further attacks by the enemy were repulsed with loss.

It was a curious incident and perhaps a fortunate one, that while the 4/Worc were advancing to this attack, the remnants of the 3/Worc were found to be retiring on the right flank. Colonel Clarke took steps to have these men collected in rear and arranged with Major Traill, who was their commanding officer, that they should take up a position covering the right flank of the 4/WorcR. This was done successfully without delay, and the two battalions settled down side by side.

April 9th.   After a spell of approximately twenty
                days in the Ypres Saliant, the Battalion
                was relieved and transported back to a
                camp some miles behind Poperinghe. We
                had, however, only been there a few hours
                when orders were received that we were to
                be ready to move off for an unknown
                destination in the morning, with the result
                that we only had about half a night's rest
                instead of, as was hoped, a few days.

April 10th.   In the morning more definite orders were
                received and we were rushed off in old
                London omnibuses through Bailleul and down
                the Armentiers Road, where we met a
                continual stream of refugees, Portugese
                and some stragglers coming back, some of
                the stragglers we collected and took along
                with us.

                ~~A few miles from Bailleul, Brig. Gen. Freyberg~~ *the Staff Captain*
                ~~passed our convoy in a car, stopped us and~~
                ~~gave orders for us to disembark, deploy~~
                ~~across the country to the right of the~~
                ~~Bailleul-Armentiers Road, and take the railway~~
                ~~line in front of Steenwerk, and consolidate~~
                ~~there. This we did, but before it was~~
                ~~possible a strenuous struggle took place~~
                ~~with the enemy, whom we first saw marching~~
                ~~down the railway embankment. Lewis gun and~~
                ~~rifle fire was immediately opened out on~~
                ~~them, and heavy casualties were inflicted~~
                ~~upon the enemy, our own casualties were only~~
                ~~slight. At this period we came in contact~~
                ~~with what was left of our 3rd Battalion, under~~
                ~~the command of Major Traill, who were placed~~
                ~~to cover our right flank.~~
                ~~The position on the railway line was consoli-~~
                ~~dated, although we were subjected to continuous~~
                ~~attacks by the enemy.~~

April 11th   Were fairly quiet, although we were at intervals
& 12th.   heavily shelled, and occasional raids endeavoured
                to penetrate our line, but our time was mainly
                spent in improving our line.

                At one period one of our officers, 2nd Lt. Gorrie,
                who with a few men was manning an advanced

Staff Captain
my account agrees
no maps
Lou Creche
I have now re-written this para - See attached.
MCC

Substitute + (attached).

shell hole, was rather seriously wounded, this had rather a demoralising effect upon these few men, who in the heat of the moment evacuated the shell hole. Lt. Rye, the battalion intelligent officer, happened to be near at the time and gathered these few men together and took them back to their evacuated position under very heavy fire. This he succeeded in doing without casualty, and then picked up 2nd Lt. Gorrie (the wounded officer) and carried him back to safety under exceedingly heavy fire.

We having seen the movements of troops on our front, I went to investigate, and arrived there just in time to see Lt. Rye landing in a safe place with the wounded officer. This was a most gallant deed and showed great initiative, and no doubt saved what might have been a very nasty situation, as had the enemy broken through at this period it would have had a very serious effect. Lt. Rye was afterwards awarded the M.C.

April 13th. During the morning of the 13th, orders were received to withdraw to the Mont de Lille during the night, and one officer from each company and myself went back to reconnoitre the position to be taken up.
At, I believe, midnight the evacuation of our position was commenced - this was carried out to such exactitude that not a shot was fired, and we were well consolidated in our new position on the Mont de Lille just as dawn broke.

April 14th. It was some little time before the enemy was seen advancing towards us, and this was done in a very clever manner, small parties of machine gunners making their way towards our new position down the hedges, and it was exceedingly difficult to watch them.
Their tactics appeared to be to get machine gun detachments through gaps in our lines and then fire on our troops from behind. They succeeded in doing this on our flank, which had rather a terrifying effect, but a small party under Capt. Bowman succeeded in

	driving them back, taking a few prisoners. We were successful in holding on to our position in spite of these continual raids until we were eventually relieved on the
April 15th.	evening of April 15th.

This relief was most welcome, as neither officers nor men had had any sleep to speak of since we went into action on the 10th April.

I cannot pass without paying a tribute to the fine spirit shown by all our officers and men during this most trying period, more especially Lt.Col. B.C. Senhause Clarke, who although he suffered terribly through lack of sleep, at all periods had the whole situation at his finger tips, and it was no doubt due to his fine example and leadership that we were successful in holding on to our position.

It was a great feat to hold up the enemy for a period of six days, which undoubtedly gave time for reorganisation behind at a very critical time.

After our relief we marched back to a well equipped Nissen Hut Camp, where the troops were given a really good hot meal and were soon between their blankets.

No sooner had we decided to settle down when the Brigade Major made an unwelcome entry into the hut occupied by Col. Clarke and myself, and informed us that the enemy had broken through the part of the line we had just left (imagine our disappointment, and even disgust, when we heard this after we had held on for nearly a week) and that we were to go up and counter attack at, I think, dawn, so that instead of having a few days rest we only had a few hours sleep. This, however, worked wonders on the men, and we went up to counter attack.

April 16th.

Fortunately, the situation was not so serious as was anticipated, and we were successful in regaining the position on Mont de Lille we had so recently left.

I do not remember how long we remained there, I think only for the one day, when we were again relieved and once again settled down to trench warfare of rather a more open character in the Vieuve Bequin Section - (Petit Sec Bois and Grand Sec Bois). We remained here for some weeks, being periodically relieved and then were sent back to near Cassell where the Battalion was re-equipped and well rested.

CONFIDENTIAL

WAR DIARY

of the

4th. BN. THE WORCESTERSHIRE REGIMENT.

From

1st. May 1918.

To

31st. May 1918.

(VOLUME NO 3)

WAR DIARY
INTELLIGENCE SUMMARY.
(Erase heading not required.)

Army Form C. 2118.

Place	Date	Hour	Summary of Events and Information	Remarks and references to Appendices
TRENCHES EAST OF HAZEBROUCK.	May 1st.		In Reserve Trenches EAST of HAZEBROUCK - Commanding Officer and Company Commanders reconnoitred towards STRAZELE with a view to counter-attack, and visited Australian positions in that area. Both artilleries very active. "X", "Y" and "Z" Coys. worked on the Reserve Line.	
	May 2nd.		"W", "Y" and "Z" Coys. worked on the Reserve Line. Both artilleries very active.	
RESERVE	May 3rd,		Major General D.E. Cayley C.M.G. visited Battalion Headquarters. Enemy's artillery particularly active at dusk, and during the night. A great deal of gas shelling, which caused a few casualties. Work on Reserve Line by "W", "X" and "Y" Coys.	
	May 4th.		Warned re Enemy attack at dawn. Battalion Stood to Arms. Our artillery put down a heavy barrage. No attack developed. Orders received to relieve the 87th. Infantry Brigade in front line posts. Work done on Reserve Line by "W", "X" and "Y" Coys.	
	May 5th.		Stood to Arms at 4.0 a.m. Again no attack developed. A very damp and misty morning. Battalion relieved 1st. K.O.S.B. and 1st. Border Regt. in the Front Line. Left sub-sector of the left sector of the 29th. Divisional Front. 2nd. Hampshires on our Right, 1st. Australian Divn. on our Left. A very wet and stormy night making a long and difficult relief. Relief not complete until 2.40 a.m. Dispositions - "Y" and "X" Coys. in Front Line, posts on Right and Left respectively. "W" Coy. in Support Line. "Z" Coy., 2 platoons in SEC BOIS Defences, 2 platoons in Reserve Line. Battalion Headquarters at Sheet 36A.N.E. E.7.b.80.65.	
STRAZEELE SECTOR.	May 6th.		86th. Brigade (the Brigade on our Right) raided Bosche, capturing one prisoner and one M.G. Bosche retaliated on our front line causing a few casualties. Capt. H.L. Grogan, M.C. Killed, 2nd. Lieut. T.P. Guy Wounded, 2nd. Lieut. H.T. Crawley, Died of Wounds. Fairly quiet day. A patrol left our front line at E.17.c.8.8. and proceeded down road to E.17.b.0.8. and laid no movement observed. A quiet day. At 10.30 p.m. a large number of Gas Projectors were fired Bosche retaliated on our front and support line, no casualties. Bridge at E.11.c.11	

Army Form C. 2118.

WAR DIARY
or
INTELLIGENCE SUMMARY.
(Erase heading not required.)

Instructions regarding War Diaries and Intelligence Summaries are contained in F. S. Regs., Part II. and the Staff Manual respectively. Title pages will be prepared in manuscript.

Place	Date	Hour	Summary of Events and Information	Remarks and references to Appendices
	May 6th. (cont).		E.11.c.11. demolished by R.E. covering party supported by "X" Coy. Lieut. G.P. O'Donovan, M.C. took over command of "X" Coy. vice Capt. H.L. Grogan, M.C. A lot of work put in on wiring our front and support lines. Work on improving trenches. Carried on with dug-out at Battalion H.Q. 150 o.r. of 2nd. Leinster Regt. working on Support Lines.	
STRAZEELE SECTOR.	May 7th.		A fairly quiet day, our guns very active. 1 Coy. Tanks (16 Lewis Guns) withdrawn from Front Line. House at E.15.a.4.9. burned down to give a field of fire for SEC BOIS Defences. Lieut. J.V.P.O'Donnor wounded. Enemy T.Ms. active. 180 Leinsters working on Support Line. 50 carried R.E. Material from front line Coy. H.Q. to front line. Wiring continued along whole front.Patrols left our lines, but came into contact with no enemy.	
	May 8th.		Enemy artillery again active. Heavy barrage placed on the Battalion on our left and further burst at 3.0 a.m. lasting for about 30 minutes. After which all was quiet. Our artillery again very active. Enemy artillery fairly active. S.O.S. Signal sent up by Battalion on our left (12.th. Bn. A.I.F.) at 10.15 p.m. The enemy placed a very heavy barrage on them at about 10 p.m., raiding them at 10.15 p.m., but without any success, driving them off, without having their line entered. Our guns were exceptionally good, and put down a very good counter-barrage. House at E.16.b.05.85 burned down to create a field of fire. Hedges burned also, for same purpose. Wiring all along front continued.	
FRONT LINE,	May 9th.		A quiet day. "X" Coy. (left front) relieved by 11th. Bn. A.I.F. "Y" Coy. relieved by "Z" Coy. "W" Coy. sidestepped with 2 platoons in Support Line, and with two in PETIT SEC BOIS.Defences. "Y" Coy., after relief, moved back to Support Line. 150 Leinsters working on wiring Support Line and carrying R.E. Material to front line. Wiring continued on front line. Hedges thinned to create field of fire.	
	May 10th.		A quiet day. A lot of work put in on thinning hedges and demolishing Chinese Camp. Wiring of front line and support continued.	

Army Form C. 2118.

WAR DIARY
INTELLIGENCE SUMMARY.
(Erase heading not required.)

Place	Date	Hour	Summary of Events and Information	Remarks and references to Appendices
FRONT LINE. STRAZEELE SECTOR.	May 11th.		Another quiet day. Work continued as on 10th. 120 Leinsters working on thinning of hedges. Work commenced on new Battalion HQ. with 1 N.C.O. and 20 men in two reliefs.	
	May 12th.		Enemy artillery more active than usual. Battalion H.Q. shelled. Work commenced on an arrow-head of wire at E.15.a. with a party of 1 N.C.O. and 20 men in 3 reliefs of 3 hours each. 120 Leinsters working on thinning hedges and carrying R.E. Material forward. Wiring continued in front and support line. Work continued on new Battalion H.Q.	
	May 13th.		Work on arrowhead continued with one officer and 20 men in 3 reliefs of 3 hours each. The Battalion was relieved by 1st. K.O.S.B. and 2nd. S.W.B., returning to GRAND HASARD CAMP on relief. Battalion arrived in camp at 2.0 a.m. on 14th.	
GRAND HASARD CAMP.	May 14th.		Rest and general cleaning up. Kit and Box Respirator inspections.	
	May 15th.		"Y" and "Z" Coys. allotted Baths from 8 a.m. to 10 a.m. Companies at the disposal of O.C. Coys. from in the morning for one hour's Drill and Musketry. A Lewis Gun Class of 16 men per Coy. commenced under Lieut. G.S. Kipps. 2 Officers and 4 N.C.O.s per Coy. attended a one day's course in the use of No. 36 Rifle Grenade Discharger. All Signallers paraded under Signalling Officer. A working party of 150 o.r. found for work on reserve lines near LA MOTTE STATION. All leather jerkins and fur coats returned to Ordnance.	
	May 16th.		Companies at the disposal of O.C. Coys. for Drill and Musketry. Each Coy. was allotted the Rifle Range for 1½ hours each for Lewis Gun and Rifle practice. All ranks instructed in the use of No. 36 Rifle Grenade Discharger. Working party found for work near LA MOTTE STATION.	
LE GRAND HASARD CAMP.	May 17th.		Headquarter Party inspected by the Commanding Officer in Fighting Order. Lewis Gun and Signalling Classes continued. The vicinity of the camp was shelled slightly during the day. Working parties of 100 o.r. for work near LA MOTTE STATION	

WAR DIARY
INTELLIGENCE SUMMARY

Army Form C. 2118.

Place	Date	Hour	Summary of Events and Information	Remarks and references to Appendices
LE GRAND HASARD CAMP.	May 17th. (Cont).		and 50 o.r. on "Elephant" shelters for Battalion H.Q. while in Support were supplied.	
	May 18th.		Lewis Gun and Signalling Classes continued. Coys. at the disposal of O.C. Companies for Drill, Musketry and Bombing. Rifle Range allotted to Coys. for 1½ hour's each. The same number of men worked on same tasks as on 17th. "W" and "X" Coys. inspected by the Commanding Officer, in Fighting Order.	
	May 19th.	H.Q.	Working Party of 1 officer and 40 o.r. found for work on new Battalion (Continued).	

Army Form C. 2118.

WAR DIARY
INTELLIGENCE SUMMARY.
(Erase heading not required.)

Instructions regarding War Diaries and Intelligence Summaries are contained in F. S. Regs., Part II. and the Staff Manual respectively. Title pages will be prepared in manuscript.

Place	Date	Hour	Summary of Events and Information	Remarks and references to Appendices
	May 19th.	(noon)	The 88th. Infantry brigade relieved the 96th. Infantry brigade in the Line, S.E. of HAZEBROUCK. The Battalion moved from LE GRAND HASARD during the afternoon, into Support. "W" Coy. relieving one company of the 1st. Royal Dublin Fusiliers "X" and "Y" Coys. each relieving a Coy. of 2nd. Royal Fusiliers. All these Companies were situated in the BOIS D'AVAL (FORET de NIEPPE). "Z" Coy. relieved one Coy. of the 2nd. Royal Fusiliers at PAROTTE. Battalion H.Q. were accomodated in unfinished "elephant" shelters. A very hot day, whole relief finished by 7.0 p.m.	
IN SUPPORT SOUTH EAST of HAZEBROUCK.	May 20th.		In support S.E. of HAZEBROUCK. Our artillery very active. brigade on our RIGHT, slightly advanced their positions, capturing about 30 prisoners. The enemy's artillery more active. During the night 20th/21st. did a considerable amount of gas shelling. Gas Helmets were worn for about an hour. Battalion H.Q. moved from the elephant shelters into buildings. R.Es. with infantry help strengthened cellars and erected "elephant" shelters within these buildings. All Companies worked on the Reserve Line and LA MOTTE Defences. Capt. R.H. Marryatt rejoined from a Course, and took over Command of LA MOTTE Defences. A very hot day.	
	May 21st.		The enemy heavy artillery very active on battery positions. Companies worked on Reserve Line and LA MOTTE Defences. A very hot day.	
	May 22nd.		Enemy much quieter, occasionally firing heavily on our battery positions. An ammunition dump near LE TIR ANGLAIS was blown up by his fire. Officers from the 2nd. Hampshire Regt. reconnoitred our positions, and all Coy. Commanders reconnoitred forward. Very hot day. All Companies work as usual on the Reserve Line and LA MOTTE Defences. Draft of 19 other ranks joined.	
	May 23rd.		Enemy artillery quieter. All Companies worked on Reserve Line and LA MOTTE Defences. Battalion moved from Support into the Front Line, relieving the 2nd. Leinster Regt. "Z" Coy. on the RIGHT, 2 Platoons of "Y" Coy. in the Centre, "W" Coy. on the LEFT, "X" Coy. and 2 Platoons of "Y" Coy in support on the LEFT, "Z" Coy. of 2nd. Hampshire Regt. in Support on the RIGHT. The remainder of the 2nd. Hampshire Regt. "Battalion in Reserve". Relief with 2nd. Leinster Regt.	

WAR DIARY
INTELLIGENCE SUMMARY.
(Erase heading not required.)

Army Form C. 2118.

Place	Date	Hour	Summary of Events and Information	Remarks and references to Appendices
FRONT LINE SOUTH EAST OF HAZEBROUCK.	May 23rd. (Cont).		Regt. completed by 11.50 p.m. A colder day with strong Westerly wind. Enemy heavily gas shelled the wood about midnight, 23/24th.	
	May 24th.		Enemy and our own artillery quiet. About 2.0 a.m. our Special Coy. R.E. liberated over 1000 drums of Gas by projectors on targets in front of our posts. A re-arrangement of troops within the Brigade took place. "Z" Coy. was relieved from the RIGHT of the Front Line by "W" Coy. 2nd. Hampshire Regt., and then moved into SWARTENBROUCK, relieving a Coy. of the 1st. Border Regt. The 2 platoons of "Y" Coy. were withdrawn to the Support Line (defended locality of E.20 Central,) and "W" Coy. extended to the RIGHT and got into touch with "W" Coy. of the 2nd. Hampshire Regt. "W" Coy. strengthened wire on its front. Draft (untrained) of 54 other ranks, from A.S.C. joined, and remained at Transport Lines	
	May 25th.		"Z" Coy's. relief completed by about 2.15 a.m. The Divisional Commander called at Headquarters during the morning. "W" Coy. worked on wire on their front. "X" and "Y" Coys. on the Support Line, and defended locality of E.20 Central. "Z" Coy. worked at night on the new Battalion H.Q., and a great deal of R.E. material was carried forward by mules. The Bosche far more active with his artillery, especially in the evening. Gas was liberated against him in the early hours of the morning. "W" Coy. sent out a patrol under 2nd. Lieut. J.C. Marriott of 1 N.C.O. and 12 men to try and obtain a prisoner. A large enemy working party was seen which scattered as soon as the patrol approached.	
	May 26th.		The enemy attacked NORTH of the Battalion, on about the LEFT of the LEFT Division, but without success. All Companies worked hard, particularly on the wire in front of the Support Line, and the SWARTENBROUCK Defences. The enemy artillery became very active during the afternoon and late at night. "W" Coy. sent out another patrol under 2nd. Lieut. G.W. Amesbury to try and obtain a prisoner, but none of the enemy were seen.	
	May 27th.		86th. Infantry Brigade made a raid about 2½ a.m. and captured three prisoners and a light M.G. Both artilleries very active. Enemy aircraft more active than previously. Work on the Support Line, M.G. bays, and Defended Locality at E.20 Central carried on with. The Battalion was relieved in the Left Front and Support Lines and SWARTENBROUCK Defences by 2 Coys. of the 2nd. Hampshire Regt. and 2	

Army Form C. 2118.

WAR DIARY
INTELLIGENCE SUMMARY.
(Erase heading not required.)

Instructions regarding War Diaries and Intelligence Summaries are contained in F. S. Regs., Part II. and the Staff Manual respectively. Title pages will be prepared in manuscript.

Place	Date	Hour	Summary of Events and Information	Remarks and references to Appendices
	May 27th.	(Cont)	2 Coys. less 1 platoon of 2nd. Leinster Regt., and then moved back into Brigade Reserve near MORBECQUE.	
SOUTH WEST of HAZEBROUCK.	May 28th.		In Brigade Reserve SOUTH WEST of HAZEBROUCK. All ranks had a complete rest. Inspection of arms, gas helmets and battle stores carried out. In the early hours of the morning the Hampshire Regt. made a raid, but were not very successful. The enemy were expected to attack, and in consequence our heavy artillery kept up a heavy harrassing fire all night. No attack on our front developed. A few H.V. shells fell near the camp. H.E. and shrapnel.	
	May 29th.		In Reserve to the Brigade. Near MORBECQUE. All Companies rested, and sports were carried out, including some very good swimming races. Enemy artillery and aircraft were very active. Three of our balloons were brought down.	
	May 30th.		In reserve to the Brigade. Near MORBECQUE. Sports of all sorts carried out. Swimming races, water polo, running and football matches, Officers versus Sergeants which the latter won. Enemy aircraft active at night, and carried out a bombing raid on back areas.	
MORBECQUE.	May 31st.		In Reserve to the Brigade - Near MORBECQUE. The Divisional Gas Officer visited the Battalion, and his G.Q.M.S. lectured all the Companies. All respirators thoroughly inspected. The Battalion moved up into support in the evening, relieving 2nd. Leinster Regt., who again relieved 2nd. Hampshire Regt. in the Front Line. Total Strength of Battalion; 47 Officers, 874 o.r. Ration Strength 51 Officers 639 o.r., Trench Strength 22 Officers, 474 o.r.	
	1st June 1918.			

Lieut. Colonel,
Commanding 4th. Bn. The Worcestershire Regiment.

COPY No. 7   4th. Battalion The Worcestershire Regiment.
                        Operation   Order   No. 24
                                        by
                              Major R. Ratliffe.

Reference Sheet 36 A. N.E.   19th. MAY 1918.

1. (a).   On the night of the 19/20th. the 88th. Infantry Brigade will
relieve the 86th. Infantry Brigade in the Right Sector of the Divisional
Front.
          When relieved the dispositions of the Brigade will be:

                2nd. Leinster Regt. in the Front Line.
                4th. Worcester Regt. in Support.
                2nd. Hampshire Regt. in Reserve.
                Brigade Headquarters at D.17.a.5.3.

   (b).   "W" Coy. will relieve 1 company of Royal Dublin Fusiliers in
E.20 central.
          "X" Coy. will relieve "Y" Coy. of Royal Fusiliers in E.19.central.
          "Y" Coy.   --do--   "Z" Coy.   ----do----   D.30 b and d.
          "Z" Coy.   --do--   "X" Coy.   ----do----   PAPOTE.

2.   Companies will march up by platoons at 200 yards distance between
platoons at the following times:
          "Z" Coy. march off at 3.0 p.m.
          "W" Coy.   ----do---   3.30 p.m.
          "X" Coy.   ----do---- 4.0 p.m.
          "Y" Coy.   ----do---   4.30 p.m.
          One limber for Lewis Guns will follow in rear of each Company.
          Headquarter party will march off at 4.0 p.m.
          Battalion Headquarters will be at D.24.a.9.7.
          Cookers will proceed in rear of the Battalion and will move off at
4.45 p.m.
          All details for the Transport Lines will march off under Lieut. G.S.
Kipps at 3.0 p.m.

3.   Details of relief have been arranged between O.C. Coys. concerned.

4.   O.C. "X" and "Y" Coys. will arrange to relieve the four Lewis Guns
in position along the BOURRE RIVER in E.25 and 26 and K.2.
          O.C. "X" Coy. will detail an Officer to be in charge of these guns.
This party will march off at 2.0 p.m.

5.   All trench stores, shovels, and work in progress and proposed, will
be handed over and receipts forwarded to Battalion H.Q.

6.   "X", "Y" and "Z" Coys. will each take in 40 shovels. These
will not be handed over on relief.
          "W" Coy. will take over 5 trench shelters.
          "Z" Coy. ----do---- 15   ---do---   and one tent.

7.   Completion of relief will be notified to Battalion Headquarters
by the code word "HILDA".

8.   A C K N O W L E D G E

---------------------------------⊙⊙⊙⊙⊙⊙⊙⊙⊙⊙---------------------------------
                              (Sgd). E.R. Smith, Capt. & A/Adjutant,
                                      4th. Bn. The Worcestershire Regiment.

Copies to:
1. C.O.
2. H.Q.
3–6. O.C. Coys.
7. O.C. R. Fus.
8. Q.M.
9. File.
10. Diary.

CONFIDENTIAL

WAR   DIARY

4th. BN. THE WORCESTERSHIRE REGT.

From   1st. JUNE 1918.
To   30th. JUNE 1918.

(Volume No 4)

WAR DIARY

Army Form C. 2118.

JUNE, 1918.

Reference Sheet 36A. N.E. 1/20,000

Place: NEAR BOIS D'AVAL AND LA MOTTE. IN SUPPORT TO 88th. INFANTRY BRIGADE

Date	Hour	Summary of Events and Information	Remarks and references to Appendices
1st. June.		In Support to the Brigade in BOIS D'AVAL and LA MOTTE. Enemy artillery far more active, particularly in SWARTENBROUCK where "Z" Coy. were and around Battalion Headquarters. "X" and "W" in the Reserve Line, and "Y" Coy. in LA MOTTE SWITCH had a quiet day, "Y" Coy. being unfortunate in having 4 men wounded by a stray shrapnel and 1 killed by H.E. "W", "X" and "Y" Coys. worked by day on the Reserve Line and Battn. H.Q. and a Strong Point SOUTH of LA MOTTE. "Z" Coy. worked by night on SWARTENBROUCK Defences and Front Line Battn. H.Q. At night the enemy shelling became far more active all round. Leave re-opened. 9 vacancies allotted Bn. for month of June. Draft of 56 o.r. joined Battalion.	

2nd. June.		Enemy artillery active during the early morning. "X" and "W" Coys. worked on the Reserve Line building breastworks and cutting brushwood etc. "Y" Coy. worked on Strong Point SOUTH of LA MOTTE, Battalion H.Q. and Brigade H.Q. "Z" Coy. on Front Line Battn. H.Q. and SWARTENBROUCK Defences. Headquarter Party with a small party from "X" Coy. worked hard on improving Support Bn. H.Q. A hot day and quite quiet during the day. Telephone notification received from Division of the following awards, given for the recent operations near BAILLEUL.
		    Lieut. Colonel B.C.S. Clarke, D.S.O. Bar to D.S.O.
		    Capt. H. Croom-Johnson, M.C. Bar to M.C.
		    Capt. D.R. Alexander, (R.A.M.C.). M.C.
		    Capt. J.E. Thorneloe. M.C.
		    2nd. Lieut. S. Gray. M.C.
		    2nd. Lieut. S.J. Rye. M.C.	

3rd. June.		With ZERO at 1 a.m., the 86th. Infantry Brigade on our LEFT, in conjunction with 1st. Australian Division carried out a minor operation and re-captured MONT MERRIS. The 2nd. Leinster Regt. to conform, advanced their posts and dug in in a new line. All objectives were gained and 32 prisoners taken by the 86th. Bde. and about 250 by the Australians. The remainder of the day both a-rtilleries carried out harassing fire on	

WAR DIARY or INTELLIGENCE SUMMARY.

JUNE 1918.

Army Form C. 2118.

Reference Sheet 36A. N.E. 1/20,000.

Place	Date	Hour	Summary of Events and Information	Remarks and references to Appendices
IN SUPPORT TO 88th. INFANTRY BRIGADE NEAR BOIS D'AVAL and LA MOTTE.	June 3rd. (Cont)		on roads and back areas. The Reserve Line and LA MOTTE SWITCH were intermittently shelled during the whole day. The usual working parties were carried by the Brigade. At 11.45 p.m. the S.O.S. Signal went up on our Left. A heavy barrage was put down by our artillery, which was quiet again after half an hour. The enemy had attempted to bomb the new posts of the 86th. Infantry Brigade, but were repulsed, leaving 6 prisoners in their (86th. Bde). hands. Draft of 23 joined Bn.	
	June 4th.		Very quiet during the whole day. Companies worked as on previous days. The Battalion was relieved in Support by 2 Companies 1st. K.O.S.B.s, 1 Coy. 1st. Border Regt., 1 Coy. S.W.B.s; 1 Coy. 2nd. R. Fusiliers and the 87th. T.M.B. took over Headquarters. Relief was completed by 10 p.m., and the Battalion moved back to Camp, between GRAND HASARD and HAZEBROUCK.	
IN CAMP BETWEEN GRAND HASARD & HAZEBROUCK.	June 5th.		Companies at the disposal of O.C. Companies for Cleaning Up, Inspections of Kit, Box Respirators etc.	
	June 6th.		Baths allotted to Battalion. All Companies bathed. Coys. at the disposal of O.C. Coys. remainder of day. A.S.C. Draft paraded under 2nd. Lieut. H.F. Boddington. Lewis Gun Class of 2 Sgts. and 4 men per Coy. commenced under Lieut. G.S. Kipps. No. 19244 Sgt. A. Mogg. awarded D.C.M.) No. 33452 Pte. P. Lewis " M.M.) For operations from 10th No. 40081 L/Cpl. H. Sansome " M.M.) - 20th. April 1918.	
	June 7th.		A.S.C. Draft and Lewis Gun Classes continued their training. All Rifle Grenadiers of "W" Coy. paraded under Lieut. H.C. Hiscock for 3 hours instruction in the use of No. 36 Rifle Grenade and Discharger. Live bombs fired. The range at GRAND HASARD was allotted to "Y" and "Z" Coys. for 1½ hours each, and to the A.S.C. Draft from 2 p.m. - 4 p.m. Remainder of the day, companies at the disposal of O.C. Coys. for training.	

Army Form C. 2118.

WAR DIARY

Instructions regarding War Diaries and Intelligence Summaries are contained in F. S. Regs., Part II. and the Staff Manual respectively. Title pages will be prepared in manuscript.

JUNE 1918.

Place	Date	Hour	Summary of Events and Information	Remarks and references to Appendices
HAZEBROUCK.	June 7th.		Total strength of Battn. 46 Officers. 833 o.r. Ration ---do---- 31 " " 682 " " Trench ---do---- 27 " " 617 " " The Drums beat "Retreat" at XV Corps Headquarters and were congratulated by the Corps Commander, Sir Lieutenant General Sir Beauvoir de Lisle, K.C.B., D.S.O.	Reference sheet 36A, N.E., 1/20,000.
IN CAMP BETWEEN LE GRAND HASARD &	June 8th.		Companies at the disposal of O.C. Companies for two hours training. The range at D.13.a.5.5. was allotted to "W" and "X" Coys. for 1½ hour's each, and to the A.S.C. Draft for two hours. The A.S.C. Draft paraded as usual under 2nd. Lt. H.F. Boddington. All Rifle Grenadiers of "X" Coy. paraded under Lt. H.C. Hiscock for instruction in the use of No. 3 Rifle Grenade and Discharger. The following platoons were inspected by the Commanding Officer, in Fighting Order. Nos. 7,9,11,13 and 15. The 29th. Divisional Band played from 5.30 p.m. to 7 p.m. in "W" and "Z" Coy's. field.	
	June 9th.		The following working parties were supplied by the Battalion. "X" Party: All Officers and 76 o.r. of "W" Coy. for work on Reserve Line from 9.30 a.m. to 2 p.m. "Y" Party: All Officers and 106 o.r. of "X" Coy. for work on Reserve Line from 10 a.m. to 2 p.m. "Z" Party: 1 Officer and 22 or H.Q. Party and 10 o.r. "X" Coy. for making forestry stakes, working from 10 a.m. to 2 p.m. "A" Party: All Officers and 120 o.r. "Y" Coy and 30 o.r. "W" Coy. for work on Reserve Line from 9.30 p.m. to 1.30 a.m.	
	June 10th.		"B" Party: All Officers and 120 o.r. "Z" Coy., 10 o.r. "X" Coy. and 20 o.r. "W" Coy. for work on Reserve Line from 9.30 p.m. to 1.30 a.m. "Y" and "Z" Coys. at the disposal of O.C. Coys. for 2 hours' Training in the morning. Voluntary Non-Conformist Service.	

Army Form C. 2118.

WAR DIARY
~~INTELLIGENCE~~ SUMMARY.
(Erase heading not required.)

Reference Sheet 36A, N.E., 1/20,000.

Place	Date	Hour	Summary of Events and Information	Remarks and references to Appendices
IN CAMP BETWEEN LE GRAND HASARD AND HAZEBROUCK.	June 10th.		Companies at the disposal of O.C. Companies for two hours' Training. A.S.C. Draft paraded under 2nd. Lieut. H.F. Boddington. Rifle Grenadiers of "Y" Coy. paraded under Lieut. H.G. Hiscock for Instruction in the use of No. 36 Rifle Grenade and Discharger. The Observers' Class (4 men per Coy). paraded under Lieut. W. Hamer. The Range at LE GRAND HASARD allotted to the A.S.C. Draft from 10.30 a.m. to 12.30 p.m. The Corps Chemical Adviser lectured to all Officers and N.C.Os. of the Brigade on Gas.	
	June 11th.		All parades as on the 10th., except the Rifle Grenadiers of "Z" Coy. paraded under Lieut. H.G. Hiscock for Instruction in the use No. 36 Rifle Grenade and Discharger. No. 24121 Pte. H. Royall awarded the Military Medal. Running and Swimming Sports and football were held between this Battalion and the 2nd. Hampshire Regt. This Battalion winning every event. A most enjoyable afternoon. Company Commanders reconnoitred the line preparatory to relieving the 1st. Royal Dublin Fusiliers.	
	June 12th.		The 88th. Infantry Brigade relieved the 86th. Infantry Brigade in the Left Sub-Sector of the Divisional Front. (VIEUX BERQUIN), this Battalion relieving the 1st. Royal Dublin Fusiliers. A quiet relief, no casualties. Front Line:- "W" Coy. on Right, "X" Coy. on Left. Support Line:- "Y" Coy. and 2 Platoons of "Z" Coy. SEC BOIS DEFENCES:- 2 Platoons of "Z" Coy. Battalion Headquarters:- E.7.b.9.6.	
FRONT LINE, VIEUX BERQUIN SECTOR.	June 13th.		Enemy M.G. and T.M.s. active in the early morning. "W" Coy. heavily bombarded by day and night. Wiring on whole front line, cutting down crops to clear field of fire in Support Line.	
	June 14th.		Received sudden orders for the Left Coy. ("X" Coy) to raid TERN FARM. "W" Coy. again very heavily shelled. T.Ms. very active.	

Army Form C. 2118.

- 5 -

WAR DIARY

~~INTELLIGENCE SUMMARY~~

(Erase heading not required.)

Instructions regarding War Diaries and Intelligence Summaries are contained in F. S. Regs., Part II. and the Staff Manual respectively. Title pages will be prepared in manuscript.

JUNE 1918.

Place	Date	Hour	Summary of Events and Information	Remarks and references to Appendices
VIEUX BERQUIN SECTOR. FRONT LINE.	June 15th.		2 Platoons of "X" Coy. under Lieut. J.S. Graves and 2/Lt. C.F. Jones attempted to raid TERN FARM at 1.15 a.m., but owing to the alertness and strength of the enemy on the right flank of the raiding party, and the weakness of the artillery support, the raiding party failed to get through the enemy wire. Lieut. J.S. Graves, Wounded and Missing, Killed and Wounded, o.r. 12. At 3.15 a.m. "W" Coy. was attacked from the front and rear suffering severe casualties, and losing their posts, the enemy having broken through from the right. Lieut. C.W. Morton, M.G., wounded. Total casualties from midnight 14th. to midnight 15th. 1 Officer Wounded 1 Officer W and M., 123 o.r. ~~Wounded~~ Killed, Wounded, and Missing. A number of these casualties were due to enemy shell fire on our own gas cylinders. The whole of the garrison from the front line was withdrawn at dusk to the support line ready for 4000 Gas Cylinders to be discharged. Owing to the change of the wind, the gas was not released, and the front line was re-occupied by "Z" Coy. and 2 Platoons of "Y" Coy. "X" Coy. and the remains of "W" staying in the Support Line.	Reference Sheet 36A. N.E. 1/20,000.
	June 16th.		Enemy artillery was again very active on our front line. The garrison of the front line was again withdrawn at dusk, preparative to the gas being discharged, but owing to the change in the wind, it was impossible for the discharge to take place, and orders were received that the gas would be let off on the first favourable opportunity, and that the post line would not be occupied, until after the discharge. Draft of 65 other ranks joined, 55 being sent to "W" Coy. The gas was discharged at 10.30 a.m. being carried by the wind in a S.E. direction, thus having no effect on our immediate front. The front line was re-occupied at 3.15 p.m. with slight opposition.	
	June 17th.		A quieter day. Work on wiring front line. 5 0 men working under M.G. Battalion at cutting down crops to create fields of fire. Front and M support lines improved.	

WAR DIARY

JUNE 1918.

Place	Date	Hour	Summary of Events and Information	Remarks and references to Appendices
FRONT LINE VIEUX BERQUIN SECTOR.	June 18th. 1918.		A much quieter day, enemy artillery not so active. Orders received to raid ANTILE FARM in conjunction with 2nd.Leinsters on Right. These orders were cancelled as far as this Battalion was concerned.	Reference Sheet 36A. N.E. 1/20,000.
	June 19th.	12.45 a.m.	At 12.45 a.m. the Leinsters raided LUG FARM with excellent artillery support, capturing one wounded German and 2 machine guns. Suffered fairly heavy casualties.	
	June 20th.		Another fairly quiet day. The Battalion was relieved by the 15th. Bn. West Yorkshire Regt. (31st. Divn.). Relief complete by 1.10 a.m. 21st. Inst.	
LA KREULE.	June 21st.		The Battalion, after completion of relief, moved back to Camp at LA KREULE. The Battalion (less Transport) paraded at 11.45 a.m. and marched to HONDEGHEM SIDING, where it entrained for LUMBRES, arriving there at 3 p.m., detrained and marched to camp at VAL DE LUMBRES.	Reference Sheets 27A. SE and 36 D. N.E. 1/20,000.
IN CAMP AT VAL DE LUMBRES.	June 22nd.		Companies were at the disposal of O.C. Companies for general cleaning up, kit inspections etc.	
	June 23rd.		Brigade Divine Service held on the parade ground in Camp.	
	June 24th.		Baths at ACQUIN allotted the Battalion for the whole day for a complete disinfection of all clothing etc. Companies at the disposal of O.C. Companies for the remainder of the day.	
	June 25th.		Musketry School Ranges allotted to the Battalion from 9 a.m. to 3p.m. 12 targets being allotted to each Company. The following practices were fired by every man:- 5 rounds Grouping at 100 yards. 5 " Application at 200 yards. 5 " Rapid at 200 yards.	

(Cont).

Army Form C. 2118.

WAR DIARY

(Erase heading not required.)

JUNE 1918.

Reference Sheets 27A. S.E. & 36D. N.E. 1/20,000.

Place	Date	Hour	Summary of Events and Information	Remarks and references to Appendices
IN CAMP AT VAL DE LUMBRES.	June 25th. (Cont).		All Lewis Gun N.C.Os. and Nos. 1 and 2 Lewis Gunners firing on Lewis Gun Range. Junior N.C.Os. Class of 8 N.C.Os. per Coy. commenced. All ranks tested their Small Box Respirators in Gas Chamber under the Divisinal Gas Officer.	
	June 26th.		The Battalion paraded as strong as possible to practice for the Brigade Ceremonial Parade. Lewis Gun Class and N.C.Os. class continued in the afternoon.	
	June 27th.		The Battalion paraded again as strong as possible for the Brigade Practice Ceremonial Parade. Lewis Gun and N.C.Os. class continued in the afternoon. Draft of 34 o.r. joined the Battalion.	
	June 28th.		The Musketry School Range again allotted the Battalion from 8 a.m. to 2 p.m., 12 targets being allotted to each Company. All men fired 5 rounds, snap-shooting at 200 yards. After this a knock-out inter-platoon competition was fired, 2 Platoons firing at each at 40 falling plates at 200 yards. No. 1 Platoon was the winning Platoon. First round of the Brigade Inter-Company Football Competition commenced. "Z" Coy. Worcs. met "Z" Coy. 2nd. Hants, beating them by 1 goal to nil. Lewis Gun and N.C.Os. Class continued. A Draft of 27 o.r. joined the Battalion.	
	June 29th.		Companies at the disposal of O.C. Companies from 9 a.m. to 1p.m. to practice shaking out into Artillery Formation and Extended Order. "W" and "X" Coys using the Training Grounds at LUMBRES, and "Y" & "Z" Coys. using the Training Area. All Signallers paraded under Capt. H.M. Clark, M.C. for training. Lewis Gun and N.C.Os. Class continued. "Y" Coy. Worcs. met "D" Coy. 2nd. Leinsters in the Brigade Football Competition beating them by 1 goal to nil.	

WAR DIARY

Army Form C. 2118.

JUNE 1918

Place	Date	Hour	Summary of Events and Information	Remarks and references to Appendices
IN CAMP AT VAL DE LUMBRES.	June 30th.		The 88th. Infantry Brigade paraded for Divine Service on the Parade Ground in Camp. The Assistant Chaplain General preached the sermon. The Army, Divisional and Brigade Commanders were all present. After the service the Brigade was inspected by the Army Commander (General Sir Herbert C.O. Plumer, G.C.B., G.C.M.G., G.C.V.O., A.D.C.) and marched past him. "W" Coy. Worcs. met "X" Coy. Worcs. in Brigade Football Competition, "W" Coy. winning by 2 goals to Nil. Strength of the Battalion:- Total Strength. 41 Officers. 880 Other Ranks. Ration Strength. 29 -do- 787 -do- Trench Strength. 24 -do- 705 -do- 1st. July 1918. [signature] Lieut. Colonel, Commanding 4th. Bn. The Worcestershire Regiment.	Reference Sheets 27A, S.E., & 36D, N.E. 1/20,000.

SECRET & CONFIDENTIAL

WAR DIARY

4th. Battalion The Worcestershire Regiment.

From: 1st. JULY 1918.
TO: 31st. JULY 1918.

(Volume no 5)

Army Form C. 2118.

WAR DIARY
INTELLIGENCE SUMMARY.
(Erase heading not required.)

Instructions regarding War Diaries and Intelligence Summaries are contained in F. S. Regs., Part II. and the Staff Manual respectively. Title pages will be prepared in manuscript.

Place	Date	Hour	Summary of Events and Information	Remarks and references to Appendices
				Reference Sheets 27A S.E. & 36D. N.E. 1/20,000. HAZEBROUCK, 5A, 1/100,000.
VAL de LUMBRES.	1st. July.		The Battalion paraded at 10.15 a.m. for the Brigade Inspection by the Divisional Commander. (Major General D.E. Cayley, C.M.G.) who presented ribbons to recipients of awards won during operations near BAILLEUL from 10th. - 20th. April 1918. The following is an extract from 29th. Divisional Routine Orders dated 2.7.18. "The G.O.C. wishes to express to Brig. Gen. B.C. Freyburg, V.C., D.S.O. and all ranks of the 88th. Infantry Brigade, his appreciation of the excellence of the turn out, steadiness and marching of the Brigade on the Ceremonial yesterday, the 1st. inst. Notification received that:- No. 202343 C.S.M. A.J. SIMKINS and No. 24221 PTE. H. ROYALL, M.M. have been awarded the M.S.M. "W" Coy. beat "B" Coy. 2nd. Leinster Regt. 2 goals - nil. and "Z" Coy. beat "X" Coy. 2nd. Hampshire Regt. 2 goals - one. in the Second Round of the Brigade inter-company Football Competition.	
	2nd. July.		Companies at the disposal of O.C. Coys. from 9 a.m. to 1 p.m. to practice shaking out into artillery formation, extended order etc. Lewis Gun, Signallers and N.C.Os' Classes continued. "Y" Coy. beat 88th. Field Ambulance in Second Round Brigade Inter-coy. Football Competition by 3 goals - nil.	
IN CAMP.	3rd. July.		Companies at the disposal of O.C. Coys. from 9 a.m. to 1 p.m. for practicing advancing in extended order etc. The Battalion on "Y" Range from 2 p.m. to 4 p.m. when inter-coy. competitions were fired at falling plates. Battalion trial sports for the Brigade Sports were held. 3rd. Bn. moved to billets about 3 miles from Camp, and taking the place of the 10th. Bn. (Disbanded) in the 19th. Divn. Draft of 5 or. joined.	
	4th. July.		Companies at the disposal of O.C. Coys. from 9 a.m. to 1 p.m. for Field Training. Lewis Gun, Signalling and N.C.Os.' Classes continued.	
	5th. July.		Companies at the disposal of O.C. Companies from 9 a.m. to 9.45 a.m. for Physical Games. The Battalion paraded at 10 a.m. for Company Field Training. Lewis	

Army Form C. 2118.

WAR DIARY

(Erase heading not required.)

Instructions regarding War Diaries and Intelligence Summaries are contained in F.S. Regs., Part II. and the Staff Manual respectively. Title pages will be prepared in manuscript.

Reference Sheets 27A S.E. & 36D. N.E., 1/20,000.
HAZEBROUCK, 5A, 1/100,000.

Place	Date	Hour	Summary of Events and Information	Remarks and references to Appendices
	July 5th. (cont).		Lewis Gun, Signalling and N.C.Os. Classes continued. "M" Coy. beat "Z" Coy. by 2 goals - nil in the Semi-Final of the Bde. inter-coy. Football Competition.	
VAL de KUMBRES.	July 6th.		Companies at the disposal of O.C. Coys. to practice a Tactical Exercise. A working party of 1 officer and 50 o.r. supplied. Brigade Sports held, commencing at 2 p.m. This Battalion winning the Brigade Cup presented by Brig.-General B.C. FREYBURG, VC., DSO, by 48 points to the 2nd. Leinsters 39 pts. "Y" Coy. beat 88th. Bde. Headquarters by 3 goals - one in the semi-final of the Brigade Inter-Company Football Competition; this leaving "M" and "Y" Coys. in the final.	
	July 7th.		The Brigade paraded at 11 a.m. for Divine Service. All Rifles and Lewis Guns inspected by Brigade Armourer's Sergeant. Brigade Boxing Competition held. This Battalion obtained 3 medals for second places.	
CAMP.	July 8th.		Companies at the disposal of O.C. Coys for practice Tactical Exercise. "M" Coy. carried out a demonstration in "Attack in Open Warfare" for Brigadier-General B.C. Freyburg, V.C., D.S.O. 2/Lt. W.G.A. Collins and draft of 23 other ranks joined the Battalion.	
IN	July 9th.		One hours' parade for all.— Coys doing P.T. & B.F. and Drill. Remainder of the day a holiday. 35 O.R. per Coy. and 10 O.R. from H.Q. were conveyed to the Div. Horse Show at LE MONT DEPIL near RACQUINGHEM. Also the Drums which competed in the Competition and took 3rd. place. No prizes were won. Lieut. E.R. Newcomb joined the Battalion for duty.	
	July 10th.		On "Y" Rifle Range - Each Coy. practiced in turn an attack on the Butts illustrating Fire and Movement. The same practice was to have been carried out during the afternoon, with ball ammunition, but owing to a heavy thunder-storm had to be cancelled. The Battalion Football Team played the 3rd. Battalion, beating them 2 goals - nil.	

Army Form C. 2118.

WAR DIARY
or
INTELLIGENCE SUMMARY.
(Erase heading not required.)

Reference Sheets 27A S.E. & 26D N.E.   1/20,000.
HAZEBROUCK 5A. 1/100,000.

Place	Date	Hour	Summary of Events and Information	Remarks and references to Appendices
VAL de LUMBRES.	July 11th.		The Battalion did Battalion Drill for one hour, forming into Mass etc., and then each Coy. did Musketry, P.T. & B.F., and Gas Drill on the ground behind "Y" Range. In the afternoon all Company Commanders accompanied the Commanding Officer for a Reconnaissance over the Training Area for a Battalion Flagged Attack. The Lewis Gun and Signalling Classes continued.	
	July 12th.		Heavy rain during the night and morning. The Battalion scheme for Flagged Attack postponed. Lewis Gun Class continued. Companies had lectures and cleaning up parades in the morning.	
	July 13th.		The Battalion paraded at 8.45 a.m. and proceeded to the Training Area and practiced the Flagged Attack. The Corps and Divisional Commanders were present.	
IN CAMP.	July 14th.		The Battalion paraded paraded at 10.45 a.m. for a Brigade Divinve Service. The Deputy Chaplain General preached the Sermon.	
	July 15th.		Baths allotted to Coys. as under:- 2 p.m. to 4 p.m. "W" Coy. 4 p.m. to 6 p.m. "X" Coy. The Battalion paraded at 9 a.m. and proceeded to Training Area and practiced the Brigade Tactical Scheme. The 88th. Field Ambulance Concert Party gave a concert for the Battalion in the Y.M.C.A. Tent, LUMBRES. All Officers and Platoon Sergeants attended a lecture by Brig.-Gen. B.C. Freyburg V.C. D.S.O. at 5 p.m. on the Brigade Tactical Scheme. Draft of 5 O.R. joined the Battalion.	
	July 16th.		The Battalion paraded as strong as possible at 8.15 a.m. to take part in the Brigade Tactical Scheme. Blank Ammunition, Green, Red, and White Verey Lights and rattles were issued to Coys. The Verey Lights being used as signals to notify progress made etc. The Corps and Divisional Commanders were present. The 4 C.Q.M.S's. and Sergt. Cook attended a demonstration at the Sch. of Cookery, LUMBRES.	

WAR DIARY
or
INTELLIGENCE SUMMARY

(Erase heading not required.)

Army Form C. 2118.

Place	Date	Hour	Summary of Events and Information	Remarks and references to Appendices
IN CAMP VAL de LUMBRES	July 17th.		Owing to heavy rain no Coy. Training was carried out. The Baths were allotted to Companies, for de-lousing, as under:- "W" Coy. 8 - 10 a.m. "Y" Coy. 10 - 12 noon. "Z" Coy. 12 - 1 p.m. & 2 p.m. - 3 p.m. "X" Coy. 3 - 5 p.m. Transport: 5 p.m. - 6 p.m. Lewis Gun and Signalling Classes continued. All N.C.Os. instructed in the use of the Compass and Map Reading. The Final of the Brigade Inter-coy. Football Competition ("W" Coy. v "Y" Coy., 4th. Worces. Regt.) was played off. Score: 2 goals all.	Reference Sheets 27A. S.E. and 36D N.E. 1/20,000. HAZEBROUCK 5A. 1/100,000.
IN CAMP VAL de LUMBRES	July 18th.	8.30 a.m.	Companies carried out the Coy. Tactical Scheme on "Y" Range, commencing at 8.30 a.m. Lewis Gun and Signalling Classes continued.	
	July 19th.		Sudden orders were received at about midnight 18th./19th. that the Battalion would move to a new area before 10 a.m. on the 19th. The Battalion paraded at 10 a.m. and proceeded by march route to PONT D'ASQUIN near WARDREQUES arriving in the new area about 5.30 p.m. Draft of 6 O.R. joined the Battalion.	
IN CAMP PONT D'ASQUIN.	July 20th.	9 a.m. and 2 p.m.	Companies were at the disposal of O.C. Coys. for inspection of Iron Rations, S.A.A., S.B. Respirators etc. The following Classes paraded at 9 a.m. and 2 p.m. :- (1) Lewis Gun. Class. (2) Signalling Class. (3) A Scouting Class of 4 men per Coy. under Capt. C. Hackett M.C., D.C.M. (4) Observers' Class under Lieut. W. Hamer.	Reference Sheet 36A. 1/40,000.
IN CAMP PONT D'ASQUIN.	July 21st.		The Battalion paraded at 9.50 a.m. for a Brigade Divine Service. Companies were at the disposal of O.C. Coys. from 10.30 a.m. to 12.30 p.m. All N.C.O's. instructed in Map Reading and use of the Compass. Lewis Gun, Signalling, Scouting, and Observers' Classes continued.	

Army Form C. 2118.

WAR DIARY
or
INTELLIGENCE SUMMARY.

(Erase heading not required.)

Instructions regarding War Diaries and Intelligence Summaries are contained in F. S. Regs., Part II. and the Staff Manual respectively. Title pages will be prepared in manuscript.

Place	Date	Hour	Summary of Events and Information	Remarks and references to Appendices
IN BILLETS NEAR ZUYTPEENE (WEST OF CASSEL.)	July 22nd.		The Battalion paraded at 9 a.m. and proceeded by march route to billets near ZUYPTEENE (WEST OF CASSEL) arriving in the new area about 12 noon, and found very little accomodation for the Battalion. 70 bivouacs were, however received. The Division transferred from XV Corps to X Corps.	Reference Sheet 27. 1/40,000. HAZEBROUCK 5A. 1/100,000.
	July 23rd.		Companies at the disposal of O.C. Coys. for individual training from 9 a.m. to 12 noon, but owing to heavy rain little training was able to be carried out. Lewis Gun, Signalling, Scouting and Observers' Classes continued.	
	July 24th.		Companies at the disposal of O.C. Companies for individual Training from 9 a.m. to 12 noon. Lewis Gun, Signalling, Scouting and Observers' Classes continued. The Commanding Officer and Second in Command reconnoitred the BLUE LINE and approaches.	
	July 25th.		Companies at the disposal of O.C. Coys. for Individual Training from 9 a.m. to 12 noon. Lewis Gun, Signalling, Scouting and Observers' Classes continued. All stretcher Bearers attended a Class of Instruction under the Medical Officer. The Adjutant, 4 Coy. Commanders and Intelligence Officer reconnoitred the BLUE LINE Approaches. 2nd. Lieut. G.W. Wright.) joined the Battalion. 2nd. Lieut. W. Hoyle.) The following Army Order was issued:- "The Left Hand salute is maximum by Warrant Officers, N.C.Os. and men is abolished. The salute will be given by all ranks with the right hand. When saluting to the side, the head will be turned towards the person saluted. In cases fof where from physical incapacity a right hand salute is impossible, the salute will be given with the left hand. The necessary amendments to the various regulations and Training manuals will be issued shortly. Inter-Platoon Football Competitions commenced. 2 Officers per Company reconnoitred the BLUE Line and approaches.	

WAR DIARY or INTELLIGENCE SUMMARY.

Army Form C. 2118.

(Erase heading not required.)

Place	Date	Hour	Summary of Events and Information	Remarks and references to Appendices
IN BILLETS NEAR ZUYTPEENE (WEST OF CASSEL).	July 26th.		Companies at the disposal of O.C. Coys. for Individual Training from 9 a.m. to 12 noon. All Classes continued. Football Competitions continued. 3 Officers or N.C.Os. per Coy. reconnoitred the BLUE LINE and approaches.	
	July 27th.		Companies at the disposal of O.C. Coys. for Individual Training from 9 a.m. to 12 noon. Classes continued. Cricket Match between Q.M. Stores and Transport.	
	July 28th.		Divine Service in the Cinema at BAVINCHOVE. The Divisional Band was present. R.C. Service in CASSEL Church. Football and cricket played in the afternoon.	
	July 29th.		Companies at the disposal of O.C. Coys. from 9 a.m. to 12 noon for Individual Training. All Classes continued. 2 Coy. Commanders, 2 Seconds in Comd. of Coys., Intelligence Officer and Transport Officer reconnoitred BLUE LINE, Assembly Areas, and Front Line WEST of BAILLEUL.	
	July 30th.		Companies at the disposal of O.C. Companies for Individual Training from 9 a.m. to 12 noon. All Classes continued. Lewis Gun Class completed its training. Cricket Match between Officers and Sergeants.	
	July 31st.		Companies at the disposal of O.C. Coys. from 9 a.m. to 12 noon for Individual Training. New Lewis Gun Class commenced. All other classes continued.	

Strength of Battalion. 31.7.18.

Total Strength. 42 Officers 922 O.R.
Ration -do- 31 " 853 "
Trench -do- 20 " 612 "

1st. August 1918. Commanding 4th. Bn. The Worcestershire Regiment.

Reference Sheet 27, 1/40,000.
HAZEBROUCK 5A, 1/100,000.

CONFIDENTIAL

WAR DIARY

of

4th Battalion The Worcestershire Regiment

From 1st August, 1918   To 31st August, 1918.

(Volume No. 6).

Army Form C. 2118.

WAR DIARY
~~INTELLIGENCE SUMMARY~~

(Erase heading not required.)

4/K Warwickshire Regt

Instructions regarding War Diaries and Intelligence Summaries are contained in F.S. Regs., Part II. and the Staff Manual respectively. Title pages will be prepared in manuscript.

Reference (SHEET 27, 1/40,000.
          (HAZEBROUCK, 5A, 1/100,000.

Place	Date	Hour	Summary of Events and Information	Remarks and references to Appendices
LA KREULE (N.of HAZE-BROUCK)	1st. August.		Preparations for move. Battalion moved at 6 p.m. by route march, and arrived at LA KREULE about 10 p.m., and were accomodated in tents and shelters	
	2nd. August.		Rained hard most of the day. At night the Battalion moved into the Line, relieving 8th. Bn. A.I.F., 2nd. Brigade, in the Right of the STRAZEELE SECTOR. Dispositions:- "W" Coy. in the Right Front Line, "X" Coy. Left Front Line, "Y" Coy. Support, "Z" Coy., Reserve. Enemy artillery active during the night on STRAZEELE, MERRIS and Battery positions. Casualties Nil. A dark night, and with the rain, it made the relief very difficult. Rear Battalion H.Q., Q.M. Stores and Transport Lines were camped on the Northern edge of HAZEBROUCK. 10% Details near WEKE MEULIN. Neucleus to the Reception Camp at EBBLINGHEM.	
FRONT LINE, STRAZEELE SECTOR.	3rd. August.		The relief not complete until 4 a.m. Not much rain during the morning, but the ground did not dry much. Showery in the afternoon and evening. Enemy quite quiet until about 10 p.m. when both artilleries were very active, giving harassing and counter-battery fire. "Y" Coy. commenced wiring their front. The two front Coys. Improved their posts, and started connecting them up. Fields of fire cleared and hedges thinned. "Z" Coy. carried forward R.E. material to "X" Coy. 2/Lt. W.G.A. Collins of "Z" Coy. wounded by M.G. fire.	
	4th. August.		Enemy artillery kept up a fairly steady harassing fire on Battery positions and back areas, forward he remained quiet. Weather was fine all day. "X" Coy. (Left Front Line) connected up their posts by traversed trench and continued wiring their front. "W" (Right Front Line) thinned hedges, connected their posts by traversed trench and wired their front. "Y" continued wiring their front - one party of about 40 carried rations to "W" and worked on their front wiring. "Z" Coy. had 40 men carrying rations to "X", and remained and dug a traversed trench connecting up the two left posts. Also R.E. material was carried up.	

Army Form C. 2118.

WAR DIARY
or
INTELLIGENCE SUMMARY
(Erase heading not required.)

Instructions regarding War Diaries and Intelligence Summaries are contained in F.S. Regs., Part II. and the Staff Manual respectively. Title pages will be prepared in manuscript.

Reference (SHEET 27, 1/40,000.
(SHEET 5A, 1/100,000. (HAZEBROUCK).

Place: FRONT LINE, STRAZEELE SECTOR, (MERRIS).

Date	Hour	Summary of Events and Information	Remarks and references to Appendices
5th. August.		Enemy artillery very lively about 2 a.m., to which all our artillery vigorously replied. Front Line Companies worked wiring and connecting front line posts. 2nd. Lieut. E.J.T. Cocks was killed and 2 O.R. of "X" Coy. wounded in an encounter with an enemy patrol in No Man's Land. During the evening rain fell very heavily making the condition of the ground very difficult for carrying parties. 2nd. Lieut. T. Bruton, MM, rejoined from leave and joined "W" Coy., relieving 2nd. Lieut. T.L. Gillespie.	
6th. August.		Rain continued till about 3.30 a.m., weather clearing up later, but continued again in the evening. An inter-company relief took place, "Y" Coy. moving into Right Front Line, "Z" Coy. Left Front Line, "W" Coy. in Support, "X" Coy. in Reserve. "Z" Coy. had 6 casualties, all wounded by shell. Work was continued, but was much hampered by the weather. Patrols were sent out with no results.	
7th. August.		About 6 a.m., the enemy, about 30 strong, attempted to rush our extreme right post (Y Coy) and the left post of the 1st. R. Dublin Fusiliers under cover of a very heavy mist. They were driven off before reaching our posts. The Divisional Commander visited Battalion H.Q. during the morning. A considerable amount of wiring and connecting up of trenches was done in the front line. Wiring was also continued on the intermediate line. (Support Coy. "W"). Reserve Company worked in the Support Line. Enemy on the whole very quiet. Our artillery did a considerable amount of harassing fire, throughout the day and night.	
8th. August.		Enemy artillery fairly lively on Battery areas, and in evening put down quite a barrage on Right Front Coy. During the afternoon Capt. C. Hackett, M.C., DCM, 2nd. Lieut. S.J. Rye, M.C. and six O.R. captured 13 prisoners and a Machine Gun from a post about 400 yards to their front. Lieut. C.G. Sneade, 2nd. Lieut. W. Pamment and a small spot captured near the same spot as above 1 Officer and 1 man. The barrage mentioned above was inretaliation.	

Army Form C. 2118.

WAR DIARY

Instructions regarding War Diaries and Intelligence Summaries are contained in F. S. Regs., Part II and the Staff Manual respectively. Title pages will be prepared in manuscript.

Place	Date	Hour	Summary of Events and Information	Remarks and references to Appendices
	9th. August.		Enemy artillery fairly active. A light field gun shelled our trenches and approaches during the early hours of the morning. Sgt. Lillis (Z Coy) was killed. Quiet during the day. 2nd. Hampshire Regt. relieved the Battalion in the Right Subsection of the Brigade Front. The Battalion moved back into Support to the Brigade, around STRAZEELE and in the Support Line. Lieut. G.T. Uren wounded by a bullet in the arm during the morning.	Reference Sheet 27 1/40,000 Hazebrouck 5A. 1/100,000
	10th. August.		Relief complete at 11.10 p.m. Present dispositions "W" Coy. Left of STRAZEELE, in Pouge Croix Switch, "X" Coy. in the Support Line, "Y" Coy. Right of STRAZEELE Avenue, "Z" Coy. STRAZEELE Defences. Bn. H.Q. PRADELLES. Quiet during the day. The Support Line ("X" Coy) was heavily shelled about 11p.m. and retaliation asked for.	
	11th. August.		A quiet day. A little shelling of back areas by enemy mostly 5.9s. A few of these were fired into PRADELLES. "X" Coy. found a small working party by day, and all Coys. worked by night under R.E. supervision, on the new Support Line. A party of 1 Officer,(2nd. Lieut. S.J. Rye MC) and 7 O.R. represented the Battalion at a Second Army Special Church Parade at which His Majesty the King attended. 2nd. Hampshire Regt. advanced their line slightly in front of MERRIS.	
	12th. August.		Enemy artillery carried out the usual harassing fire on back areas. "X" Coy found by day a similar party to yesterday for digging in the new Support Line. "W", "X", XXX and "Z", "Y" Coy. were relieved in their position in STRAZEELE Field Coy., R.E.) parties by night under R.E. supervion (427th. Kent Avenue by a Company of the 2nd. R. Fusiliers and moved NORTH of the Village n into the COURT CROIX SWITCH. Move completed by 10.30 p.m., and the day was hot and fine.	
	13th. August.		Enemy artillery normal. Working parties as usual including "Y" Coy. Weather fine.	

Army Form C. 2118.

- 4 -

WAR DIARY
or
INTELLIGENCE SUMMARY

(Erase heading not required.)

Instructions regarding War Diaries and Intelligence Summaries are contained in F.S. Regs., Part II. and the Staff Manual respectively. Title pages will be prepared in manuscript.

Reference { Sheet 27. 1/40,000.
            { HAZEBROUCK, 5A, 1/100,000.

Place	Date	Hour	Summary of Events and Information	Remarks and references to Appendices
IN CAMP NEAR LA KREULE (N. of HAZE-BROUCK).	14th August.		Enemy artillery fairly quiet. No day working party. Weather very hot. 88th. Infantry Brigade were relieved by 87th. Infantry Brigade, 1st. Border Regt. relieving the Battalion. Relief completed about 12.45 a.m.	
	15th August.		In Camp near LA KREULE, N. of HAZEBROUCK. Brigade in reserve to the Division. General cleaning up and inspection. Major Reilly returned to 2nd. Hampshire Regiment. Lieut. Col. B.C.S. Clarke, DSO, resumed command. The 29th. Divisional Diamond Troupe are performing nightly in the barn opposite the H.Q. Mess.	
	16th August.		Companies at the disposal of O.C. Companies for inspection and drill. A cricket match was played in the evening, Officers v Sergeants, which resulted in a win for the Sergeants.	
	17th August.		Companies at the disposal of O.C. Coys. "Y" Coy. moved up into STRAZEELE Defences and came under command of O.C. 2nd. Hampshire Regt., to support a minor operation the 87th. Inf. Bde. were carrying out with the 9th. Divn. "X" Coy. went up to the Support Line on a carrying party at night.	
IN SUPPORT NEAR STRAZEELE.	18th August.		(In Divisional Reserve near LA KREULE, N of HAZEBROUCK, with "Y" Coy. in the STRAZEELE Defences under the Command of O.C. 2nd. Hampshire Regt.). "W" and "Z" Coys. attended Church Parade on the Diamond Troupe Barn. The Drums took part in a Brigade Massed Drum Practice, and in the afternoon played Retreat at the camp of the 12th. N. Staffordshire Regt. (Lt. Col. Kitching) near STAPLE. At 11.0 a.m. the attack of the 9th. Divn. and 87th. Brigade commenced. All objectives were taken with slight casualties. (The OUTTERSTEENE RIDGE). Over 600 prisoners were captured. At 6 p.m. the remaining 3 companies of the Battalion moved up into the "Z" Line (old support line) relieving the 2nd. Hampshire Regt., who moved forward, having 2 companies in the Front Line. "Y" Coy. reverted to the command of O.C. 4th. Worcestershires (Capt. R.H. Marryatt). "Z" Coy. was detailed for a carrying party, and carried R.E. material and S.A.A. etc. forward to the 87th. Brigade. 10 Officers, 349 O.R. unwounded, and 41 O.R. wounded, making a total of	

WAR DIARY
INTELLIGENCE SUMMARY

(Erase heading not required.)

Reference Sheet HAZEBROUCK 5A, 1/100,000.

Place	Date	Hour	Summary of Events and Information	Remarks and references to Appendices
IN LINE "Z"	18th. Aug.	(Co.) O.R.	400 prisoners were taken by the Division alone. About 8 Officers and 227 unwounded were taken by the 9th. Divn.	
IN STRAZEELE DEFENCES & "Z" LINE	19th. August.		Enemy artillery fairly active, particularly to the NORTH. Our artillery replied to a S.O.S. call about 11 a.m. At 5 p.m. the 86th. Brigade with 31st Divn. took part in a minor operation with complete success. All objectives taken, and advancing the line beyond LABIS FARM. 1 Officer per Coy. and 1 N.C.O. per platoon sent forward about midnight to reconnoitre the sector held by the 2nd. S.W. Borderers with a view to relieving them on the night 20/21st.	
	20th. August.		Weather cloudy, enemy artillery very active, firing on forward and back areas including STRAZEELE. Also Enemy Aircraft very busy during the day, several low-flying planes coming over our lines. Moved up into the Front Line and relieved 2nd. S.W. Bs. in Right Sub-section of the Brigade front. (Left Sector of the Division). "W" Coy. Right Front Line, "X" Coy. Left Front Line, "Z" Coy. Close Support, "Y" Coy. Reserve. Relief complete 1 a.m. 21st. Enemy M.Gs. active about 11 p.m. sweeping road through OUTTERSTEENE village. Major J.R. Frend, D.S.O., 2nd. Leinster Regt., took over command of the Battalion. Draft of 6 O.R. joined Battalion.	
IN FRONT LINE OUTTERSTEENE.	21st. August.		A heavy barrage was going on from about 1 a.m. to 2 a.m. well to the NORTH, presumably LOCRE. Relief complete of S.W.Bs. at 1 a.m. Enemy quiet. Weather hot, bright sunshine. MERRIS shelled at intervals. During the day and night the two support Coys. were shelled heavily every two hours. Our heavies retaliated each time. Battalion H.Q. moved forward to hopfield, N. of MERRIS F.1.b.3.8. "Y" Coy. sent one platoon to work on Battalion H.Q., the remainder of the Coy. working on their own front line. "Z" worked with "X" connecting posts, "W" also worked connecting posts. Both forward Coys. "W" and "X", had patrols out, the former under Lieut. G.S. Kipps who found no enemy within 600 yards of their line. "X" established a post at KISMET HOUSE, F.9.b.1.4. E.A. busy during the day. Enemy apparently withdrawing;further SOUTH he has gone back behind MERVILLE.	

Army Form C. 2118.

WAR DIARY
or
INTELLIGENCE SUMMARY

(Erase heading not required.)

Reference SHEET HAZEBROUCK, X 5A, 1/100,000.

Place	Date	Hour	Summary of Events and Information	Remarks and references to Appendices
FRONT LINE. OUTTERSTEENE.	22nd. August.		A heavy barrage was put down by the enemy on the Support Coys. about 2 a.m. and 4 a.m., also on MERRIS. One stray shell fell direct on "W" Coy's H.Q. killing outright Lieut. G.S. Kipps, Cr. Sgt. Andrews, Cpl. Green, Ptes. Dixey and Towler, wounding 2/Lt. G.W. Wright and Pte. Thomas, and shaking 5 more. Throughout the day the enemy artillery was very active, intermittently shelling the Support Coys. Our artillery replied on to their Batteries. L/Sgt. Surman and Cpl. Cook were awarded a Bar to the M.M., Sgt. Lawley, Pte. Phipps, Pte. Johnson,& Pte. Marsh the M.M., all of "W" Coy. for their exploits on 8th. August. The usual working parties were found by Coys. for digging, connecting posts and work on Battalion H.Q. Lieut. E.R. Newcomb, 1 N.C.O. and 3 men went on a daylight patrol and made a good reconnaissance along the South side of the Railway. Enemy artillery still active at night. Lieut. Colonel Tudor Fitzjohn, D.S.O. joined Battalion at the Transport Lines.	
	23rd. August.		The usual early morning artillery strafes were carried out by the enemy to which our Batteries replied. During the day our artillery were far more active and the enemy much quieter, but from 9 p.m. onwards, especially between 11 p.m. and midnight, the enemy artillery was very active, and sent over some Mustard Gas on the Support Coy's area. Capt. R.H. Marryatt and 2/Lt. J.L.P. Talbot returned to the Transport Lines prior to going on leave, leaving only 13 officers in the line, including Major. J.R. Frend, D.S.O. The 2nd. Hampshire Regt. relieved the 2nd. Leinster Regt on our left.	
	24th. August.		Normal morning. During the afternoon and night the enemy put over a lot of gas, using mustard, phyosgyene and lachrymatory, several men of "X", "Y" and "Z" Coys.were sent to the M.O. in consequence. At one time 8 enemy balloons were up on the Corps Front, in spite of the fact that during the day 7 enemy balloons were brought down. One of our airmen was seen to be brought down by A.A. fire in the enemy's lines. Weather remaining hot and dry.	

WAR DIARY
INTELLIGENCE SUMMARY

Army Form C. 2118.

Reference Sheet HAZEBROUCK, S.A., 1/100,000.

Place	Date	Hour	Summary of Events and Information	Remarks and references to Appendices
IN FRONT LINE, OUTTERSTEENE.	25th. August.		Very heavy dew and the mist hung about until nearly 9 a.m. The enemy sent over a lot of gas during the day in the Support Areas causing a lot of casualties. Major J.R. Frend, DSO, left the Battalion and Lieut. Colonel Tudor Fitzjohn, D.S.O. assumed command. Rained hard during the night. An Officers' reconnoitring party of 1st. Border Regt. visited the Battalion prior to relieving us. All Companies worked on the front line, deepening trenches, cutting fire-steps, and connecting up KISMET Post. A little wire was also erected. A re-distribution of troops took place, "Z" Coy. and 2 platoons of "Y" Coy. held the front line, 2 Platoons of "Y" Coy. in close support, "X" Coy. in the old British Front Line SOUTH of MERRIS, "W" Coy. moved back to the COURTE CROIX SWITCH. Lieut. Colonel Tudor Fitzjohn, D.S.O. took over command of the Battalion vice Lieut. Colonel B.C.S. Clarke, D.S.O. to the U.K.	
	26th. August.		Wet and damp morning, quiet during the day. 1st. Border Regt. relieved the Battalion in the Right Sector of the Brigade front. Relief completed by 11.30 p.m. The Battalion moved back to camp near LA KREULE (Diamond Troupe Camp). A draft of 21 O.R. joined the Battalion.	
IN CAMP NEAR LA KREULE, N. of HAZEBROUCK.	27th. August.		A general cleaning up was carried out by Companies, and inspection. Deficiencies were made up.	
	28th. August.		Companies at the disposal of O.C. Companies for Platoon Training. All Companies bathed at 29th. Division Baths, LA KREULE, and were issued with a clean suit of underclothing. Armourer Sergt. from Division inspected the rifles and Lewis Guns of "W" and "Z" Coys. Brigade Gas N.C.O. inspected the whole of the Battalion Small Box Respirators. Captain C. Hackett, M.C., D.C.M. and 2nd Lieut. S.J. Rye, M.C., received a Bar to their M.C., and Lieut. C.G. Sneade a M.C. for their exploits on 8th. August.	

WAR DIARY
or
INTELLIGENCE SUMMARY.
(Erase heading not required.)

Army Form C. 2118.

Reference Sheet HAZEBROUCK, &, 1/100,000.

Place	Date	Hour	Summary of Events and Information	Remarks and references to Appendices
NORTH OF HAZEBROUCK.	29th. August.		Companies at the disposal of O.C. Companies for Platoon Training from 9 a.m. to 12 noon, and 2 p.m. to 3 p.m. L.G.Class of 6 O.R. per Coy. commenced under Lieut. H.F. Boddington. Lieut. L. Walker joined for duty.	
	30th. August.		Companies at the disposal of O.C. Companies for Platoon Training from 9 a.m. to 12 noon and 2 p.m. to 3 p.m. Lewis Gun Class continued. All Signallers paraded under Sgt. Sheasby from 9 a.m. to 12 noon, and 2 p.m. to 3 p.m. All Platoon Commanders attended a Lecture by the Brigade Major on Map Reading and use of Compasses.	
IN CAMP NEAR LA KREULE,	31st. August.		Companies at the disposal of O.C. Companies for Platoon Training from 9 a.m. to 12 noon. Lewis Gun and Signalling Classes continued. Orders received at 12.45 p.m. that the Battalion was to be prepared to embuss at 7 p.m. to BAILLEUL to relieve the 31st. Division in the line. These orders were all cancelled at 3.15 p.m. 2/Lieuts. D.L. Townes and R.H. Warren rejoined the Battalion for duty. Final of the Brigade Inter-Coy. Football Competition (commenced at LUMBRES in July) played between "W" and "Y" Coys., 4th. Worcestershire Regiment. Result. Y (long won, I good one)	

Battalion Strength. 31.8.18.

	Officers.	O.R.
Total Strength.	40	875
Ration Strength.	25	703
Trench Strength.	20	554

1.9.18.

[signature] Lieut. Colonel,
Commanding 4th. Bn. The Worcestershire Regiment.

CONFIDENTIAL.

WAR DIARY

of

4th Battalion, The Worcestershire Regiment.

From 1st September To 30th September, 1918.

(VOLUME NO 7).

Army Form C. 2118.

Instructions regarding War Diaries and Intelligence Summaries are contained in F.S. Regs., Part II. and the Staff Manual respectively. Title pages will be prepared in manuscript.

WAR DIARY
or
INTELLIGENCE SUMMARY.
(Erase heading not required.)

REFERENCE SHEET № 28, 1/40,000.
MERRIS, Ed. 2A., LOCAL, 1/20,000.

Place	Date	Hour	Summary of Events and Information	Remarks and references to Appendices
IN ACTION SOUTH WEST OF BAILLEUL.	Sept. 1st.		The Battalion, with remainder of 88th. Infantry Brigade, and "B" Coy. 29th. M.G. Bn. embussed on the HAZEBROUCK - LA KREULE ROAD at 6 a.m. for the SQUARE at BAILLEUL, via CAESTRE, METEREN. Owing to demolition on the road East of METEREN, it was impossible to proceed by bus to BAILLEUL. The Brigade therefore debussed East of METEREN and marched to the Assembly Area on the reverse slope of the REVELSBERG SPUR, arriving there about 10 a.m. The Xth. Corps were at this time on the Western outskirts of NEUVE EGLISE and were pushing forward in the direction of MESSINES. The role of the Brigade was to move forward and fill in any gaps which might occur between the Xth. Corps Right Flank and the 87th. Infantry Brigade Left Flank. At 10.50 a.m. "W" Coy. were sent forward and got in touch with the Inniskillings (109th. Inf. Bde.) on their Left and the 2nd. Borders (87th. Inf. Bde.) on their Right, and endeavoured to move forward in conjunction with these troops on their flanks. They succeeded in getting as far as GOUGH HOUSE (S.30.a.2.5.) where they met with M.G. fire from their Right. The troops on the Right were also held up by M.G. fire. At 12.20 p.m. "X" Coy. were sent forward to support "W" Coy. 1 section of 18 pounders and 1 section of 4.5 howitzers got into position at COMMET CAMP (S.29.a.4.5.) the officer in charge getting into touch with O.C. "W" Coy. and doing useful work. "Y" Coy. and "Z" Coy. moved forward at 1.30 p.m. and 1.45 p.m. respectively, taking up positions in the Valley about S.29.a.&.c. Battalion H.Q. moved up at 2 p.m. and was established at COMMET CAMP (S.29.a.4.5.) A very large mine went up at about 5.30 p.m. near DE SEULE CROSS ROADS. At about 6.30 p.m. the Brigade on our Right captured STEENWERKE and LA CRECHE capturing 11 prisoners. 2 escaped French and 1 escaped Italian prisoners were also captured, and gave the information that the enemy were only holding on with M.Gs. at 500 yds. distance, with no support this side of ARMENTIERES. Capt. C. Hackett M.C., D.C.M., Wounded. 2nd. Lieut. T. Bruton, M.M. Killed. C.S.M. G.C. Key Wounded. At dusk our line was again advanced to a line running from about S.24.d.8.2. to S.30.d.0.5. Owing to resistance from M.Gs. we could get no further.	

Army Form C. 2118.

WAR DIARY
or
INTELLIGENCE SUMMARY.
(Erase heading not required.)

Instructions regarding War Diaries and Intelligence Summaries are contained in F.S. Regs., Part II. and the Staff Manual respectively. Title pages will be prepared in manuscript.

REFERENCE SHEET 28 S.W., 1/20,000.

Place	Date	Hour	Summary of Events and Information	Remarks and references to Appendices
26.	Sept. 2nd.		At about 1 a.m. our line was again advanced, but met with considerable resistance from M.Gs. from ENGLISH and EMPIRE LINES. The following line was taken up before dawn. T.28.d.5.3. to T.20.c.4.2. At dawn another attempt was made to get further forward, but owing to heavy M.G. fire from ENGLISH and EMPIRE Lines, the advance was held up. At 3 p.m. we advanced our line, under artillery support, to a line running from T.20.b.8.8. to T.26.b.7.5. In this advance we captured 7 M.Gs. and 7 prisoners. 20 German dead were also counted. At 6 p.m. another artillery barrage our line was advanced to a line from T.21.a.3.8. to T.27.a.6.4. Again a considerable number of enemy dead were counted. 2/Lt. V.C. Cornish Wd.	
	Sept. 3rd.		At 3 a.m. the final objective was reached without any further opposition. The final objective being the old G.H.Q. Line from T.22.a.3.8. The Divisional and Brigade Commanders congratulated the Battalion on its good work in reaching this line. Up to this time the 2nd. Hampshires and the 2nd. Leinsters were in Brigade Reserve. At 3 p.m. the 2nd. Hampshires moved forward to the G.H.Q. Line, preparatory to making an attempt to push forward to road from T.23.b.85.15 to T.17.b.1.8. At 5 p.m. the 2nd. Hampshires, under artillery support, advanced to line running T.17.b.1.9. down road to T.23.b.8.1. 2nd. Lieut. D.L. Downes Wounded. At midnight the 2nd. Leinsters moved forward from Brigade Reserve to a position of assembly just in front of the G.H.Q. line.	
	Sept. 4th.		At 8 a.m. the 2nd. Hampshires and 2nd. Leinsters, under artillery support, attacked on a 2000 yard front. The first objective was taken by 11 a.m. 2nd. objective not taken owing to strong enemy resistance. Line now runs U.13.d.5.2. - U.16.d.60.40. thence along trench in U.13.d.&.b. to road, thence along trench from U.13.a.85.85 along trench to U.12.c.85.85. Over 100 prisoners taken, many M.Gs. and some Trench Mortars also captured. At 1.15 p.m. Brigade H.Q. notified us that Companies were to be ready to move at short notice, as the 2nd. Leinsters had reported the enemy massing for a counter-attack. At 1.30 p.m. 2 Companies moved forward and reinforced the 2nd. Leinsters and 2nd. Hampshires (who had suffered fairly heavy casualties) At about 2.30 p.m. the enemy counter-attacked but did not succeed in penetrating	

IN ACTION WEST OF BAILLEUL.

WAR DIARY or INTELLIGENCE SUMMARY

Army Form C. 2118.

REFERENCE SHEET HAZEBROUCK 5A, 1/100,000.
Reference Sheet 28, 1/40,000.

Place	Date	Hour	Summary of Events and Information	Remarks and references to Appendices
	Sept. 4th. (cont).		our lines, except on the extreme left, where he entered the trench and was taken prisoner. At 6 p.m. "Y" Coy. moved up into support to the 2nd. Leinsters. Enemy shelled fairly heavily on front line, G.H.Q. line and approaches to front line during the night. 3 enemy observation balloons brought down in flames. 1 British aeroplane brought down, falling just behind the old G.H.Q. line, both the pilot and observer being wounded.	
	Sept. 5th.		No further attempt was made to advance our line. The Brigade was relieved by 94th. Inf. Bde., 31st. Divn. This Battalion being relieved by 2 Coys. 24th R.W.F. and 1 Coy. K.O.R.R. After relief the Battalion stayed the night in fields near COMMET CAMP (S.29.a.4.5.) where the men had a hot meal.	
	Sept. 6th.		At 5 a.m. the Battalion moved off by Companies at 5 minutes interval to a Camp South West of BAILLEUL, arriving there about 7 a.m. All ranks resting.	
IN CAMP SOUTH WEST OF BAILLEUL.	Sept. 7th.		Kit, S.A.A., S.B. Respirators and Battle Stores inspections, and general cleaning up. A very heavy thunderstorm at about 3.30 p.m., which resulted in a number of tents being blown down.	
	Sept. 8th.		Another very dull and wet day. Baths allotted to Companies. Church Parade for two Coys. held in the open.	
	Sept. 9th.		Companies at the disposal of O.C. Companies for Platoon Training and anti-gas drill. Another very wet and windy day. Lewis Gun Class continued under Lieut. H.F. Boddington. Draft of 17 O.R. joined the Battalion.	
	Sept. 10th.		The Brigade Armourer Sergeant inspected all rifles and Lewis Guns of the Battalion. The Brigade P.T. & B.F. Instructor visited the Battalion, and took each Coy. for one hour at a time. 16 Rifle Grenadiers per Coy. parade under 2nd. Lieut. J.C. Marriott for instruction in the use of the No. 36 Rifle Grenade and Discharger. The remainder of the parade hours Coys. were at the disposal of O.C. Companies. Lewis Gun Class continued.	

Army Form C. 2118.

WAR DIARY
or
INTELLIGENCE SUMMARY.
(Erase heading not required.)

Place	Date	Hour	Summary of Events and Information	Remarks and references to Appendices
	Sept. 10th. (Cont).		Warning order received to be prepared to move to HAZEBROUCK Area on 11th. inst.	
	Sept. 11th.		Advance party of Lieut. H.F. Boddington, 4 C.Q.M.S. & 1 N.C.O. for H.Q. proceeded on bicycles to HAZEBROUCK where they met the Staff Captain. At 2.15 p.m. the Battalion paraded, and proceeded by march route to HAZEBROUCK, a distance of about 10 miles, arriving in the new area about 6 p.m. Heavy rain during the morning, but cleared up about 12.30 p.m. Themen were billeted in an evacuated hospital. Lieut. H.N. Newey, 2nd. Lieuts. E.A. Wood and J. Hipkiss joined the Battalion for duty, also draft of 22 O.R.	REFERENCE SHEET HAZEBROUCK 5A, 1/100,000. 36 A., 1/40,000. 27, 1/40,000.
HAZEBROUCK.	Sept. 12th.		Companies at the disposal of O.C. Companies for Platoon Training from 9 a.m. to 12 noon, and from 2 p.m. to 5 p.m. Lewis Gun and Rifle Grenade Classes continued. A very wet day.	
IN BILLETS,	Sept. 13th.		Companies at the disposal of O.C. Companies for Platoon Training from 9 a.m. to 12 noon and from 2 p.m. to 5 p.m. Lewis Gun Class continued. All X Company and 5 H.Q. Runners Instructed in Map Reading.	
	Sept. 14th.		Companies at the disposal of O.C. Companies for Platoon Training on Training Area from 9 a.m. to 12 noon and from 2 p.m. to 5 p.m. Lewis Gun and Runners Classes continued. All Rifle Grenadiers of "W" Coy. instructed in firing No. 36 Rifle Grenades from 2 – 4 p.m. All Signallers training from 2 – 4 p.m. No. 42121 Pte. H. Morris awarded the M.M. Draft of 14 O.R. joined the Battalion	
	Sept. 15th.		Divine Service held in the Hospital Theatre. Non-Conformists and Roman Catholics also had a service. Very fine day.	
	Sept. 16th.		Baths allotted to Companies as follows: "W" Coy. 8 – 9.30 a.m., "X" Coy. 9.30 – 11.0 a.m., "Y" Coy. 11.0 a.m. to 12.30 p.m., "Z" Coy. 12.30 p.m. to 2 p.m. Remainder of the day, Companies were at the disposal of O.C. Coys. for Platoon Training. All Classes continued. All C.S.Ms. and Platoon Sergeants instructed in Map Reading and use of the Compass. Diamond Troupe performing nightly in the Cinema Hall.	

Army Form C. 2118.

WAR DIARY
or
INTELLIGENCE SUMMARY

(Erase heading not required.)

REFERENCE:- Sheet HAZEBROUCK, 5A, 1/100,000. Sheet 27, 1/40,000.

Place	Date	Hour	Summary of Events and Information	Remarks and references to Appendices
IN BILLETS AT HAZEBROUCK.	Sept. 17th.		Companies at the disposal of O.C. Coys. from 9 a.m. to 10.30 a.m. for Platoon Training on the Training Area. At 10.30 a.m. the Battalion assembled and did a small scheme, practicing advancing under a barrage, re-organising, and advancing with advance guard. Classes continued in the afternoon. 2nd. Lieut. D.L. Downes rejoined Battalion. Draft of 58 O.R. joined Battalion.	
	Sept. 18th.		Companies at the disposal of O.C. Companies for Platoon Training on the Training Area from 9 a.m. to 12 noon, and from 2 p.m. to 3 p.m. Classes continued.	
	Sept. 19th.		Training as on previous day.	
	Sept. 20th.		Battalion carried out a scheme practising following up the retreating enemy, and pushing back his rear-guards. A successful morning. Commanding Officer proceeded with the Brigadier, O.C. 2nd. Hants, and O.C. 2nd. Leinsters by car, and reconnoitred the new area.	
	Sept. 21st.		Companies at the disposal of O.C. Coys. for final inspections, and preparations for the move. At 6.30 p.m. the Battalion (less transport) paraded and proceeded by march route to HONDEGHEM STATION (Metre Guage) where it entrained (H.Q., "Z", and 3 platoons "Y" Coy. on the first train leaving at 7.45 p.m. One platoon "Y", "W" and "X" Coys. on the second train leaving at 8.15 p.m.). The Battalion detrained at ST. JAN TER BIEZEN and marched to ROAD CAMP. Bn. all in Camp by 11.30 p.m. The Transport moved by road, arriving in Camp at 1.15 a.m. 22nd. inst. The Division transferred to IInd. Corps.	
IN CAMP AT ST. JAN TER BIEZEN.	Sept. 22nd.		Divine Service held in the Y.M.C.A. Hut at 10 a.m., after which Coys. were at the disposal of O.C. Coys. for Route Marches and Physical Games. The Corps Commander (IInd. Corps) Lieut. General Sir Claud Jacob, K.C.B. visited the Battalion and met all the Commanding Officers, Seconds in Command, and Adjutants and Company Commanders of the Brigade. The Commanding Officer, Adjutant, Intelligence Officer, and the 4 Coy. Commanders reconnoitred the front line.	

Army Form C. 2118.

WAR DIARY
or
INTELLIGENCE SUMMARY.
(Erase heading not required.)

Place	Date	Hour	Summary of Events and Information	Remarks and references to Appendices
ST. JAN TER BIEZEN. IN CAMP AT	Sept. 23rd.		Companies at the disposal of O.C. Coys. for Physical Games and Route Marches. The Adjutant and 4 Coy. Commanders again reconnoitred the Front line preparatory to taking over, from the 86th. and 87th. Infantry Brigades.	
	Sept. 24th.	11 a.m.	Baths allotted to Companies as follows:- "X" 8. - 9.30 a.m., "Y" 9.30 - 11 a.m., "Z" 11 - 12 noon, "W" 1 - 1.30 p.m., "HQ" 1.30 - 2.0 p.m. Remainder of the day Companies at the disposal of O.C. Coys. for Route Marches and Physical Games. 1 Officer, 1 Sgt. and 1 runner per Coy., Signalling Officer and 2 signallers left Brigade H.Q. at 11.30 a.m. by lorry and were conveyed forward as advance party for the relief. At 6.15 p.m. the Battalion paraded and proceeded by march route to LANCASTER SIDING, thence to GODRICH SIDING, YPRES, by metre guage railway. This Battalion relieved the 1st. K.O.S.B. and 1st Coys. 1st. Lancs. Fus. in the ZILLEBEKE Sector. The 9th. Division being on our Right. Disposition of Companies :-	
			Front Line (Right). "X" Coy.	
			--do-- (Centre). "Y" Coy.	
			--do-- (Left). "Z" Coy.	
			Support Line. "W" Coy.	
			Battalion H.Q. in the RAMPARTS of YPRES (I.14.b.2.8.). 2nd. Leinsters in Brigade Support, 2nd. Hampshires in Brigade Reserve. A quiet and rapid relief. Relief complete by 2.30 p.m. 25th. inst.	
ZILLEBEKE SECTOR. IN FRONT LINE.	Sept. 25th.		Heavy rain storms commencing at about 4 a.m., and lasting till 10 a.m., after which it cleared up a little. An exceptionally quiet morning. At 3.30 p.m. a daylight patrol of Sgt. Jones and 2 men left our Right Front Line Post and proceeded in an Easterly direction to a Pill Box at I.22.b.8.2. where they saw signs of enemy occupation. One revolver round was fired into the Pill Box, the enemy fired back. Another round was then fired by the patrol, whereupon 6 of the enemy emerged from the Pill Box and were captured. Again at 4 p.m. another daylight patrol under 2nd. Lieut. R.H.Warren, M.M. with 2 men proceeded to the same Pill Box and captured 9 more enemy and a M.G., making a total of 15 in all belonging to the 28th. Bav. Regt. Front Line posts improved, and shelters cleaned and repaired. A little gas shelling on ZILLEBEKE LANE during the night.	

REFERENCE HAZEBROUCK 5A, 1/100,000.
SHEET 28 N.W. 4., 1/20,000.

Army Form C. 2118.

WAR DIARY
or
INTELLIGENCE SUMMARY.
(Erase heading not required.)

REFERENCE SHEET, HAZEBROUCK, 5A, 1/100,000.
SHEET, 28, N.W. 4., 1/20,000.

Place	Date	Hour	Summary of Events and Information	Remarks and references to Appendices
IN SUPPORT, BOBSTAY CASTLE (YPRES). IN LINE ZILLEBEKE SECTOR.	Sept. 26th		Just before dawn the enemy fired two M.Gs. on a party carrying breakfasts, to the Front Line P.sts. At 6 a.m. two enemy were observed advancing to our Right Post. These two were immediately fired at, one being observed to fall, the other surrendering. He belonged to Corps Troops, and was advancing with his listening set, as during the past 14 days he had been unable to intercept any of our messages. A quiet day. The Battalion was relieved by the 2nd. S.W.Bs. and 1 Coy. 1st. Lancs. Fus. Relief complete by 1 a.m. After relief the Battalion moved back to BOBSTAY CASTLE (H.12.a. & C.). Notification received that the undermentioned had been awarded the M.M. for operations East of BAILLEUL from 1st. to 5th. Sept. 1918. 15321 Sgt. A. Bright. 41788 Sgt. H. Carpenter. 26087 Sgt. C. Hands. 42549 L/C. C. Westcott. 53164 L/C. J. Young. 36097 Pte. J. Field. 20229 Pte. W. Goode. 15809 Pte. W. Griffiths. 42480 Pte. W. Humphries. 23678 Pte. E. Pipe. 42095 Pte. E. Workman.	

Instructions regarding War Diaries and Intelligence Summaries are contained in F.S. Regs., Part II. and the Staff Manual respectively. Title pages will be prepared in manuscript.

Army Form C. 2118.

WAR DIARY
or
INTELLIGENCE SUMMARY.
(Erase heading not required.)

Instructions regarding War Diaries and Intelligence Summaries are contained in F. S. Regs., Part II. and the Staff Manual respectively. Title pages will be prepared in manuscript.

REFERENCE SHEET: 28, 1/40,000.
N.W. 4., 1/20,000.

Place	Date	Hour	Summary of Events and Information	Remarks and references to Appendices
EAST OF YPRES.	27th. Sept.		All ranks rested as much as possible. Battle stores, flares etc., issued. Hot soup issued at 7 p.m. At 9 p.m. the Battalion moved off as from BOBSTAY CASTLE to positions of assembly in the YPRES DEFENCES (East of YPRES) preparatory to attacking in the early morning of the 28th. inst. Pack mule train moved to GOLDFISH CHATEAU in the evening.	
BOBSTAY CASTLE. from YPRES, along MENIN ROAD.	28th. Sept.		Hot tea sent up to assembly trench at 4 a.m., in food containers, in order that every man should have a hot drink before "jumping off". At ZERO Hour (5.30 a.m.) the 29th. Division in conjunction with the Belgians and the 9th. Division on the Left, and the 35th. Division on the Right, attacked the enemy EAST of YPRES. The 86th. and 87th. Infantry Brigades advancing without much resistance to the TOWER HAMLETS - POLDERHOEK line. This Battalion moved forward from the position of assembly at 6.15 a.m. in the following order. "V", "X", "W", "Z", H.Q. to the position of concentration (STIRLING CASTLE) J.13. central, arriving there about 8.30 a.m. At 9.25 a.m. the Battalion leap-frogged through the 87th. Brigade and advanced down, and on the flanks of the MENIN ROAD, pressing through INVERNESS COPSE, and capturing GHELUVELT, taking a large number of prisoners and field guns. Owing to the heavy artillery not ceasing their fire, and the fact that our flanks were so much exposed, we were unable to advance further than a line running through KRUISEECKE CROSS ROADS. During this attack the 2nd. Hampshires were in Support, and the 2nd. Leinsters in Reserve. At about 2 p.m. the enemy was seen forming up, and it was thought that he was preparing to make a counter attack. He was heavily engaged with rifle and M.G. fire. No counter attack was launched. At dusk the 2nd. Leinsters advanced a short distance through our line, and were then held up by M.G. fire. The 2nd. Hampshires still remained in Support. Lieut. W. Hamer wounded. A very wet day.	
ADVANCE ON GHELUVELT				
AU ROSSIGNOL CABt. (K.31.a.).	29th. Sept.		At dawn this Battalion again attacked under a very slight artillery barrage. In spite of heavy enemy M.G. fire we succeeded in capturing the ridge at AU ROSSIGNOL CABt. (K.31.a.), a very useful piece of ground. A line was then taken up in the valley. During the day many attempts were made to capture the KOELENBERG RIDGE (K.32.a.), but owing to it being very strongly held we met with no success except for capturing 50 or 60 prisoners. At 7 p.m. we again attacked the Ridge, this time under an artillery barrage, but owing to exception-	

Army Form C. 2118.

WAR DIARY
or
INTELLIGENCE SUMMARY.
(Erase heading not required.)

Place	Date	Hour	Summary of Events and Information	Remarks and references to Appendices
AU ROSSIGNOL CABT. (K.31.a.).	29th. Sept. (Cont).		-ally heavy M.G. and rifle fire only a very little ground was gained. The line taken up ran from K.25.c.5.4. to K.31.a.0.8. Another 25 prisoners taken. We suffered rather heavy casualties. Capt. G.P.O. Donovan, M.C. Wounded. Capt. G. Hackett, M.C., D.C.M. Wounded. Lieut. H.N. Newey. Wounded. 2nd. Lieut. J. Cowherd, M.C. Killed. 2nd. Lieut. D.L. Downes, Wounded. 2nd. Lieut. J.C. Marriott, Wounded. The Hampshires and Leinsters still remained in Support and Reserve. Wheeled transport moved up to BOBSTAY CASTLE on afternoon of 29th. Only Battle Stores and Rations brought up, remainder being left at PESELHOEK. A fine morning, but wet remainder of day.	
KOELENBERG RIDGE (K.32 c.2 a.).	30th. Sept.		At dawn the Battalion again pushed forward and took the KOELENBERG RIDGE (K.32.c.and d.) and advanced under heavy M.G. and artillery fire to a line running approximately from Q.4.c.7.0. to Q.4.a.2.1., in front of GHELUWE. Owing to exceedingly heavy Artillery, T.M. and M.G. fire it was impossible to advance further than this. Two Coys. of the 2nd. Leinsters advanced and took up a position on our left, and one Coy. on our Right, during the afternoon. The 2nd. Hampshires took over the line from this Battalion and one Coy. of the 2nd. Leinsters. The Battalion, after relief, moving back to Pill Boxes and shelters on the reverse slope of the KOELENBERG RIDGE. Total casualties from 27th. inst. (approx). 1 Officer killed, 6 wounded, 31 O.R. Killed, 117 wounded, 19 missing, 6 sick. The following message received from Lieut. General Sir Beauvoir de Lisle (Comdg. XVth. Corps) "Well done the 29th. Division. - I knew you would do great things". The Pack Train moved from the School, YPRES, to GHELUVELT. Great coats and mobile reserve of Ammunition also moved up by limber. Latter journey took 15 hours, owing to roads being blocked with traffic and wounded. Roads in very bad condition owing to heavy rain. A very wet day.	

Army Form C. 2118.

- 10 -

WAR DIARY
or
INTELLIGENCE SUMMARY.
(Erase heading not required.)

Place	Date	Hour	Summary of Events and Information	Remarks and references to Appendices

	2nd. Oct. 1918.		Battalion Strength. (Approx.).
			
			        Off. O.R.
			Total. 53 716
			Ration. 19 561
			Trench. 13 391
			
			                     Lieut. Colonel,
			Commanding 4th. Bn. The Worcestershire Regiment.	

Instructions regarding War Diaries and Intelligence Summaries are contained in F.S. Regs., Part II. and the Staff Manual respectively. Title pages will be prepared in manuscript.

SECRET & CONFIDENTIAL.

WAR   DIARY

4th. Battalion The Worcestershire Regiment.

From

1st. October 1918.

To

31st. October 1918.

(VOLUME NO 8)

Army Form C. 2118.

WAR DIARY
or
INTELLIGENCE SUMMARY.
(Erase heading not required.)

Instructions regarding War Diaries and Intelligence Summaries are contained in F. S. Regs., Part II. and the Staff Manual respectively. Title pages will be prepared in manuscript.

Place	Date	Hour	Summary of Events and Information	Remarks and references to Appendices
KEMMELBERG RIDGE. IN SUPPORT	Oct. 1st.		The Battalion remained in position (Support to Brigade) on the KEMMELBERG RIDGE, the 2nd. Hampshire Regiment being in the front line and 2nd. Leinster Regt. in reserve. The line was not advanced during the day. A finer day. Enemy heavily shelled our positions during the afternoon and night, we suffered a few casualties. 2nd. Lieut. A. Pasco wounded.	REFERENCE SHEET 28, 1/40,000.
OUDE KRUISUICK.	Oct. 2nd.		The 2nd. Hampshires, in conjunction with the 41st. Division on the Right, attacked the enemy under an artillery barrage. The 2nd. Hampshires succeeded in taking the village of GHELUVE, capturing a number of prisoners. At 10.30 "Z" Coy. was sent up to support the 2nd. Hampshires and moved into position on their left flank, remaining in that position until relieved by the 87th. Infantry Brigade. This Brigade was relieved by the 87th. Inf. Bde. the Battalion moving back without a relief to camp near OUDE KRUISUICK. The relief was considerably delayed owing to the enemy counter-attacking the Brigade on our right. No ground was, however, lost.	
DIRTY BUCKET CAMP. (Near BRANDHOEK)	Oct. 3rd.		The Battalion moved back to DIRTY BUCKET CAMP, leaving OUDE KRUISUICK at 16.00 and proceeding to BURR CROSS ROADS by march route, where it entrained on a Light Railway at 18.30 for BRAKE CAMP, arriving there about 23.50.	
	Oct. 4th.		Baths allotted to Companies. Men issued with winter underclothing. Jerkins and blankets were also received. Companies at the disposal of O.C. Coys. for cleaning up, inspections, etc.	
YPRES.	Oct. 5th.		Reconnoitring party of C.O., Adjt., and 4 Coy. Commanders proceeded by lorry to reconnoitre the front line on the BROODSEINDE SECTOR. The Battalion was conveyed in lorries from DIRTY BUCKET CAMP to YPRES, arriving at YPRES by 16.30. Lieut. H.S. Smith, Lieut. T.L. Gillespie, and 2nd. Lieut. F.L. Booth awarded the Military Cross. Draft of 44 O.R. joined Battalion.	
IN BILLETS	Oct. 6th.		Companies at the disposal of O.C. Coys. "X", "Y" & "Z" Coys. moved their billets from the Infantry Barracks to shelters and cellars near the STATION. Reconnoitring parties of 1 Officer per Coy. proceeded to Front Line.	

Army Form C. 2118.

WAR DIARY
or
INTELLIGENCE SUMMARY.
(Erase heading not required.)

- 2 -

REFERENCE SHEET 28, 1/40,000.
SHEET 28 N.E., 1/20,000.

Place	Date	Hour	Summary of Events and Information	Remarks and references to Appendices
WESTHOEK. IN CAMP AT	Oct. 7th.		The Battalion moved by march route at 10.00 from YPRES to WESTHOEK, arriving at new area by 12.00, where the Battalion was accomodated in dug-outs and shelters. Reconnoitring parties of 1 officer per Coy. proceeded to Front Line. S.B. Respirators inspected by Divisional Gas Officer.	
	Oct. 8th.		Companies at the disposal of O.C. Coys. for 1 hour's gas drill, handling of arms and lectures. 2nd. Lieut. J. Baxter joined Battalion.	
LEDEGHEM SECTOR. IN FRONT LINE	Oct. 9th.		Companies at the disposal of O.C. Coys. for making preparations for relief. The Battalion paraded at 13.00 and proceeded by march route to concentration area behind KEIBERG RIDGE (T.25.b.) arriving there at 15.00. Here two days' rations were issued and Battalion had tea. At 17.30 the Battalion moved off and proceeded to relieve the 1st. R. Dublin Fusiliers in the line. (LEDEGHEM SECTOR). Relief completed by 23.58. A fairly quiet relief. Dispositions :- "W" Coy. in Front Line on Right. "Y" Coy. ---do--- Left. "X" Coy. in Support. "Z" Coy. in Reserve. Battalion Headquarters situated at L.i.c.10.05.	
	Oct. 10th.		A quiet day. Artillery activity on both sides normal. At dusk the 1st. R. Irish Fusiliers, 36th. Division, (Division on our Right) took over 350 yards of our line on the Right. This Battalion taking over 300 yards of line from the 2nd. Leinsters on the Left. "W" and "Y" Coys. then combining their H.Q. in RAYMOND FARM. Capt. E.P. Bennett, V.C., M.C. joined the Bn. for one month's attachment.	
BECELAERE. IN CAMP	Oct. 11th.		Our artillery put down a barrage on our right just before dawn. The enemy retaliated very heavily along the 9th. Divl., 29th. Divl., and 36th. Divl. fronts. Enemy artillery very active most of the day. The Battalion was relieved by the 1st. K.O.S.B., arriving back in camp at J.12.d.7.8. at about 23.45., and were accomodated in huts and shelters. A very wet night.	

WAR DIARY
or
INTELLIGENCE SUMMARY
(Erase heading not required.)

Army Form C. 2118.

Reference Sheets: Tournai 2, 1/100,000; 28, 1/40,000; 29, N.W. 1/20,000.

Place	Date	Hour	Summary of Events and Information	Remarks and references to Appendices
IN CAMP BECLAERE.	12th. Oct.		Companies at the disposal of O.C. Companies for inspections, Drill and Feet Rubbing. A very wet day. Capt. D.J.F. MacCarthy, Lieut. C.G. Weld, and draft of 41 O.R. joined Battalion.	
	13th. Oct.		The Battalion moved into assembly positions with the remainder of the 29th. Division, South West of LEDEGHEM.	
GENERAL ADVANCE on COURTRAI.	14th. Oct.	05.55	At 05.55 the 29th. Division in conjunction with the 9th. Division and Belgians on our left, and the 36th. Division on our Right attacked the enemy, the final objective being the Railway Line running from COURTRAI to GHENT. The 88th. Infantry Brigade attacked on the right of the Divisional Front, and the 86th. Infantry Brigade on the Left, the 87th. being in Reserve. The 2nd. Leinster Regt. being the assault Battalion, the 4th. Worcestershire Regt. in Support, and the 2nd. Hampshire Regt. in Reserve. The barrage opened at ZERO minus 3 minutes, ZERO being 05.35, and the 2nd. Leinsters attacked, this Battalion moving up closely behind them, and owing to the intensity of the smoke barrage, the majority of the Battalion, including Battalion H.Q. found themselves attacking with the 2nd. Leinsters in the front line. At about 09.00 the first objective was taken by ½ Coy. 2nd. Leinsters and ½ Coy. 4th. Worcesters. At 09.15 Battalion H.Q., Coy. H.Q. of "Z" Coy. and a platoon of "X" Coy. reached the first objective, many prisoners, field guns and M.Gs. being captured. Owing to the obscurity of the situation and the thinness of our line, it was impossible to continue the advance. About an hour later the remainder of the Battalion joined, and a line was established, and an endeavour to move forward made, but this was impossible owing to heavy M.G. resistance and fire from enemy field Guns, with open sights. These were fired at by rifles and Lewis Guns, and at about 13.00 our field guns were in forward positions, and they also continued the fire. At about 15.00 the 2nd. Hampshires leap-frogged through this Battalion and moved forward to a line running from G.8.d.85.20. to G.14.b. central (approx) and were in touch with 86th. Brigade on the Left at G.8.d.85.20 and the 2nd. Inniskillings on Right at G.14.b.8.9. This Battalion moved forward in Support to 2nd. Hampshires. At 16.15, instructions were received to concentrate the Battalion in an area in square G.9.d. for the night, this was done, and Battalion H.Q. were situated	

Army Form C. 2118.

WAR DIARY
or
INTELLIGENCE SUMMARY.
(Erase heading not required.)

- 4 -

Place	Date	Hour	Summary of Events and Information	Remarks and references to Appendices
	14th Oct. (Cont)		In a farm at K.12.c.9.5. (Sheet 28 N.E.). Rations were delivered to Coys. by 20.00.	
			Casualties from Zero Hour:-	
			Lieut. C.G. Snea de, M.C. Killed.	
			2/Lt. J.L.P. Talbot, Died of Wounds.	
			Capt. E.P. Bennett, V.C.; M.C. Wounded.	
			2nd. Lieut. S.J. Rye, M.C. Wounded at duty.	
			Lieut. A.V. Colledge, N.Y.D.(Gas.)	
			11 O.R. Killed.	
			82 " Wounded.	
			28 " Missing.	
			5 " Sick.	
			1 " N.Y.D. (Gas).	
GENERAL ADVANCE ON RIVER LYS.	15th Oct.		At 09.00 the 87th. Infantry Brigade leap-frogged through the 86th. and 88th. Brigades, and attacked under a barrage, with the Railway Line running through G. 18 central as the first objective, and the river LYS as the final objective. The 2nd. Leinsters moved forward in Support to the 87th. Bde. and this Battalion received orders to be ready to leap-frog through the 2nd. Leinsters at short notice.	
			Very shortly after Zero Hour the enemy put down a fairly heavy barrage, including a large proportion of smoke shells. The 87th. Bde. succeeded in making good a line running (approx) from H.9.d.00. to H.14.d.0.0.	
			The Brigade moved forward to farms in the vicinity of G.9., this Battalion being in vicinity of Square G.10.c.	
	16th Oct.		The 87th. Brigade attacked under an artillery barrage at 05.30, in conjunction with troops on our right, and left, and established a line on the River LYS. The 88th. Inf. Bde. relieved the 87th. Inf. Bde. in the afternoon, this Battalion relieving the 1st. Border Regt. in Support, Battalion H.Q. being situated at G.18.a.7.6. and the Companies in farms in squares G. 12., H. 7 & 13. Blankets and rations delivered about 18.00. A large	

Army Form C. 2118.

- 5 -

WAR DIARY
or
INTELLIGENCE SUMMARY.
(Erase heading not required.)

REFERENCE SHEETS :- COURTRAI, 1/100,000.
TOURNAI, 1/100,000.
29 N.W., 1/20,000.

Place	Date	Hour	Summary of Events and Information	Remarks and references to Appendices
	16th. Oct. (Cont).		number of civilians were released on 15th. and 16th. Enemy guns active during the night.	
	17th. Oct.		The enemy launched a counter-attack on the troops of the 9th. Divn., the line of which crossed the LYS in squares H. 16. c. & d. The enemy were repulsed, and suffered heavy casualties. No less than 4 enemy divisions were identified. The enemy's guns were very active all day. The Battalion relieved the 27th. Inf. Bde. (9th. Div) in the line, (CUERNE Sector), relief complete by 20.45. Dispositions :- Headquarters: FARM HOUSE at H.9.b.5.4. "W" Coy. in front line on left. "Z" Coy. --do--- in centre. "Y" Coy. --do--- on right. "X" Coy. in Support. 2nd. Hampshires on our Right, and Belgian Army on our Left. A covering party of 2 officers, and 4 Lewis Guns and teams each from 2nd. Hampshires and 4th. Worcesters, was supplied to cover the withdrawal of troops of the 9th. Divn. from the South Side of the LYS.	
	18th. Oct.		Enemy guns active, especially on CUERNE all day. Battalion H.Q. shelled at intervals during the day.	
	19th. Oct.		Enemy guns aga in very active shelling CUERNE with Gas and H.E. continuously all day. Orders were received for the 88th. Bde. to be relieved by the 86th. Bde. These were, however, cancelled, and orders issued for the Brigade to cross the river LYS during the night, preparatory to an attack in the morning. At 16.00 the 2nd. Hampshires crossed the river LYS in pontoons and established a line along the HERLEBEKE - COURTRAI Road. A little M.G. resistance was experienced. By 18.00 the R.E's had erected one infantry bridge by which the 2nd. Leinsters crossed the LYS. This Battalion	
	20th.Oct.		followed the 2nd. Leinsters across at 02.15 and took up a line along the HERLEBEKE - COURTRAI Road, the 2nd. Hampshires and 2nd. Leinsters having by this time made good the Railway Line.	

ADVANCE ON & CROSSING OF THE LYS.

Army Form C. 2118.

WAR DIARY
or
INTELLIGENCE SUMMARY.

(*Erase heading not required.*)

REFERENCE SHEETS : TOURNAI 1/100,000.
29 N.W. 1/20,000.

Place	Date	Hour	Summary of Events and Information	Remarks and references to Appendices
CROSSING OF RIVER LYS, ADVANCE ON STACEGHEM & ST. LOUIS.	Oct.	20th	At 06.00 an artillery barrage opened, under which this Brigade (with the 86th. in Support and 87th. in Reserve) attacked the enemy in conjunction with 9th. Divn. and 36th. Divn. on our Left, and the 35th. Divn. on our Right, the final objective being a line running from D.9. central and I.35. central. The Brigade attacked with the 2nd. Leinsters on the right, the 2nd. Hampshires on the left, and the 4th. Worcesters in Support. This Battalion advanced with "W" Coy. on the Left, "Z" in the Centre, and "Y" on the Right. "X" Coy., at Zero Hour, mopped up HERLEBEKE, after which they moved up in support to the Battalion. Owing to gaps which occurred in the line during the advance, "Y" and "W" Coys. joined the front line, "Y" Coy. taking STACEGHEM. The line of the ESSCHER Keskuxm Road from I.32. central to I.27.a.0.8. was made good by 09.50. At 12.30 the 9th. Divn. were seen to cross over the Ridge North of ST. LOUIS (I.34.), "X" Coy. was then immediately pushed forward to occupy the ridge from ST. LOUIS to the South. At 14.00, a Company of the 2nd. Hampshires moved up and came on the right of "X" Coy. Owing to heavy M.G. fire it was impossible to push on further. At about 15.00 the 86th. Bde. passed through the 88th. Bde. but were unable to advance the line more than 200 yards. At dusk the 88th. Bde. moved back to billets at STACEGHEM and became Bde. in Reserve, the 87th. Bde. being in Support.	
IN BILLETS AT STACEGHEM.	Oct.	21st	Men rested as much as possible. General cleaning up and inspection of Battle Stores, S.B. respirators etc. Nucleus rejoined the Battalion.	
	Oct.	22nd	Companies at the disposal of O.C. Coys. for cleaning up and inspections Baths allotted to Coys. as follows :- "W" Coy. 11.30 - 12.30. "X" Coy. 13.15 - 14.00. "Y" Coy. 14.00 - 14.45. "Z" Coy. 14.45 - 15.30.	

WAR DIARY
INTELLIGENCE SUMMARY

Army Form C. 2118.

Reference TOURNAI, 1/100,000.

Place	Date	Hour	Summary of Events and Information	Remarks and references to Appendices
IN BILLETS AT STACEGHEM.	Oct. 23rd.		Companies at the disposal of O.C. Companies for training Lewis Gunners, Handling of Arms, Drill etc. Notification received that the undermentioned were awarded the following decorations by the Corps Commander for gallantry and devotion to duty during operations from 28.9.18 to 3.10.18. 40431 Cpl. Taylor G.A. Bar to Military Medal. The Military Medal. 12720 Sgt. J. Coombes. 241761 Pte. Workman A. 202674 Pte. Hurley H. 41080 " Laycock J. 201902 Sgt. Jones C.G. (5/N.Staffs. attd. 203362 " Chancellor F.J. 4/Worc). 202522 " Ballard M. 222213 Pte. Snow. J. 40409 " Mason H. 8955 Cpl. Smith H. 42101 L/C. Kerslake L. 200928 Pte. Bullock B. 1148 " Adey W. (Attd. 88th. Bde. H.C.) 12258 " Downing J. New clothing and boots fitted. The Divisional Commander visited the Battalion.	
	Oct. 24th.		Companies at the disposal of O.C. Companies for training Lewis Gunners, Handling of Arms, Drill and Physical Games. From 09.00 to 12.00 and from 14.00 to 15.30. Transport and Q.M. Stores moved from near HRULE to STACEGHEM.	
	Oct. 25th.		Training as on previous day. Warning Order received that the Brigade would move to MOUSCRON tomorrow, 26th., whence it will move to CROIX (S.W. of ROUBAIX) for a period of rest and training.	
	Oct. 26th.		The Battalion moved by march route from STACEGHEM to NEUVILLE, via COURTRAI, arriving in new area by 12.45.	
NEUVILLE.	Oct. 27th.		The Battalion moved from NEUVILLE to CROIX by march route via TOURCOING and ROUBAIX, marching past the Corps Commander (Lieut. General Sir Beauvoir de Lisle, K.C.B., K.C.M.G., K.C.M.G., A.D.C.) (XV Corps) en route. Arrived in new	

Army Form C. 2118.

WAR DIARY
or
INTELLIGENCE SUMMARY.

(Erase heading not required.)

Reference Sheet TOURNAI, 1/100,000.
36, 1/40,000.

Place	Date	Hour	Summary of Events and Information	Remarks and references to Appendices
IN BILLETS AT CROIX (NEAR ROUBAIX).	Oct. 27th. (Cont).		area by 12.45. The whole Battalion was accomodated in a Factory.	
	Oct. 28th.		The Battalion paraded as strong as possible at 10.00 and marched to parade ground to practise for the Brigade Ceremonial Parade. Companies were at the disposal of O.C. Coys. from 14.00 to 15.00 for steadying drill etc.	
	Oct. 29th.		The whole Battalion worked from 07.00 to 11.00 on the Railway Line.	
	Oct. 30th.		The Battalion paraded at 09.30 for a Practice Brigade Ceremonial Parade. The Brigadier expressed his satisfaction on the turn-out and drill. Lieut. W. Wooldridge joined Bn.	
	Oct. 31st.		Baths were allotted to Companies as follows:- "W" Coy. 08.00 to 09.15. "X" Coy. 09.15 to 10.30. "Y" Coy. 10.30 to 11.45. "Z" Coy. 11.45 to 13.00. All Transport Personnel attended a Lecture by the Corps Horse Adviser. Battalion Strength, 31st. October 1918. Officers. O.R. Battalion Strength. 29 616. Ration Strength. 18 478. Trench Strength. 14 313.	
	1st. Nov. 1918.		Major, Commanding 4th. Bn. The Worcestershire Regt.	

CONFIDENTIAL.

WAR DIARY

of

4th Battalion The Worcestershire Regiment

From 1st November, 1918 To 30th November, 1918.

(VOLUME NO. 9).

Army Form C. 2118.

WAR DIARY
or
INTELLIGENCE SUMMARY
(Erase heading not required.)

Instructions regarding War Diaries and Intelligence Summaries are contained in F.S. Regs., Part II. and the Staff Manual respectively. Title pages will be prepared in manuscript.

REFERENCE SHEETS : 36 & 37, Edn. 6, 1/40,000.
TOURNAI 5, 1/100,000.

Place	Date	Hour	Summary of Events and Information	Remarks and references to Appendices
IN BILLETS AT CROIX.	1st. Nov.		The Battalion paraded at 13.30 for a Brigade Ceremonial Parade and was inspected by the Corps Commander. After the inspection the Corps Commander expressed his appreciation of the smartness of the Brigade after the past two months heavy fighting. Companies were at the disposal of O.C. Companies from 09.00 to 12.00. 2nd. Lieut. N.M. Goodman and draft of 208 O.R. joined the Battalion.	
	2nd. Nov.		The Battalion, less the draft, paraded at 09.30 and marched to Training Area for Company training. Draft was the disposal of O.C. Coys. for kit inspections, etc., Companies were at the disposal of O.C. Coys. from 14.00 to 15.00. A Lewis Gun Class was commenced under Lieut. F.F. Boddington, and a Signalling Class under Cpl. Sig. Edwards. Lieut. W. Wooldridge joined the Battalion.	
	3rd. Nov.		Church Parade held in the large hall, HOLDEN'S WORKS, at 10.00. Holy Communion celebrated in the English Church at 11.45, and a voluntary service held at 15.00. Presbyterians and Non-Conformists Services held in the BISCUITERIE at 10.30. Roman Catholic Service in the Church at 10.30. All the draft had a bath and clean change of underclothing.	
	4th. Nov.		The Battalion paraded at 09.00 and marched to the Training Area for Company and Platoon training. At 11.30 the Battalion formed up and did 30 minutes Ceremonial and Battalion Drill. Lewis Gun and Signalling Classes continued. /An N.C.Os. Class under the Adjutant commenced.	

(Continued).

Army Form C. 2118.

WAR DIARY
or
INTELLIGENCE SUMMARY.
(Erase heading not required.)

REFERENCE SHEETS : 36 & 57 Edn. 6, 1/40,000.
JOURNAL 5, 1/100,000.

Place	Date	Hour	Summary of Events and Information	Remarks and references to Appendices
IN BILLETS AT CROIX.	4th. Nov.		(Cont). The Field Marshal Commanding-in-Chief has, under authority granted by His Majesty the King, awarded the following decorations for operations near CHELINELT from 28th. Sept. to 3rd. Oct. 1918.	
			BAR to the DISTINGUISHED SERVICE ORDER.	
			Lieut. Col. Tudor Fitzjohn, D.S.O.	
			BAR to the MILITARY CROSS.	
			Capt. J.E. Thorneloe, M.C.	
			THE MILITARY CROSS.	
			Capt. A.H. Bowman.	
			2nd. Lieut. R.H. Warren, M.M.	
			THE DISTINGUISHED CONDUCT MEDAL.	
			No. 41794 C.S.M. W. Russon.	
			No. 39708 Sgt. W.J. Smith, M.M.	
			No. 41518 Pte. A.E. Hughes.	
			2nd. Lieut. W. Burd, D.C.M. and 2nd. Lieut. G. Watson joined.	
	5th. Nov.		Owing to heavy rain Companies were at the disposal of O.C. Coys. In billets. Lewis Gun, Signalling and N.C.Os' Classes continued.	

WAR DIARY or INTELLIGENCE SUMMARY

Army Form C. 2118.

(Erase heading not required.)

Instructions regarding War Diaries and Intelligence Summaries are contained in F. S. Regs., Part II. and the Staff Manual respectively. Title pages will be prepared in manuscript.

Place	Date	Hour	Summary of Events and Information	Remarks and references to Appendices
PETIT TOURCOING	6th Nov	06.30	The Battalion moved at 06.30 from CROIX by march route via ROUBAIX – TOMBROER – BULLEGHEM to PETIT TOURCOING where we billeted over an area of about 2000 yards, arriving in the new area about 14.30, a very wet day – raining continuously from 09.00 to about 21.00	1/40,000 1/100,000
IN LINE NEAR RIVER L'ESCAUT	7th Nov		Reconnoitring parties sent from each coy to reconnoitre routes forward to front line. At 14.00 the Battalion paraded and moved forward to the line "X" Coy relieving 1 Coy 29th D.L.I. (14th Div) over the river L'ESCAUT in U.30 and 24. The remaining 3 coys did not relieve any unit but were located as under W Coy in Support, "Y" and "Z" in Reserve. A quiet relief 1 casualty.	Reference Sheets 29 d 4 27
IN LINE NEAR RIVER L'ESCAUT	8th Nov	03.00	At 03.00 a patrol left our right (or) and proceeded forward to the Bank at the GRAND COURANT, turned left-handed and proceeded along the Bank for 2000 yards and returned. The object of the patrol being to ascertain whether any of the enemy were between L'ESCAUT and the GRAND COURANT – no enemy was seen or heard. The enemy was reported to be withdrawing on I Army Front and TOURNAI was also reported evacuated, a patrol therefore was sent out by "X" Coy to endeavour to cross the GRAND COURANT to see if the enemy had withdrawn.	Reference Sheets 29 d 4 27 Journal 1/100,000

continued

WAR DIARY
or
INTELLIGENCE SUMMARY.
(Erase heading not required.)

Army Form C. 2118.

Instructions regarding War Diaries and Intelligence Summaries are contained in F. S. Regs., Part II. and the Staff Manual respectively. Title pages will be prepared in manuscript.

Place	Date	Hour	Summary of Events and Information	Remarks and references to Appendices
IN LINE	9th Nov		At about 00:01 "X" Coy arrived the river and took up a position along the road running parallel to the river. "W" & "Z" Coys followed the last man of Y Coy crossing the river by about 01:00. "W" and "Y" Coys took up a position on approx. line of B.Line from D5C to D9C. At about 11:30 orders were issued for W & Y Coys to move forward and take up a position along the road from D29 B88 to D16 D6.3, and was in position by 13.00. X & Z Coys took up a position along the road running from D14 central to D9 central, at about 15.30 W & Y Coys were ordered to take the position along the road from D29 D00 to D24 central and were in position by 16.30 at 17.30 W & Y Coys moved forward and took up positions on high ground in K1A & K26 E2&6 X Coy were in Reserve in billets at D23 D.4. Y Coy in Reserve in billets at D24 D68. A Battn was up by 0.200 10 inst. No enemy position was met during the day. Civilians report the enemy were withdrawing to high ground E18 & E24 covering party. "A" Squadron "4th Dragoon Guards" 10 cyclists as	1/100,000 2 & Lieuts 1 warrant off 24 Sgts Lewis G
ST SAUVEUR	10th Nov		The Batt continued the advance in Column of Route in the following order 2/H & S 2/Leins 4/4 Worcs. The Batt advancing S.E through E2.D & moved forward at 11:30. By 15.00 ST SAUVEUR was reached without any enemy opposition. The 2/Leins & this Batt were billeted for the night in the village	

/cont'd

WAR DIARY
or
INTELLIGENCE SUMMARY.
(Erase heading not required.)

Army Form C. 2118.

Place	Date	Hour	Summary of Events and Information	Remarks and references to Appendices
L E S S I N E S	10th Nov		of ST SAUVEUR. The 2/H.&I.s taking up an outpost line along the road east of BOIS D'HUBERMONT. The cavalry patrols reached LAMANAIDE and WIDDESQ and established standing patrol there but were fired on. Rations up by 12 midnight.	
	11th Nov		The BN. Bde continued the advance, the advance being covered by "A" Squadron 1st D.G's and 10th Hussars. The Bde advanced in the following order 4/ Worc's 2/ Jun 2/ H.&I.s. The Battalion formed up in St SAUVEUR at 08:30 and moved forward with LESSINES as the objective. Just as the Battalion was about to move off, information was received that the enemy had given in unconditionally to the Armistice to be signed when the Battalion reached the outskirts of the BOIS D'HUBERMONT near at 09:50. Information was received that the armistice of that hostilities would cease at 11:00. At 10:15 the Bn. reached LESSINES & made good the crossing over the River DENDRE. The Battalion continued the advance and reached LESSINES by 1500 amid great enthusiasm. The Battalion. Thousands of civilians crowding the streets. At 11:30 Z Coy took up an outpost line across the DENDRE. W, X & Y Coys being billeted in the town.	1/100/000 36 Reference Sheet T QUIRNAI 5
	12th Nov		Continued at the disposal of Bde. Bdgs. Z Coy was for general cleaning up. The S.B.R. In Pelotons. – On the 11th Nov relieved Z Coy on the outpost line. Y Coy took up a position on the 12 platoons in the outpost line from LOCK No.4 (E16.d.9.0) to H.5.0.9.9 including the other line X will X Coy .... all crossings. On the night from C17-22 to C.29.d.7.4. the remainder of the Bn. being all the crossings across the river. Remainder of Coy in Billets on w.&.b.3.9.x by took up a position the outpost line will Will be west at C.16.d.8.2. Z Coy returned to billets near C16.d.35. CONT'D	

Army Form C. 2118.

WAR DIARY
or
INTELLIGENCE SUMMARY.
(Erase heading not required.)

Place	Date	Hour	Summary of Events and Information	Remarks and references to Appendices
In fields LESSINES	Nov 13th		The Battalion took up an outpost line along the road running NORTH and SOUTH through squares C.12.a.7.c, C.18.a.r.c, C.24.a.r.c, with X Coy on the right, & W Coy on the left. Y Coy withdrawing to billets near C.16.b.3.6. Z Coy remained in their billets.	SL. 38. 1/40,000 ST TOURNAI S. 1/100,000
	Nov 14th		Coys at the disposal of OC Coys from 10.00 to 12.00 and from 14.00 to 15.00 for Standing Orders, Physical Games &c. 2nd Lt J Salter joined the Battalion. The following Awards were received for operations from 14th to 20th Oct 1918, at LEDEGHEM and STACEGHEM. Bar to the M.M. 39676 Sergt S Heath M.M. The Military Medal 238029 Sgt E S Skrimshaw 242360 Pte S H Dean 144456 Pte H Norton 12277 " (A/S) J Egginton H1150 " A E Higgins 45226 " A Benell 20367 " A Salter 36612 " T/S J Tartans 19620 " E Beacock 53148 " (A/L) C Kelly 15791 " A E Robinson 47696 " 3 Underwood 24720 " Grant	Reference

WAR DIARY
or
INTELLIGENCE SUMMARY.

Army Form C. 2118.

Place	Date	Hour	Summary of Events and Information	Remarks and references to Appendices
LESSINES	Nov 14th	(cont)	The 2nd Hampshire Regt relieved the 2 Coys 1st Worcestershire Regt in the out post line, these 2 Coys returning to billets. See C.16.b. Baths allotted to Coys as under:-	
	Nov 15th		W 0900 to 10.00	
			X 10.00 to 11.00	
			Y 11.00 to 12.00	
			Z 12.00 to 13.00	
			For the remainder of the day, coys were at the disposal of OsC of Coys. Standing of Arms Drill & Physical Exercise.	TOURNAI 5, 1/100,000 St 38, 1/40,000
De Lettes	Nov 16th		The Battalion paraded in slow & Quick time for a Battalion Parade. 10.00	
	Nov 17th		The Battalion paraded at 11.55 & marched to L'École Communale for Divine Service. Non Conformists & Presbyterians paraded at 10.00 for Divine Service. Roman Catholics paraded at 08.55 and marched to St Géréon's Church for Mass. Lieut J A Gurney & Lt B Bowerband & the 2 Lt Guy Gurbay W W Gillatton joined	Reference ✓

W G Gillatton joined

J A Gurney

WAR DIARY
or
INTELLIGENCE SUMMARY.

(Erase heading not required.)

Army Form C. 2118.

Place	Date	Hour	Summary of Events and Information	Remarks and references to Appendices
LESSINES – ENGHIEN	Nov 11th		In accordance with the terms of the Armistice the 29th Division advanced as part of the Allied force to occupy the territory evacuated by the enemy. The 86th Inf Bde group as advance Guard marched to Ath via ENGHIEN. 4th Worcestershire Regt with 1 platoon 1/1st Cyclists, 2 Sections 2 Gun Bays formed the advanced guard. followed by 2nd Hampshires. 2nd Leinsters. 88th Trench Mortars 497th Field Coy RE. 29th Bn MG Corps. 88th TMB No 4 Coy Div Train. The Battalion paraded at 06.00 and moved off with 2 Coys as Vanguard and Wand X Coy's as Mainguard, the cyclists overtaking the Bn's Army Advance Markers. Battalion in billets by 12.45, 2 Coys putting out 2 platoons on outpost. Also 2 platoons being relieved by 2nd Hampshires at 15.00	TOURNAIS. 1/100.000 BRUSSELS. 1/100.000 Reference Sheets

WAR DIARY or INTELLIGENCE SUMMARY.

Army Form C. 2118.

(Erase heading not required.)

Place	Date	Hour	Summary of Events and Information	Remarks and references to Appendices
ENGHIEN	Nov 19th		Companies at the disposal of Oc.Coys from 10.00 to 12.00 for Handling of Arms, Physical Games.	
			1 Platoon of Coy relieved 1 Platoon 2nd Hants on outpost at NOVES.	
	Nov 20th		Companies at the disposal of Oc.Coys for Physical Games, Handling of Arms Drill. All men issued with clean underclothing.	
	Nov 21st		The march to the frontier was commenced, the Brigade moving to BRAINE-LE-CHATEAU via SAINTES and TUBIZE.	
			Coys. C.Mounts, 2nd M.G. Coy, m.e., 2nd Battalion moving MT. N.[?]village and 100 OR. Together with 100 OR from the 2nd Hampshire and 2nd Leinsters proceeded to BRUSSELS in order to take part in the procession when the King of Belgium entered that city.	BRUSSELS, G. 1/100,000. Reference Sheet.
BRAINE-LE-CHATEAU	Nov 22nd		Coys at the disposal of Oc.Coys for Handling of Arms Drill, Physical Games from 10.00 to 12.00.	
			The King of Belgium entered BRUSSELS followed by Bntsh, American, French & Belgian troops, all of whom received a wonderful reception. Prince Albert and Queen also took part in the procession. A large percentage of officers from the Bn. were formed in BRUSSELS to see the procession.	Reference Sheet

Army Form C. 2118.

WAR DIARY
or
INTELLIGENCE SUMMARY.

(Erase heading not required.)

Instructions regarding War Diaries and Intelligence Summaries are contained in F. S. Regs., Part II. and the Staff Manual respectively. Title pages will be prepared in manuscript.

Place	Date	Hour	Summary of Events and Information	Remarks and references to Appendices
ST LAMBERT	23rd Nov		The march to the front was continued, the Battalion arriving at ST LAMBERT marching through the Battlefield of WATERLOO a number of photographs including a cinematograph were taken of the Battalion marching through. All in billets by 18.15	
	24th Nov		Troops at the disposal of 66 bgs for Physical Drill & Handling of arms. The rifles of "W" Coy were inspected by the Armourer Sergeant. The Commanding Officer and 2nd in Command attended a Staff Ride under the Divisional Commander around the Battlefield of WATERLOO	
LIMELETTE	25th Nov		The Battalion moved to LIMELETTE via CEROUX - MOUSTY and OTTIGNIES. All in billets by 13.45.	
	26th Nov		Troops at the disposal of 66 bgs for Drill and Physical from the Armourer Sergeant inspected the rifles of "X" Coy	
WALHAIN ST PAUL	27th Nov		The Battalion moved to WALHAIN ST PAUL. All in billets by 13.45.	
EGHEZEE	28th Nov		The Battalion moved from WALHAIN ST PAUL to EGHEZEE via PERWEZ and GRAND ROSIERE a distance of 23 Kilometres. All in billets by 14.30.	
ANTHEIT	29th Nov		The Battalion moved to ANTHEIT via BIERWART LAVOIR and WANZE a distance of 25 Kilometres. All in billets by 15.05	
WARZEE	30th Nov		The Battalion moved to WARZEE via HUY and STREE a distance of 23 Kilometres. Transport was brigaded and moved independently. All in billets by 16.45.	

1/12/18

[signature]
Lieut Colonel
Commanding 1/5 The Yorkshire Regt

SECRET & CONFIDENTIAL.

WAR DIARY

4th. Battalion The Worcestershire Regiment

From

1st. DECEMBER 1918

To

31st. DECEMBER 1918.

(VOLUME No 10)

-o-o-o-o-o-o-o-o-o-o-o-o-o-o-o-o-o-o-o-o-o-o-o-o-o-o-o-o-

Army Form C. 2118.

WAR DIARY
or
INTELLIGENCE-SUMMARY.

(Erase heading not required.)

Instructions regarding War Diaries and Intelligence Summaries are contained in F.S. Regs., Part II. and the Staff Manual respectively. Title pages will be prepared in manuscript.

UK Warwickshire Regt

Place	Date	Hour	Summary of Events and Information	Remarks and references to Appendices
				reference sheets MARCHE 1/100,000 GERMANY K 1/100,000 J.L. & I.W. GERMANY 1/100,000
AYWAILLE	Dec. 1.		The Battalion moved to AYWAILLE via COMBLAIN and FAIRON a distance of 24 kilometres, a halt was observed from 12.30 to 13.00 during which the tea ration was consumed.	
	2.		Baths were allotted to Companies - no clean clothing available - remainder of day Companies were at the disposal of O.C. Companies for cleaning up.	
	3.		Companies at the disposal of O.C. Companies for Drill, Handling of Arms, Physical Games and general cleaning up by platoons. Rate of Exchange for one month fixed at 1 mark = 70 cms (French money). A number of Officers, N.C.O.s and men visited LA GROTTE at REMOUCHAMPES.	
LA REID	4.		The Battalion moved from AYWAILLE to LA REID via SOUGNE HALTE, a distance of 9 kilometres. The transport was brigaded and marched in rear of Brigade owing to hills.	
MALMEDY	5.		The Battalion moved from LA REID to MALMEDY via SPA - FRANCORCHAMPS a distance of 36 kilometres. At SPA a considerable number of German soldiers were seen being members of the Armistice Commission. A halt was observed between 12.30 and 13.00 during which time the tea ration was consumed. The Battalion crossed the frontier at 14.00. arriving in Billets at about 15.30.	
ELSENBORN	6.		The Battalion moved to ELSENBORN via BAUGNE - WEISMES, a distance of 18 kilometres.	
SIMMERATH	7.		The Battalion moved to SIMMERATH via KELTER HERBERG - MONTJOIE a distance of 24 kilometres. The usual half hour halt was observed at 12.30.	
EMBKEN	8.		The Battalion moved to EMBKEN via SCHMIDT - NIDEGHEM a distance of about 29 kilometres. The usual halt was observed at 12.30.	

Army Form C. 2118.

WAR DIARY
or
INTELLIGENCE SUMMARY.
(Erase heading not required.)

Instructions regarding War Diaries and Intelligence Summaries are contained in F. S. Regs., Part II. and the Staff Manual respectively. Title pages will be prepared in manuscript.

Reference Sheets 3M4 3L. GERMANY 1/100.000.

Place	Date	Hour	Summary of Events and Information	Remarks and references to Appendices
LECHENICH	Decr. 9.		The Battalion moved to LECHENICH via TUNTERSDORF - ZULPICH - WEILER, a distance of 21 kilometres. The usual halt of 30 minutes observed.	
	10.		The Battalion moved to FRECHEN via KIERDORF - MODRATH a distance of 16 kilometres.	
	11.		Baths were allotted to Companies as under. Z Company 09.00. to 11.00. Y Company 11.00. to 13.00. X Company 13.00. to 14.00. Companies at the disposal of O.C.Companies for general cleaning up ready for march past Army Commander.	
F R E C H E N	12.		Companies at the disposal of O.C. Companies for cleaning up etc Baths allotted to X and W Companies from 11.30 to 12.00 and 12.00 to 14.00. The following French Decorations have been awarded to the under mentioned Officers and N.C.O.s Croix de Guere a L'Ordre Division. Lieut. Colonel Tudor Fitzjohn, D.S.O. Croix de Guere a L'Ordre Brigade. Captain G.P. O'Donovan MC. Croix de Guere a L'Ordre Regiment - No. 11590. C.S.M. B.Loone MM. No. 488 15. Cpl C.Orbell A Colour Party consisting of Lieut.E.R.Newcombe MC. Lieut H.F. Boddington a/R.S.M. Samson D.C.M. No 11460 Cpl Hall MM. and No 12520 Pte Cotton proceeded to Worcester to escort the Colours to Germany.	
MULHEIM	13.		The Battalion moved from FRECHEN to MULHEIM via LIND - COLOGNE a distance of 15 kilos. Heavy rain in early morning until about 12 noon. The Brigade marched past the Corps Commander on the HOLZZOLLERN BRIDGE.	

Army Form C. 2118.

WAR DIARY
or
INTELLIGENCE SUMMARY.
(Erase heading not required.) 4th Worcestershire Regt

Instructions regarding War Diaries and Intelligence Summaries are contained in F. S. Regs., Part II. and the Staff Manual respectively. Title pages will be prepared in manuscript.

Reference Sheets 2M-2L GERMANY 1/100,000

Place	Date	Hour	Summary of Events and Information	Remarks and references to Appendices
	Dec 14.		The Battalion Brigade was congratulated on its turn out and on the way it marched past. The whole Battalion was billeted in a large school.	
	15.		The Commanding Officer inspected the kits of the Battalion. Armourer Sergeant inspected "Z" Company's rifles. The remainder of the day Companies at the disposal of O.C. Companies.	
BERG GLADBACH			The Battalion moved from MULHEIM to BERG GLADBACH via DELBRUCK a distance of 10 kilos. Under Authority delegated by the Field Marshall Commander-in-Chief the Corps Commander has awarded the M.M. to the under mentioned N.C.O.s and men	
			46191 L/Cpl Carter	
			12601 Pte J.Willetts	
			18052 L/Cpl A.Waite	
			15963 Pte H.Bayliss	
			40421 Pte J.H.Rollings	
ALTENBERG	16.		The Battalion moved from BERG GLADBACK to ALTENBERG via ODENTHAL a distance of 7 kilometres	
	17.		Companies at the disposal of O.C. Companies for handling of arms, physical games and Lewis Gun classes. All Signallers paraded under Sergt Sneasby outside Orderly Room.	
	18.		Rate of Exchange fixed at :- 5 marks equals 2/8 or 3 francs 50 cms. The Battalion moved from ALTENBERG to WERMELSKERCHEN the final destination of Brigade via BLECHER and HILGEN. Raining hard all day. On arrival "Z" Company took over two posts from 2nd Leinster Regt	
WERMELSKERCHEN	19.		Companies at the disposal of O.C. Companies for general cleaning up and rearranging Billets. "W" Company and Drums were billetted in 1 School. "X" and "Y" were billeted in one school and the two platoons of "Z" Company not on outpost were in one large house	
	20.		Companies at the disposal of O.C. Companies for handling of Arms, Drill Physical Games and Company Lewis Gun Classes.	

Army Form C. 2118.

WAR DIARY
or
INTELLIGENCE SUMMARY
(Erase heading not required.)

Instructions regarding War Diaries and Intelligence Summaries are contained in F.S. Regs., Part II. and the Staff Manual respectively. Title pages will be prepared in manuscript.

1/4 Warwickshire Regt

Place	Date	Hour	Summary of Events and Information	Remarks and references to Appendices
	Decr 20.		2/Lt G.G. Royal joined the Battalion.	Reference Sheet Germany, SK 1/100,000
	21.		Companies at the disposal of O.C. Companies from 09.00 to 12.00 for Kit inspections and cleaning up. The Diamond Troupe commenced their evening performances.	
	22.		The Battalion paraded at 11.20 for Divine Service and marched to the Church.	
	23.		Companies at the disposal of O.C. Companies from 0,9.00 to 12.00 for Drill, Physical Games and Company Lewis Gun Classes. 1 Estaminet was reserved for Warrant Officers and Sergeants 1 for Corporals and two for L/Corporals and men A Battalion Officers Mess was commenced.	
	24.		The Commanding Officer inspected Companies as under in full Marching Order. "W" Company and Signallers 09.30. "X" Company 10.00. "Y" Company 10.30. "Z" Company 11.00. 2nd Lieutenants C.F.Twining and H.P. Park joined Battalion.	
	25.		The Battalion paraded for Divine Service at 11.20 for Church Parade in the Church. Owing to the Poultry etc. not arriving Xmas Dinners were indefinitely postponed.	
	26.		Companies at the disposal of O.C. Companies. "W" Company relieved the two Platoons of "Z" Company on outpost.	

Army Form C. 2118.

WAR DIARY
or
INTELLIGENCE SUMMARY.

(Erase heading not required.)

Reference sheet Germany & K 1/100,000

Place	Date	Hour	Summary of Events and Information	Remarks and references to Appendices
WERMELSKIRCH	Dec. 27.		Companies at the disposal of O.C. Companies from 09.15 to 12.15. for Drill, Physical Games etc Company Lewis Gun classes continued. A1-1 N.C.O.s incharge of Lewis Gun Teams paraded for instruction. All Signallers paraded for instruction	
	28.		Company at the disposal of O.C. Companies from 9.15 to 12.15. for Drill, Handling of Arms, and Physical Games. Lewis Gun Classes continued. Captain E.R.Smith awarded the M.C. 2nd Lieut. R.H.Warren MC.MM. appointed Battalion Education Officer. 2nd Lieut. J.R.Hall joined the Battalion. Baths allotted "Y" Company for 1½ hours.	
	29.		Baths allotted to "W", "X" and "Z" Companies for 1½ hours each. "Y" Company attended Church Parade.	
	30.		Battalion (less "X" Company) route march in battle order from 9.30 to 11.30. "X" Company, company training.	
	31.		Companies at the disposal of O.C. Companies from 9-15 to 12.00 and from 14.00 to 15.00 for handling ofarms, physical games etc. Classes continued.	
			Battalion Strength. Officers O.R.	
			Trench Strength 25 511	
			Ration 3 39 671	
			Total 42 777	

Hugh Fitzjohn
Lieutenant Colonel
Commanding 4th Bn The Worcestershire Regt.

1st January 1919.

SOUTHERN (LATE 29TH) DIVN.
88TH INFY BDE

4TH BN WORCESTER REGT.
JAN - APR 1919

SOUTHERN (LATE 29TH) DIVN.
88TH INFY BDE

****

(VOLUME NO. 11).

From 1st January To 31st January, 1919.

4th Battalion The Worcestershire Regiment

of

WAR DIARY

CONFIDENTIAL.

Army Form C. 2118.

WAR DIARY
or
INTELLIGENCE SUMMARY
(Erase heading not required.)

Instructions regarding War Diaries and Intelligence Summaries are contained in F. S. Regs., Part II. and the Staff Manual respectively. Title pages will be prepared in manuscript.

4th Inniskilling Regt.

Reference Sheet Germany 1/100,000 Sheet 2 K

Place: Hermee - Richen

Place	Date	Hour	Summary of Events and Information	Remarks and references to Appendices
	1 Jan.1919		Companies under Coy.Commanders from 9.15 to 12.00. Signalling and Lewis Gun Classes continued.	
	2nd Jan.		A whole holiday - men given their Christmas Dinner, less the turkeys, which arrived at Division bad.	
	3rd Jan.		The Corps Commander (11 Corps) visited the Battn., inspecting billets institutes etc., He expressed his appreciation. Platoons under platoon Commanders from 09.15 to 10.45, and Companies under Coy.Commanders from 11.00 to 12.00. 09.30 to 11.30 Signal Class continued. "W" Coy. instructed in guard mounting etc., by R. S. M.	
	4th Jan.		Interior economy and kit inspections. Rate of exchange 5 marks - 2/4d. or 3 francs.	
	5th Jan.		Divine Service 11.30. The Battalion (less X Coy) paraded for Brigade Church Parade at Wermelskirchen.	
	6th Jan.		09.15 - 10.30 Platoons under Platoon Commanders. 09.30 - 12.15 All Signallers under Sergt. Sheasby. 10.45 - 12.15 Coys. at disposal of Coy., Commanders. 14.00 - 15.00 Coy. Lewis Gun Classes. Saluting & Handling of Arms.	
	7th Jan.		Battalion Parade. Notification received that G.O.C. 29th Division, would inspect the Battalion on 9th instant. The Battalion paraded at 10.20 as strong as possible, and marched to Football Ground to practice Ceremonial Drill. 14.00 - 15.30. Special Lewis Gun Class under Cpl.Toney.- All N.C.Os. in charge of Lewis Gun Teams. Companies at disposal od O.C. Coys., for handling of Arms and Saluting.	
	8th Jan.		Battalion Parade at 11.00. Practice for G.O.C's. Inspection. Order of march Drums, "W" "X", Colours, "Y" & "Z". Dress: Drill Order. The Colours were on parade (cased) for the first time since their arrival from England)	

WAR DIARY
or
INTELLIGENCE SUMMARY.

(Erase heading not required.)

Army Form C. 2118.

- 2 -

Place	Date	Hour	Summary of Events and Information	Remarks and references to Appendices
	8th Jan.	(Contd) 14.00 15.30.	Battalion Lewis Gun Class Continued. Companies at disposal of O.C.Coys.	
	9th Jan.	09.30.	The Battalion paraded as strong as possible outside Orderly Room, Drums, "W", "X", "Y", "Z" Stretcher Bearers (under Medical Officer) and marched to No. 1. Football Ground for inspection and presentation of Medal Ribbons by Maj.Gen. D.E.Cayley, C.B.,C.M.G. The Divisional Commander presented the Croix-de-Guerre to Lieut.Colonel Tudor Fitzjohn, D.S.O, and C.S.M. C.Loone, M.M. The King colours were on parade anducased for the first time. Party and Escort were as follows:- King's Colour. Lieut. H.F. Boddington. Regtl. Colour. Lieut. J. Watt. Escort:- C.Q.M.S. J.Dossett, Sgt.A.Baker, Sgt.C.Healey	Reference Sheet
	10th Jan.	09.15 to 10.30. 10.45 to 12.00 09.15 to 10.30 14.00 to 15.30 09.30 to 12.15	Platoons under Platoon Commanders. Coys. under Company Commanders. Lewis Gunners under Coy.Lewis Gun N.C.Os. Company Drill. All Signallers paraded under Sgt. Sig.Sheasby.	
	11th Jan.		"Z" Coy. 2nd. Hampshire Regt., relieved "X" Coy at BERGISCH BORN "X" Coy. returned to WERMELSKIRCHEN. "W" & "Z" Coys., Interior economy and kit inspection. "Y" Coy. relieved one platoon 2nd. Hampshire Regt. at TALESPERRE.	
	12th Jan.	11.30	Divine Service The Battalion(less "Y" Coy) paraded for Brigade Church Parade at Wermelskirchen. Capt. & Adjt. J. Thorncloe, M.C. left the Battn. for demobolisation. He was carried Shoulder High to the station, Drums, Officers, Headquarters attended to wish him goodbye.	

Army Form C. 2118.

WAR DIARY
or
INTELLIGENCE SUMMARY.
(Erase heading not required.)

Instructions regarding War Diaries and Intelligence Summaries are contained in F. S. Regs., Part II. and the Staff Manual respectively. Title pages will be prepared in manuscript.

Place	Date	Hour	Summary of Events and Information	Remarks and references to Appendices
	13 Jan. 1919.		09.15 to 10.30. Platoons under Platoon Commanders.	
			09.30 to 12.30 Signallers under Sgt.Sig.Sheasby.	
			10.45 to 12.15 Coys. under Coy. Commanders.	
			14.00 to 15.00 Coy.Lewis Gun Classes, saluting & handling of arms under company arrangements. Battalion paraded by companies for Baths at FACTION SCHOOL & COMMUNAL KITCHEN BATHS.	
	14th Jan.		Battalion paraded for route march from 09.30 to 12.00. Dress: Battle Order.	
			14.00 to 15.00. N.C.Os. in charge of Lewis Gun teams under Cpl. Toney for instruction. Saluting & handling of Arms under Company arrangements	
	15th Jan.		09.15 to 10.30 Companies under Coy. arrangements.	
			09.30 to 12.15 All Signallers under Sgt.Sig.Sheasby outside Orderly Room.	
			10.45 to 12.00 Platoons under Platoon Commanders.	
			14.00 to 15.30 Lewis Gun Classes under Coy.Lewis Gun N.C.Os. Lecture by Company Commanders.	
	16th Jan.		09.15 to 10.30 Platoons under Platoon Commanders.	
			09.15 to 10.30. Lewis Gunners under Coy.Lewis Gun N.C.Os.	
			09.30 to 12.15 Signallers under Sgt.Sig.Sheasby outside Orderly Room.	Notification received that Major R.A.Mangall #1728 Sgt.Cartwright#059 Sgt.Shersby C. 24728 Sgt Rawlinson.N.M.C 112534 Sgt Glover. have been awarded Med.Belgium.
	17th Jan.		Battalion paraded for Route March at 09.30 to 12.30. Dress. Battle Order.	
			14.00 to 15.30. Lectures by Platoon Commanders.	
	18th Jan.		Interior economy and kit inspections. The Commanding Officer inspected the kits of "X" and "Z" Companies.	
	19th Jan.		The Battalion paraded for Divine Service at WERMELSKIRCHEN at 11.30.	

WAR DIARY
or
INTELLIGENCE SUMMARY.
(Erase heading not required.)

Army Form C. 2118.

Instructions regarding War Diaries and Intelligence Summaries are contained in F. S. Regs., Part II. and the Staff Manual respectively. Title pages will be prepared in manuscript.

Place	Date	Hour	Summary of Events and Information	Remarks and references to Appendices
Mandelsloh	20th Jan.1919.	09.15 to 10.30 10.45 to 12.00 14.00 to 15.30	Companies under Coy. Commanders. Platoons under Platoon Commanders. Lewis Gun Classes and Lecture by Company Commanders.	
			Battalion, Coy. Football Competition. "Z" Coy. beat "W" Coy. 3 - 2.	
	21st Jan.	09.30 to 12.15 09.15 to 12.30 14.00 to 15.30	Signallers under Sgt. Sig. Sheasby. "W" "X" & "Z" Coys. under company Commanders. "Y" Coy. Sports.	Reference Sheet Germany 1/100.000
			Football Competition. "Y" Coy. beat "X" Coy. 3 - 2.	
	22nd Jan.	9.15 to 12.30	"W" & "Z" Coys. Baths, Fumigating of clothes and blankets. 14.15.30 Coys. under company commanders.	
	23rd Jan.	9.15 to 10.30 10.45 to 12.00 14.00 to 15.30 09.15 to 10.30 09.15 to 12.15	Coys. under Company Commanders. Platoons under Platoon Commanders. Company Drill. Lewis Gunners under Lewis Gun N.C.Os. Signallers under Sgt. Sig. Sheasby.	
	24th Jan.	09.30 to 12.30	Company Route Marches. 30 men per company, 15 drummers & 10 signallers attended Lecture on "Alsace Lorraine & German Mentality". 14.00 to 15.30 Coy. Lewis Gun Classes, saluting and handling of arms under company arrangements.	
	25th Jan.		Interior economy and kit inspections. The Commanding Officer Inspected the kits of "W" Coy. and the Drums.	
	26th Jan.	11.20.	The Battalion paraded for Divine Service at Wermelskirchen at	
	27th Jan.	09.15 to 12.30.	Coys under Company Commanders,	

Army Form C. 2118.

WAR DIARY
INTELLIGENCE SUMMARY
(Erase heading not required.)

Instructions regarding War Diaries and Intelligence Summaries are contained in F. S. Regs., Part II. and the Staff Manual respectively. Title pages will be prepared in manuscript.

Place	Date	Hour	Summary of Events and Information	Remarks and references to Appendices
Vernice Bracken	1919. Jany. 28.		The Battalion (less "Y" Coy) paraded in Column of Route on the Road outside Orderly Room facing South, in the following order, Signallers, Drums, "X", "Z" and "W" Coys. Dress. Battle Order, less steel helmets, ground sheets rolled and fastened on belts. "X" Company found 2 parties for work on range consisting of 1 officer and 24 O.Rs. 14.00 - 15.30 Lectures by Platoon Commanders.	Sheet 2. R.
	29th Jan.		09.15 - 10.30 Platoons under Platoon Commanders. 09.30 - 12.15 Signallers under Sgt.Sig.Sheasby. 10.45 - 12.15 Companies under Company Commanders. 14.00 - 15.00 Company Lewis Gun Classes, saluting & handling of arms under Company arrangements.	Germany 1/100,000
	30th Jan.		"W" Company found 2 working parties for work on range consisting of 1 officer and 24 O.Rs. from 08.00 to 12.00. 09.15 - 10.30 Platoons under Platoon Commanders. 09.30 - 12.15 All Signallers under Sgt.Sig.Sheasby. 10.45 - 12.00 Platoons under Platoon Commanders. 14.00 - 15.30 Lewis Gun Classes under company Lewis Gun N.C.Os. Lecture by Company Commanders.	Germany
	31st Jan.		09.30 Battalion Route March. Dress .Battle Order, less steel helmets, ground sheets rolled and fastened on belts. Signallers parade at head of Battalion under Sgt.Sig.Sheasby. 14.00 - 15.30 Coy. Lewis Gun Classes, saluting and handling of Arms under Company arrangements.	

Tudor Majestu Lt.R.
Com Oy 4 Worcestershire Rgt.

SECRET & CONFIDENTIAL.

WAR DIARY

4th. Battalion The Worcestershire Regiment.

From
1st. February 1919
To
28th. February 1919.

(Volume No. 12.)

Army Form C. 2118.

WAR DIARY
or
INTELLIGENCE SUMMARY
(Erase heading not required.)

Instructions regarding War Diaries and Intelligence Summaries are contained in F. S. Regs., Part II. and the Staff Manual respectively. Title pages will be prepared in manuscript.

Place	Date	Hour	Summary of Events and Information	Remarks and references to Appendices
WERMELSKIRCHEN.	Feb. 1st.		Interior economy and kit inspections.	
	Feb. 2nd.		The Battalion, less "Y" Coy., parade for a Brigade Church Parade at WERMELSKIRCHEN.	
	Feb. 3rd.		The Baths at Faction School were allotted to "X", Y and "Z" Coys. Baths at Communal Kitchen allotted "W" Coy. Remainder of the day spent in saluting drill, handling of arms, and recreational training.	
	Feb. 4th.		The Battalion paraded at 09:30 for a Route March, in battle order, less steel helmets. Lecture by Company Commanders from 14.00 to 15.30. "Z" Coy. found a working party of 2 N.C.Os., and 20 O.R. under R.Es. for work on the range, during the morning.	
	Feb. 5th.	09.15 – 10.30.	Companies under Company Commanders.	
		09.15 – 12.30.	Signallers under Sgt. Sig. Sheasby.	
		10.45 – 12.00.	Platoons under Platoon Commanders.	
		14.00 – 15.30.	Lewis Gun Classes under Lewis Gun N.C.Os.	
		14.00 – 15.30.	Lectures by Company Commanders.	
			Major (A/Lieut. Colonel) Tudor Fitzjohn, DSO, proceeded to Divisional Headquarters.	
	Feb. 6th.	09.15 – 10.30.	Platoons under Platoon Commanders.	
		09.15 – 10.30.	Lewis Gunners under Lewis Gun N.C.Os.	
		10.45 – 12.00.	Companies under Company Commanders.	
		14.00 – 15.30.	Company Drill.	
		09.30 – 12.30.	Signallers under Sgt. Sig. Sheasby.	
			Major J.R. Freand, 2nd. Leinster Regt. joined, and took over command of the Bn.	

Army Form C. 2118.

WAR DIARY
or
INTELLIGENCE SUMMARY.
(Erase heading not required.)

Instructions regarding War Diaries and Intelligence Summaries are contained in F. S. Regs., Part II. and the Staff Manual respectively. Title pages will be prepared in manuscript.

Place	Date	Hour	Summary of Events and Information	Remarks and references to Appendices
WERMELSKIRCHEN.	Feb. 7th.		The Battalion paraded for a Route March at 09.30. Dress: Battle Order, less Steel Helmets. In the afternoon Platoons were taken by Platoon Commanders, and instruction given to Lewis Gun Classes under Lewis Gun N.C.Os.	Reference Sheet 2 M., "GERMANY, 1/100,000".
	Feb. 8th.		"W" Coy. found a working party, from 08.00 to 12.00, of 2 N.C.Os. and 20 O.R. for work on the Range under the R.E. Remainder of the Battalion: Interior economy and kit inspections.	
	Feb. 9th.		Brigadier General B.G. Freyburg, V.C., D.S.O. left the 88th. Infantry Brigade. In the morning the Officers of the Battalion, and the Brigade Staff had a photo. group taken at Brigade Headquarters. On the Brigadier leaving WERMELSKIRCHEN, the Battalion turned out and man-handled his motor-car through the streets of the town. The Drums, at the same time, played lively airs.	
DHUNN.	Feb. 10th.		The Battalion relieved the 2nd. Bn. Hampshire Regiment in DHUNN. Relief complete by 12.10. The Battalion was disposed as under:- Battalion Headquarters and "X" Coy: DHUNN. "W" Coy. BERGISCH BORN. "Y" Coy. HALZENBERG. Z Coy. HUELSEN. A road guard of 1 Officer, 3 N.C.Os., and 27 O.R. is found by X Coy. at DREIBAUME.	
	Feb. 11th.		Major J.P. Frend, DSO, 2nd. Leinster Regt., relinquished command of the Bn., which was taken over by Major R.H. Marryatt. Companies at the disposal of O.C. Companies.	
	Feb. 12th.		Companies at the disposal of O.C. Companies.	
	Feb. 13th.		Companies at the disposal of O.C. Companies.	

WAR DIARY
INTELLIGENCE SUMMARY

Army Form C. 2118.

(Erase heading not required.)

Instructions regarding War Diaries and Intelligence Summaries are contained in F.S. Regs., Part II. and the Staff Manual respectively. Title pages will be prepared in manuscript.

Reference Sheet 2 M, GERMANY, 1/100,000.

Place	Date	Hour	Summary of Events and Information	Remarks and references to Appendices
DHUUN	Feb. 14th		Companies at the disposal of O.C. Companies. Capt. H.S. Smith, M.C., (4th. Northants attd 4th. Worcestershire Regt.) demobilized.	
	Feb. 15th		Interior economy and kit inspections.	
	Feb. 16th		The Battalion (less "W" Coy) paraded at 09.15 for Divine Service at DHUNN. The Commanding Officer presented the Belgian Croix de Guerre to Sgt. Sig. Sheasby.	
	Feb. 17th		The Baths at the Communal Kitchen, and the Faction School, WERMELS KIRCHE, were allotted the Battalion all day.	
	Feb. 18th		Companies at the disposal of O.C. Companies. The Concert Party of the 2nd. Hampshires gave a performance in the evening to the Battalion.	
	Feb. 19th		Companies at the disposal of O.C. Companies. The Brigade Boxing Tournament Finals took place in the afternoon. L/Cpl. Philpotts winning the Welter Weight Competition for the Battalion.	
	Feb. 20th		Companies at the disposal of O.C. Companies.	
	Feb. 21st		Companies at the disposal of O.C. Companies.	
	Feb. 22nd		Interior economy and kit inspections.	
	Feb. 23rd		The 2nd. Hampshires left the Brigade en route for England, and were replaced by the 2/4th. Hampshires. The Battalion (less "W" Coy) paraded at 09.15 for Divine Service at DHUNN. The Battalion played the 2nd. Leinsters in the Second Round of the Divisional Football Competition. Result: 2 Goals all.	
	Feb. 24th		The Baths at Communal Kitchen, and the Faction School, WERMELS KIRKKIRCHEN, were allotted the Battalion all day. Battalion replays 2 Leinster in Divisional Football Competition, and Lost 1-3.	

Army Form C. 2118.

WAR DIARY
or
INTELLIGENCE SUMMARY
(Erase heading not required.)

Reference S.est. 2 M., GERMANY, 1/100,000.

Place	Date	Hour	Summary of Events and Information	Remarks and references to Appendices
DUINN.	Feb. 25th.		Companies at the disposal of O.C. Companies. The Concert Party of 19th. Royal Hussars gave a concert to the Battalion in the evening.	
	Feb. 26th.		Companies at the disposal of O.C. Companies. "A" Coy. started wiring the locality of HULSEN.	
	Feb. 27th.		Companies at the disposal of O.C. Companies. Lieut. A.V. College proceeded to the U.K. for two months leave, prior to proceeding overseas for duty. Lecture by Capt. Lloyd, R.A.F. on Aeroplane Reconnaissance.	
	Feb. 28th.		Companies at the disposal of O.C. Companies. First Day Divisional Boxing Competition (Finals) at BERG GLADBACH. About 70 Officers and O.R. proceeded as spectators by motor lorries.	

[signature] Major,
1st. March 1919. Comdg. 4th. Bn. Worcestershire Regiment.

29 Division
88 Infantry Brigade
4 Battalion Worcestershire Regiment
March 1919 Missing

SECRET & CONFIDENTIAL.

WAR DIARY.

4th Battalion The Worcestershire Regiment.

From. 1st April. 1919.
To. 30th April. 1919.

Army Form C. 2118.

WAR DIARY
or
INTELLIGENCE SUMMARY

(Erase heading not required.)

Instructions regarding War Diaries and Intelligence Summaries are contained in F. S. Regs., Part II. and the Staff Manual respectively. Title pages will be prepared in manuscript.

Place	Date	Hour	Summary of Events and Information	Remarks and references to Appendices
MULHEIM (GERMANY)	April 1st.		Companies at disposal of O.C.Coys.	
	2nd.		Companies at disposal of O.C.Coys.	
	3rd		Companies at disposal of O.C.Coys.	
	4th		Companies at disposal of O.C.Coys.	
	5th.		Companies at disposal of O.C.Coys. Lieut.Colonel.R.H.Marryatt rejoined the battalion and assumed command.	
	6th.		Companies at disposal of O.C.Coys.	
	7th.		Companies at disposal of O.C.Coys.	
	8th.		Companies at disposal of O.C.Coys.	
	9th.		Companies at disposal of O.C.Coys.	
	10th.		The Battalion was reduced to Cadre strength, Capt.E.R.Newcomb.M.C. 2nd Lieuts J.Baxter.M.M., E.A.Wood, H.P.Park, E.F.Twining, J.R.Hall, A.H.Wright and G.A.Monks with a draft of 184 O.R's proceeded to Concentration Camp COLOGNE for dispersal and demobilisation. Brigadier-General D.E.Cayley.C.B.; C.M.G., came to say good-bye to the battalion.	
ATH (BELGIUM)	11th.		The Cadre consisting of 6 Officers and 61 O.R's entrained at Cologne for Ath (Belgium).	
	12th.		The Cadre arrived at Ath, being accomodated in the Belgian barracks.	
	13th.		The transport, mobilisation stores, equipment & etc were taken over from the 1st Battn The Worcestershire Regt, and all transport etc repainted 4th Battn The Worcestershire Regiment.	

WAR DIARY
or
INTELLIGENCE SUMMARY.

(Erase heading not required.)

Army Form C. 2118.

Instructions regarding War Diaries and Intelligence Summaries are contained in F. S. Regs., Part II. and the Staff Manual respectively. Title pages will be prepared in manuscript.

Place: ATH (BELGIUM)

Place	Date	Hour	Summary of Events and Information	Remarks and references to Appendices
	April 11.14th.		Cadre at disposal of the Orderly Officer.	
	" 15th.		Cadre at disposal of the Orderly Officer.	
	" 16th.		1st Battalion Worcestershire Regiment entrained for Dunkirk en route to England, being played to the station by the Drums of this Battalion.	
	" 17th.		Cadre at disposal of the Orderly Officer.	
	" 18th.		Cadre at disposal of the Orderly Officer.	
	" 19th.		Cadre at disposal of the Orderly Officer.	
	" 20th.		Cadre at disposal of the Orderly Officer.	
	" 21st.		Cadre at disposal of the Orderly Officer.	
	" 22nd.		Cadre at disposal of the Orderly Officer.	
	" 23rd.		Cadre at disposal of the Orderly Officer.	
	" 24th.		Cadre at disposal of the Orderly Officer.	
	" 25th.		Cadre at disposal of the Orderly Officer.	
	" 26th.		Cadre at disposal of the Orderly Officer.	
	" 27th.		Cadre at disposal of the Orderly Officer.	
	" 28th.		Cadre at disposal of the Orderly Officer.	
	" 29th.		Cadre at disposal of the Orderly Officer.	
	" 30th.		Cadre at disposal of the Orderly Officer.	

WO 95/23001 3

29TH DIVISION
88TH INFY BDE

1-5TH BN ROYAL SCOTS
1916 MAR - ~~APR~~ JUNE 1916

To 32 DIV
14 Bde

Amalgamated with
6; R Scots

29th Division.
98th Infantry Brigade.

Arrived MARSEILLES from EGYPT 22.3.16.

Y_____

1/5th BATTALION

ROYAL SCOTS

MARCH 1 9 1 6

Apr "

29

1/5 Royal Scots

Vol I B.E.F
from M.E.F

29 Div
58 Bde

Army Form C. 2118.

WAR DIARY
or
INTELLIGENCE SUMMARY.
(Erase heading not required.)

Instructions regarding War Diaries and Intelligence Summaries are contained in F. S. Regs., Part II. and the Staff Manual respectively. Title pages will be prepared in manuscript.

Place	Date	Hour	Summary of Events and Information	Remarks and references to Appendices
Suez	9.3.16	—	Divisional Attack practice in the desert.	
"	10.3.16	—	Physical training, Musketry. Parade for practice of tactical movements :- "Infantry in attack over open ground".	
"	11.3.16	—	Tactical exercises with the Brigade.	
"	12.3.16	—	Usual Routine. Brigade and Lewis Gun detachments practised firing at point N.W. of Camp, about 2 miles out, facing the Ataka Mountains.	
"	13.3.16	—	Usual Routine.	
H.M.T. "Glenart"	14.3.16	—	Battalion marched from present Camp, Suez, to Port Tewfik and embarked on board H.M. "Glenart", weighed anchor, and moved up the Suez canal in the evening.	
"	15.3.16	—	Reached Port Said about 9.30 a.m. Officers allowed ashore in afternoon.	
"	16.3.16	—	Left Port Said this morning at 8 a.m. Route marching exercises carried out.	
"	17.3.16	—	Rounds. Route marching exercises. Lectures on Sanitation etc in the Trenches.	
"	18.3.16	—	Usual Routine.	
"	19.3.16	—	Church Parade. Sighted Malta, but did not enter Grand Harbour.	
"	20.3.16	—	Usual Routine :- Route marching exercises, Lectures on Gas Helmets, etc.	
"	21.3.16	—	Usual Routine.	
Marseilles	22.3.16	—	Reached Marseilles, France this morning. The Battalion disembarked, and in the evening entrained for Pontville. Lt. Murdoch, Quartermaster, reported from leave in Britain this day.	
"	23.3.16	—	Travelled all this day. Received light refreshments at certain points on the line.	
"	24.3.16	—	"	
Ailly le Clocher	25.3.16	—	Arrived at destination early this morning, the Battalion marched to Billets in the village of Ailly le Haut Clocher. Lieut. J. Newlands rejoined the Battalion with transport personnel and grooms.	

Army Form C. 2118.

WAR DIARY
or
INTELLIGENCE SUMMARY.
(Erase heading not required.)

Instructions regarding War Diaries and Intelligence Summaries are contained in F. S. Regs., Part II. and the Staff Manual respectively. Title pages will be prepared in manuscript.

Place	Date	Hour	Summary of Events and Information	Remarks and references to Appendices
Pully L'hôpital Blocker	26.3.16		Physical Drill and Route marching. Lecture on war conditions in Gallipoli and France (difference of). Usual routine.	
"	27.3.16		Usual routine.	
"	28.3.16		Battalion took part in Brigade Route march. 2/Lt Graham and Mackie returned to duty with Battalion from special duty with transports.	
"	29.3.16		Physical drill, Rifle exercises, Aiming drill etc. Lecture on Prevention of frostbite.	
"	30.3.16		Physical drill, Route marching. Lts. J.A. Watts left for No Stab?	
"	31.3.16		Usual routine.	
"	1.4.16		The Battalion moved from Billets in Pully L'hôpital to take up new Billets. Arrived at Bonneville in evening and Billeted there.	

Bonneville
3.4.16

J. Begg Lieut
a/Adjutant 1/5th Royal Scots

Army Form C. 2118.

WAR DIARY
or
INTELLIGENCE SUMMARY.
(Erase heading not required.)

Instructions regarding War Diaries and Intelligence Summaries are contained in F.S. Regs., Part II. and the Staff Manual respectively. Title pages will be prepared in manuscript.

Hour, Date, Place	Summary of Events and Information	Remarks and references to Appendices
1st March 1916. Suez.	Usual Routine :- (Company and Platoon drills, bombing and machine gun class, Route marching)	
2nd March. Suez.	C.O's Route march to Port Tewfik, where the process of disinfecting the men's clothing was carried out. 2/Lt. Graham and Mackie with two servants left for Port Said for embarkation duty.	
3rd March. Suez.	Usual Routine. 2/Lt. T. Nueland (Hampshire Regt) and servant proceeded to Alexandria today. Lieut. W.K. Darling (2nd Bn. Cheshire while commanding "Z Coy". 12th Hampshire Regt) reported for duty with Bn.	
4th March. Suez.	Firing at the rifle range. 2/Lt. R.D. Neel and 2/Lt. J. Anderson returned from Lewis Gun Instruction at Ismailia.	
5th " "	Church Parade. Firing at the Rifle range continued.	
6th " "	Firing at the Rifle range.	
7th " "	Extended Order drill and practising marching in line. Lt. E.J. Barendine detached from the 1/4th and M.C. Company and reported to the 1st Border Regt. Lt. Morson attached for instruction to Lewis Gun Section. Lt. Johnston attached to Machine Gun Company vice Lt. Barendine. Lt. Brunt is reported to the Battalion from the 2nd S.H.B.	
8th " "	Battalion inspected by G.O.C. 29th Division. Lt. Corran is reported to the Battalion from the 2nd Hants Regt and detailed as Assembly Officer 88th Brigade. Lt. Wigman reported to Bn. for duty. Lt. Darling detailed as Orderly Officer. Lt. J. Stagg detailed as Musketry Officer.	

(73989) W4141—463. 400,000. 9/14. H.&J.Ltd. Forms/C. 2118/10.

29th Division.

88th Infantry Brigade

Battalion went to G.H.Q. 24th April 1916.

L

1/5th BATTALION

ROYAL SCOTS

APRIL 1916

Army Form C. 2118.

WAR DIARY
or
INTELLIGENCE SUMMARY.
(Erase heading not required.)

Place	Date	Hour	Summary of Events and Information	Remarks and references to Appendices
Rouen	9-5-16		Usual Routine. 1/Lieut. Harnish sick, sent to hospital.	
"	10-5-16		" "	
"	11-5-16		3 Officers and 62 Other Ranks received 1/6th Gordons at New Ammunition Depot.	
"	12-5-16		Usual Routine. Furnished a funeral party.	
"	13-5-16		Usual Routine.	
"	14-5-16		Church Parade.	
"	15-5-16		Usual Routine.	
"	16-5-16		" "	
"	17-5-16		" "	
"	18-5-16		Lieut. J. G. Hislop 1/5th Royal Scots attached for duty in Rouen.	
"	19-5-16		Usual Routine.	
"	20-5-16		Remainder of Battalion moved down to Caserne Lupel, Rouen.	
"	21-5-16		Usual Routine.	
"	22-5-16		" Furnished funeral party. Rev. Capt. E. C. Houlston attached No. 6 General Hospital.	
"	23-5-16		" Furnished funeral party.	
"	24-5-16		" Draft of 41 men from 3/5 Royal Scots.	
"	25-5-16		" 1/Lieut Palmer E. B. to hospital	
"	26-5-16		"	
"	27-5-16		Church Parade. Capt. J. W. Robertson & Lieut. W. Gunnison with 32 Other Ranks	
"	28-5-16		detached for duty to Abancourt.	

Army Form C. 2118.

WAR DIARY
or
INTELLIGENCE SUMMARY.
(Erase heading not required.)

Instructions regarding War Diaries and Intelligence Summaries are contained in F. S. Regs., Part II. and the Staff Manual respectively. Title pages will be prepared in manuscript.

Place	Date	Hour	Summary of Events and Information	Remarks and references to Appendices
Rouen	29th		Usual Routine	
"	30th		" "	
"	31st		" "	

1st June 1916
Rouen.

D. M. Ryan
Lieut Colonel
Commanding 1/5th Bn. The Royal Scots

WAR DIARY
INTELLIGENCE SUMMARY

Army Form C. 2118

1/5 Royal Scots

Place	Date	Hour	Summary of Events and Information	Remarks and references to Appendices
Rouen	1.6.16		The usual Physical Training Parades were carried out from 6.30am to 9am. There were no further parades. The Officers and men being on detached Guards in, and near Rouen carried on as before.	
	3.6.16		For the next few days the same programme was followed.	
	5.6.16		On the 5th Lt. Colonel B.C. McLagan and Capt. B. Maitland attended a R.E.E.M. at Caudebec.	
	6.6.16		Major R.H. Griffiths, 2nd i/c Battn. of 1/5th Royal Scots left on the night of the 6th for duty with 2nd i/c Royal Regt. For many months previous to Lt. McLagan taking over command of the Battalion, Major Griffiths held the position of Commanding Officer, and was present with the 5th through some hard fighting at Cape Helles and Suvla.	
	11.6.16		The Battalion moved this morning from billets in the town of Rouen to camp at the 4th Inf. Base Depot, a few miles out. The Guards were relieved from the various duties by 4th Royal Scots.	
Hedin	13.6.16		On the 13th the Battalion paraded in full marching order and entrained at Gare du Nord Station. Travelling throughout that day, Hedin was reached just after midnight, and from the station the Battalion marched to Billets in the little village of Leewary.	
Le Quesnoy	15.6.16		During the four days stay there the Bn. was engaged in training. On the forenoon of the 15th a draft of 13 officers and 460 other ranks from the 16th R.Sc. 1/4 Royal Scots were attached. The Commanding Officer addressed the members of the drafts, and then the Officers and men were detailed to assist the 116 Companies with the 1/5th men. The numerous Battalion afterwards marched past the Commanding Officer.	
Amiens Rubenpré	17.6.16		By the afternoon of the 17th the Bn. was again on the move. Entraining at Hedin and travelling all night, the South of France was reached, on the morning of Sunday 18th. Breakfasts and cooked rations were served on a field adjoining the railway siding; after which the march to the village of Rubenpré was about 11. was commenced on the way, and Rubenpré was reached in the evening without the Battalion was attached for duties &c. to 49th Division (Maj Gen Reune's)	
Puchvillers	19.6.16		On the afternoon of the 19th a move was made to the village of Puchvillers where the Bn. was immediately required to take its share at different spots with working parties, loading and unloading ammunition &c., and in supplying various guards and small fatigue parties.	

Army Form C. 2118.

WAR DIARY
or
INTELLIGENCE SUMMARY.
(Erase heading not required.)

Instructions regarding War Diaries and Intelligence Summaries are contained in F.S. Regs., Part II. and the Staff Manual respectively. Title pages will be prepared in manuscript.

Place	Date	Hour	Summary of Events and Information	Remarks and references to Appendices
Pucheviller	20.6.16		From the 20th onwards to the end of the month the Battalion furnished working parties of varying sizes to perform duties at many points round Brons Pucheviller. Consequently there was little opportunity for training of any description.	
	23.6.16		On the 23rd Lieut C. M. Nicholas R.A.M.C. who filled the position of Medical Officer for a considerable period, left for duty as a Corvette Clearing Station, & Lieut Nicholas relinquished duty in his place.	
	24.6.16		On the 24th Lieut W. Stewart proceeded to Boulogne to visit Major R.H. Knype 2nd W. to 3rd Sept Regiment, who was wounded while serving with the Bn. & which he had so recently transferred.	
	30.6.16		Usual fatigues. &c	

Pucheviller.
B.E.F.

D. Wyn
Lieut-Colonel
Commanding 1/5th Bn. The Royal Scots (S.S.R.)

Army Form C. 2118.

WAR DIARY
or
INTELLIGENCE SUMMARY.
(Erase heading not required.)

1/5 RS

Instructions regarding War Diaries and Intelligence Summaries are contained in F.S. Regs., Part II. and the Staff Manual respectively. Title pages will be prepared in manuscript.

Place	Date	Hour	Summary of Events and Information	Remarks and references to Appendices
Billon L'Abbaye France	1-4-16		The Battalion moved from Billets in Ailly L'Abbaye and arrived in new Billets at Bonneville that evening.	
Bonneville	2-4-16		The usual instructional Classes in proper method of adjusting and wearing Gas Helmets were carried out. On this date Capts. L. Radcliffe and Capt. J.K. Robertson with 140 Other Ranks proceeded to Britain on leave.	
"	3-4-16		Captain Mc.Cloud. (R.A.M.C.) Capt. J. Gibson and Lieut. J.I. Robinson (Adjutant) rejoined from leave in Britain.	
"	4-4-16		On this day the Battalion marched out of Billets in Bonneville to Argoeuves going via Brilleux Manin, Vauchelles and La Arthie; During the march the Battalion marched past the Corps Commander Lieut. General Sir Hubert Gough. Arrived at Argoeuves about 6 p.m.	
Argoeuves	5-4-16		On the morning of the 5th 2 Officers and 125 Other Ranks commenced the work of Railway Construction near the village of Argoeuves. This work was carried on throughout the remainder of the time on which the Battalion was stationed at Argoeuves.	
"	6-4-16		On this date 2nd Lt. J.W.K. Darling was detailed as Battalion Intelligence Officer. Captain Mc.Cloud, 2nd Lt. Gibson, Stewart and Darling accompanied by 4 senior N.C.O.s visited the front line trenches for instruction. Major J.C. McLagan D.S.O. & later rejoined the Battalion for duty.	
"	7-4-16		The party visiting the front line trenches on this day consisted of Major McLagan, Lts. Bishop and Stephen, and 2nd Lt. Palmer.	
"	8-4-16		On this day Major R.H. Griffiths and 2nd Lt. Millar Cowan & Doulton visited the front line trenches. Capt. A.N. McRae rejoined the Battalion from Egypt.	
"	9-4-16		Leave was again allotted to the Battalion, and on this occasion 2nd Lt. Darling, 1t. Cowan and Bother ranks to left for Britain.	
"	10-4-16		To-day the party visiting the front line trenches consisted of 2nd Lts. Jamieson, Reid, Elder & Kerr. Captain Roulston (Chaplain) 2nd Lt. Muir and 2 other ranks went on leave to Britain. This evening the Battalion paraded in full marching order, and accompanied by transport and Field Kitchen moved up to the Reserve area. The Men manned the trenches at Bresletown and after carrying out duties on advanced posts etc. returned in the early morning to Argoeuves	

WAR DIARY
or
INTELLIGENCE SUMMARY.
(Erase heading not required.)

Army Form C. 2118.

Instructions regarding War Diaries and Intelligence Summaries are contained in F.S. Regs., Part II. and the Staff Manual respectively. Title pages will be prepared in manuscript.

Place	Date	Hour	Summary of Events and Information	Remarks and references to Appendices
Angres	11-4-16		The Officers and men of the Battalion attended a Gas Demonstration on these two days.	
"	12-4-16			
"	13-4-16		This evening the Battalion paraded and marched from Billets in Angres to new Billets at Beauvais. Lt. J. Graham was left behind as Town Commandant of Angres.	
Beauvais	14-4-16		To-day a working party of 6 Officers and 200 other ranks paraded, and moving up to the Communication Trenches commenced work on a certain portion thereof. During the period in which the Battalion was Billeted at Beauvais took zone covered out trenches and day on their dugout and Communication trenches. The working parties were greatly inconvenienced during the operation by the extremely inclement weather, the trenches filling up with water in many places.	
"	15-4-16		Captain Radcliffe, Capt. Robertson and 1/4 other ranks rejoined the Batt: from leave in Britain. Captain Nethercutt and a draft of 29 nco's and men reported for duty with the Regiment. Major R.W. Griffiths to-day relinquished Command of Batt: The men not engaged in work in the trenches were occupied in Gas Helmet Drill, and the usual Schools of Instruction. To-day Major P.C. Milligan D.S.O. took over the Command of Battalion. (authority: Telegram War Office)	
"	16-4-16			
"	17-4-16		The Battalion arranged under new Company scheme paraded at the respective Alarm Posts	
"	18-4-16		5 Officers and 45 other ranks attended a Gas demonstration in the Chateau near village of Verdrel this morning. Lt. Garling, M.C. men and Corpn with 5 other ranks rejoined the Battalion from leave in Britain. 4 n.c.o's reported to the Brigade for duty as Bde. Intelligence Officer. Nil errors reported	
"	19-4-16		4 n.c.o's reported from leave to-day	
"	20-4-16		To-day the Officers in the Batt: unable to ride commenced a course of horsemanship under the Transport Officer.	

Army Form C. 2118.

WAR DIARY
or
INTELLIGENCE SUMMARY.
(Erase heading not required.)

Instructions regarding War Diaries and Intelligence Summaries are contained in F. S. Regs., Part II. and the Staff Manual respectively. Title pages will be prepared in manuscript.

Place	Date	Hour	Summary of Events and Information	Remarks and references to Appendices
Beauvais	21-4-16		This morning all ranks paraded under their respective Commanders and proceeded to the Divisional Baths at Ackeux, where each individual bathed and received clean under clothing.	
"	22-4-16			
"	23-4-16		Church Parade was conducted in the little village Church Beauvais this morning and in the evening a voluntary service was held. Captain & M.C. Bland and Lieut. B. Bowen proceeded to Flixecourt to-day for a course of Special Instruction for one month (at 4th Army School of Instruction.)	
"	24-4-16		This morning the Battalion paraded in full marching order and moved to Doullens and was inspected en route by Brigadier General Caley, arriving Doullens about 4 o'clock in the afternoon. Billets in Doullens.	
Doullens	25-4-16		To-day 15 Officers and 188 other ranks proceeded this morning to guard duties at 3rd old 4th Army Railheads.	
"	26-4-16		This morning the Battalion were inspected by Lieut- General Sir Aylmer Hunter Weston and commended for the heroic deeds performed throughout the Gallipoli Campaign. Various Grenade drills were carried out by the Bn. to-day.	
"	27-4-16		The remainder of Battalion not on Guard duties furnished Escorts for prisoners on both days.	
"	28-4-16			
"	29-4-16		Intimation received that Major J.C. McLagan D.S.O. had been Gazetted Lieut-Colonel (extract London Gazette 27-4-16) dating from 15-4-16.	
"	30-4-16		Church Parade held this morning in Y.M.C.A. Hall Doullens. In the forenoon a draft of 47 men arrived from Rouen. Little afternoon a Lecture was delivered to the Battalion by Brigade Major Jordan on the War.	

J.R. Moron
Lieutenant
Adjutant 1/5 Bn. The Royal Scots.

Doullens
3-1-6-16.

W0 95/23091

SOUTHERN (LATE 29TH) DIVN
88TH INFY BDE

2/4TH BN HAMPSHIRE REGT
MAY - OCT 1919

From 62 DIV 186 BDE

VOLUME No. 23.

SECRET.

WAR DIARY
OF THE
2/4TH BATTALION,
THE HAMPSHIRE REGIMENT.

PERIOD

FROM :- MAY 1st, 1919. TO :- MAY 31st, 1919.

J. H. Thomas Capt.

for ——— LIEUT.-COLONEL,
COMMANDING 2/4th BATTALION, THE HAMPSHIRE REGIMENT.

WERMELSKIRCHEN.
JUNE 1st, 1919.

Army Form C. 2118.

WAR DIARY

INTELLIGENCE SUMMARY 2/4th Battn. The Hampshire Regiment.

VOLUME 23.

(Erase heading not required.)

Instructions regarding War Diaries and Intelligence Summaries are contained in F.S. Regs., Part II. and the Staff Manual respectively. Title pages will be prepared in manuscript.

Place	Date	Hour	Summary of Events and Information	Remarks and references to Appendices
WERMELSKIR- CHEN.	May 1st- 31st.		The Battalion less "A" Company, at WERMELSKIRCHEN. "A" Company on Outpost duty at TALSPERRE.	
	23rd.		2/Lieutenant S.H.KINGSMILL appointed Captain & Adjutant.	
	27th.		The Battalion, less "A" Company was this morning inspected by the Commander-in-Chief, General Sir WILLIAM R.ROBERTSON, G.C.B., K.C.V.O., D.S.O., A.D.C. The following Special Order of the Day was afterwards issued :- "The Commander-in-Chief has asked me to convey to the 2/4th and 15th Battalions, The Hampshire Regiment, his appreciation of the excellence of the turnout, and steadiness on Parade this morning. He considers that it reflects the highest credit on the Officers and All Ranks of these Battalions - I wish to add my congratulations to All Ranks of these Battalions, on what was a splendid performance, and to thank them for the hard work of preparation which the Parade entailed. (Signed) D.E.CAYLEY, Brig.-Gen.; Commdg. 3rd Southern Infantry Brigade." During the past month, Training has proceeded very satisfactorily. The additional hours Parade in the afternoon has been dropped. Classes have been held daily in Signalling, Scouting and Lewis Gun work. 50 yards Rifle Ranges have been constructed for each Company, and practise has been proceeding daily. The Open Air Baths at EIFGEN have been much appreciated by the men who have, during the month, shewn exceptional keenness in their turnout, Training and Games. Education is now only compulsory for those who do not hold 3rd Army Class Army Certificates, and is limited to 6 hours per week. The Qualifying Examination was held on May 5th, 1919 and 36% of the Battalion passed the Test. An Examination has also taken place on the basis of the 2nd Class Standard, and resulted in 15% of the Battalion qualifying.	

Army Form C. 2118.

WAR DIARY
or
INTELLIGENCE SUMMARY.

(Erase heading not required.)

SHEET -2-
VOLUME 23.

Instructions regarding War Diaries and Intelligence Summaries are contained in F. S. Regs., Part II. and the Staff Manual respectively. Title pages will be prepared in manuscript.

Place	Date	Hour	Summary of Events and Information	Remarks and references to Appendices
WERMELSKIR-CHEN.	May 1919.			
	12th.		FOOTBALL & RESULTS.	
			SIX A SIDE.	
			No. 14 Platoon beat No. 10 Platoon by 4 Points.	
			7 " " " 13 " " 2 "	
			3 " " " 5 " " 2 "	
			1 " " " 9 " " 6 "	
			4 " " " 18 " " 4 "	
			2 " " " 11 " " 6 "	
	25th.		BATTALION MATCH.	
			2/4th Bn. The Hampshire Regiment VERSUS Machine Gun Corps.	
			2/4th Hants. won. 3 to NIL.	
	30th.		"D" Company, 2/4th Hampshires VERSUS "A" Company, 15th Hampshires.	
			2/4th Hants. won 4 to NIL.	

WERMELSKIRCHEN.
June 1st, 1919.

J. L. Thomas as Capt. for
Lieut: Colonel.
Commanding 2/4th Battn. The Hampshire Regiment.

VOLUME. 25.

WAR DIARY

of

2/4th BATTALION, THE HAMPSHIRE REGIMENT

From :- 1st June 1919.
To :- 30th June 1919.

N.C. Rew-Pearce
Major,
Commanding 2/4th Battalion, The Hampshire Regiment.

SECRET.

Army Form C. 2118.

WAR DIARY

INTELLIGENCE SUMMARY
(Erase heading not required.)

2/4th BATTALION, THE HAMPSHIRE REGIMENT.

Volumn. 25.

Instructions regarding War Diaries and Intelligence Summaries are contained in F. S. Regs, Part II. and the Staff Manual respectively. Title pages will be prepared in manuscript.

Place	Date	Hour	Summary of Events and Information	Remarks and references to Appendices
WERMELS-KIRCHEN.	June 1st.		The Battalion, less 'A' Coy at WERMELSKIRCHEN. 'A' Coy on Outpost duty TALSPERRE.	
	June 3rd.		In honour of the King's Birthday the Battalion paraded for Brigade Ceremonial under Brigadier General D.E.CAYLEY, C.B., C.M.G. - A football match was played in the afternoon, 13 platoon (D.Coy) being the winners of Knock out Competition. In the evening an open air Concert was given by the Battalion Concert Party.	
	June 6th.		Football. On this day 'D' Coy of this Battalion played 'A' Coy of the 15th Hants, 'D' Coy winning 4 goals to 1.	
	June 8th.		Cricket. Battalion Cricket team played 72nd R.F.A., at , the score being 2/4th Hants 65, 72nd R.F.A. 66.(66)	
	June 13th.		Battalion Cricket Team played S.D.M.T. at Mulheim, score".2/4th Hants. 49. SDMT Coy. 51.	
DHUNN.	June 16th.		The Battalion, less 'A' Coy, relieved the 51st Battalion, Hampshire Regiment on Outpost Duty. "A" Company remaining at TALSPERRE, 'B' Company taking over the BERGISH BORN area. 'C' " " " BREIBAUMEN 'D' " " " HALZENBURG 'HQ'Coy. less advanced HQuarters. DHUNN. Advanced HQ. SUPPELBACH.	
WERMELSKIR-CHEN.	June 18th.		The Battalion were relieved by the 51st Battalion, Warwick Regiment, and proceeded to WERMELSKIRCHEN to billets for the night. Advanced H.Q. remaining that night at SUPPELBACH. Blankets and tents were despatched to MULHEIM and all surplus kit and stores deposited in a Brigade Dump at WERMELSKIRCHEN.	
HUNGER.	June 19th.		The 3rd Southern Infantry Brigade moved to BURG. The 2/4th Hampshire Regiment in the rear of the Column. The Battalion billeted at HUNGER, and adjoining hamlets of NEUENFLUGEL, POHLHAUSEN, STALZENBERG.	
	June 27th.		The Battalion in HUNGER awaiting the decision of the Germans with regard to the signing of the Peace Treaty.	
			Continued:-	

Army Form C. 2118.

WAR DIARY
of
INTELLIGENCE SUMMARY 2/4th BATTALION THE HAMPSHIRE REGIMENT.
VOLUMN. 25.

(Erase heading not required.)

Instructions regarding War Diaries and Intelligence Summaries are contained in F. S. Regs., Part II. and the Staff Manual respectively. Title pages will be prepared in manuscript.

Place	Date	Hour	Summary of Events and Information	Remarks and references to Appendices
HUNGER.	June 28th		Peace Signed. No demonstrations whatever were made either by ourselves or the civilians.	
	June 30th		This day saw the first of the withdrawals of troops concentrated on the Perimeter line being 'A' Day. On 'C' Day we move back to the area we vacated on June 18th.	

HUNGER.
July 2nd 1919.

[signature]
Major.
Commanding 2/4th Battalion Hampshire Regiment.

SECRET.

VOLUME No. 26.

WAR *⊙* DIARY

2/4TH BATTALION, THE HAMPSHIRE REGIMENT.
⊙

PERIOD

FROM :— 1ST JULY 1919. *⊙* TO :— 31ST JULY 1919.

[signature] LIEUT. COLONEL,
COMMANDING 2/4TH BATTALION, THE HAMPSHIRE REGIMENT.

[stamp: SUPPELBACH, 2ND AUGUST, 1919.]

Army Form C. 2118.

WAR DIARY
or
INTELLIGENCE SUMMARY.
(Erase heading not required.)

2/4th BATTALION. THE HAMPSHIRE REGIMENT.

VOLUM. NO:26.

Place	Date	Hour	Summary of Events and Information	Remarks and references to Appendices
HUNGER.	JULY 1-3.		The Battalion billeted at HUNGER.	
SUPPELBACH.	JULY 3rd.		The Battalion moved back from HUNGER and relieved the 51st Battalion, The Warwickshire Regiment on Outpost Duty; our "A" Company taking over the TALSPERRE Area. "B" ... BERGISH BORN Area. "C" ... BUCHHOLZEN. "D" ... HALZENBERG. "HQ" ... DHUNN. Advanced "HQ" ... SUPPELBACH.	
	JULY 5-12.		A period of fine weather; a certain amount of shooting on ranges, and some Cricket was played at BUCHHOLZEN.	
	JULY 13-20.		A period of Company Sports. Very successful meetings and much keenness shown.	
	JULY 21-26.		A wet period, culminating in Battalion Sports on the 26th. "C" Company won the Athletic Cup with 20 points. "A" Company were the runnersup with 15 points.	
	JULY 27-31.		A wet period; but some Cricket was played. During our month on Outpost Duty, the discomforts of wet weather under canvas have been great; but have been borne cheerfully.	

SUPPELBACH.
August 2nd 1919.

Newton Lieut. Colonel.
Commanding 2/4th Battalion, The Hampshire Regiment.

VOLUMN NO: 28.

2/4TH BATTALION, THE HAMPSHIRE REGIMENT.

"WAR DIARY"

AUGUST 1919.

SECRET.

VOLUME No. 27.

C O P Y.
****

W A R   D I A R Y   O F   T H E

2/4TH BATTALION, THE HAMPSHIRE REGIMENT.

****

P E R I O D.

F R O M :- 1ST AUGUST 1919.   T O :- 31ST AUGUST 1919.

****

H.Drew
Lieut. Colonel,
Commanding 2/4th Battalion, The Hampshire Regiment.

WERMELSKIRCHEN,
September 2nd 1919.

WAR DIARY
or
INTELLIGENCE SUMMARY.

(Erase heading not required.)

2/4th Battalion, The Hampshire Regiment.   Volum No. 27.

COPY.

Place	Date	Hour	Summary of Events and Information	Remarks and references to Appendices
SUPPELBACH.	Aug. 1-2.		The Battalion on Outpost Duty :- our "A" Company at 'tALSPERRE. "B" " BERGISCH BORN. "C" " BUCHHOLZEN. "D" " HALZENBURGH. "HQ" " DHUNN. "HQ" " SUPPELBACH.	
WERMELSKIRCHEN.	Aug. 3.		The Battalion relieved by the 15th Battalion The Hampshire Regiment, and moved into Billets in Eastern Area of WERMELSKIRCHEN.	
	Aug. 4-15.		A period of fine weather, and a certain amount of cricket played on the Battalion Ground at WERMELSKIRCHEN.	
	Aug. 16-19.		Lieut.-Gen. Sir CLAUD JACOB, K.C.B., K.C.M.G., Commanding II Army Corps, with Major-Gen. Sir W.C.HENNEKER, K.C.B., D.S.O., Commanding Southern Division, inspected the Battalion on No. 1 Football Ground. After the Inspection the Battalion was congratulated on the splendid turn-out, and the steadiness of the Men on Parade.	
	Aug. 20-31.		The Battalion commenced firing the General Musketry Course on the Brigade Range, firing taking place in the morning as well as the afternoon, and continuing until the end of the end of the month.	

WERMELSKIRCHEN.
September 2rd, 1919.

Lieut. Colonel,
Commanding 2/4th Battalion, the Hampshire Regiment.

Army Form C. 2118.

WAR DIARY
or
INTELLIGENCE SUMMARY.

(Erase heading not required.) 2/4th BATTALION, THE HAMPSHIRE REGIMENT.

VOLUMN NO: 27.

Instructions regarding War Diaries and Intelligence Summaries are contained in F. S. Regs., Part II. and the Staff Manual respectively. Title pages will be prepared in manuscript.

Place	Date	Hour	Summary of Events and Information	Remarks and references to Appendices

SUPPELBACH.	Aug. 1-2		The Battalion on Outpost duty:- our "A" Company at TALSPERRE.
			                                       "B" " BERGISH BORN.
			                                       "C" " BUCHHOLZEN.
			                                       "D" " HALZENBURG.
			                                       "HQ" " DHUNN.
			                   Advanced. "HQ" SUPPELBACH.	

WERMELSKIRCHEN.	Aug. 3.		The Battalion relieved by the 15th Hampshire Regiment, and moved into Billets in Eastern Area of WERMELSKIRCHEN.	
WERMELSKIRCHEN.	Aug. 4-15.		A period of fine weather, and a certain amount of Cricket played on the Battalion Ground at WERMELSKIRCHEN.	
WERMELSKIRCHEN.	Aug. 16-19.		Lieutenant-General Sir CLAUD JACOB, K.C.B., K.C.M.G., Commanding II Army Corps, with Major General Sir W.C. HENNEKER., K.C.B., D.S.O., Commanding Southern Division, inspected the Battalion on No: 1. Football Ground. After the Inspection the Battalion was congratulated on the splendid turn-out, and the steadiness of the men on Parade.	
WERMELSKIRCHEN.	Aug. 20-31.		The Battalion Commenced firing the General Musketry Course on the Brigade Range, Firing taking place in the morning as well as the afternoon, and continuing until the end of the month.	

1919.

                                                 Lieut. Colonel.

Commanding 2/4th Battalion Hampshire Regiment.

SECRET.

VOLUME No. 28.

2/4TH HAMPSHIRE REGIMENT.
No. W.D.
Date 2.10.19.

W A R   D I A R Y

O F   T H E

2/4th BATTALION, THE HAMPSHIRE REGIMENT.

P E R I O D.

FROM :- SEPTEMBER 1st, 1919.   TO :-   SEPTEMBER 30th, 1919.

Hutton
Lieut. Colonel,
Commanding 2/4th Battalion, The Hampshire Regiment.

WERMELSKIRCHEN.
October 2nd, 1919.

Army Form C. 2118.

WAR DIARY
or
INTELLIGENCE SUMMARY.

2/4th Battalion, The Hampshire Regiment.

VOLUME No. 28.

(Erase heading not required.)

Instructions regarding War Diaries and Intelligence Summaries are contained in F. S. Regs., Part II. and the Staff Manual respectively. Title pages will be prepared in manuscript.

Place	Date	Hour	Summary of Events and Information	Remarks and references to Appendices
WERMELSKIRCHEN.	Sept. 1-7th.		The Battalion in Billets in the EASTERN Area of WERMELSKIRCHEN, and continuing the Firing of The GENERAL MUSKETRY COURSE.	
	8th.		The MUSKETRY COURSE concluded, and the Average Points scored leaves the Battalion holding 2nd Place amongst the Units of the Division, whom have completed the COURSE.	
	9-17th.		A Period of Fine hot weather during several Cricket Matches were played, both at Home and away.	
	18th.		A very regretable accident occurred during a demonstration by the 3rd Southern L.T.M.B. at which "B" & "C" Companies were present. A Premature Explosion causing the deaths of Sgt. CHIPLING, Cpl. HOWE and Pte. PIWELL of this Unit, as well as causing injuries to 9 Other Ranks.	
	19-29th.		Training in progress for Events in the Divisional Competition.	
	30th.		Transport Turn-Out Event took place in connection with the Divisional Competition, this Unit gaining 1st Place in the Brigade.	
			DEMOBILISATION during this Month has proceeded apace. - 3 Officers and 211 Other Ranks have been sent for dispersal to the United Kingdom. EDUCATION has progressed satisfactorily, Candidates in the Special and 1st Class Army Certificates having been successful.	

2/4TH HAMPSHIRE REGIMENT.

WERMELSKIRCHEN.
October 2nd, 1919.

Lieut. Colonel,
Commanding 2/4th Battalion, The Hampshire Regiment.

Army Form C. 2118.

WAR DIARY
or
INTELLIGENCE SUMMARY.

(Erase heading not required) 2/4th Battalion, The Hampshire Regiment.

Summary of Events and Information   VOLUME NO: 29.

Place	Date	Hour	Summary of Events and Information	Remarks and references to Appendices
WERMELSKIRCHEN.	Oct. 1st–24th.		Battalion in Billets in WERMELSKIRCHEN. On the 23rd inst. The G.O.C. 3rd Southern Infantry Brigade, Brigadier-General D.E.CAYLEY, C.B., C.M.G. addressed the Battalion previous to its disbandment. In a well chosen speech he complimented the Battalion on its work, smart turn-out and discipline whilst with the 3rd Southern Infantry Brigade. He wished ALL Ranks success where ever they might find themselves in the future. After three hearty cheers for the General had been given, and the General had left, the Commanding Officer, Lieut. Colonel H.SIDNEY, D.S.O., T.D. thanked ALL Ranks for the hearty support that had been given him and expressed his best wishes for their future; three hearty cheers were then given. On the 24th the Battalion sent the following Officers to the 51st Battalion, The Hampshire Regiment :- Lieut. (A/Capt) R.J.SCOTT, M.C., Lieut. (A/Capt) W.L. CLARKE, 2/Lt (A/Capt) W.GIBBONS, M.C., Lieut. (A/Capt) C.D.WOOLDRIDGE, Lieutenants H.L.WILLSHER, M.C., R.A.GIBB, F.C.ISAACS, R.T.ANDERSON, W.S.STONER, V.R.HARDING, 2/Lieutenants T.H.BENNETT, H.F. WHEELER, M.C., J.R.STEVENS, E.M.NEIL, M.C., C.NEWMAN, A.W.PALMER, H.C.BRIDGER, and 266 OTHER RANKS. 163 OTHER RANKS proceeded to the 15th Battalion, The Hampshire Regiment. 2/Lieut. R.J.HERITAGE proceeded to the 52nd Battalion, The Royal Warwickshire Regiment.	
	30th–31st.		At MIDNIGHT 30/31st OCTOBER 1919, the 2/4th Battalion, The Hampshire Regiment, T.F. brought its Record of 4 Years 10½ Months Service Overseas to a close. The following Officers who had not been disposed of, being attached to the 15th Battalion, The Hampshire Regiment :- Lieut. Colonel H.SIDNEY, D.S.O., T.D.; Major H.C.WESTMORLAND, D.S.O.; Lieut. (A/Capt) J.L.THOMAS, Lieut. & Q.M. S.A.THOMSON, Lieutenants C.F.WOOLHOUSE, W.KILLIN, R.L.J.BOWEN, H.HODGSON, 2/Lieutenants R.R.DEAR, M.C.M., A.GOSLIN, I.J.LOW. As a matter of interest the following left England with the Battalion, 12/4/1914, and were with the Battalion the whole Period the Battalion was in existence Serving in INDIA, EGYPT, PALESTINE, FRANCE & GERMANY. 200294 Sgt. Q.R.S. COUSINS W.H., 201289 Cpl. COX H., 200988 Pte. DENTON C.V. 201149 Sgt. DIXON A., 201207 R.Q.M.S. EMBERTON J.M., 201028 L/Cpl. GRIGG E., 201108 Pte. HUTCHINGS C., 200644 Sgt. Dmr. JAMES S., 201174 Pte. LAVERSUCH G., 200100 Sgt. MEADEN G., 200871 Pte. OAKLEY C., 201487 Pte. WESTBROOK E.; 201253 C.S.M. SAMWAYS C., 200613 Ste. BONE W.	
	31st.		Lieutenant (A/Captain) & Adjutant S.H.KINGSMILL proceeded to the 51st Battalion, The Hampshire Regiment.	

H. Sidney
Lieut. Colonel,
Commanding 2/4th Battalion, The Hampshire Regiment.

W9a5/2309/5

SOUTHERN (LATE 29TH) DIVN
88TH INFY BDE

15TH BN HAMPSHIRE REGT

MAY - SEP 1919

FROM 41 DIV 122 BDE

Army Form C. 2118.

WAR DIARY
or
INTELLIGENCE SUMMARY.
(Erase heading not required.)

MAY 1919.

Place	Date	Hour	Summary of Events and Information	Remarks and references to Appendices
SUPPELBACH	3rd		Weekly Strength 64 Officers 1116 O.Rks.	
	4th		Divine Service.	
	5th		Baths.	
	6th		Baths.	
	7th		Baths.	
	8th		Baths.	
	9th		Divisional Guard found by "C" Company. Capt. G.C. Oxborrow M.C. rejoined the Battalion and assumes command of "C" Company from this date.	
	10th		Weekly Strength 64 Officers 1088 O.Rks.	
	11th		Divine Service.	
	12th		Musketry Results for week ending 11th May as follows:—	
			DELIBERATE RAPID. No. of men fired.	
			"A" Company 13.3 9.5 110	
			"C" " 11.9 9.7 145	
			"D" " 11.3 9.6 122	
			"B" " 6.9 6.5 100	

Army Form C. 2118.

WAR DIARY
or
INTELLIGENCE SUMMARY.
(Erase heading not required.)

Place	Date	Hour	Summary of Events and Information	Remarks and references to Appendices
SUPPELBACH	12th		Eight best shots :-	
			G. D. R. Total.	
			"A" 20252 Pte Reeves R. 2" 20 13 35	
			"A" 29817 L.C. Preiss O. 3" 20 15 35	
			"D" 57808 A/Sgt.Combs H.J. 2" 16 18 34	
			"A" 45606 Pte Dollor W. 2" 20 14 34	
			"D" 7075 " Palmer J. 2" 15 19 34	
			"C" 02367 " Harry F.G. 2" 18 15 34	
			"C" 12955 L.C. Jeffreys R. 2" 18 15 34	
			"C" 51401 Pte. Thyer W.W. 2" 18 15 34	
	15th		Battalion relieved by 51st Bn Hampshire Regt and marched to billets at Wermelskirchen. Copy of operation orders attached.	
WERMELSKIRCHEN	15th		Companies disposal Company Commanders. Lecture by Mr. Edgar Bollingham at Diamond Troupe Hall, Wermelskirchen. Subject "The Course of Defiance". Lieut.Col.Hon R. Brand D.S.O. joined Battalion this date.	
	16th		Lieut Col Hon R. Brand D.S.O. assumes command of Battalion this date. Company Commanders Conference.	
	17th		Weekly Strength 64 Officers 1035 O.Rks.	
	18th		Divine Service at Parish Church - Wermelskirchen.	
	19th		Baths. Kit Inspection.	
	20th		Company and Specialist Training.	
	21st		Company and Specialist Training.	

Army Form C. 2118.

WAR DIARY
or
INTELLIGENCE SUMMARY.

(Erase heading not required.)

Instructions regarding War Diaries and Intelligence Summaries are contained in F. S. Regs., Part II. and the Staff Manual respectively. Title pages will be prepared in manuscript.

Place	Date	Hour	Summary of Events and Information	Remarks and references to Appendices
WERMELSKIRCHEN	22nd		Battalion Route March. SUPPELBACH - BUCHOLZEN - "T" roads S of the B in BERGISH BORN WERMELSKIRCHEN.	
	23rd		Company and Specialist Training. Lecture by Mr. F.W. Gill at Diamond Troupe Hall, Wermelskirchen. Subject "THE EXPERIENCES OF A CYCLING VAGABOND".	
	24th		Marching Order Parades and Ceremonial Parades. Weekly Strength 61 Officers 1113 O.Rks.	
	25th		Divine Service at Parish Church. Wermelskirchen.	
	26th		Battalion paraded for Commander-in-Chief's inspection. Baths.	
	27th		Company and Specialist Training. "B" Company inspected by C.O.	
	28th		Company and Specialist Training. Gymnasium alloted to Companies.	
	29th		Battalion Route March. EIPRINGHAUSEN - X roads N of DHUNN - WOLLERSBERG - HINTERCHUFF - ECKRINGHAUSEN - WERMELSKIRCHEN.	
	30th		Company and Specialist Training. "D" Company inspected by C.O.	
	31st		Films on Venereal Disease at Diamond Troupe Hall, Wermelskirchen. Weekly Strength 61 Officers 1113 O.Rks.	

R. Brand, Lt Colonel
en cd 15-B. Hants Regt

Army Form C. 2118.

WAR DIARY
or
INTELLIGENCE SUMMARY.
(Erase heading not required.)

Instructions regarding War Diaries and Intelligence Summaries are contained in F.S. Regs., Part II. and the Staff Manual respectively. Title pages will be prepared in manuscript.

Place	Date	Hour	Summary of Events and Information	Remarks and references to Appendices
Wermelskirchen.	1/6/19.		Divine Service at Parish Church WERMELSKIRCHEN.	
"	2/6/19.		Baths. Kit Inspection.	
"	3/6/19.		H.M. THE KING'S BIRTHDAY. Day observed as a whole holiday. Battalion Sports cancelled owing to rain.	
"	4/6/19.		Company and Specialist Training. Lecture by Archdeacon DYER M.A. Subject, "Burma & Burmese".	
"	5/6/19.		Battalion Route March cancelled owing to rain.	
"	6/6/19.		Southern Divisional Race Meeting at KALK, COLOGNE. Special train ran.	
"	7/6/19.		Second and last day of Southern Divisional Race Meeting. WEEKLY STRENGTH. 60 Officers, 1,114 Other Ranks.	
"	8/6/19.		Divine Service at Parish Church WERMELSKIRCHEN.	
"	9/6/19.		BANK HOLIDAY. Day observed as a whole holiday. Sports in afternoon. The KING has been pleased to confer on Lieut. Colonel The Hon R. Brand D.S.O. the most Distinguished Order of the C.M.G. (London Gazette 3/6/19)	
"	10/6/19.		Battalion, Company and Specialist Training.	
"	11/6/19.		Tactical training for Companies.	
"	12/6/19.		Battalion, Company and Specialist Training. Major T.P. THYNE M.C. assumes command of "B" Company from this date.	
"	13/6/19.		Battalion, Company and Specialist Training. Lecture at Diamond Troupe Hall.	
"	14/6/19.		Full Marching Order Inspections. Transport inspected by the Commanding Officer. WEEKLY STRENGTH. 54 Officers, 1,115 Other Ranks.	

R. Brand
Lieut.-Colonel
Commanding 15th (S) Battn. Hampshire Regt.

Army Form C. 2118.

WAR DIARY
or
INTELLIGENCE SUMMARY.
(Erase heading not required.)

Instructions regarding War Diaries and Intelligence Summaries are contained in F. S. Regs., Part II. and the Staff Manual respectively. Title pages will be prepared in manuscript.

Place	Date	Hour	Summary of Events and Information	Remarks and references to Appendices
Wermelskirchen.	15/6/19.		Divine Service at Parish Church WERMELSKIRCHEN. "C" Company's Sports in the morning and afternoon.	
"	16/6/19.		Baths. Kit Inspection.	
"	17/6/19.		Conference at Brigade Headquarters for Commanding Officers and Adjutants.	
"	18/6/19.		Fighting Order Inspections and Gas Helmet Inspections. Conference for all Officers at Headquarters Mess with reference to future movements of the Battalion.	
"	19/6/19.		Battalion moved to BURG. Route WERMELSKIRCHEN - HUNGER - BURG.	
Burg.	20/6/19.		Companies at disposal of Company Commanders. Conference held at Headquarter Mess to discuss future movements of Battalion.	
"	21/6/19.		Companies at disposal of Company Commanders. WEEKLY STRENGTH. 54 Officers, 1,118 Other Ranks.	
"	22/6/19.		Divine Service for the Battalion, less "C" Company, on field at rear of Orderly Room 1045 hours.	
"	23/6/19.		Company and Specialist Training.	
"	24/6/19.		Companies at disposal of Company Commanders.	
"	25/6/19.		Field Firing carried out by all Companies in the morning.	
"	26/6/19.		Companies at the disposal of Company Commanders.	
"	27/6/19.		Companies at the disposal of Company Commanders.	
"	28/6/19.		Wire from Brigade 2030 hours, PEACE SIGNED. General rejoicings in BURG. Companies at the disposal of Company Commanders, also Specialist Training.	WEEKLY STRENGTH 54 Officers, 1,122 Other Ranks.

R.P. Brand Lieut-Colonel
Commanding 15th (S) Batln. Hampshire Regt.

Army Form C. 2118.

WAR DIARY
or
INTELLIGENCE SUMMARY.
(Erase heading not required.)

Place	Date	Hour	Summary of Events and Information	Remarks and references to Appendices
Burg.	29/6/19.		Divine Service at 1115 hours at BURG Parish Church. Battalion Sports Meeting at 1000 hours to arrange for Battalion Sports on 2/7/19.	
"	30/6/19.		Baths. Companies at the disposal of Company Commanders.	

R. Shaw
Lieut. Colonel
Commanding 15th. Battalion Hampshire Regt.

Army Form C. 2118.

WAR DIARY
or
INTELLIGENCE SUMMARY.
(Erase heading not required.)

Instructions regarding War Diaries and Intelligence Summaries are contained in F.S. Regs., Part II. and the Staff Manual respectively. Title pages will be prepared in manuscript.

Place	Date	Hour	Summary of Events and Information	Remarks and references to Appendices
BURG	1/7/19		Battalion moved back BURG-WERMELSKIRCHEN. Route followed BURG-KELLERS MUHL-PREYERSMUHL-WERMELSKIRCHEN.	
WERMELSKIRCHEN	2/7/19		Battalion Sports at WERMELSKIRCHEN. No Training. Heats run off in morning. Finals in afternoon. Brigadier General D.E. CAYLEY C.B., C.M.G. *(?)*, 3rd Southern Infantry Brigade presented the Cup, given by the Officers of the 15th Hants., to the winning Platoon (No 9)	
do	3/7/19		Companies at the disposal of Company Commanders.	
do	4/7/19		Whole holiday for the Battalion in celebration of Peace. Battalion Sports team left for RATH HEUMAR in the afternoon, having been challenged by the 41st M.G.C.	
do	5/7/19		Companies at the disposal of Company Commanders. Battalion took part in the Sports in accordance with the challenge, and won by the following points (at RATH HEUMAR) 15th Bn HAMPSHIRE Regt. 58.33 41st M.G.C. 43.66 WEEKLY STRENGTH. OFFICERS 49 O.R. 1053	
do	6/7/19		Divine Service at WERMELSKIRCHEN Parish Church 1130 hrs for the whole Battalion.	

Army Form C. 2118.

WAR DIARY
or
INTELLIGENCE SUMMARY.
(*Erase heading not required.*)

Place	Date	Hour	Summary of Events and Information	Remarks and references to Appendices
WERMELSKIRCHEN	7/7/19		Companies at the disposal of Company Commanders. Brigadier General D.E. CAYLEY C.B. C.M.G. 3rd Southern Infantry Brigade inspected billets. "C" Company placed in isolation from this date. Capt J.L. Spencer MC and 4 O.Rks. go to Paris today to take part in the Victory March therm.	
do	8/7/19		Companies at the disposal of Company Commanders. Peace celebrations in the Officers Mess.	
do	9/7/19		Companies at the disposal of Company Commanders.	
do	10/7/19		Companies at the disposal of Company Commanders.	
do	11/7/19		Companies at the disposal of Company Commanders. Sports meeting held at the Recreation Room concerning the coming Brigade Sports.	
do	12/7/19		Companies at the disposal of Company Commanders. Several Officers and O.Rks. visited Divisional Races at MERHEIM. WEEKLY STRENGTH OFFICERS 48 O.Rks. 1051	
do	13/7/19		Divine Service for Battalion less "C" Company in WERMELSKIRCHEN Parish Church 1130 Hrs. Cross Country Run for Battalion cancelled.	
do	14/7/19		Companies at the disposal of Company Commanders. Battalion Cross Country Run took place at 1730 hrs today. Lieut O.V. HART MC came in first. No 16 Platoon won this event, having the first 10 men foremost amongst the competitors.	
do	15/7/19		No Military Training carried out in the morning. Educational Examination.	

Army Form C. 2118.

WAR DIARY
or
INTELLIGENCE SUMMARY.
(Erase heading not required.)

Instructions regarding War Diaries and Intelligence Summaries are contained in F. S. Regs., Part II. and the Staff Manual respectively. Title pages will be prepared in manuscript.

Place	Date	Hour	Summary of Events and Information	Remarks and references to Appendices
WERMELSKIRCHEN	16/7/19		Companies at the disposal of Company Commanders. In accordance with the invitation, several Officers visited DABRINGHAUSEN to see the 29th M.G.C. Sports.	
do	17/7/19		Companies at the disposal of Company Commanders. Tactical Training carried out by all Companies during the Training hours. Battalion Inter Platoon "TUG-OF-WAR" competition started today.	
do	18/7/19		Companies at the disposal of Company Commanders. Tactical Training carried out during the morning work.	
do	19/7/19		Day observed as a whole holiday (PEACE DAY) TUG-OF-WAR (Inter Platoon) Semi Finals. No 1 v No 16 No 3 v No 13 Platoons respectively. No 13 & 16 Platoons won their respective pulls. An entertainment; a party sent out by Miss Lena Ashwell; performed at the Cinema at 1800 hrs today. Lieut McIlveen left Battalion today for Home Service. Capt C.W. Guppy took over duties of Q.M. in Lieut McIlveen's place. WEEKLY STRENGTH OFFICERS 48 O. Rks. 1052	
do	20/7/19		Divine Service for Battalion (less "C" Coy) in WERMELSKIRCHEN Parish Church 1130 hrs.	
do	21/7/19		Companies at the disposal of Company Commanders. TUG-OF-WAR Final. No 13 Platoon v No 16 Platoon No 16 won the Battalion Inter Platoon TUG-OF-WAR.	

signature for Capt.
1.1

Army Form C. 2118.

WAR DIARY
or
INTELLIGENCE SUMMARY.
(Erase heading not required.)

Place	Date	Hour	Summary of Events and Information	Remarks and references to Appendices
WERMELSKIRCHEN	22/7/19		Companies at the disposal of Company Commanders.	
do	23/7/19		Companies at the disposal of Company Commanders. Battalion aquatic Sports at EIFGEN.	
do	24/7/19		Companies at the disposal of Company Commanders. Battalion Heats for Brigade Sports run off. 15th Hants Concert Party's First Performance 1830 hours. Sports Meeting concerning monthly subscriptions at 1750 hrs today.	
do	25/7/19		Companies at the disposal of Company Commanders. Brigade Cross Country Run. Cpl Porter of "C" Coy. came in first. Lieut O.V.Hart MC came in third. The Battalion won this event, the last man coming in 29th. Brigade Tug-of-War Heats. L 15th HAMPSHIRE REGIMENT v BRIGADE H.Q. H 51st HAMPSHIRE REGIMENT Bde v H.Q 2/4th HAMPSHIRE Regt. The winners of L & H were 15th Hampshire Regt and 15th Hampshire Regiment respectively. A Concert was given in the evening by the Rhine Choral Society at the Diamond Troupe Hall.	
do	26/7/19		Companies at the disposal of Company Commanders. 51st HAMPSHIRE REGIMENTAL SPORTS took place. WEEKLY STRENGTH OFFICERS 47 O. Rks. 1045	
do	27/7/19		Divine Service in Parish Church WERMELSKIRCHEN. "TUG-OF-WAR" finals in the afternoon at 1500 hours. In the morning 15th Hants pulled 2/4th Hants, 15th Hants won. In the afternoon 15th Hants pulled M.G.C. 15th Hants won.	

Army Form C. 2118.

WAR DIARY
or
INTELLIGENCE SUMMARY.
(Erase heading not required.)

Place	Date	Hour	Summary of Events and Information	Remarks and references to Appendices
WERMELSKIRCHEN	28/7/19		Companies at the disposal of Company Commanders. Divisional Cross Country Run at ODENTHAL. 15th Hampshire won this event. This race was run on the same principles as previous Cross Country Runs mentioned this month. Lieut C.V. Hart MC was the first to come in for this Battalion finishing fourth.	
do	29/7/19		Companies at the disposal of Company Commanders. Tatical Training carried out by all companies during the morning.	
do	30/7/19		Companies at the disposal of Company Commanders. Brigade Aquatic Sports at EIFGEN. RESULTS:- 15th Hants. Regt. 27 Points. 51st Hants. Regt. 8 " 2/4th Hants.Regt. 4 "	
do	31/7/19		Day observed as a whole holiday on account of the Brigade Sports - the first day. 15th Hants Regt 36 points 2/4th Hants Regt 13 " 51st Hants Regtt 10 " Brigade 7 "	

I.J. Parker Captain,
for Captain, ~~Lieut-Colonel~~,
Commanding 15th Bn Hampshire Regiment.

Army Form C. 2118.

WAR DIARY
or
INTELLIGENCE SUMMARY.
(Erase heading not required.)

15th (S) BATT.
HAMPSHIRE REGT.

Instructions regarding War Diaries and Intelligence Summaries are contained in F.S. Regs., Part II. and the Staff Manual respectively. Title pages will be prepared in manuscript.

Place	Date	Hour	Summary of Events and Information	Remarks and references to Appendices
Wermelskirchen	1/8/19.		Day observed as a whole holiday on account of Minden Day. 15th Hampshire Regiment defeated the other Battalions in the 2nd day of the Brigade Sports by a large margin. Lieut. G.V. Hart M.C. carried-off the individual prize with 9 points. Great rejoicings by the 15th Hampshire Regiment after the Sports. "C" Company out of isolation from this date.	
"	2/8/19.		Companies atvthe disposal of Company Commanders. Concert party at the cinema today.	
"	3/8/19.		Divine Service in Wermelskirchen Parish Church at 1130 hours. Capt C.C. OXBORROW takes charge of Battalion and Lieut. Colonel Hon R.BRAND C.M.G.,D.S.O. assumes command of Brigade. WEEKLY STRENGTH, 47 Officers, 1046 Other Ranks.	
"	4/8/19.		Battalion moved to the outpost line to relieve 2/4th Hampshire Regiment. Company Areas, "A" Company, HALZENBERG. "B" Company, TALSPERRE. "C" Company, BERGISCH BORN. "D" Company, BUCHOLZEN. Battalion Headquarters, SUPPELBACH.	
Suppelbach.	5/8/19.		Companies carried on Training in their respective areas. Lieut. Colonel Hon R. BRAND C.M.G.,D.S.O. (acting Brigadier) inspected the outpost line in the morning.	
"	6/8/19.		Companies carried on Training in their respective areas. Major M.H. STONEY D.S.O. assumes command of the Battalion having returned from leave and Capt C.C. OXBORROW M.C. takes over command of "C" Company.	
"	7/8/19.		Companies carried on Training in their respective areas. Battalion Sports Team left for KALK.	

Army Form C. 2118.

WAR DIARY
or
INTELLIGENCE SUMMARY.
(Erase heading not required.)

Instructions regarding War Diaries and Intelligence Summaries are contained in F. S. Regs., Part II. and the Staff Manual respectively. Title pages will be prepared in manuscript.

Place	Date	Hour	Summary of Events and Information	Remarks and references to Appendices
Suppelbach.	8/8/19.		Companies carried on Training in their respective areas. 1st day of Divisional Sports at KALK. Lieut. F.C. ELLIOTT won the 2nd prize for Jumping (Horses). Finals to be run off on the 9th inst. Special Train ran for the Sports.	
"	9/8/19.		Companies carried on Training in their respective areas. Several Officers and Other Ranks again visited KALK to see the Divisional Sports. Lieut. PURSEY (15th Hants) won the Divisional High Jump.	
"	10/8/19.		Church Parade at BUCHOLZEN. Sports Team returned from KALK. WEEKLY STRENGTH, 47 Officers, 1045 Other Ranks.	
"	11/8/19.		Companies carried on Training in their respective areas.	
"	12/8/19.		Companies carried on Training in their respective areas. 15th Hants Officers had their photo taken.	
"	13/8/19.		Companies carried on Training in their respective areas.	
"	14/8/19.		Companies carried on Training in their respective areas. Capt. C.C. OXBORROW M.C. and Capt. J.L. SPENCER M.C. leave Battalion for service with a regular Battalion of the Hampshire Regiment.	
"	15/8/19.		Companies carried on Training in their respective areas.	
"	16/8/19.		Companies carried on Training in their respective areas. Major H.C. WESTMORELAND D.S.O. 2/4th Hampshire Regiment assumes temporary command of this Battalion. The 41st Battalion Machine Gun Corps held their sports against the 15th Hampshire Regt, the former winning the majority of points.	

Army Form C. 2118.

WAR DIARY
or
INTELLIGENCE SUMMARY.
(Erase heading not required.)

Instructions regarding War Diaries and Intelligence Summaries are contained in F. S. Regs., Part II. and the Staff Manual respectively. Title pages will be prepared in manuscript.

Place	Date	Hour	Summary of Events and Information	Remarks and references to Appendices
Suppelbach	17/8/19.		Divine Service for all denominations. Major H.H. STONEY D.S.O. and Major T.P. THUNE M.C. leave the Battalion, the former for command of the 51st Warwickshire Regiment and the latter for demobilization. WEEKLY STRENGTH, 42 Officers, 1045 Other Ranks.	
"	18/8/19.		Companies carried on Training in their respective areas.	
"	19/8/19.		Companies carried on Training in their respective areas. Representatives of the Army Council inspected the outpost line during the afternoon.	
"	20/8/19.		Companies carried on Training in their respective areas.	
"	21/8/19.		Companies carried on Training in their respective areas. "The Fragments" gave a concert at the cinema, DHUNN.	
"	22/8/19.		Companies carried on Training in their respective areas.	
"	23/8/19.		Companies carried on Training in their respective areas.	
"	24/8/19.		Divine Service for all denominations. WEEKLY STRENGTH, 42 Officers, 1042 Other Ranks.	
"	25/8/19.		Companies carried on Training in their respective areas.	
"	26/8/19.		Companies carried on Training in their respective areas.	
"	27/8/19.		Companies carried on Training in their respective areas.	
"	28/8/19.		Companies carried on Training in their respective areas.	

Army Form C. 2118.

WAR DIARY
or
INTELLIGENCE SUMMARY.
(Erase heading not required.)

Instructions regarding War Diaries and Intelligence Summaries are contained in F.S. Regs., Part II. and the Staff Manual respectively. Title pages will be prepared in manuscript.

Place	Date	Hour	Summary of Events and Information	Remarks and references to Appendices
Suppelbach.	29/8/19.		Companies carried on Training in their respective areas. Battalion Horse Show at HALZENBERG today.	
"	30/8/19.		Companies carried on Training in their respective areas. Several Officers visited the COLOGNE races.	
"	31/8/19.		Divine Service for all denominations. Cricket Match, 15th Hants. v. 51st Hants. Result, win for 51st Hants. WEEKLY STRENGTH, 41 Officers, 1010 Other Ranks.	

Lieut. Colonel
Commanding 15th Bn. Hampshire Regmt.

Army Form C. 2118.

WAR DIARY
or
INTELLIGENCE SUMMARY.
(Erase heading not required.)

Instructions regarding War Diaries and Intelligence Summaries are contained in F.S. Regs., Part II. and the Staff Manual respectively. Title pages will be prepared in manuscript.

Place	Date	Hour	Summary of Events and Information	Remarks and references to Appendices
Suppelbach.	1/9/19.		Companies carried on training in their respective areas.	
"	2/9/19.		Companies carried on training in their respective areas.	
"	3/9/19.		Companies carried on training in their respective areas.	
"	4/9/19.		Battalion relieved by the 51st Bn. Hampshire Regiment and returned to WERMELSKIRCHEN. Lieut. Colonel The Hon R. Brand C.M.G.,D.S.O. assumed command of the Battalion from this date and also Brigade.	
Wermelskirchen.	5/9/19.		Major H.U. WESTMORELAND D.S.O. returned to the 2/4th Bn. Hampshire Regiment. Day spent by Battalion in clearing up billets. The Commanding Officer inspected the billets of the Battalion during the morning.	
"	6/9/19.		Companies at the disposal of Company Commanders.	
"	7/9/19.		Divine Service in WERMELSKIRCHEN Parish Church at 1130 hours. WEEKLY STRENGTH, 39 Officers, 1004 Other Ranks.	
"	8/9/19.		Companies at the disposal of Company Commanders. The Commanding Officer inspected "C" Company. The Sports team left for II Corps Sports, REHL, COLOGNE.	
"	9/9/19.		Companies at the disposal of Company Commanders. Light Trench Morter exhibition for "C" Company. Corps Sports at COLOGNE. The Commanding Officer inspected "A" Company.	

Army Form C. 2118.

WAR DIARY
or
INTELLIGENCE SUMMARY.
(Erase heading not required.)

Instructions regarding War Diaries and Intelligence Summaries are contained in F. S. Regs., Part II. and the Staff Manual respectively. Title pages will be prepared in manuscript.

Place	Date	Hour	Summary of Events and Information	Remarks and references to Appendices
Wermelskirchen	10/9/19.		Companies at the disposal of Company Commanders. The Commanding Officer inspected "D" Company. Last day of the Corps Sports at RHYLL. The Battalion team won the Cross Country run, C.Q.M.S. AVEY securing first place. Capt. H.G.J. IONE M.C. won the hurdles race.	
"	11/9/19.		Companies at the disposal of Company Commanders. The Commanding Officer inspected "B" Company. Light Trench Mortar exhibition to "D" & "A" Companies at 0900 – 1030 hours and 1100 – 1230 hours respectively.	
"	12/9/19.		Companies at the disposal of Company Commanders. "A" Company commenced firing the Rhine Army Musketry Course (General) from 0900 hours to 1230 hours. "B" Company commenced in the afternoon from 1400 hours to 1700 hours at HINTERHUFE.	
"	13/9/19.		Companies at the disposal of Company Commanders. "C" & "D" Companies commenced firing the Rhine Army General Musketry Course at HINTEREUFE from 0830 hours to 1230 hours. Miss Doris Cloud's Concert Party performed at the Cinema at 1930 hours today.	
"	14/9/19.		Divine Service at WERMELSKIRCHEN Parish Church at 1130 hours. WEEKLY STRENGTH. 57 Officers. 951 Other Ranks.	
"	15/9/19.		Companies at the disposal of Company Commanders. "B" Company continued firing the General Musketry Course at HINTERHUFE. The Commanding Officer inspected Battalion Headquarters. Major H.E. HUFFER M.C. joined the Battalion today and took over the duties of 2nd in Command.	

Army Form C. 2118.

WAR DIARY
or
INTELLIGENCE SUMMARY.
(Erase heading not required.)

Instructions regarding War Diaries and Intelligence Summaries are contained in F. S. Regs., Part II. and the Staff Manual respectively. Title pages will be prepared in manuscript.

Place	Date	Hour	Summary of Events and Information	Remarks and references to Appendices
Wermelskirchen.	16/9/19.		Companies at the disposal of Company Commanders. "C" & "D" Companies continued firing the General Musketry Course from 0650 hours to 1330 hours. The Sports team representing the Battalion left for COLOGNE to take part in the Rhine Army Championships. Cross Country Team	
"	17/9/19.		Companies carried on training. "A" & "B" Companies continued firing the General Musketry Course from 0900 hours to 1330 hours.	
"	18/9/19.		Companies at the disposal of Company Commanders. "C" & "D" Companies continued firing the General Musketry Course. At 1000 hours this morning a very serious accident happened on the 3rd Southern Infantry Brigade Light Trench Mortar Battery Demonstration Field. This accident was due to a premature explosion. 3 men were killed and 15 wounded. Today the Battalion won the Rhine Army Cross Country Race at COLOGNE.	
"	19/9/19.		Companies at the disposal of Company Commanders. Sports team returned from COLOGNE.	
"	20/9/19.		Companies at the disposal of Company Commanders.	
"	21/9/19.		Battalion attended Divine Service at WERMELSKIRCHEN Parish Church at 1130 hours. WEEKLY STRENGTH, 34 Officers, 748 Other Ranks.	
"	22/9/19.		Companies at the disposal of Company Commanders. The Southern Divisional Concert Party, "The Fragments", gave a performance at the cinema at 1800 hours today.	
"	23/9/19.		Companies at the disposal of Company Commanders.	
"	24/9/19.		Companies at the disposal of Company Commanders. Miss Coate's Concert Party performed at the cinema at 1830 hours.	
"	25/9/19.		Companies at the disposal of Company Commanders.	

Army Form C. 2118.

WAR DIARY
or
INTELLIGENCE SUMMARY.

(Erase heading not required.)

Instructions regarding War Diaries and Intelligence Summaries are contained in F. S. Regs., Part II. and the Staff Manual respectively. Title pages will be prepared in manuscript.

Place	Date	Hour	Summary of Events and Information	Remarks and references to Appendices
Wermelskirchen.	26/9/19.		Companies at the disposal of Company Commanders. Several Officers went to the American Horse Show at WIESBADEN today.	
"	27/9/19.		Companies at the disposal of Company Commanders.	
"	28/9/19.		Divine Service for Battalion at WERMELSKIRCHEN Parish Church at 1140 hours today. WEEKLY STRENGTH, 32 Officers, 811 Other Ranks.	
"	29/9/19.		Companies at the disposal of Company Commanders.	
"	30/9/19.		Companies at the disposal of Company Commanders. The Divisional Commander inspected the Transport.	The Transport was inspected by the Brig. Gen. R.D. Light Division for the purpose awarding points in the Div. Championship.

M. Maud. Lieut. Colonel.
Commanding 15th Bn. Hampshire Regiment.

woas|2309|6

SOUTHERN (LATE 29TH) DIVN
88TH INFY BDE

51ST BN HAMPSHIRE REGT
MAY - DEC 1919
1919. MAY - OCT

SOUTHERN (LATE 29TH) DIVN
88TH INFY BDE

Army Form C. 2118.

WAR DIARY
or
INTELLIGENCE SUMMARY

(Erase heading not required.)

51st Battalion The HAMPSHIRE REGIMENT

Instructions regarding War Diaries and Intelligence Summaries are contained in F.S. Regs., Part II. and the Staff Manual respectively. Title Pages will be prepared in manuscript.

Place	Date	Hour	Summary of Events and Information	Remarks and references to Appendices
WERMELSKIRCHEN	1st to 14th May 1919.		Battalion remained in support, and carried out ordinary training.	Map reference. REMSCHEID 1/25,000
--do--	15.5.1919.		Battalion moved into Outpost Line in relief of 15th Battalion Hampshire Regiment, and took over line from BERGISCH-BORN to FURD, inclusive. Battn Headquarters at SUPPELBACH. "A" Company NEUENHAUS. "B" Company BERGISCH-BORN. "C" Company BUCHHOLZEN. "D" Company HALZENBERG.	
	15th to 31st		Remained in this Position and carried out ordinary Training.	
	30.4.1919.		Captain.(A/Major) K.R.O'BRIEN. M.C. The LONDON REGIMENT, appointed Temporary Major whilst employed as 2nd in Command to Battalion.	
	26.5.1919.		Lieutenant J.M.H. GOODWIN. Royal Engineers, joined Battalion for duty as Education Officer.	
	3.5.1919.		RE-INFORCEMENTS. One Other Ranks from General Base Depot ETAPLES.	

STRUCK OFF STRENGTH DURING MONTH. To U.K. for Demob; Lieutenant J.G.SMITHSON and 120 O.Ranks.
To U.K. (Invalids) 2 Other Ranks.

STRENGTH OF BATTALION Officers. W.O's Sergts Corpls. Dmrs. Privates. Total.
                       39   6   50   58   16   804   965.

Lieutenant Colonel
Commanding, 51st Bn Hampshire Regiment.

Army Form C. 2118.

WAR DIARY
or
INTELLIGENCE SUMMARY

(Erase heading not required.)

5 1st Battalion The HAMPSHIRE REGIMENT

Instructions regarding War Diaries and Intelligence Summaries are contained in F. S. Regs., Part II. and the Staff Manual respectively. Title Pages will be prepared in manuscript.

Place	Date	Hour	Summary of Events and Information	Remarks and references to Appendices
	15th June 1919.		Battalion in Out Post, and carried out ordinary Training.	
	16th June 1919.		Battalion relieved by 2/4th Battalion The Hampshire Regiment and moved back into support to WERMELSKIRCHEN.	
	18th June 1919.		"A" and "C" Companies moved up in relief of the whole of the 1/5th Devon Regiment on Perimeter Line. Remainder of Battalion remained in support.	
	19th June 1919.		Battn H.Q. and "B" and "D" Companies moved to KELLERSHAMMER, BURG, under WUPPER	
	21st. June 1919.		"D" Company took over Out Post Line from BERGISCH-BURN to TALSPERRE inclusive. After this move had been completed the Battalion held the line as follows:-	
			"D" Company. BERGISCH-BURN to TALSPERRE inclusive.	
			"A" Company. TALSPERRE to KELLERSHAMMER both places exclusive.	
			"C" Company. KELLERSHAMMER to EAST side of KAISER WILHELM BRIDGE over WUPPER RIVER inclusive.	
			Bn H.Q. and "B" Company in Reserve at KELLERSHAMMER.	
	22nd to 30.June 1919.		Remained in above Positions and carried out ordinary Training.	
			REINFORCEMENTS 1. O.R. From Details Battn The Hampshire Regiment.	
			CASUALTIES (Offrs) 2Lieut. A.C.SMITH (On Course of Instrn U.K.) Struck off Strength.	
			2 Lieut. G.H.HICKMAN Demobilized.	
			(O.Rks). To. U.K. (Sick) 3.	
			To. Home Estab: 1.	
			Transferred to other Units 13.	
			To U.K. Demobilized 3	
			TOTAL. O.R. 20.	

STRENGTH OF BATTALION

Officers	W.O's	Sergts	Corpls	Drummers	Privates	TOTAL.
37	6	49	51	16	785	944

Lieutenant Colonel,
Commanding, 51st Bn Hampshire Regiment.

2449 Wt. W14957/M90 750,000 1/16 J.B.C. & A. Forms/C.2118/12.

Army Form C. 2118.

WAR DIARY
or
INTELLIGENCE SUMMARY

(Erase heading not required.)

51st BATTALION THE HAMPSHIRE REGIMENT

Place	Date	Hour	Summary of Events and Information	Remarks and references to Appendices
KELLSHAMMER. BURG on the WUPPER	1.7.1919.		Battalion Headquarters and "B" Company, moved back to WERMELSKIRCHEN.	
	2.7.1919.		"A" "C" and "D" Companies, were relieved on the Perimeter by the 1/5th DEVONSHIRE REGIMENT, and moved back to WERMELSKIRCHEN.	
WERMELSKIRCHEN.	3 to 31.7.1919.		The Battalion remained in Billets at WERMELSKIRCHEN, and carried out ordinary Training.	
--do--	28.7.1919.		The Divisional Commander, (MAJOR GENERAL SIR W.C.G.HENEKER. K.C.B. D.S.O.) Inspected the Battalion.	
			REINFORCEMENTS. OFFICERS. From. 51st R.Warwick Regiment. 2nd Lieutenant H.E. Cave.	
			2nd Lieutenant A. Peyton.	
			Lieutenant. H.M.S. Bailey.	
			From. 52nd R.Warwick Regiment Lieutenant. C. Chitty.	
			2nd Lieutenant S.R. Hepworth	
			2nd Lieutenant L. Griffen	
			2nd Lieutenant W.G. Smith.	
			OTHER RANKS....N I L.	
			CASUALTIES OFFICERS. To. 51st Bn Devonshire Regiment. 2nd Lieutenant R.E. Geddes	
			To. 9th East Surrey Regiment. Lieutenant H.M.S. Bailey.	
			OTHER RANKS Invalided to U.K............ 1.	
			Demobilized............ 5.	
			Transferred to Other Units... 6.	
			TOTAL. 12.	
			STRENGTH OF THE BATTALION. Officers. W.O's. Sergts. Corpls. Dmrs. Privates. Total.	
			42. 5 52 51 16 770 936.	

Lieut. Colonel.
Commanding 51st Hampshire Regt.
1.8.1919.

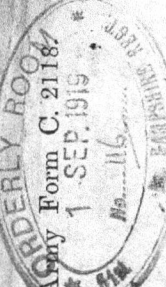

WAR DIARY
or
INTELLIGENCE SUMMARY

(Erase heading not required.)

51st BATTALION THE HAMPSHIRE REGIMENT.

Army Form C. 2118.

Place	Date	Hour	Summary of Events and Information	Remarks and references to Appendices
WERMELSKIRCHEN.	1 to 4.8.1919		The Battalion remained in billets at WERMELSKIRCHEN, and carried out ordinary Training.	
	5.8.1919		The Battalion moved to DELLBRUCK.	
DELLBRUCK.	6 to 15.8.1919		The Battalion fired The General Musketry Course	
	16.8.1919		The Battalion moved back to WERMELSKIRCHEN.	
WERMELSKIRCHEN.	17 to 31.8.1919		The Battalion remained in billets at WERMELSKIRCHEN, and carried out ordinary Training.	

REINFORCEMENTS. OFFICERS. NIL.

OTHER RANKS From 1st Bn. The Hampshire Regiment. 6.

CASUALTIES

OFFICERS
To Reserve Bn. The Hampshire Regiment 2/Lt. A.J. Bather
 2/Lt. H.C. Phillips
 2/Lt. A. Sturgess
Placed on the Establishment of Southern Lt. J.M.H. Goodwin
Divisional Education School

OTHER RANKS
Demobilised 11
Transferred to Other Units 64
 Total 75

STRENGTH OF BATTALION Officers W.O's. Sergts. Corpls. Dmrs. Privates TOTAL.
 38   5   47   49   15   709   863

Lieutenant Colonel
Commanding 51st Bn. Hampshire Regiment.
1.9.1919.

Original Army Form C. 2118.

WAR DIARY or INTELLIGENCE SUMMARY

(Erase heading not required.)

51st BATTN THE HAMPSHIRE REGIMENT

SEPTEMBER 1919.

Instructions regarding War Diaries and Intelligence Summaries are contained in F.S. Regs., Part II. and the Staff Manual respectively. Title Pages will be prepared in manuscript.

Place	Date	Hour	Summary of Events and Information	Remarks and references to Appendices
WERMELSKIRCHEN.	1--3-9-1919.		Battalion in Billets. Carried out Ordinary Trainings.	
	4-9-1919.		The Battalion moved into the Out Post Line, in relief of the 15th Bn HAMPSHIRE REGIMENT. and took over the Line from TALSPERRE to PURD inclusive. Battn Headquarters, DHUNN. "D" Company, TALSPERRE, "A" Company, BERGISBORN. "C" Company, BUCHHOLZEN. "B" Company, HALZENBURG. (Factory, 250 Metres,	Map Reference REMSCHEID 1/25.000
	30-9-1919.		3 Platoons "A" Company, moved back into Billets at WERMELSKIRCHEN. M, of B in ELBRINGHAUSEN).	
	5--30-9-1919.		The remainder of the Battalion remained in the positions as above and carried out Ordinary Training ...	
			REINFORCEMENTS:- OFFICERS. NIL. OTHER RANKS..... 1.	
			CASUALTIES:- OFFICERS. Lieut W.A.G.Downer, K.Liverpools } Posted to Lieut A.S. Bates K.R.R.Corps. } Home Establishment. 2/Lieut. G.A.Gray. Essex Regiment. Posted to R.A.O.C. COLOGNE.	
			OTHER RANKS. Accidently Killed. 1. Invalided to U.K. 3. Demobilized........ 70. Transferred......... 34. ------ TOTAL.......... 108.	
			STRENGTH OF BATTALION. Officers. W.O's Sergts. Corpls Dmrs. Privates TOTAL. 35 5 42 41 14 718 ✗ 753.	✗ Includes 2.Privates Transferred but not struck off strength.

[signature]
LT. COLONEL,
COMMANDING 51st Bn. HAMPSHIRE REGT

Army Form C. 2118.

WAR DIARY
or
INTELLIGENCE SUMMARY
(Erase heading not required.)

Instructions regarding War Diaries and Intelligence Summaries are contained in F. S. Regs., Part II. and the Staff Manual respectively. Title Pages will be prepared in manuscript.

Place	Date	Hour	Summary of Events and Information	Remarks and references to Appendices
DHUNN	1-6 -10-19. 7-10-19.		Battalion in Outpost Line and carried out ordinary training. Battalion Headquarters, 1 platoon of "A" Company and "C" Company withdrew to WIPPELLSKIRCHEN and occupied billets as follows :- Battalion Headquarters :- "C" Area. "C" Company :- School 250 yards N.W. of B in ELBRINGHAUSEN. 1 Platoon of "A" Company joined Company at Factory 250 yards N. of B in ELBRINGHAUSEN. "B" Company, with H.Q. at DHUNN, occupied HAARHAUSEN and DRIEBUKEN each with 1 platoon, remaining 2 platoons at DHUNN. "D" Company, with H.Q. at TALSPERRE, occupied BERGISCH-BORN with 1 Platoon, MEBUSMUHLE with 1 Platoon, 2 Sections at WATER-WORKS, and remainder of Company in reserve at TALSPERRE.	RE SCHEID 1/25,000.

WIPPELLSKIRCHEN	28-10-19.		Battalion took over the 1st Southern Infantry Brigade Perimeter with "A" and "C" Companies as under :-
			"A" Company from 51st R.Warwick Regt - WIPPERFELD to LAUSPURF.
			"C" " from 51st R.Warwick Regt - JUNKERMUHLE to FURTH.
			Disposition of these Companies after this move :-
			"A" Company :- Company H.Q. and 2 platoons - WIPPERFELD.
			          " " " " 2 " - LAUSPURF.
			"C" Company :- Company H.Q. and 2 " - JUNKERMUHLE.
			          " " " " 1 " - FURTH.
			          " " " " 1 " - FURTH.
			
			"D" Company handed over the Line TALSPERRE to BERGISCH-BORN to 51st Devon Regt and withdrew to WER-ELSKIRCHEN and occupied the Factory 250 yards N. of B in ELBRINGHAUSEN.
			
			(Continued)
				REMSCHEID 1/25,000.

Army Form C. 2118.

WAR DIARY
or
INTELLIGENCE SUMMARY

(Erase heading not required.)

Instructions regarding War Diaries and Intelligence Summaries are contained in F. S. Regs., Part II. and the Staff Manual respectively. Title Pages will be prepared in manuscript.

Place	Date	Hour	Summary of Events and Information	Remarks and references to Appendices
			REINFORCEMENTS:- OFFICERS :- A/Capt.R.J.SCOTT, A/Capt.W.GIBBONS MC, A/Capt.W.L.CLARKE, Lieutenants W.S.STONER, C.D.WOOLDRIDGE, E.L.WILLSHER MC, R.A.GIBB, F.C.ISAACS, R.T.ANDERSON, 2/Lieutenants J.R.STEVENS, A.W.PALMER, V.R.HARDING, C.NEWMAN, T.H.BENNETT, S.H.KINGS ILL, H.C.BRIDGER, E.A.NELL MC, H.F.WADHAMS. (From 2/4th BATTALION, THE HAMPSHIRE REGIMENT).- Capt.H.G.J.ICKE, Lieutenants R.K.TITLEY, C.KNEEBONE, T.W.GRAINSTREET, 2/Lieutenant P.J.BOYD. (From 15th BATTALION, THE HAMPSHIRE REGIMENT).- OTHER RANKS :- R.S.M. G.H.DEWEY from 1st HAMPSHIRE Regiment 269 Other Ranks from 2/4th BATTALION, THE HAMPSHIRE Regiment. 187 " " " 15th " " " CASUALTIES:- OFFICERS :- Capt. C.MEIGHAN, Capt. C.A.OGIER MC, Lieutenants R.S.LEDGARD, H.ORTON, W.R.REDWAY, A.L.GRIOTT LL, A.PETTON, J.H.PERRY MC, B.EVANS MC, J.SCOTT, J.R.SHARP, N.BOTHING, J.L.GRIFFIN MC, 2/Lieutenants J.G.EUSTACE & S.R.HEPWORTH. All Demobilized. To 51st R.Warwick Regiment :- Captain D.L.WAGHORN MC, DCM. To H.Q. Southern Division :- Captain W.A.STANBRICK and Lieut.F.J.JANAWAY MC. OTHER RANKS :- Demobilized 56. Transferred 21. ------ TOTAL 77 ====== Strength of Battalion :- Offrs. W.Os.Sgts. Cpls. Dmrs. Ptes. TOTAL. 46 5 40 46 15 982 1138.	

[signature] Lieut.Colonel,
for Commanding 51st HAMPSHIRE Regiment.

www.ingramcontent.com/pod-product-compliance
Lightning Source LLC
Chambersburg PA
CBHW080837010526
44114CB00017B/2327